Dynamic Models for Volatility and Heavy Tails

The volatility of financial returns changes over time and, for the last thirty years, Generalized Autoregressive Conditional Heteroscedasticity (GARCH) models have provided the principal means of analyzing, modelling and monitoring such changes. Taking into account that financial returns typically exhibit heavy tails – that is, extreme values can occur from time to time – Andrew C. Harvey's new book shows how a small but radical change in the way GARCH models are formulated leads to a resolution of many of the theoretical problems inherent in the statistical theory. The approach can also be applied to other aspects of volatility, such as those arising from data on the range of returns and the time between trades. Furthermore, the more general class of Dynamic Conditional Score models extends to robust modelling of outliers in the levels of time series and to the treatment of time-varying relationships. As such, there are applications not only to financial data but also to macroeconomic time series and to time series in other disciplines. The statistical theory draws on basic principles of maximum likelihood estimation and, by doing so, leads to an elegant and unified treatment of nonlinear time-series modelling. The practical value of the proposed models is illustrated by fitting them to real data sets.

Andrew C. Harvey is Professor of Econometrics at the University of Cambridge and a Fellow of Corpus Christi College. He is a Fellow of the Econometric Society and of the British Academy. He has published more than 100 articles in journals and edited volumes and is the author of three books, *The Econometric Analysis of Time Series*, *Time Series Models* and *Forecasting and Structural Time Series Models and the Kalman Filter* (Cambridge University Press, 1989). He is one of the developers of the STAMP computer package.

Econometric Society Monographs

Editors:

Rosa L. Matzkin, University of California, Los Angeles
George J. Mailath, University of Pennsylvania

The Econometric Society is an international society for the advancement of economic theory in relation to statistics and mathematics. The Econometric Society Monograph series is designed to promote the publication of original research contribution of high quality in mathematical economics and theoretical and applied econometrics.

Other titles in the series:

G. S. Maddala, *Limited dependent and qualitative variables in econometrics*, 9780521241434, 9780521338257
Gerard Debreu, *Mathematical economics: Twenty papers of Gerard Debreu*, 9780521237369, 9780521335614
Jean-Michel Grandmont, *Money and value: A reconsideration of classical and neoclassical monetary economics*, 9780521251419, 9780521313643
Franklin M. Fisher, *Disequilibrium foundations of equilibrium economics*, 9780521378567
Andreu Mas-Colell, *The theory of general equilibrium: A differentiable approach*, 9780521265140, 9780521388702
Truman F. Bewley, Editor, *Advances in econometrics – Fifth World Congress (Volume I)*, 9780521467261
Truman F. Bewley, Editor, *Advances in econometrics – Fifth World Congress (Volume II)*, 9780521467254
Hervé Moulin, *Axioms of cooperative decision making*, 9780521360555, 9780521424585
L. G. Godfrey, *Misspecification tests in econometrics: The Lagrange multiplier principle and other approaches*, 9780521424592
Tony Lancaster, *The econometric analysis of transition data*, 9780521437899
Alvin E. Roth and Marilda A. Oliviera Sotomayor, Editors, *Two-sided matching: A study in game-theoretic modeling and analysis*, 9780521437882
Wolfgang Härdle, *Applied nonparametric regression*, 9780521429504
Jean-Jacques Laffont, Editor, *Advances in economic theory – Sixth World Congress (Volume I)*, 9780521484596
Jean-Jacques Laffont, Editor, *Advances in economic theory – Sixth World Congress (Volume II)*, 9780521484602
Halbert White, *Estimation, inference and specification*, 9780521252805, 9780521574464
Christopher Sims, Editor, *Advances in econometrics – Sixth World Congress (Volume I)*, 9780521444590, 9780521566100
Christopher Sims, Editor, *Advances in econometrics – Sixth World Congress (Volume II)*, 9780521444606, 9780521566094
Roger Guesnerie, *A contribution to the pure theory of taxation*, 9780521629560
David M. Kreps and Kenneth F. Wallis, Editors, *Advances in economics and econometrics – Seventh World Congress (Volume I)*, 9780521589833
David M. Kreps and Kenneth F. Wallis, Editors, *Advances in economics and econometrics – Seventh World Congress (Volume II)*, 9780521589826
David M. Kreps and Kenneth F. Wallis, Editors, *Advances in economics and econometrics – Seventh World Congress (Volume III)*, 9780521580137, 9780521589819
Donald P. Jacobs, Ehud Kalai, and Morton I. Kamien, Editors, *Frontiers of research in economic theory: The Nancy L. Schwartz Memorial Lectures, 1983–1997*, 9780521632225, 9780521635387
A. Colin Cameron and Pravin K. Trivedi, *Regression analysis of count data*, 9780521632010, 9780521635677
Steinar Strom, Editor, *Econometrics and economic theory in the 20th century: The Ragnar Frisch Centennial Symposium*, 9780521633239, 9780521633659

Continued on page following the index

Dynamic Models for Volatility and Heavy Tails

With Applications to Financial and Economic Time Series

Andrew C. Harvey
University of Cambridge

CAMBRIDGE
UNIVERSITY PRESS

CAMBRIDGE
UNIVERSITY PRESS

32 Avenue of the Americas, New York NY 10013-2473, USA

Cambridge University Press is part of the University of Cambridge.

It furthers the University's mission by disseminating knowledge in the pursuit of education, learning and research at the highest international levels of excellence.

www.cambridge.org
Information on this title: www.cambridge.org/9781107034723

First published 2013

A catalogue record for this publication is available from the British Library

Library of Congress Cataloguing in Publication data

Harvey, A. C. (Andrew C.)
Dynamic models for volatility and heavy tails : with applications to financial and economic time series / Andrew C. Harvey.
p. cm. – (Econometric society monographs)
Includes bibliographical references and index.
ISBN 978-1-107-03472-3 (hbk.) – ISBN 978-1-107-63002-4 (pbk.)
1. Econometrics. 2. Finance – Mathematical models. 3. Time-series analysis. I. Title.
HB139.H369 2013
330.01′5195–dc23 2012036508

ISBN 978-1-107-03472-3 Hardback
ISBN 978-1-107-63002-4 Paperback

Contents

Preface

This book sets out a class of nonlinear time series models designed to extract a dynamic signal from noisy observations. The signal may be the level of a series or it may be a measure of scale. Changing scale is of considerable importance in financial time series where volatility clustering is an established stylized fact. Generalized autoregressive conditional heteroscedasticity (GARCH) models are widely used to extract the current variance of a series. However, using variance (or rather, standard deviation) as a measure of scale may not be appropriate for non-Gaussian (conditional) distributions. This is of some importance, because another established feature of financial returns is that they are characterized by heavy tails.

The dynamic equations in GARCH models are filters. Just as the filters for linear Gaussian location models are linear combinations of past observations, so GARCH filters, because of their Gaussian origins, are usually linear combinations of past squared observations. The models described here replace the observations or their squares by the score of the conditional distribution. Furthermore, when modelling scale, an exponential link function is employed, as in exponential GARCH (EGARCH), thereby ensuring that the filtered scale remains positive. The unifying feature of the models in the proposed class is that the asymptotic distribution of the maximum likelihood estimators is established by a single theorem that delivers an explicit analytic expression for the asymptotic covariance matrix of the estimators. Furthermore, the conditions under which the asymptotics go through are relatively straightforward to verify. There is no such general theory for GARCH models: analytic expressions for the asymptotic covariance matrix of the maximum likelihood estimators cannot be found even in the most basic cases, and for some models, most notably EGARCH, there is no asymptotic theory except for very special cases that are never used in practice.

Other properties of the proposed models may be found. These include analytic expressions for moments, autocorrelation functions and multistep forecasts. The properties, particularly for the volatility models, which employ an exponential link function, are more general than is usually the case. For example, expressions for unconditional moments, autocorrelations and the conditional moments of multistep predictive distributions can be obtained for absolute values of the observations raised to any power.

The generality of the approach is further illustrated by consideration of dynamic models for non-negative variables. Such models have been used for modelling duration, range and realized volatility in finance. Again, the use of an exponential link function combined with a dynamic equation driven by the conditional score gives a range of analytic results similar to those obtained with the new class of EGARCH models.

Estimating a dynamic level embedded in noise is explicitly an exercise in signal extraction. A general treatment of Gaussian models is based on the state space form and the Kalman filter. When the noise comes from a heavy-tailed distribution, such as Student's t, the filter proposed here can be regarded as an approximation to a filter for the signal plus noise model that can only be obtained by computer simulation techniques, as in Durbin and Koopman (2012). However, its properties are obtained by treating it as a model in its own right. Such a model is said to be observation-driven, as opposed to the unobserved components model, which is parameter-driven. Turning to scale, GARCH models are not usually seen as vehicles for signal extraction, but this is precisely what they are. That this is the case becomes clearer if they are viewed as observation-driven approximations to parameter-driven stochastic volatility models. Indeed, this was part of the original motivation for the formulation of EGARCH models. The development of the class of observation-driven models in this book acknowledges the link with parameter-driven models, and in doing so, it takes a step towards a unified theory of nonlinear time series models.

The book assumes that the reader is familiar with the basic ideas and technicalities of time series. The mathematics is not too demanding given a good understanding of statistical concepts such as conditional distributions and maximum likelihood estimation. Hence it should be accessible to graduate students in the more technical areas of economics and finance, as well as to statisticians. Sections marked with an asterisk (*) are more technical and/or tangential to the main argument and can be skipped without loss of continuity.

The idea of using the score to drive the dynamics in non-Gaussian models is not new, but up to now has had no firm theoretical foundation. The research for this book began in 2008 with a working paper I wrote with a student, Tirthankar Chakravarty, on EGARCH models. At the same time, Siem-Jan Koopman and his co-workers were independently developing a range of score-driven models.[1] They also produced a working paper in 2008. Because Siem-Jan and I have co-authored many papers on unobserved component models, it is perhaps not too surprising that we hit on the same idea, albeit by different routes. One of the difficulties we faced was that the models lacked a convincing asymptotic

[1] Rather than the term dynamic conditional score (DCS) models, which I use here, Creal, Koopman and Lucas (2011) prefer the name generalized autoregressive score (GAS). However, despite the attraction of the acronym, the term 'autoregressive' seems to me to convey a more limited dynamic structure than is actually the case.

theory for maximum likelihood estimation. Fortunately, a six-month visit to Carlos III University in Madrid in 2010 provided me with the inspiration to develop the necessary theory. I'm grateful to the Bank of Santander for its support under the Carlos III program for Chairs of Excellence. Further work was done when I was a visiting Fernand Braudel Fellow at the European University Institute in Florence towards the end of 2011. It was there, in the garden of the Villa San Paolo, that Anders Rahbek gave me a memorable tutorial on the finer points of advanced asymptotic theory for time series. I'm grateful to Anders and to all the other colleagues who have provided comments and support during the work on the project. These include Philipp Andres, Tirthankar Chakravarty, Frank Diebold, Rob Engle, Gloria Gonzalez-Rivera, Peter Hansen, Stan Hurn, Ryoko Ito, Siem-Jan Koopman, Alessandra Luati, Mark Salmon, Steve Satchell, Richard Smith, Genaro Sucarrat, Abderrahim Taamou, Stephen Thiele and Paolo Zaffaroni. Universities at which the ideas were presented include Oxford, Warwick, Queensland, Monash, Hanover, EUI, Carlos III, Alicante, New York, Columbia and Pennsylvania. Special thanks go to Esther Ruiz at Carlos III and Mardi Dungey at the University of Tasmania, where I spent three weeks in December 2010. Finally I'd like to thank Rosa Matzkin and two anonymous readers for their helpful and constructive comments, and Peihang Lu for editorial assistance.

Acronyms and Abbreviations

ACD	autoregressive conditional duration
ACF	autocorrelation function
AIC	Akaike information criterion
APARCH	asymmetric power ARCH
ARCH	autoregressive conditional heterocedasticity
ARIMA	autoregressive integrated moving average
BIC	Bayesian information criterion
CAViaR	conditional autoregressive value at risk by regression quantiles
CDF	cumulative distribution function
CPI	consumer price index
CV	coefficient of variation
DCC	dynamic conditional correlation
DCS	dynamic conditional score
EGARCH	exponential GARCH
ES	expected shortfall
EWMA	exponentially weighted moving average
GARCH	generalised autoregressive conditional heteroscedasticity
GED	general error distribution
GG	generalised gamma
IF	innovations form
IGARCH	integrated GARCH
IID	independent and identically distributed
IRW	integrated random walk
KF	Kalman filter
LIE	law of iterated expectations
LM	Lagrange multiplier
LR	likelihood ratio
MA	moving average
MCMC	Markov chain Monte Carlo
MD	martingale difference
MEM	multiplicative error models
MGF	moment generating function

ML	maximum likelihood
MMSE	minimum mean square error (estimate)
MSE	mean square error
NID	normally and independently distributed
PDF	probability distribution function
PIT	probability-integral transform
QARMA	quasi-ARMA
QML	quasi-maximum likelihood
QQ	quantile-quantile
RMSE	root mean square error
SD	standard deviation
SE	standard error
SRE	stochastic recurrence equation
SSF	state space form
STM	structural time series model
SV	stochastic volatility
UC	unobserved components
VaR	value at risk
WN	white noise

CHAPTER 1

Introduction

The aim of this monograph is to set out a unified and comprehensive theory for a class of nonlinear time series models that can deal with dynamic distributions. The emphasis is on models in which the conditional distribution of an observation may be heavy-tailed and the location and/or scale changes over time. The defining feature of these models is that the dynamics are driven by the score of the conditional distribution. When a suitable link function is employed for the changing parameter, analytic expressions may be derived for unconditional moments, autocorrelations and moments of multistep forecasts. Furthermore, a full asymptotic distribution theory for maximum likelihood estimators can be developed, including analytic expressions for asymptotic covariance matrices of the estimators.

The class of what we call *dynamic conditional score* (DCS) models includes standard linear time series models observed with an error that may be subject to outliers, models which capture changing conditional variance and models for non-negative variables. The last two of these are of considerable importance in financial econometrics, where they are used for forecasting volatility. A guiding principle underlying the proposed class of models is that of signal extraction. When combined with basic ideas of maximum likelihood estimation, the signal extraction approach leads to models which, in contrast to many in the literature, are relatively simple and yield analytic expressions for their principal features.

For estimating location, DCS models are closely related to the unobserved components models described in Harvey (1989). Such models can be handled using state space methods, and they are easily accessible using the STAMP package of Koopman et al. (2009). For estimating scale, the models are close to stochastic volatility models, in which the variance is treated as an unobserved component. The close ties with unobserved component and stochastic volatility models provide insight into the structure of the DCS models, particularly with respect to modelling trend and seasonality, and into possible restrictions on the parameters.

The reference to location and scale rather than mean and variance is deliberate. Location and scale apply to all distributions, whereas mean and variance may not always exist, a point which is particularly relevant when dealing with heavy tails. Furthermore, although a knowledge of the mean and variance of a Gaussian distribution tells us all there is to know, this is not the case with many other distributions. Focussing too much attention on mean and variance is unwise, particularly in financial econometrics. By a similar token, correlation measures the strength of the relationship between two variables in a Gaussian world, but the more general concept of association is of wider relevance, as witnessed by the recent upsurge of interest in copulas.

Section 1.1 introduces a very basic, but important, unobserved components time series model. The idea of signal extraction for Gaussian models is explained, and the Kalman filter is written down in a form that leads to the development of a more general filter, based on the score of a conditional distribution for each observation. Some basic definitions are noted in Section 1.2, before moving on to a discussion of volatility models in Section 1.3. The relevance of dynamic conditional score models for volatility modelling is explained in Section 1.4, and the implications of outlying observations for conventional and DCS filters are explored. Section 1.5 stresses the importance of modelling the full conditional distribution of an observation, rather than just its first two moments. The last section outlines the contents of each chapter.

1.1 UNOBSERVED COMPONENTS AND FILTERS

Autoregressive integrated moving average (ARIMA) models focus on forecasting future values of a series. A more general framework is given by the signal plus noise paradigm. Signal extraction is of interest in itself, and once the problem has been solved, the forecasting solution follows.

A simple Gaussian signal plus noise model for a sample of T observations, $y_t, t = 1, .., T$, is

$$y_t = \mu_t + \varepsilon_t, \quad \varepsilon_t \sim NID\left(0, \sigma_\varepsilon^2\right), \quad t = 1, \ldots, T, \tag{1.1}$$

$$\mu_{t+1} = \phi\mu_t + \eta_t, \quad \eta_t \sim NID\left(0, \sigma_\eta^2\right),$$

where ϕ is the autoregressive parameter, the irregular and signal disturbances, ε_t and η_t respectively, are mutually and serially independent and the notation $NID\left(0, \sigma^2\right)$ denotes normally and independently distributed with mean zero and variance σ^2. The *signal-noise ratio*, $q = \sigma_\eta^2/\sigma_\varepsilon^2$, plays a key role in determining how observations should be weighted for prediction and signal extraction. The *reduced form* of (1.1) is an $ARMA(1, 1)$ process,

$$y_t = \phi y_{t-1} + \xi_t - \theta\xi_{t-1}, \quad \xi_t \sim NID\left(0, \sigma^2\right), \quad t = 1, \ldots, T, \tag{1.2}$$

but with restrictions on θ. For example, when $\phi = 1$, $0 \leq \theta \leq 1$. The forecasts from the unobserved components (UC) model and reduced form are the same. An autoregressive approximation to the reduced form is possible, but, if q is close to zero, a large number of lags may be needed for the approximation to yield acceptable forecasts.

The UC model in (1.1) is effectively in state space form (SSF), and as such, it may be handled by the Kalman filter (KF); see Harvey (1989). The parameters ϕ and q can be estimated by maximum likelihood, with the likelihood function constructed from the one-step-ahead prediction errors. The KF can be expressed as a single equation which combines the estimator of μ_t based on information at time $t-1$ with the t-th observation in order to produce the best estimator of μ_{t+1}. Writing this equation together with an equation that defines the one-step-ahead prediction error, v_t, gives the *innovations form* (IF) of the Kalman filter:

$$\begin{aligned} y_t &= \mu_{t|t-1} + v_t, \quad t = 1, \ldots, T, \\ \mu_{t+1|t} &= \phi\mu_{t|t-1} + k_t v_t. \end{aligned} \tag{1.3}$$

The Kalman gain, k_t, depends on ϕ and q. In the steady-state, k_t is constant. Setting it equal to a parameter, κ, and rearranging gives the ARMA model, (1.2), with $\xi_t = v_t$ and $\phi - \kappa = \theta$. A pure autoregressive (AR) model is a special case in which $\kappa = \phi$, so that $\mu_{t|t-1} = \phi y_{t-1}$.

Now suppose that the noise in a UC model comes from a heavy-tailed distribution, such as Student's t. Such a distribution can give rise to observations which, when judged against the yardstick of a Gaussian distribution, are considered to be outliers. In the case of (1.1), the reduced form is still an $ARMA(1,1)$ process, but with disturbances which, although they are serially uncorrelated, are not independently and identically distributed. Allowing the disturbances to have a heavy-tailed distribution does not deal with the problem. A large value of ε_t only affects the current observation, but in the reduced form, it is incorporated into the level and takes time to work through the system. To be specific, the AR representation of an $ARMA(1,1)$ process is

$$y_t = (\phi - \theta)\sum_{j=1}^{\infty}\phi^{j-1}y_{t-j} + \xi_t = \mu_{t|t-1} + \xi_t.$$

If the t-th observation is contaminated by adding an arbitrary amount, C, then, after τ periods, the prediction of the next observation is still contaminated by C because it contains the quantity $(\phi - \theta)\phi^{\tau}C$.

An ARMA or AR model in which the disturbances are allowed to have a heavy-tailed distribution is designed to handle *innovation outliers*, as opposed to *additive outliers*. There is a good deal of discussion of outliers, and how to handle them, in the robustness literature; see, for example, the book by Maronna, Martin and Yohai (2006, Chapter 8) and the recent article by Muler, Pena and Yohai (2009) on robust estimation for ARMA models. The view taken here is that a model-based approach is not only simpler, both conceptually and computationally, than the usual robust methods, but is also more amenable to diagnostic checking and generalization.

Simulation methods, such as Markov chain Monte Carlo (MCMC), importance sampling and particle filtering, provide the basis for a direct attack on models that are nonlinear and/or non-Gaussian. The aim is to extend the Kalman filtering and smoothing algorithms that have proved so effective in handling linear Gaussian models. Considerable progress has been made in recent years; see Robert and Casella (2010), Durbin and Koopman (2012) and Koopman, Lucas and Schartha (2012). However, the fact remains that simulation-based estimation can be time-consuming and subject to a degree of uncertainty. In addition, the statistical properties of the estimators are not easy to establish.

The approach here begins by writing down the distribution of the t-th observation, conditional on past observations. Time-varying parameters are then updated by a suitably defined filter. Such a model is what Cox (1981) called *observation-driven*. In a linear Gaussian UC model, which is *parameter-driven* in Cox's terminology, the KF is driven by the one-step-ahead prediction error, as in (1.3). The main ingredient in the filter developed here for non-Gaussian distributions is the replacement of v_t in the KF equation by a variable, u_t, that is proportional to the score of the conditional distribution, that is the logarithm of the probability density function at time t differentiated with respect to $\mu_{t|t-1}$. Thus the second equation in (1.3) becomes

$$\mu_{t+1|t} = \phi\mu_{t|t-1} + \kappa u_t,$$

where κ is treated as an unknown parameter.

Why the score? If the signal in (1.1) were fixed, that is $\phi = 1$ and $\sigma_\eta^2 = 0$ so $\mu_t = \mu$, the sample mean, $\widehat{\mu}$, would satisfy the condition

$$\sum_{t=1}^{T}(y_t - \widehat{\mu}) = 0.$$

The maximum likelihood (ML) estimator is obtained by differentiating the log-likelihood function with respect to μ and setting the resulting derivative, the score, equal to zero. When the observations are normally distributed, the ML estimator is the same as the sample mean, the moment estimator. However, for a non-Gaussian distribution, the moment estimator and the ML estimator differ. Once the signal in a Gaussian model becomes dynamic, as in (1.1), its estimate can be updated with each new observation using the Kalman filter. With a non-normal distribution, exact updating is no longer possible, but the fact that ML estimation in the static case sets the score to zero provides a rationale for replacing the prediction error, which has mean zero, by the score, which for each individual observation also has mean zero. The resulting filter might, therefore, be regarded as an approximation to the computer-intensive solution for the UC model, and the evidence presented later lends support to this notion. Further theoretical support comes from the conditional mode approach to smoothing for nonlinear models. Indeed the argument presented in Sub-section 3.7.3 is a more comprehensive one.

The attraction of treating the filter driven by the score of the conditional distribution as a model in its own right is that it becomes possible to derive the asymptotic distribution of the ML estimator and to generalize in various directions. Thus the same approach can then be used to model scale, using an exponential link function, and to model location and scale for non-negative variables. The first equation in (1.3) is then nonlinear. The justification for the class of dynamic conditional score models is not that they approximate corresponding UC models, but rather that their statistical properties are both comprehensive and straightforward.

The use of the score of the conditional distribution to robustify the Kalman filter was originally proposed by Masreliez (1975). However, it has often been argued that a crucial assumption made by Masreliez (concerning the approximate normality of the prior at each time step) is, to quote Schick and Mitter (1994, p. 1054), 'insufficiently justified and remains controversial'. Nevertheless, they note that the procedure 'has been found to perform well both in simulation studies and with real data'. Schick and Mitter (1994) suggested a generalization of the Masreliez filter based on somewhat stronger theoretical foundations. The observation noise is assumed to come from a contaminated normal distribution, and the resulting estimator employs banks of Kalman filters and smoothers weighted by posterior probabilities. As a result, it is considerably more complicated than the Masreliez filter. Once the realm of computationally intensive techniques has been entered, it seems better to adopt the simulation-based methods alluded to earlier.

The situations tackled by Masreliez are more complicated than those considered here because the system matrices in the state space model may be time-varying. The models in this monograph are simpler in structure, and as a result, the use of the score to drive the dynamics can be put on much firmer statistical foundations.

1.2 INDEPENDENCE, WHITE NOISE AND MARTINGALE DIFFERENCES

The study of models that are not linear and Gaussian requires a careful distinction to be made between the concepts of independence, uncorrelatedness and martingale differences. But before proceeding, some basic statistical results need to be stated. The proofs can be found in many introductory time series and econometrics texts.

1.2.1 The Law of Iterated Expectations and Optimal Predictions

A key element in some of the statistical derivations that follow is the *law of iterated expectations* (LIE). Suppose that it is difficult to find the expected value of a random variable, y, but evaluating its expectation conditional on another random variable, x, is straightforward. Then $E(y)$ may be obtained as

$$E(y) = E_x[E(y \mid x)],$$

because

$$E_x[E(y|x)] = \int \left[\int yf(y|x)\,dy \right] f(x)\,dx$$
$$= \iint yf(y,x)\,dy\,dx = E(y).$$

The above process may be generalized and repeated. Thus, if $g(y_t)$ is a function of y_t, an expected value several steps ahead can be found from the sequence of one-step-ahead conditional expectations because

$$\underset{t-j}{E}[g(y_t)] = \underset{t-j}{E} \cdots \underset{t-1}{E}[g(y_t)], \quad j = 2, 3, \ldots.$$

The unconditional expectation is found by letting $j \to \infty$. The expectation of a function of the observation at time $T+\ell$ based on information available at time T is given by setting $t = T+\ell$ and $j = \ell$ so

$$\underset{T}{E}[g(y_{T+\ell})] = \underset{T}{E} \cdots \underset{T+\ell-1}{E}[g(y_{T+\ell})], \qquad \ell = 2, 3, \ldots. \tag{1.4}$$

When the objective is to predict a future observation based on current information, the conditional expectation, $E_T(y_{T+\ell})$, $\ell = 1, 2, 3, \ldots$, is optimal in the sense that it minimizes the mean square error (MSE) of the prediction error; see, for example, Harvey (1993, p. 33). As such, it is called the minimum mean square error (MMSE) predictor. For nonlinear models, expression (1.4) is of considerable practical importance for finding MMSE predictors.

1.2.2 Definitions and Properties

The following important definitions should be noted.

Definition 1 *White noise (WN) variables are serially uncorrelated with constant mean and variance.*

Definition 2 *A martingale difference (MD) has a zero (or constant) conditional expectation, that is,*

$$\underset{t-1}{E}(y_t) = E(y_t \mid Y_{t-1}) = 0.$$

It is also necessary for the unconditional expectation of the absolute value to be finite, that is, $E|y_t| < \infty$; see Davidson (2000, pp. 121–2).

Definition 3 *Strict white noise variables are independent and identically distributed (IID).*

The relationship between a martingale difference and the two kinds of white noise is given by the following proposition.

Proposition 1 *(a) All zero mean independent sequences are martingale differences and (b) all martingale differences are white noise, provided that the variance is finite. In neither case is the converse true.*

Proof. Part (a) requires no proof. Part (b) follows because all MDs have zero unconditional mean and are serially uncorrelated. Specifically

$$E(y_t) = E[E(y_t \mid Y_{t-1})] = 0$$

and y_t is uncorrelated with any function of past observations because

$$E[y_t f(Y_{t-1}) \mid Y_{t-1}] = f(Y_{t-1}) E(y_t \mid Y_{t-1}) = 0.$$

Hence the unconditional expectation of $y_t f(Y_{t-1})$ is zero.

The heteroscedastic models introduced in the next section produce observations that are MDs but not IID. That a WN sequence is not necessarily an MD can be demonstrated by a simple example showing that there may be a nontrivial nonlinear predictor. To be specific, the observations in the model

$$y_t = \varepsilon_t + \beta\varepsilon_{t-1}\varepsilon_{t-2}, \quad \varepsilon_t \sim IID(0, \sigma^2), \qquad t = 1, \ldots, T,$$

where ε_0 and ε_{-1} are fixed and known, are white noise, but not an MD because $E(y_{T+1} \mid Y_T) = \beta\varepsilon_T\varepsilon_{T-1}$. ■

Remark 1 *When a variable is normally distributed, the distinction between WN, strict WN and MDs disappears, the reason being that a normal distribution is fully described by its first two moments. Thus Gaussian white noise is strict white noise.*

A *linear process* is usually defined as one that can be written as an infinite moving average in $IID(0, \sigma^2)$ disturbances, with the sum of the squares of the coefficients being finite, that is,

$$y_t = \sum_{j=0}^{\infty} \psi_j \varepsilon_{t-j}, \quad \sum_{j=0}^{\infty} \psi_j^2 < \infty, \quad \varepsilon_t \sim IID(0, \sigma^2). \tag{1.5}$$

More generally, a linear process may be defined as a linear combination of past observations and/or strict white noise disturbances, with appropriately defined initial conditions.[1] For a stationary process, the representation in (1.5) means that all the information about the dynamics is in the autocorrelation function (ACF). Furthermore, the minimum mean square error predictor of $y_{T+\ell}$ is linear, and its MSE is $\sigma^2 \sum_{j=0}^{\ell-1} \psi_j^2$. However, unless the disturbances are Gaussian, the linearity of (1.5) is of limited practical value since it is not usually possible to derive the multistep predictive distribution. On the other hand, the optimal forecasts in a model which is a linear function of current and past MDs are the same as in a model in which the MDs are replaced by strict WN, and if the conditional variances are constant, the MSEs are the same.

1.3 VOLATILITY

If dividends and other payments are ignored, financial returns can be defined as the first differences of the logarithm of the price; see Taylor (2005, Chapter 2 and pp. 100–2). When markets are working efficiently, returns are martingale differences. In other words, they should not be predictable on the basis of past information. However, returns are not usually independent, and so features

[1] For further discussion, see Terasvirta et al. (2010, pp. 1–2).

of the conditional distribution apart from the mean may be predictable. In particular, nontrivial predictions can be made for the variance or scale.

1.3.1 Stochastic Volatility

The variance in *stochastic volatility* (SV) models is driven by an unobserved process. The first-order model, with the mean of the observations, y_t, $t = 1, .., T$, assumed to be zero, is

$$y_t = \sigma_t \varepsilon_t, \quad \sigma_t^2 = \exp(2\lambda_t), \quad \varepsilon_t \sim IID(0, 1) \tag{1.6}$$

$$\lambda_{t+1} = \delta + \phi\lambda_t + \eta_t, \quad \eta_t \sim NID\left(0, \sigma_\eta^2\right),$$

where the disturbances ε_t and η_t are mutually independent. Leverage effects, which enable σ_t^2 to respond asymmetrically to positive and negative values of y_t, can be introduced by allowing ε_t and η_t to be correlated, as in Harvey and Shephard (1996). Shephard and Andersen (2009) discuss the relationship between SV models and continuous time models in the finance literature.

The *exponential link function* ensures that the variance remains positive and the restrictions needed for λ_t and y_t to be stationary are straightforward; for (1.6), $|\phi| < 1$. Furthermore, analytic expressions for moments and ACFs of the absolute values of the observations raised to any power can be derived.

Unfortunately, direct maximum likelihood estimation of the SV model is not possible. A procedure can be based on the linear state space form obtained by taking logarithms of the absolute values of the demeaned observations to give the following measurement equation:

$$\ln|y_t| = \lambda_t + \ln|\varepsilon_t|, \quad t = 1, \ldots, T. \tag{1.7}$$

The parameters in the model are then estimated by using the Kalman filter, as in Harvey, Ruiz and Shephard (1994). However, there is a loss in efficiency because the distribution of $\ln|\varepsilon_t|$ is far from Gaussian. Efficient estimation can be achieved by computer-intensive methods, as described in Creal (2012), Andrieu et al. (2011) and Durbin and Koopman (2012).

1.3.2 Generalized Autoregressive Conditional Heteroscedasticity

The *generalized autoregressive conditional heteroscedasticity* (GARCH) model, introduced, as ARCH, by Engle (1982) and generalized by Bollerslev (1986) and Taylor (1986), is the classic way of modelling changes in the volatility of returns. It does so by letting the variance be a linear function of past squared observations. The first-order model, $GARCH(1, 1)$, is

$$y_t = \sigma_{t|t-1}\varepsilon_t, \quad \varepsilon_t \sim NID(0, 1) \tag{1.8}$$

and

$$\sigma_{t|t-1}^2 = \delta + \beta\sigma_{t-1|t-2}^2 + \alpha y_{t-1}^2, \quad \delta > 0, \beta \geq 0, \alpha \geq 0. \tag{1.9}$$

The conditions on α and β ensure that the variance remains positive. The sum of α and β is typically close to one, and the *integrated GARCH* (IGARCH) model is obtained when the sum is equal to one. The variance in IGARCH is an exponentially weighted moving average of past squared observations and, as such, is often used by practitioners.

The model may be extended by adding lags of the variance and the squared observations. Heavy tails are accommodated by letting the conditional distribution be Student's t, as proposed by Bollerslev (1987). The $GARCH(1, 1) - t$ model has become something of an industry standard.

Leverage effects, which enable $\sigma^2_{t|t-1}$ to respond asymmetrically to positive and negative values of y_t, are typically incorporated into GARCH models by including a variable in which the squared observations are multiplied by an indicator that takes a value of unity when an observation is negative and is zero otherwise; see Taylor (2005, pp. 220–1). The technique is often known as GJR, after the originators, Glosten, Jagannanthan and Runckle (1993).

The autocorrelations of squared observations may be obtained relatively easily, as they obey an ARMA process. For example, for $GARCH(1, 1)$ with zero mean

$$y_t^2 = \gamma + \phi y_{t-1}^2 + v_t + \theta^* v_{t-1}, \tag{1.10}$$

where v_t is white noise, $\phi = \alpha + \beta$ and $\theta^* = -\beta$. The drawback to working with squared observations is that outlying observations can seriously weaken the serial correlation. The autocorrelations of absolute values tend to be larger and so provide a better vehicle for detecting dynamic volatility and assessing its nature.

The principal advantage of GARCH models over SV models is that, because they are observation-driven, the likelihood function is immediately available.

1.3.3 Exponential GARCH

Nelson (1991) introduced the exponential GARCH (EGARCH) model in which the dynamic equation for volatility is formulated in terms of the logarithm of the conditional variance in (1.8). The leading case is

$$\ln \sigma^2_{t|t-1} = \delta + \phi \ln \sigma^2_{t-1|t-2} + \alpha\left[|\varepsilon_{t-1}| - E\,|\varepsilon_{t-1}|\right] + \alpha^* \varepsilon_{t-1}, \tag{1.11}$$

where α and α^* are parameters and, for a Gaussian model, $E\,|\varepsilon_t| = \sqrt{2/\pi}$. The role of ε_t is to capture leverage effects. As in the SV model, the exponential link function ensures that the variance is always positive. Indeed, the model has a structure similar to that of the SV model because $|\varepsilon_{t-1}| - E\,|\varepsilon_{t-1}|$, like ε_{t-1}, is an MD. Stationarity restrictions are similar to those in the SV model; for example, in the preceding equation, $|\phi| < 1$. The exponential link permits models that would be problematic with GARCH because of the need to ensure a positive variance. In particular, cycles and seasonal effects are possible.

Nelson (1991) noted that if the conditional distribution of the observations is Student's t, with finite degrees of freedom, the conditions needed for the existence of the moments of $\sigma^2_{t|t-1}$ and y_t are rarely satisfied in practice. Hence the model is of little practical value because, without a first moment, even the sample mean is inconsistent. The lack of moments for Student's t and the fact that there is no asymptotic theory for ML has limited the application of EGARCH.

1.3.4 Variance, Scale and Outliers

Substituting repeatedly for the conditional variance in (1.9) gives an infinite autoregression in squared observations. In an $ARCH(p)$ model, forecasts are made directly from a finite number of past squared observations – hence the name ARCH. From our perspective, the reason that GARCH is more plausible than $ARCH(p)$ is that estimating variance is an exercise in signal extraction, and as such, the conditional variance cannot normally be a finite autoregression. The $ARCH(1)$ model is particularly problematic, as it is based on a single squared observation which is bound to be a poor estimator of variance.

The great strength of the GARCH filter is its simple interpretation as an estimate of variance constructed by weighting the squared observations. This is also its weakness, because a linear combination of past squares (even if infinite) may not be a good choice for modelling dynamics when the conditional distribution is non-Gaussian. This stems from the fact that the sample variance in a static model can be very inefficient. Indeed, for some heavy-tailed distributions, the variance may not exist. The difficulties can be avoided by modelling scale instead. Since scale is necessarily positive (as is variance), an exponential link function is appropriate. Furthermore, a model for the logarithm of volatility may be regarded as an approximation to an SV model. This reasoning led to Nelson proposing EGARCH. The only flaw was to use absolute values in the dynamic equation. Replacing the absolute value by the score resolves the problem.

Outliers present a practical problem for GARCH models, even if the conditional distribution is allowed to have heavy tails, as in GARCH-t. The reason is that a large value becomes embedded in the conditional variance and typically takes a long time to work through. This is the same difficulty that was noted earlier in connection with additive outliers.

1.3.5 Location/Scale Models

Many variables are intrinsically non-negative. Examples in finance include duration, range, realized volatility and spreads; see, for example, Brownlees and Gallo (2010) and Russell and Engle (2010). Other situations in economics in which distributions for non-negative variables are appropriate are in the study of incomes and the size of firms; the book by Kleiber and Kotz (2003) describes many case studies.

Engle (2002) introduced a class of *multiplicative error models* (MEMs) for time series modelling of non-negative variables. In these models, the conditional mean, $\mu_{t|t-1}$, is driven by a GARCH-type equation, and so

$$y_t = \varepsilon_t \mu_{t|t-1}, \qquad 0 \leq y_t < \infty, \quad t = 1, \ldots, T,$$

where ε_t has a distribution with mean one and, analogous to $GARCH(1, 1)$,

$$\mu_{t|t-1} = \delta + \beta \mu_{t-1|t-2} + \alpha y_{t-1}, \quad \delta > 0, \beta \geq 0, \alpha \geq 0. \tag{1.12}$$

The gamma distribution is often used for ε_t, with the exponential distribution being an important special case. The gamma distribution does not have a heavy tail, so distributions such as the Weibull and Burr may sometimes be preferred. Nevertheless, the fact that the observations enter directly into the dynamic equation means that observations which would be considered as outliers for a gamma distribution can become embedded in the predictions. Thus the linearity of (1.12) must be questioned, just as the use of a linear combination of squares was questioned for GARCH.

An exponential link function is sometimes used to ensure that $\mu_{t|t-1}$ remains positive; see, for example, Brandt and Jones (2006). However, an exponential link does not, in itself, deal with the problem noted at the end of the previous paragraph.

1.4 DYNAMIC CONDITIONAL SCORE MODELS

An *observation-driven* model is set up in terms of a conditional distribution for the *t-th* observation. Thus

$$f(y_t|\theta_{t|t-1}, Y_{t-1}), \qquad t = 1, \ldots, T, \tag{1.13}$$

$$\theta_{t+1|t} = g(\theta_{t|t-1}, \theta_{t-1|t-2}, \ldots, Y_t)$$

where Y_t denotes observations up to, and including y_t, and $\theta_{t|t-1}$ is a parameter that changes over time. The second equation in (1.13) may be regarded as a data-generating process or as a way of writing a filter that approximates a nonlinear UC model. In both cases, the notation $\theta_{t+1|t}$ stresses its status as a parameter of the conditional distribution and as a filter that is a function of past observations.[2] The likelihood function for an observation-driven model is immediately available because the joint density of a set of T observations is

$$L(\boldsymbol{\psi}) = \prod_{t=1}^{T} f(y_t|Y_{t-1}; \boldsymbol{\psi}),$$

where $\boldsymbol{\psi}$ denotes a vector of unknown constant parameters.

[2] Andersen et al. (2006) use the same notation for the conditional variance in their survey on GARCH models.

The first-order Gaussian GARCH model, (1.8) and (1.9), is an observation-driven model in which $\theta_{t|t-1} = \sigma^2_{t|t-1}$. As such, it may be written

$$y_t \mid Y_{t-1} \sim NID\left(0, \sigma^2_{t|t-1}\right)$$

$$\sigma^2_{t+1|t} = \delta + \phi\sigma^2_{t|t-1} + \alpha v_t, \quad \delta > 0,\ \phi \geq \alpha,\ \alpha \geq 0, \tag{1.14}$$

where $\phi = \alpha + \beta$ and $v_t = y_t^2 - \sigma^2_{t|t-1}$ is a martingale difference. Writing the dynamic equation with $\sigma^2_{t+1|t}$, as opposed to $\sigma^2_{t|t-1}$, on the left-hand side stresses the link with signal extraction.

Once the assumption of Gaussianity is dropped, the case for weighting the squared observations is much weaker. In a DCS model, $\sigma^2_{t+1|t}$ depends on current and past values of a variable, u_t, that is defined as being proportional to the score of the conditional distribution at time t. This variable is an MD by construction. When y_t has a conditional t distribution with ν degrees of freedom, the DCS modification replaces v_t in the conditional variance equation, (1.14), by another MD, $v_t = \sigma^2_{t|t-1}u_t$, where

$$u_t = \frac{(\nu+1)y_t^2}{(\nu-2)\sigma^2_{t|t-1} + y_t^2} - 1, \quad -1 \leq u_t \leq \nu, \quad \nu > 2. \tag{1.15}$$

This model is called *Beta-t-GARCH* because u_t is a linear function of a variable with a beta distribution. Note that u_t is the score standardized by dividing by the information quantity, $I(\sigma^2_{t|t-1}) = \sigma^{-4}_{t|t-1}$, and then multiplying by two. When $\nu = \infty$, $u_t = y_t^2/\sigma^2_{t|t-1} - 1$ and the standard GARCH model, (1.14), is obtained by setting $v_t = \sigma^2_{t|t-1}u_t$.

Figure 1.1 shows the *impact curve* for Beta-t-GARCH as a plot of the conditional score function, u, against y for t – distributions with $\nu = 3$ and 10 and for the normal distribution ($\nu = \infty$). In all cases the variance is unity. When $\nu = 3$, an extreme observation has only a moderate impact, whereas if it were treated as coming from a normal distribution, it would imply a significant change in the variance. As $|y_t| \to \infty$, $u_t \to \nu$ so u_t is bounded for finite ν, as is the robust conditional variance equation proposed by Muler and Yohai (2008, p. 2922).

The DCS volatility models have particularly attractive properties when an exponential link function is used. In the Gaussian case, this implies that the dynamic equation applies to $\ln \sigma^2_{t+1|t}$, as in EGARCH. For the t distribution, it is better to work with the scale, which, for $\nu > 2$, is related to the standard deviation by the formula, $\varphi_{t+1|t} = (\nu-2)^{1/2}\sigma_{t+1|t}$. The dynamic equation is then set up for the logarithm of scale, $\lambda_{t+1|t} = \ln \varphi_{t+1|t}$, and so the first-order model is

$$\lambda_{t+1|t} = \delta + \phi\lambda_{t|t-1} + \kappa u_t, \qquad t = 1, \ldots, T, \tag{1.16}$$

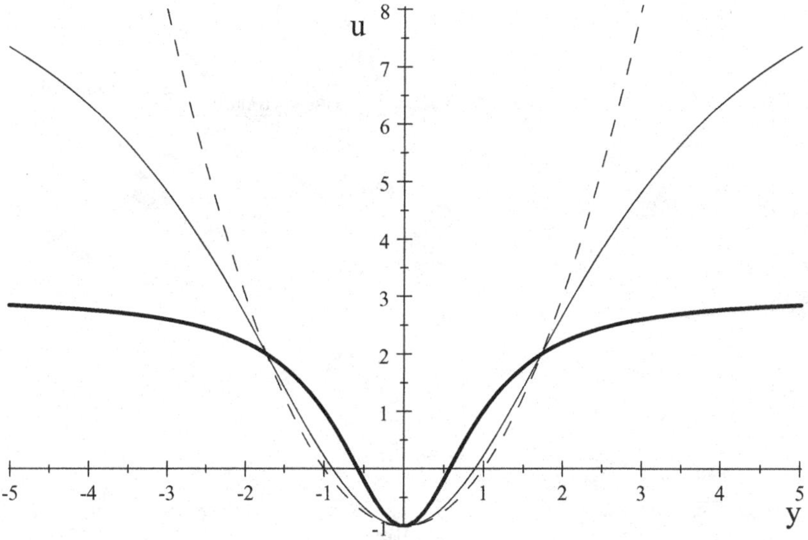

Figure 1.1. Impact of score for t_ν with $\nu = 3$ (thick), $\nu = 10$ (thin) and $\nu = \infty$ (dashed).

where

$$u_t = \frac{(\nu + 1)y_t^2}{\nu \exp(2\lambda_{t|t-1}) + y_t^2} - 1, \quad -1 \leq u_t \leq \nu, \quad \nu > 0,$$

is just the conditional score. Like (1.15), it has a beta distribution, but the crucial point is that it enters directly into the dynamic equation, whereas (1.15) is multiplied by $\sigma^2_{t|t-1}$. The class of models obtained by combining the conditional score with an exponential link function is called *Beta-t-EGARCH*. A complementary class is based on the general error distribution distribution. The conditional score then has a gamma distribution, leading to the name *Gamma-GED-EGARCH*.

Example 1 *On Thursday, 28 September 2000, the computer firm Apple issued a profit warning, which led the value of the stock to plunge from an end-of-trading value of \$26.75 to \$12.88 on the subsequent day. This change corresponds to a drop of about 73% in the log-difference. In terms of volatility, the fall was a one-off event, because it apparently had no effect on the variability of the price changes on the following days. Figure 1.2 plots absolute demeaned returns, the fitted conditional standard deviations of a $GARCH(1,1)$-t model (with leverage) and the fitted conditional standard deviations of the corresponding Beta-t-EGARCH model; see Harvey and Sucarrat (2012) and Example 17 for further analysis. As is clear from the figure, the GARCH forecasts of one-step standard deviations exceed absolute returns for almost two months after the*

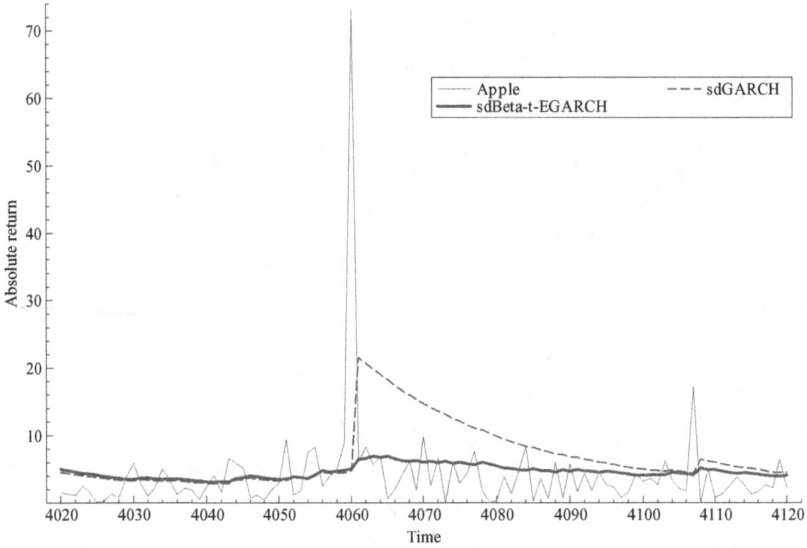

Figure 1.2. Absolute values of demeaned Apple returns with filtered GARCH-t and Beta-t-EGARCH.

event. By contrast, the Beta-t-EGARCH forecasts remain in the same range of variation as the absolute returns.

Similar considerations arise when dealing with location/scale models. Again, u_t is chosen so as to be proportional to the conditional score. Figure 1.3 shows a plot of u_t against y for a standardized log-logistic distribution, with a shape parameter of three, and contrasts it with the response for a gamma distribution, which is linear. Although the DCS approach for a gamma distribution is consistent with the conditional mean dynamic equation of (1.12), it suggests a dampening down of the impact of a large observation from a log-logistic.

Remark 2 *There is a considerable literature on QML estimation of GARCH models. In this context, QML estimates the parameters under the assumption of Gaussianity. Similarly, QML can be used to estimate the parameters in an ARMA model. QML is then essentially just least squares. For a location/scale model, QML is based on the exponential distribution. The estimators can be shown to be consistent for certain distributions other than the assumed one, and asymptotically correct standard errors can be computed.*[3] *However, QML is of little use when the dynamic equation is incorrect.*

[3] Standard QML asymptotic theory breaks down for GARCH models with heavy-tailed distributions (specifically those without fourth moments), and modified bootstrap procedures have to be used, as in Hall and Yao (2003).

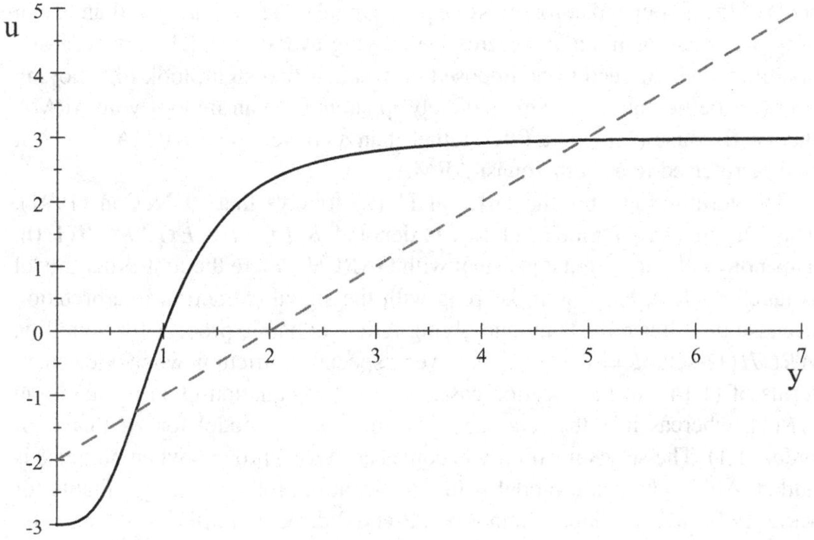

Figure 1.3. Impact of score for a log-logistic distribution and a gamma distribution (dashed), with shape parameters $\nu = 3$ and $\gamma = 2$, respectively.

In this monograph, attention is directed towards score-driven models for which an asymptotic distribution for the ML estimator can be derived. The asymptotics work because the score and its first derivative are distributed independently of the time-varying parameter(s) and have finite first and second moments. The main theorem is set out in Chapter 2 and then applied in the next three chapters, which deal respectively with location models, scale models (primarily EGARCH), and location/scale models. Other properties of the proposed models may also be found. In particular, there are analytic expressions for moments, autocorrelation functions, and multistep forecasts, together with their mean square errors. The properties, particularly for the volatility models which employ an exponential link function, are more general than is usually the case; expressions for unconditional moments, autocorrelations, and the conditional moments of multistep predictive distributions can be found for absolute values of the observations raised to any power.

For modelling volatility, the popularity of $GARCH(1, 1)$ suggests that the first-order model, (1.16), will be the most widely used in practice. More generally, a linear dynamic model of order (p, r) for a parameter $\theta_{t|t-1}$ may be defined as

$$\theta_{t+1|t} = \delta + \phi_1\theta_{t|t-1} + \cdots + \phi_p\theta_{t-p+1|t-p} + \kappa_0 u_t + \kappa_1 u_{t-1} + \cdots + \kappa_r u_{t-r}, \quad (1.17)$$

where $p \geq 0$ and $r \geq 0$ are finite integers and $\delta, \phi_1, .., \phi_p, \kappa_0, .., \kappa_r$ are (fixed) parameters. Stationarity (both strict and covariance) of $\theta_{t|t-1}$ requires that the roots of the associated autoregressive polynomial equation[4] are less than one in absolute value, as in an autoregressive-moving average model. However, any conditions which need to be imposed on what, at first sight, look like moving average coefficients are not immediately apparent from an analogy with ARMA theory. Because (1.17) is a filter, rather than a conventional ARMA model, it will be referred to as being quasi-ARMA.

The terminology for the order of (1.17) follows that of Nelson (1991). Thus the first-order model, (1.16), is denoted $Beta-t-EGARCH(1,0)$. This nomenclature is not consistent with GARCH, where the first-order model is labelled (1,1), but it is in keeping with the signal extraction interpretation because the filter reflects an underlying AR(1) dynamic process for volatility. $ARCH(1)$ sets $\phi = \kappa$, which is a very special restriction when viewed in terms of (1.14). In the location case, the level in equation (1.1) is clearly an $AR(1)$, whereas it is the reduced form, the ARMA model for y_t, that is of order (1,1). The series itself only becomes an $AR(1)$ process when no noise is added. Although such a model is fine for location, it is not really suitable for variance because variance cannot be observed directly. Further discussion on these matters can be found in Appendix D.

Although equation (1.17) generalizes DCS models in the ARMA direction, another possibility is to develop DCS models that mirror the unobserved component, or structural time series models, that are implemented in the STAMP package of Koopman et al. (2009). Such models typically include trend, seasonal and cyclical components for capturing movements in location. The DCS approach leads to a filter that is suitable for a heavy-tailed irregular component. Furthermore, the use of an exponential link function allows the inclusion of trend, seasonal and cyclical components in dynamic volatility models, without the attendant difficulties experienced with GARCH because of the need to ensure a positive variance.

1.5 DISTRIBUTIONS AND QUANTILES

Once the Gaussian assumption is dropped, the question arises as to why the focus should be on mean and variance. Admittedly, the mean is rather basic, but the attraction of the variance is limited because attention is typically on certain quantiles or indeed the whole distribution.

One of the reasons for the interest in quantiles is that they define, or help to define, certain measures of risk. In particular, *value at risk* (VaR) for a return, y, is

$$\Pr(y \leq VaR_\tau(y)) = \tau,$$

[4] The associated autoregressive polynomial equation is $x^p - \phi_1 x^{p-1} - \cdots - \phi_p = 0$. The roots may be complex conjugates. Hence the reference to absolute value (or modulus).

so $VaR_{\tau}(y)$ is just the τ-th quantile; see, for example, Tsay (2010). *Expected shortfall* (ES), defined as

$$ES_{\tau}(y) = E[y \mid y > VaR_{\tau}(y)),$$

is often preferred to VaR because it aggregates risks in a coherent manner.

For tabulated distributions, such as the normal and t, the quantiles can be read off directly, and so VaR for the one-step-ahead conditional distribution is readily available. Sometimes analytic expressions are available for quantiles. The quantile function for a given distribution function, $F(y)$, is $F^{-1}(\tau)$, $0 \leq \tau \leq 1$.

Multistep predictive distributions for DCS models are easily simulated, and hence VaR and ES can be calculated to a required degree of precision. In a similar way, expected loss can be computed by simulation for any loss function and the results employed in decision making; see Harvey (1989, pp. 222–26).

What happens if we are not prepared to assume a distribution? The attraction of QML estimation for GARCH is that it is consistent, even if the distribution is not normal. As a result, many researchers are more comfortable with QML than with an approach that assumes a specific distribution; see the remarks in Gregory and Reeves (2010, p. 553). However, setting aside the point that QML values consistency more than efficiency and a desire to explore different model specifications, the implied focus on variance is of limited value if what is required is knowledge of the quantiles. In any case, as was pointed out in Remark 2, the argument that QML is robust to misspecification misses the point because it assumes that the specification of the conditional variance as a linear combination of squares is correct.

A better approach to relaxing the dependence on distributional assumptions is to develop nonparametric methods for time series data. Rather than weighting squared observations, as in GARCH, weighting patterns implied by dynamics models can be applied to the kernels that are typically used for density estimation. Thus the whole distribution is tracked as it changes over time, and at the same time, features of the distribution, such as quantiles, can be extracted. Proceeding in this way raises various issues. For example, is it better to model the quantiles directly, and how well is tail behaviour captured?

1.6 PLAN OF BOOK

The plan of this book is as follows. Chapter 2 provides some basic theory, beginning with a review of Student's t and general error distributions. The principles of maximum likelihood estimation are discussed. The asymptotic theory for the properties of the maximum likelihood estimators of the parameters in the DCS class is then developed.

Chapters 3, 4 and 5 set out the theory for location, scale and location/scale models. For the reader primarily interested in volatility, the core material is in Chapters 4 and 5. Attention is initially focussed on stationary time series, after which it is shown how trend and seasonal components may be handled by drawing on parallels with the unobserved component, or structural, time series models that have been successfully applied to modelling the level of Gaussian time series. The technical manipulations rest mainly on standard properties of the beta and gamma distributions. Once this is appreciated, most of the results and formulae follow in a straightforward and elegant fashion. Indeed the fact that the mathematics is so transparent is a strong indication that the statistical structure of the class of models is a sound one. However, the appeal of the mathematics should not detract from the main purpose of the models, which is to deal with heavy-tailed distributions in a manner that is efficient, both statistically and from the practical perspective.

Chapter 6 indicates how the ideas of the earlier chapters might be extended to nonparametric estimation of changing distributions. Chapter 7 provides an introduction to the challenges associated with modelling multivariate time series. The DCS approach leads to an appealing way of modelling changing correlation, as well as changing scale. In fact, tackling model construction for dynamic relationships as an exercise in changing correlation, rather than through the usual route of time-varying regression parameters, seems to be the best way forward. Further development leads to the replacement of correlation by the more general concept of association and the opportunities afforded by the modelling of dynamic copulas.

CHAPTER 2

Statistical Distributions and Asymptotic Theory

The asymptotic distribution theory for a wide range of dynamic conditional score models is of crucial importance in showing their viability. The information matrix can be obtained explicitly, and the proof of the asymptotic normality of the maximum likelihood estimators is relatively straightforward. This contrasts with the situation for most other classes of nonlinear dynamic models. For example, no explicit information matrix is available for the most commonly used GARCH models, whereas for EGARCH models there is virtually no asymptotic theory for ML estimation.

Section 2.1 reviews the properties of the distributions that feature most prominently in this book. The interconnections between the various distributions provide the building blocks for the theory that follows. Maximum likelihood estimation is discussed for static models before moving on to the main theorems in Section 2.3. It is shown that, for the class of models in question, the information matrix breaks down into two parts. One part is the information matrix of the static model, whereas the other is a matrix linked to the equation for the dynamics. This second matrix depends on properties of the conditional score. Its form is the same for all the models described in Chapters 3, 4 and 5, and the sections on asymptotic theory in these chapters simply link up the two components of the information matrix to give the full picture. The asymptotic theory points to certain restrictions on the dynamic parameters, and the form taken by these restrictions is investigated in later chapters. Section 2.4 indicates how to extend the results on asymptotic theory for the first-order dynamic equation to more complex models. Lagrange multiplier tests against serial correlation are derived in Section 2.5. Methods for assessing goodness of fit are also discussed. The last section introduces explanatory variables into the models.

2.1 DISTRIBUTIONS

Student's t distribution and the general error distribution play a key role in the ensuing development. Both include the Gaussian distribution as a special case. Beta and gamma distributions feature in the score and its derivatives. Hence their properties are invoked in deriving expressions for moments and ACFs of the series, as well as in obtaining asymptotic distributions of ML estimators.

2.1.1 Student's *t* Distribution

The t_ν distribution with a location of μ and scale of φ has probability density function (PDF)

$$f(y;\mu,\varphi,\nu)=\frac{\Gamma\left((\nu+1)/2\right)}{\Gamma\left(\nu/2\right)\varphi\sqrt{\pi\nu}}\left(1+\frac{(y-\mu)^2}{\nu\varphi^2}\right)^{-(\nu+1)/2}, \quad \varphi,\nu>0, \tag{2.1}$$

where ν is the degrees of freedom and $\Gamma(.)$ is the gamma function. Moments exist only up to and including $\nu-1$; see (2.12). Thus the mean is finite when $\nu>1$. Because the distribution is symmetric, the mean is equal to the median (which always exists). For $\nu>2$, the variance is

$$\sigma^2=\{\nu/(\nu-2)\}\varphi^2. \tag{2.2}$$

The excess kurtosis, that is the amount by which the normal distribution's kurtosis of three is exceeded, is $6/(\nu-4)$, provided that $\nu>4$.

The Cauchy distribution is t_1 and famously has no moments. Its PDF is

$$f(y)=\frac{1}{\pi\varphi}\left(1+\frac{(y-\mu)^2}{\varphi^2}\right)^{-1}.$$

The standardized PDF, that is, $\mu=0$ and $\varphi=1$, is plotted together with that of the normal in Figure 2.1. The tails of the Cauchy distribution are much heavier than those of the normal.

When observations are from a t_ν distribution in which ν is small, the sample mean is a very inefficient estimator of μ. For example, with $\nu=3$, the efficiency is one-half. The sample variance is even more inefficient. Specifically,

$$Eff(variance)=(\nu+3)(\nu-4)/\{\nu(\nu-1)\}, \quad \nu>4.$$

The efficiencies of the mean and variance are plotted against ν in Figure 2.2. The efficiency of the variance plummets once ν reaches single figures; for $\nu=6$, which is not unusual for financial returns, it is 0.60. The efficiency of the median,

$$Eff(median)=\left(\frac{2\Gamma\left((\nu+1)/2\right)}{\Gamma(1/2)\,\Gamma(\nu/2)\,\nu^{1/2}}\right)^2\frac{\nu+3}{\nu+1}, \quad \nu>0,$$

is also shown. The median always has a limiting normal distribution, whereas the mean needs $\nu>2$. For a Cauchy distribution, the median has an efficiency of 0.81.

Efficient estimators are obtained by maximum likelihood, as described in Section 2.2.

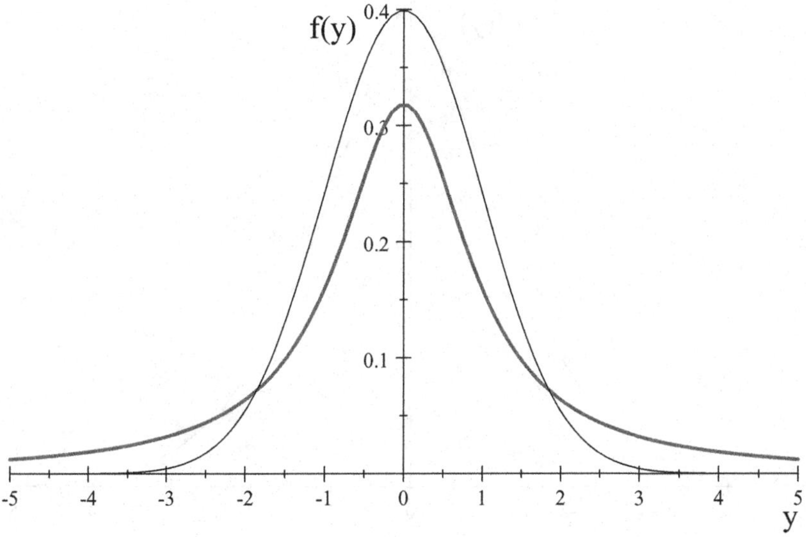

Figure 2.1. Cauchy (thick line) and Gaussian distributions.

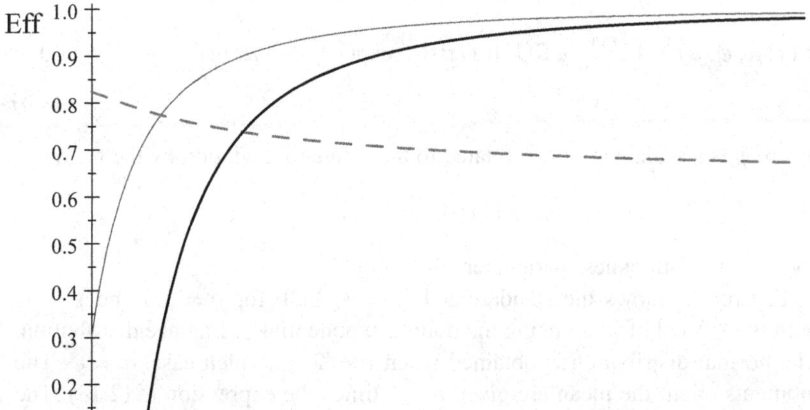

Figure 2.2. Efficiencies of sample mean (top), median (- - -) and variance for a t_ν distribution.

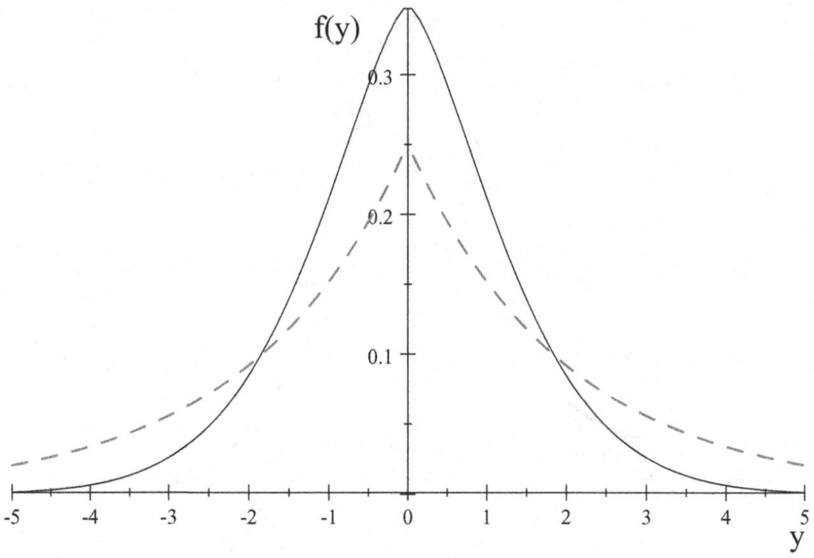

Figure 2.3. GED distributions with $\upsilon = 1.5$ and $\upsilon = 1$ (dashed).

2.1.2 General Error Distribution

The PDF of the general error distribution, denoted *GED*(υ), is

$$f\,(y;\mu,\varphi,\upsilon) = \left[2^{1+1/\upsilon}\varphi\Gamma(1+1/\upsilon)\right]^{-1}\exp(-\left|(y-\mu)/\varphi\right|^{\upsilon}/2),\ \varphi,\upsilon>0, \tag{2.3}$$

where φ is a scale parameter, related to the standard deviation by the formula

$$\sigma = 2^{1/\upsilon}(\Gamma\,(3/\upsilon)\,/\,\Gamma\,(1/\upsilon))^{1/2}\varphi,$$

and υ is a tail-thickness parameter.

Figure 2.3 shows the standardized ($\varphi = 1$) PDF for $\upsilon = 1.5$ and $\upsilon = 1$, with the second of these being the double exponential or Laplace distribution. The normal distribution is obtained when $\upsilon = 2$, in which case, $\sigma = \varphi$. The moments about the mean are given by φ^c times the expression in (2.13). The kurtosis is $\Gamma\,(5/\upsilon)\,\Gamma\,(1/\upsilon)$, so for $\upsilon = 1$, the excess kurtosis is nine.

2.1.3 Beta Distribution

When b has a $beta(\alpha,\beta)$ distribution, the PDF is

$$f(b) = \frac{1}{B(\alpha,\beta)}b^{\alpha-1}(1-b)^{\beta-1},\quad 0\le b\le 1,\quad \alpha,\beta>0, \tag{2.4}$$

where $B(\alpha,\beta) = \Gamma(\alpha)\Gamma(\beta)/\,\Gamma(\alpha+\beta)$ is the beta function.

Lemma 1 *When b has a beta(α, β) distribution and $w(b)$ is a function of b with finite expectation,*

$$E[b^h(1-b)^k w(b)] = \frac{B(\alpha+h, \beta+k)}{B(\alpha, \beta)} E[w(b)], \quad h > -\alpha, k > -\beta,$$

where the expectation on the right-hand side is now understood to be with respect to a beta$(\alpha + h, \beta + k)$ distribution.

Proof. The PDF of b is as in (2.4), so

$$\begin{aligned} &E(b^h(1-b)^k w(b)) \\ &= \frac{1}{B(\alpha, \beta)} \int b^h (1-b)^k b^{\alpha-1} (1-b)^{\beta-1} w(b) db, \quad h > -\alpha, \quad k > -\beta, \\ &= \frac{B(\alpha+h, \beta+k)}{B(\alpha, \beta)} \frac{1}{B(\alpha+h, \beta+k)} \int b^{\alpha-1+h} (1-b)^{\beta-1+k} w(b) db. \quad \blacksquare \end{aligned}$$

Note that h and k do not need to be integers. Setting $w(b) = 1$ gives the following important corollary.

Corollary 1 *When b has a beta(α, β) distribution*

$$E(b^h(1-b)^k) = \frac{B(\alpha+h, \beta+k)}{B(\alpha, \beta)}, \quad h > -\alpha, k > -\beta \tag{2.5}$$

and the moments are obtained by setting $k = 0$.

The mean is $\alpha/(\alpha + \beta)$. More generally, the formula in (2.5) can simplify significantly for small h and k.

Example 2 *For a beta$(1/2, \nu/2)$ distribution*

$$E(b(1-b)) = \frac{\Gamma(\alpha+1)\Gamma(\beta+1)}{\Gamma(\alpha+\beta+2)} \frac{\Gamma(\alpha+\beta)}{\Gamma(\alpha)\Gamma(\beta)} = \frac{\alpha\beta}{(\alpha+\beta+1)(\alpha+\beta)} \tag{2.6}$$

$$= \frac{(1/2)(\nu/2)}{(1/2+\nu/2+1)(1/2+\nu/2)} = \frac{\nu}{(\nu+3)(\nu+1)}. \tag{2.7}$$

The moment-generating function (MGF) of a beta distribution plays a key role in deriving results in later chapters. Suppose b has a beta(α, β) distribution and c is a finite number. Then,

$$M_\beta(c; \alpha, \beta) = E(e^{cb}) = 1 + \sum_{k=1}^{\infty} \left(\prod_{r=0}^{k-1} \frac{\alpha+r}{\alpha+\beta+r} \right) \frac{c^k}{k!}, \quad \alpha, \beta > 0. \tag{2.8}$$

The above expression is Kummer's (confluent hypergeometric) function, ${}_1F_1(\alpha; \beta; c)$; see Slater (1965, p. 504). It is available as a standard routine in many packages.

Finally, note that when b has a beta(α, β) distribution, the distribution of $1 - b$ is beta(β, α).

2.1.4 Gamma Distribution

The gamma distribution will feature in its own right in Chapter 5. In Chapters 3 and 4, its role is in connection with the t and general error distributions, especially the latter.

The PDF of a $gamma(\alpha, \gamma)$ variable is

$$f(g) = \alpha^{-\gamma} g^{\gamma-1} e^{-g/\alpha} / \Gamma(\gamma), \quad 0 \leq g < \infty, \quad \alpha, \gamma > 0, \tag{2.9}$$

where α is the scale parameter and γ is the shape parameter. The chi-square distribution with ν degrees of freedom is $gamma(2, \nu/2)$. Setting $\gamma = 1$ gives the exponential distribution.

The moments of all orders exist, with the raw moments given by

$$E(g^h) = \alpha^h \Gamma(h + \gamma) / \Gamma(\gamma), \quad h > 0. \tag{2.10}$$

Hence the mean is $\gamma\alpha$ and the variance is $\gamma\alpha^2$. The MGF is

$$M(c; \alpha, \gamma) = E(e^{cg}) = (1 - \alpha c)^{-\gamma}, \quad -\infty < c < 1/\alpha, \quad \gamma > 0. \tag{2.11}$$

There are a number of important connections between the gamma and other distributions.

Lemma 2 *The expected value of the absolute value of a standardized t_ν variate, ε_t, raised to a power c is*

$$E(|\varepsilon_t|^c) = \nu^{c/2}\Gamma(c/2+1/2)\Gamma(-c/2+\nu/2)/(\Gamma(1/2)\Gamma(\nu/2)), \quad -1 < c < \nu. \tag{2.12}$$

Proof. When ε_t is t_ν, $|\varepsilon_t|^c$ can be expressed in terms of the ratio of chi-square variables raised to the power $c/2$. The expected value of a chi-square with f degrees of freedom raised to the power $c/2$ is $2^{c/2}\Gamma(c/2 + f/2)/\Gamma(f/2)$, $c > -f$. ■

Lemma 3 *If z is $gamma(\theta, \alpha)$ and w is $gamma(\theta, \beta)$, then $x = z/(w + z)$ is $beta(\alpha, \beta)$.*

Corollary 2 *The variable $(t^2/\nu)/(1 + t^2/\nu)$ has a $beta(1/2, \nu/2)$ distribution, whereas $1/(1 + t^2/\nu)$ has a $beta(\nu/2, 1/2)$ distribution.*

Proof. *Because t^2/ν is the ratio of a squared standard normal to a χ^2_ν, it follows from Lemma 3 that $(t^2/\nu)/(1 + t^2/\nu) = (z/w)/(1 + z/w) = z/(w + z)$. Similarly, $1/(1 + t^2/\nu) = w/(w + z)$.* ■

Lemma 4 *For the GED, $|(y - \mu)/\varphi|^\upsilon$ has a $gamma(2, 1/\upsilon)$ distribution*

The preceding result can be easily proved by change of variable. The next result is immediate.

Corollary 3 *The expected value of the absolute value of a standardized $GED(\upsilon)$ variate raised to a power c is*

$$E(|(y-\mu)/\varphi|^c) = 2^{c/\upsilon}\Gamma((c+1)/\upsilon)/\Gamma(1/\upsilon), \quad c > -1, \quad \upsilon > 0. \tag{2.13}$$

The preceding expression gives the even (central) moments of a GED variate. The odd central moments are zero.

2.2 MAXIMUM LIKELIHOOD

Let $y_t, t = 1, \ldots, T$, be a set of time series observations, each of which is drawn from a distribution with probability density function $f(y_t; \boldsymbol{\theta})$, where $\boldsymbol{\theta}$ is a vector of parameters. When the observations are IID, the joint density function is just the product of the individual density functions. The likelihood function has the same form as the joint density function. For practical and theoretical reasons, it is more convenient to work with the logarithm of the likelihood function, and so

$$\ln L(\boldsymbol{\theta}; y_1, .., y_T) = \sum_{t=1}^{T} \ln f(y_t; \boldsymbol{\theta}).$$

The likelihood function differs from the joint density function in that the observations are taken as given, whereas $\boldsymbol{\theta}$ is variable. The aim is to find the value of $\boldsymbol{\theta}$ that makes the sample 'most likely'. The global maximum likelihood estimator, $\widetilde{\boldsymbol{\theta}}$, maximizes $\ln L(\boldsymbol{\theta})$ over the full parameter space. Provided that $\ln L(\boldsymbol{\theta})$ is differentiable at the true parameter value, $\widetilde{\boldsymbol{\theta}}$ will be given by solving the likelihood equations,

$$\frac{\partial \ln L(\boldsymbol{\theta})}{\partial \boldsymbol{\theta}} = \mathbf{0}. \tag{2.14}$$

Remark 3 *It is possible for the supremum of the likelihood function to be on a boundary, in which case solving the likelihood equation(s) may not yield the ML estimator. The random walk plus noise model, (1.1) with $\phi = 1$, provides an example; see Shephard and Harvey (1990).*

The properties of an ML estimator are usually straightforward to derive when it can be written in closed form.

Example 3 *The mean and variance in the Poisson distribution,*

$$f(y) = \mu^y e^{-\mu}/y!, \qquad y = 0, 1, 2, \ldots,$$

are both μ. The log-likelihood function for T independent observations is

$$\ln L(\mu) = \ln \mu \sum y_t - T\mu - \sum \ln y_t!$$

and so the ML estimator of μ is just the sample mean, that is, $\widetilde{\mu} = \overline{y}$. Thus the properties of the ML estimator are readily found, because, from Khinchine's *theorem, $\overline{y}$ is consistent, as it is the average of IID observations with finite mean, and the variance of the mean is μ/T. Asymptotic normality follows from a standard central limit theorem.*

The information matrix for a single observation is

$$\mathbf{I}(\boldsymbol{\theta}_0) = E_0\left(\frac{\partial \ln f}{\partial \boldsymbol{\theta}}\frac{\partial \ln f}{\partial \boldsymbol{\theta}'}\right) = -E_0\left(\frac{\partial^2 \ln f}{\partial \boldsymbol{\theta}\partial \boldsymbol{\theta}'}\right), \quad t = 1, \ldots, T, \qquad (2.15)$$

where the expectation is taken at the true value of $\boldsymbol{\theta}$, denoted $\boldsymbol{\theta}_0$. The full information matrix is $T.\mathbf{I}(\boldsymbol{\theta}_0)$. Provided that $f(y_t;\boldsymbol{\theta})$ satisfies certain regularity conditions, $\widetilde{\boldsymbol{\theta}}$ is a consistent estimator of $\boldsymbol{\theta}_0$, and it is asymptotically normal in the sense that $\sqrt{T}(\widetilde{\boldsymbol{\theta}} - \boldsymbol{\theta}_0)$ converges in distribution to a multivariate normal, with mean vector zero and covariance matrix $\mathbf{I}^{-1}(\boldsymbol{\theta}_0)$. The information matrix is positive definite, provided that the model is identifiable.

Example 4 *The information quantity for the Poisson distribution is*

$$I(\mu_0) = -E_0\left(\frac{\partial^2 \ln f}{\partial \mu^2}\right) = \frac{1}{\mu_0}.$$

In this case, $1/I(\mu_0)$ gives the small sample variance.

The vector in (2.14) is called the score of the likelihood function and, as such, is a function of $\boldsymbol{\theta}$ for a given set of observations. The score for a single observation plays a prominent role in the formulation of DCS models, but the statistical properties of these models are derived with respect to the score vector, $\partial \ln f(y_t;\boldsymbol{\theta})/\partial\boldsymbol{\theta}$, where the observations are random variables, just as they are in the formulae for the information matrix, (2.15).

The normal equations will often be nonlinear, in which case they must be solved by a numerical optimization procedure. There may be more than one solution to a particular likelihood equation, but only the global maximum yields the ML estimator. The location parameter in a Cauchy distribution provides an example, as discussed by Newey and McFadden (1994, p. 2117).

Remark 4 *There are different sets of regularity conditions, according to the nature of the problem. A very general treatment can be found in Newey and McFadden (1994). For the purposes of dealing with the dynamic models considered here, the most practical set of conditions seems to be those adapted from Jensen and Rahbek (2004). These conditions are set out in the final sub-section.*

2.2.1 Student's *t* Distribution

When observations are from a t_ν distribution, the logarithm of the PDF, the log-density, is

$$\ln f(y_t;\mu,\varphi,\nu) = \ln\Gamma\left((\nu+1)/2\right) - \frac{1}{2}\ln\pi - \ln\Gamma\left(\nu/2\right) \qquad (2.16)$$
$$-\frac{1}{2}\ln\nu - \ln\varphi - \frac{(\nu+1)}{2}\ln\left(1+\frac{(y_t-\mu)^2}{\nu\varphi^2}\right).$$

The information matrix[1] is

$$\mathbf{I}\begin{pmatrix}\mu\\ \varphi^2\\ \nu\end{pmatrix}=\begin{bmatrix}\frac{\nu+1}{\nu+3}\varphi^{-2} & 0 & 0\\ 0 & \frac{\nu}{2\varphi^4(\nu+3)} & \frac{1}{2\varphi^2(\nu+3)(\nu+1)}\\ 0 & \frac{1}{2\varphi^2(\nu+3)(\nu+1)} & h(\nu)/2\end{bmatrix},$$

where

$$h(\nu)=\frac{1}{2}\psi'(\nu/2)-\frac{1}{2}\psi'((\nu+1)/2)-\frac{\nu+5}{\nu(\nu+3)(\nu+1)}, \tag{2.17}$$

with $\psi'(.)$ being the trigamma function[2]; see, for example, Taylor and Verblya (2004) and Lin and Wang (2009). As will be seen in due course, the derivation depends on recognizing that the first derivatives of $\ln f$ with respect to μ and φ^2 are both simple functions of a variable with a beta distribution. If the parameterization is in terms of the variance rather than the squared scale, then, assuming $\nu > 2$, the only change to the information matrix is that σ^2 replaces φ^2 and the first element, associated with μ, is multiplied by $(\nu-2)/\nu$. The familiar information matrix for the mean and variance of a normal distribution is obtained as a limiting case.

The parameter λ, where $\varphi = \exp(\lambda)$, will normally be employed here when modelling dynamic scale. The information matrix is then

$$\mathbf{I}\begin{pmatrix}\mu\\ \lambda\\ \nu\end{pmatrix}=\begin{bmatrix}\frac{\nu+1}{\nu+3}\exp(-2\lambda) & 0 & 0\\ 0 & \frac{2\nu}{\nu+3} & \frac{1}{(\nu+3)(\nu+1)}\\ 0 & \frac{1}{(\nu+3)(\nu+1)} & h(\nu)/2\end{bmatrix}, \tag{2.18}$$

and a scale parameter no longer appears in the lower block. This feature of the link function turns out to be of crucial importance. The mathematics underlying the derivation (2.18) can be explained as follows. Assume for simplicity that μ is known to be zero. The score with respect to λ for a single observation,

$$\frac{\partial \ln f(y_t;\lambda,\nu)}{\partial\lambda}=\frac{(\nu+1)y_t^2}{\nu\exp(2\lambda)+y_t^2}-1,\quad t=1,\ldots,T,$$

may be expressed as

$$\frac{\partial \ln f(y_t;\lambda,\nu)}{\partial\lambda}=(\nu+1)b(y_t;\lambda,\nu)-1, \tag{2.19}$$

where

$$b(y_t;\lambda,\nu)=\frac{y_t^2/\nu\exp(2\lambda)}{1+y_t^2/\nu\exp(2\lambda)},\quad 0\le b\le 1,\quad 0<\nu<\infty. \tag{2.20}$$

[1] The information matrix is evaluated at the true parameter value, $\boldsymbol{\theta}_0$, but the subscript is often dropped.

[2] The digamma and trigamma functions appear in several formulae in this book. They are defined as the first and second derivatives, respectively, of the logarithm of the gamma function.

The result that $b(y_t; \lambda_0, \nu_0)$ is distributed as $beta(1/2, \nu/2)$ follows immediately from Corollary 2. Because $E(b) = 1/(\nu+1)$ and $Var(b) = 2\nu/\{(\nu+3)(\nu+1)^2\}$, the score has zero mean and variance $2\nu/(\nu+3)$. The variance is the second diagonal element in (2.18). The other elements in the information matrix can be similarly found.

2.2.2 General Error Distribution

The log-density for the t-th observation from a GED is

$$\ln f(y_t; \mu, \lambda, \upsilon) = -\left(1+\upsilon^{-1}\right)\ln 2 - \ln\Gamma(1+\upsilon^{-1}) - \ln\varphi - \frac{1}{2\varphi^{\upsilon}}\left|y_t-\mu\right|^{\upsilon}. \quad (2.21)$$

The score for μ is

$$\frac{\partial \ln f(y_t; \mu, \lambda, \upsilon)}{\partial\mu} = \frac{\upsilon}{2\varphi^{\upsilon}} sgn(y-\mu)\left|y_t-\mu\right|^{\upsilon-1}, \quad t=1,\ldots,T,$$

but when $\upsilon < 2$, the log-density is not differentiable with respect to μ at $y_t = \mu$, so the score is not continuous. When $1 < \upsilon < 2$, the asymptotic theory for μ follows from the argument in Zhu and Zinde-Walsh (2009). Note that they transform the scale differently so the formulae in their information matrix differ slightly from those here.

The information matrix when scale is parameterized with an exponential link function, so that $\lambda = \ln\varphi$, is

$$\mathbf{I}\begin{pmatrix}\mu\\ \lambda\\ \upsilon\end{pmatrix} = \begin{bmatrix}(\upsilon/2)^2\exp(-2\lambda\upsilon) & 0 & 0\\ 0 & \upsilon & j(\upsilon)\\ 0 & j(\upsilon) & \upsilon^{-3}\ln 2 + g(\upsilon) + h(\upsilon)\end{bmatrix},$$

where

$$j(\upsilon) = -\upsilon^{-1}(1+0.5\Gamma(2/\upsilon)\psi(2/\upsilon)/\Gamma(1/\upsilon)),$$

$$g(\upsilon) = 2\upsilon^{-3}\psi(1+1/\upsilon) + \upsilon^{-4}\psi'(1+1/\upsilon)$$

and

$$h(\upsilon) = \frac{\Gamma(2/\upsilon)((\psi(2/\upsilon))^2 - \psi'(2/\upsilon))}{2\upsilon^2\Gamma(1/\upsilon)};$$

see Appendix C. As in (2.18), the elements in the lower block are independent of scale.

When $\upsilon = 1$,

$$\frac{\partial \ln f(y_t; \mu, \lambda, \upsilon)}{\partial\mu} = \frac{1}{2\varphi} sgn(y_t-\mu)$$

and the ML estimator of μ is the sample median. The general expression for the asymptotic variance of the sample median is $(2f(0))^{-2}$, where $f(0)$ is the PDF at μ; see Koenker (2005). For the Laplace distribution, the asymptotic variance, $4\varphi^2$, given by the preceding formula is the same as that obtained from the information matrix.

Problems with non-differentiability do not arise when μ is known and the ML estimator of scale is being considered. Suppose, for the sake of illustration, that $\mu = 0$ in (2.21) and υ is known. Differentiating the full log-likelihood function with respect to φ gives the score

$$\frac{\partial L}{\partial \varphi} = \sum_{t=1}^{T} \left[-\frac{1}{\varphi} + \frac{\upsilon}{2\varphi^{\upsilon+1}} |y_t|^{\upsilon} \right].$$

Setting the score to zero yields the ML estimator

$$\widetilde{\varphi} = \left(\frac{\upsilon}{2} \frac{\sum |y_t|^{\upsilon}}{T} \right)^{1/\upsilon}. \tag{2.22}$$

The fact that there is a closed-form expression for $\widetilde{\varphi}$ means that proving consistency and asymptotic normality is straightforward. The properties of $\widetilde{\lambda}$ then follow as $\widetilde{\lambda} = \ln \widetilde{\varphi}$.

2.2.3 Gamma Distribution

The log-likelihood function for a gamma distribution is

$$\ln L(\alpha, \gamma) = -\gamma T \ln \alpha + (\gamma - 1) \sum \ln y_t - \sum y_t/\alpha - T \ln \Gamma(\gamma).$$

The ML estimator of α is $\widetilde{\gamma}$ times the sample mean, but $\widetilde{\gamma}$ has to be computed by numerical optimization. The information matrix depends on α and γ, but if the parameterization is changed to the logarithm of the scale, that is $\alpha = \exp \lambda$, where $-\infty < \lambda < \infty$, it depends only on γ and is given by

$$\mathbf{I}\begin{pmatrix} \widetilde{\lambda} \\ \widetilde{\gamma} \end{pmatrix} = \begin{bmatrix} \gamma & 1 \\ 1 & \psi'(\gamma) \end{bmatrix}, \tag{2.23}$$

where the trigamma function, $\psi'(\gamma)$, appears from differentiating $\ln \Gamma(\gamma)$ twice.

The scale parameter may be replaced by the mean, $\mu = \alpha\gamma$, in which case its ML estimator is just the sample mean. Thus an efficient estimator can be obtained without actually estimating γ. The information matrix is, of course, diagonal. If μ is parameterized in terms of its logarithm, λ^*, then $\alpha = \gamma^{-1} \exp \lambda^*$, and the information matrix is

$$\mathbf{I}\begin{pmatrix} \widetilde{\lambda}^* \\ \widetilde{\gamma} \end{pmatrix} = \begin{bmatrix} \gamma & 0 \\ 0 & \psi'(\gamma) - 1/\gamma \end{bmatrix}.$$

Inverting the preceding information matrices confirms that the asymptotic variance of $\widetilde{\gamma}$ is the same in both cases.

2.2.4 Consistency and Asymptotic Normality*

The proof of consistency and for a wide range of DCS models can be based on Lemma 1 in Jensen and Rahbek (2004, p. 1206). This sub-section shows how the conditions apply to some static models.[3] A simplified, single parameter version of the lemma is that $\widetilde{\theta}$, the global maximum of the likelihood function, is consistent and asymptotically normal, in the sense that the limiting distribution of $\sqrt{T}(\widetilde{\theta} - \theta_0)$ is normal, with mean zero and variance $1/I(\theta_0)$, provided the following conditions hold.

(i) $\ln L(\theta)$ is three times continuously differentiable for θ.
(ii) The true parameter value, θ_0, is an interior point of the compact parameter space.
(iii) As $T \to \infty$, $(1/\sqrt{T})\partial \ln L(\theta_0)/\partial\theta \to N(0, I(\theta_0))$, where $I(\theta_0)$ is positive. (The subscript on θ_0 in $\partial \ln L(\theta_0)/\partial\theta$ indicates that the derivative is evaluated at θ_0.)
(iv) As $T \to \infty$, $(-1/T)\partial^2 \ln L(\theta_0)/\partial\theta^2 \xrightarrow{P} I(\theta_0)$.
(v) If $N(\theta_0)$ is a neighborhood of θ_0,

$$\sup_{\theta \in N(\theta_0)} \left| \frac{\partial^3 \ln L(\theta)}{T.\partial\theta^3} \right| \leq c_T, \tag{2.24}$$

where c_T is a random variable which converges in probability to a bounded positive constant, that is, $0 \leq c_T \xrightarrow{P} c$, $0 < c < \infty$.

Remark 5 *Condition (ii) rules out boundary values, such as $\sigma_\varepsilon^2 = 0$ in (1.1), although it is often possible to develop a (nonstandard) asymptotic theory in such cases. The classic reference is Chernoff (1954), but see the discussion on unobserved components models in Harvey (1989). The compactness assumption rules out parameter values that are invalid because the model is not identifiable. Verifying (v) is not usually easy, but it turns out to be relatively straightforward for models in this book in which the third derivative of the log-likelihood function is bounded because it depends on a variable, beta distributed at the true parameter values, that must always lie between zero and one.*

Student's t Distribution

For the estimation of λ, the logarithm of scale, for a Student's t distribution, differentiating the log-density three times shows that condition (i) is satisfied. Condition (ii) simply requires that λ_0 be finite because the parameter space is $-\infty < \lambda < \infty$.

Because the scores in (2.19) are IID, with zero mean and finite variance at λ_0, condition (iii) follows from a basic central limit theorem (Lindberg-Levy). As regards (iv), differentiating (2.19) yields

$$\frac{\partial^2 \ln f(y_t;\lambda)}{\partial\lambda^2} = -2(\nu + 1)b(1 - b), \quad t = 1, \ldots, T, \tag{2.25}$$

[3] For a static model, the conditions are not very different from those in textbooks such as Greene (2012, Definition 14.3, p. 555).

which, like the scores, are IID random variables, but with expectation $-2\nu/(\nu+3)$; see (2.7). Thus their mean converges in probability to minus $I(\lambda_0)$ by Khinchine's theorem.

Finally, the third derivative of the log-likelihood for the t-th observation is

$$\frac{\partial^3 \ln f(y_t;\lambda)}{\partial\lambda^3} = 4(\nu+1)b(1-b) - 8(\nu+1)b^2(1-b). \qquad (2.26)$$

For any admissible λ, the structure of b is such that $0 \leq b \leq 1$; see (2.20). Hence $0 \leq b(1-b) \leq 1$ and $0 \leq b^2(1-b) \leq 1$, and so $\partial^3 \ln f(y_t;\lambda)/\partial\lambda^3$ is bounded for any admissible λ. Condition (v) is satisfied without the need to introduce a bounding random variable, c_T, into the argument.

When ν is unknown, it is straightforward to adapt the preceding arguments to verify the conditions.

General Error Distribution

Consider the GED model with $\mu = 0$ and υ known. Although the existence of a closed-form expression for the ML estimator of scale means that the full set of regularity conditions is not needed to establish its properties, it is worth showing that they hold as a prelude to proving consistency and asymptotic normality for the more complicated dynamic model introduced in the next section. The single observation score with respect to λ is

$$\begin{aligned}\frac{\partial \ln f(y_t;\lambda)}{\partial\lambda} &= \frac{\upsilon}{2}\,|y_t \exp(-\lambda)|^{\upsilon} - 1\\ &= (\upsilon/2)g - 1, \quad t = 1,\ldots,T, \quad -\infty < \lambda < \infty,\end{aligned}$$

where $g = g(y_t;\lambda)$ has a $gamma(2, 1/\upsilon)$ distribution at $\lambda = \lambda_0$; see Lemma 4. The expectation of the score is zero, as it should be, and the variance is υ. Clearly, conditions (i) to (iii) hold. The second derivative is

$$\partial^2 \ln f(y_t;\lambda)/\partial\lambda^2 = -(\upsilon^2/2)\,|y_t \exp(-\lambda)|^{\upsilon} = -(\upsilon^2/2)g,$$

which is also gamma distributed at λ_0. Hence (iv) holds. As regards (v),

$$\partial^3 \ln f(y_t;\lambda)/\partial\lambda^3 = (\upsilon^3/2)\,|y_t \exp(-\lambda)|^{\upsilon} = (\upsilon^3/2)g.$$

Now write

$$g(y_t;\lambda) = g(y_t;\lambda_0)\exp(\upsilon(\lambda_0 - \lambda)).$$

If a value λ^* is chosen so that $\lambda_0 - \lambda^* > \lambda_0 - \lambda$, then $g(y_t;\lambda)\exp(\upsilon(\lambda - \lambda^*)) > g(y_t;\lambda)$, and we can construct a random variable, $g(y_t;\lambda^*)$, that will uniformly bound $g(\lambda)$ from above. Because $g(y_t;\lambda_0)$ has a finite first moment (indeed all moments are finite), it follows from Khinchine's theorem that $\sup_{\lambda\in N(\lambda_0)}\left|T^{-1}\partial^3 \ln L/\partial\lambda^3\right|$ is bounded by a random variable that converges to a positive, finite quantity, that is,

$$\frac{\upsilon^3}{2T}\sum_{t=1}^{T} g(y_t;\lambda^*) = \frac{\upsilon^3}{2T}\exp(\upsilon(\lambda_0 - \lambda^*))\sum_{t=1}^{T} g(y_t;\lambda_0) \xrightarrow{P} \upsilon^2 \exp(\upsilon(\lambda_0 - \lambda^*)) = c,$$

where $0 < c < \infty$.

2.3 MAXIMUM LIKELIHOOD ESTIMATION OF DYNAMIC CONDITIONAL SCORE MODELS

In DCS models, some or all of the parameters are time-varying, and the distribution of y_t is defined conditional on these parameters. For a single time-varying parameter, as in (1.13), the dynamics are driven by the conditional score. A crucial requirement – though not the only one – for establishing results on asymptotic distributions of ML estimators of the parameters governing the movements in $\theta_{t|t-1}$ is that it does not appear in the expression for its information quantity. The fulfillment of this condition may require a careful choice of link function. The first sub-section sets out a basic lemma on the information matrix and the second sub-section derives its form for the first-order model. The third sub-section reworks the result for a more common, but as it turns out, less elegant dynamic specification. The asymptotic distribution of the maximum likelihood estimator is stated in Sub-section 2.3.4 and proved in the following sub-section. Following a brief discussion on nonstationarity, the result on the information matrix is generalized in Sub-section 2.3.7.

2.3.1 An Information Matrix Lemma

Suppose initially that there is just one parameter, θ, in a static model. Define

$$u_t = k.\partial \ln f(y_t;\theta)/\partial\theta, \quad t = 1, \ldots, T,$$

where k is a finite constant which may be the information quantity, thereby yielding the standardized score, or some other constant, including unity. The derivative $\partial \ln f(y_t;\theta)/\partial\theta$ is a random variable which has zero mean at the true parameter value, θ_0. Similarly, u_t has zero mean at $\theta = \theta_0$, and its variance, σ_u^2, is finite under standard regularity conditions.

The *information quantity*[4] for a single observation is

$$\begin{aligned} I(\theta_0) &= -E(\partial^2 \ln f/\partial\theta^2) = E[(\partial \ln f/\partial\theta)^2] \\ &= E(u_t^2)/k^2 = \sigma_u^2/k^2 < \infty. \end{aligned} \tag{2.27}$$

If, for a particular choice of link function, $I(\theta_0)$ does not depend on θ_0, the following condition is satisfied.

Condition 1 *The variance of the score in the static model is finite and does not depend on θ_0.*

Now let $\theta = \theta_{t|t-1}$ evolve over time as a function of past observations and past values of the score of the conditional distribution. Because the conditional score depends on past observations through $\theta_{t|t-1}$, it can be broken down into

[4] The information quantity is the name given to the information matrix when it consists of a single element.

two parts:

$$\frac{\partial \ln f_t(y_t \mid Y_{t-1};\boldsymbol{\psi})}{\partial \boldsymbol{\psi}} = \frac{\partial \ln f_t(y_t;\theta_{t|t-1})}{\partial \theta_{t|t-1}}\frac{\partial \theta_{t|t-1}}{\partial \boldsymbol{\psi}}, \tag{2.28}$$

where the notation $f_t(y_t;\theta_{t|t-1})$ indicates that the distribution of y_t depends on the time-varying parameter, $\theta_{t|t-1}$, and $\boldsymbol{\psi}$ denotes the vector of parameters governing the dynamics. Because $\theta_{t|t-1}$ and its derivatives depend only on past information, the distribution of the score conditional on information at time $t-1$ is the same as its unconditional distribution and so is time invariant.

The preceding decomposition of the conditional score leads to the following result.

Lemma 5 *Consider a model with a single time-varying parameter, $\theta_{t|t-1}$, which satisfies an equation that depends on variables which are fixed at time $t-1$. The process is governed by a set of fixed parameters, $\boldsymbol{\psi}$. If Condition 1 holds, then the conditional score for the t-th observation, $\partial \ln f_t(y_t \mid Y_{t-1};\boldsymbol{\psi})/\partial\boldsymbol{\psi}$, is a MD at $\boldsymbol{\psi} = \boldsymbol{\psi}_0$, with conditional covariance matrix*

$$E_{t-1}\left(\frac{\partial \ln f_t(y_t \mid Y_{t-1};\boldsymbol{\psi})}{\partial \boldsymbol{\psi}}\right)\left(\frac{\partial \ln f_t(y_t \mid Y_{t-1};\boldsymbol{\psi})}{\partial \boldsymbol{\psi}}\right)'$$
$$= I.\left(\frac{\partial \theta_{t|t-1}}{\partial \boldsymbol{\psi}}\frac{\partial \theta_{t|t-1}}{\partial \boldsymbol{\psi}'}\right), \quad t = 1,\ldots,T, \tag{2.29}$$

where the information quantitly, I, is constant over time and independent of $\boldsymbol{\psi}$.

Proof. The fact that the score in (2.28) is an MD is confirmed by the fact that the derivative of the time-varying parameter, $\partial\theta_{t|t-1}/\partial\boldsymbol{\psi}$, is fixed at time $t-1$, and the expected value of the score in the static model is zero.

The conditional covariance matrix of the score is found by writing its outer product as

$$\left(\frac{\partial \ln f_t}{\partial \theta_{t|t-1}}\frac{\partial \theta_{t|t-1}}{\partial \boldsymbol{\psi}}\right)\left(\frac{\partial \ln f_t}{\partial \theta_{t|t-1}}\frac{\partial \theta_{t|t-1}}{\partial \boldsymbol{\psi}}\right)' = \left(\frac{\partial \ln f_t}{\partial \theta_{t|t-1}}\right)^2\left(\frac{\partial \theta_{t|t-1}}{\partial \boldsymbol{\psi}}\frac{\partial \theta_{t|t-1}}{\partial \boldsymbol{\psi}'}\right).$$

Now take expectations conditional on information at time $t-1$. If $E_{t-1}(\partial \ln f_t/\partial\theta_{t|t-1})^2$ does not depend on $\theta_{t|t-1}$, it is fixed and equal to the unconditional expectation in the static model, that is, (2.27). Therefore, because $\theta_{t|t-1}$ is fixed at time $t-1$,

$$E_{t-1}\left[\left(\frac{\partial \ln f_t}{\partial \theta_{t|t-1}}\frac{\partial \theta_{t|t-1}}{\partial \boldsymbol{\psi}}\right)\left(\frac{\partial \ln f_t}{\partial \theta_{t|t-1}}\frac{\partial \theta_{t|t-1}}{\partial \boldsymbol{\psi}}\right)'\right]$$
$$= \left[E\left(\frac{\partial \ln f_t}{\partial \theta}\right)^2\right]\frac{\partial \theta_{t|t-1}}{\partial \boldsymbol{\psi}}\frac{\partial \theta_{t|t-1}}{\partial \boldsymbol{\psi}'}. \quad \blacksquare$$

Corollary 4 *The information matrix for the model of Lemma 5 is*

$$\mathbf{I}(\boldsymbol{\psi}) = I.\mathbf{D}(\boldsymbol{\psi}), \quad \textit{where} \quad \mathbf{D}(\boldsymbol{\psi}) = E\left(\frac{\partial\theta_{t|t-1}}{\partial\boldsymbol{\psi}}\frac{\partial\theta_{t|t-1}}{\partial\boldsymbol{\psi}'}\right).$$

The next sub-section shows how to find the unconditional expectations of the elements in the outer product matrix of derivatives.

2.3.2 Information Matrix for the First-Order Model

In this sub-section, the information matrix at time t is derived for the first-order model,

$$\theta_{t+1|t} = \delta + \phi\theta_{t|t-1} + \kappa u_t, \quad |\phi| < 1, \quad \kappa \neq 0, \quad t = 1, \ldots, T, \tag{2.30}$$

and shown to be positive definite when the model is identifiable. Unless ϕ is known to be zero, the condition $\kappa \neq 0$ is necessary for identifiability. The assumption that $|\phi| < 1$ enables $\theta_{t|t-1}$ to be expressed as an infinite moving average in the $u_t^{\prime}s$. Because the $u_t^{\prime}s$ are MDs and hence WN, $\theta_{t|t-1}$ is weakly stationary, with an unconditional mean of $\omega = \delta/(1-\phi)$ and an unconditional variance of $\sigma_u^2/(1-\phi^2)$. The process is assumed to have started in the infinite past, though for practical purposes, $\theta_{1|0}$ may be set equal to the unconditional mean.

Although (2.30) is the conventional formulation of a first-order dynamic model, it turns out that the information matrix takes a simpler form if the paramerization is in terms of ω rather than δ. Thus

$$\theta_{t+1|t} = \omega + \theta_{t+1|t}^{\dagger}, \quad \theta_{t+1|t}^{\dagger} = \phi\theta_{t|t-1}^{\dagger} + \kappa u_t, \qquad t = 1, \ldots, T, \tag{2.31}$$

where setting $\theta_{1|0}^{\dagger} = 0$ is the same as setting $\theta_{1|0} = \omega$. The complications arise because u_t depends on $\theta_{t|t-1}$ and hence on the parameters in $\boldsymbol{\psi}$. Differentiating (2.31) and noting that $\partial\theta_{t|t-1}/\partial\kappa = \partial\theta_{t|t-1}^{\dagger}/\partial\kappa$, $\partial\theta_{t|t-1}/\partial\phi = \partial\theta_{t|t-1}^{\dagger}/\partial\phi$, but $\partial\theta_{t|t-1}/\partial\omega = 1 + \partial\theta_{t|t-1}^{\dagger}/\partial\omega$, the vector $\partial\theta_{t+1|t}/\partial\boldsymbol{\psi}$ becomes

$$\frac{\partial\theta_{t+1|t}}{\partial\kappa} = \phi\frac{\partial\theta_{t|t-1}}{\partial\kappa} + \kappa\frac{\partial u_t}{\partial\kappa} + u_t \tag{2.32}$$

$$\frac{\partial\theta_{t+1|t}}{\partial\phi} = \phi\frac{\partial\theta_{t|t-1}}{\partial\phi} + \kappa\frac{\partial u_t}{\partial\phi} + \theta_{t|t-1} - \omega$$

$$\frac{\partial\theta_{t+1|t}}{\partial\omega} = \phi\frac{\partial\theta_{t|t-1}}{\partial\omega} + \kappa\frac{\partial u_t}{\partial\omega} + 1 - \phi.$$

However,

$$\frac{\partial u_t}{\partial\kappa} = \frac{\partial u_t}{\partial\theta_{t|t-1}}\frac{\partial\theta_{t|t-1}}{\partial\kappa},$$

and similarly for the other two derivatives. Therefore,

$$\frac{\partial \theta_{t+1|t}}{\partial \kappa} = x_t \frac{\partial \theta_{t|t-1}}{\partial \kappa} + u_t \tag{2.33}$$

$$\frac{\partial \theta_{t+1|t}}{\partial \phi} = x_t \frac{\partial \theta_{t|t-1}}{\partial \phi} + \theta_{t|t-1} - \omega$$

$$\frac{\partial \theta_{t+1|t}}{\partial \omega} = x_t \frac{\partial \theta_{t|t-1}}{\partial \omega} + 1 - \phi,$$

where

$$x_t = \phi + \kappa \frac{\partial u_t}{\partial \theta_{t|t-1}}, \qquad t = 1, \ldots, T. \tag{2.34}$$

The next condition, which generalizes Condition 1, is needed for the information matrix of $\boldsymbol{\psi}$ to be derived.

Condition 2 *For the static model, the score and its first derivative, or equivalently u_t and u_t', where $u_t' = \partial u_t / \partial \theta$, have finite second moments and covariance that are time-invariant and do not depend on θ, that is, $E(u_t^{2-k} u_t'^k) < \infty$, $k = 0, 1, 2$.*

The preceding condition states that $E(u_t u_t') < \infty$ and $E(u_t'^2) < \infty$ as well as $E(u_t^2) < \infty$. The last condition is the same as Condition 1, as is the fact that the mean of u_t' is time invariant.

The following definitions are needed:

$$a = E_{t-1}(x_t) = \phi + \kappa E_{t-1}\left(\frac{\partial u_t}{\partial \theta_{t|t-1}}\right) = \phi + \kappa E\left(\frac{\partial u_t}{\partial \theta}\right) \tag{2.35}$$

$$b = E_{t-1}(x_t^2) = \phi^2 + 2\phi\kappa E\left(\frac{\partial u_t}{\partial \theta}\right) + \kappa^2 E\left(\frac{\partial u_t}{\partial \theta}\right)^2 \geq 0$$

$$c = E_{t-1}(u_t x_t) = \kappa E\left(u_t \frac{\partial u_t}{\partial \theta}\right).$$

The expectations in the preceding formulae[5] exist in view of Condition 2. Because they are time-invariant, the unconditional expectations can replace conditional ones.

The following lemma is a prerequisite for Theorem 1.

[5] Note that when b_t is used to denote a beta variable in a dynamic model, it will have a time subscript.

Lemma 6 *When the process for $\theta_{t|t-1}$ starts in the infinite past and $|a| < 1$,*

$$E\left(\frac{\partial \theta_{t+1|t}}{\partial \kappa}\right) = 0, \qquad t = \cdots 0, 1, \ldots, T, \tag{2.36}$$

$$E\left(\frac{\partial \theta_{t+1|t}}{\partial \phi}\right) = 0,$$

$$E\left(\frac{\partial \theta_{t+1|t}}{\partial \omega}\right) = \frac{1-\phi}{1-a}.$$

Proof. Taking the conditional expectations of the first equation in (2.32) gives

$$E_{t-1}\left(\frac{\partial \theta_{t+1|t}}{\partial \kappa}\right) = E_{t-1}\left(x_t \frac{\partial \theta_{t|t-1}}{\partial \kappa} + u_t\right) = a\frac{\partial \theta_{t|t-1}}{\partial \kappa} + 0$$

and, from the law of iterated expectations, the expectation at time $t-2$ is given by

$$\begin{aligned} E_{t-2}E_{t-1}\left(\frac{\partial \theta_{t+1|t}}{\partial \kappa}\right) &= aE_{t-2}\left(\frac{\partial \theta_{t|t-1}}{\partial \kappa}\right) \\ &= aE_{t-2}\left(x_{t-1}\frac{\partial \theta_{t-1|t-1}}{\partial \kappa} + u_{t-1}\right) = a^2\frac{\partial \theta_{t-1|t-2}}{\partial \kappa}. \end{aligned}$$

Hence, if $|a| < 1$,

$$\lim_{n\to\infty} E_{t-n}\left(\frac{\partial \theta_{t+1|t}}{\partial \kappa}\right) = 0, \quad t = \cdots 0, 1, \ldots, T.$$

As regards ω,

$$E_{t-1}\left(\frac{\partial \theta_{t+1|t}}{\partial \omega}\right) = a\frac{\partial \theta_{t|t-1}}{\partial \omega} + 1 - \phi. \tag{2.37}$$

We can continue to evaluate this expression by substituting for $\partial\theta_{t|t-1}/\partial\omega$, taking conditional expectations at time $t-2$, and then repeating this process. Once a solution has been shown to exist, the result can be confirmed by taking unconditional expectations in (2.37) to give

$$E\left(\frac{\partial \theta_{t+1|t}}{\partial \omega}\right) = \frac{1-\phi}{1-a}.$$

Similarly, taking conditional expectations of $\partial\theta_{t+1|t}/\partial\phi$ at time $t-1$ gives

$$E_{t-1}\left(\frac{\partial \theta_{t+1|t}}{\partial \phi}\right) = a\frac{\partial \theta_{t|t-1}}{\partial \phi} + (\theta_{t|t-1} - \omega), \tag{2.38}$$

and then the unconditional expectation yields

$$E\left(\frac{\partial \theta_{t+1|t}}{\partial \phi}\right) = 0, \quad t = \cdots 0, 1, \ldots, T. \quad \blacksquare$$

The preceding Lemma requires that $|a| < 1$. The result on the information matrix below requires $b < 1$, and fulfillment of this condition implies $|a| < 1$. That this is the case follows directly from the Cauchy-Schwarz inequality $E(x_t^2) \geq [E\,|x_t|)]^2$.

Theorem 1 *Assume that Condition 2 holds and that $b < 1$. Then the information matrix for a single observation is time-invariant and given by*

$$\mathbf{I}(\boldsymbol{\psi}) = I.\mathbf{D}(\boldsymbol{\psi}) = (\sigma_u^2/k^2)\mathbf{D}(\boldsymbol{\psi}), \tag{2.39}$$

where

$$\mathbf{D}(\boldsymbol{\psi}) = \mathbf{D}\begin{pmatrix}\kappa \\ \phi \\ \omega\end{pmatrix} = \frac{1}{1-b}\begin{bmatrix} A & D & E \\ D & B & F \\ E & F & C \end{bmatrix}, \tag{2.40}$$

with

$$A = \sigma_u^2, \qquad B = \frac{\kappa^2\sigma_u^2(1+a\phi)}{(1-\phi^2)(1-a\phi)}, \qquad C = \frac{(1-\phi)^2(1+a)}{1-a},$$

$$D = \frac{a\kappa\sigma_u^2}{1-a\phi}, \qquad E = \frac{c(1-\phi)}{1-a} \qquad \textit{and} \qquad F = \frac{ac\kappa(1-\phi)}{(1-a)(1-a\phi)}.$$

Proof. For a single observation, the information matrix, the covariance matrix of the score, is obtained by taking the unconditional expectation of (2.29) and then combining it with the formula for $\mathbf{D}(\boldsymbol{\psi})$, which is derived in Appendix A. The derivation of the first term, A, is given here to illustrate the method. This term is the unconditional expectation of the square of the first derivative in (2.33). To evaluate it, first take conditional expectations at time $t-1$, to obtain

$$\begin{aligned} E_{t-1}\left(\frac{\partial\theta_{t+1|t}}{\partial\kappa}\right)^2 &= E_{t-1}\left(x_t\frac{\partial\theta_{t|t-1}}{\partial\kappa} + u_t\right)^2 \\ &= b\left(\frac{\partial\theta_{t|t-1}}{\partial\kappa}\right)^2 + 2c\frac{\partial\theta_{t|t-1}}{\partial\kappa} + \sigma_u^2. \end{aligned} \tag{2.41}$$

It follows from Lemma 6 that the unconditional expectation of the second term is zero. Eliminating this term and taking expectations at $t-2$ gives

$$\begin{aligned} E_{t-2}\left(\frac{\partial\theta_{t+1|t}}{\partial\kappa}\right)^2 &= bE_{t-2}\left(x_{t-1}\frac{\partial\theta_{t-1|t-2}}{\partial\kappa} + u_{t-1}\right)^2 + \sigma_u^2 \\ &= b^2\left(\frac{\partial\theta_{t-1|t-2}}{\partial\kappa}\right)^2 + 2cb\frac{\partial\theta_{t-1|t-2}}{\partial\kappa} + b\sigma_u^2 + \sigma_u^2. \end{aligned}$$

Again, the second term can be eliminated, and it is clear that

$$\lim_{n\to\infty} E_{t-n}\left(\frac{\partial\theta_{t+1|t}}{\partial\kappa}\right)^2 = \frac{\sigma_u^2}{1-b}.$$

Taking unconditional expectations in (2.41) gives the same result. The derivatives are all evaluated in this way in Appendix A. ∎

Corollary 5 *If κ is zero, $B = 0$ in (2.40), and so $\mathbf{D}(\kappa, \phi, \omega)$ is singular, and the model is not identifiable. When $\kappa \neq 0$, all three parameters are locally identified, so long as $b < 1$, even if $\phi = 0$. On the other hand, if ϕ is known, both κ and ω are locally identifiable, even if $\kappa = 0$.*

Remark 6 *An expression for the information matrix enables ML estimates to be computed by the method of scoring. Analytic derivatives are constructed recursively by using (2.32) combined with (2.28).*

2.3.3 Information Matrix with the δ Parameterization*

For the model in which the constant is parameterized as in (2.30),

$$\begin{aligned}\frac{\partial \theta_{t+1|t}}{\partial \kappa} &= x_t \frac{\partial \theta_{t|t-1}}{\partial \kappa} + u_t \\ \frac{\partial \theta_{t+1|t}}{\partial \phi} &= x_t \frac{\partial \theta_{t|t-1}}{\partial \phi} + \theta_{t|t-1} \\ \frac{\partial \theta_{t+1|t}}{\partial \delta} &= x_t \frac{\partial \theta_{t|t-1}}{\partial \delta} + 1,\end{aligned} \tag{2.42}$$

leading to a modification of Lemma 6.

Lemma 7 *When the process for $\theta_{t|t-1}$ starts in the infinite past and $|a| < 1$,*

$$\begin{aligned}E\left(\frac{\partial \theta_{t+1|t}}{\partial \kappa}\right) &= 0, \qquad t = \cdots 0, 1, \ldots, T, \\ E\left(\frac{\partial \theta_{t+1|t}}{\partial \phi}\right) &= \frac{\delta}{(1-a)(1-\phi)}, \\ E\left(\frac{\partial \theta_{t+1|t}}{\partial \delta}\right) &= \frac{1}{1-a}.\end{aligned} \tag{2.43}$$

The information matrix is given by the following modification of Theorem 1.

Theorem 2 *Assume that Condition 2 holds and that $b < 1$. Then the information matrix for a single observation is time-invariant and given by (2.39), with*

$$\mathbf{D}(\boldsymbol{\psi}) = \mathbf{D}\begin{pmatrix}\kappa \\ \phi \\ \delta\end{pmatrix} = \frac{1}{1-b}\begin{bmatrix} A & D & E \\ D & B & F \\ E & F & C\end{bmatrix}, \tag{2.44}$$

where $A = \sigma_u^2$,

$$B = \frac{(1+a\phi)\kappa^2\sigma_u^2}{(1-a\phi)(1-\phi^2)} + \frac{(1+a\phi)\delta^2}{(1-a\phi)(1-\phi)^2} + \frac{2a\delta(\delta+\kappa c)}{(1-\phi)(1-a)(1-a\phi)},$$

$$C = (1+a)/(1-a), \quad D = \frac{a\kappa\sigma_u^2}{1-a\phi} + \frac{c\delta}{(1-\phi)(1-a)},$$

$$E = c/(1-a), \quad F = \frac{a\kappa c}{(1-a)(1-a\phi)} + \frac{\delta(1+a)}{(1-\phi)(1-a)}.$$

The proof is set out in Appendix A.2.

Remark 7 *The information matrix based on (2.40) is much simpler and is independent of the parameter ω, whereas (2.44) depends on δ. This difference might seem surprising at first sight, but in fact, a similar contrast appears in the information matrices for a simple Gaussian AR(1) model, which can be formulated as*

$$y_t = \omega(1-\phi) + \phi y_{t-1} + \varepsilon_t \quad or \quad y_t = \delta + \phi y_{t-1} + \varepsilon_t, \quad |\phi| < 1. \tag{2.45}$$

On inverting the information matrices obtained from (2.40) and (2.44), it is found that the sub-matrices corresponding to the covariance matrix of $(\widetilde{\kappa}, \widetilde{\phi})$ are the same. Indeed, it would be somewhat worrying if they were not. The only terms in the inverse of (2.44) that depend on δ are those connected to $\widetilde{\delta}$. It is easy to verify that the same is true in (2.45), where the asymptotic variance of $\widetilde{\phi}$ is always $(1-\phi^2)/T$.

2.3.4 Asymptotic Distribution

Provided that $\widetilde{\boldsymbol{\psi}}$, the ML estimator of $\boldsymbol{\psi}$, is the global maximum of the likelihood function and $\mathbf{I}^{-1}(\boldsymbol{\psi}_0)$ is positive definite, the expectation is that it is consistent, and the limiting distribution of $\sqrt{T}(\widetilde{\boldsymbol{\psi}} - \boldsymbol{\psi}_0)$ is multivariate normal with mean vector zero and covariance matrix

$$Var(\widetilde{\boldsymbol{\psi}}) = \mathbf{I}^{-1}(\boldsymbol{\psi}_0) = I^{-1}\mathbf{D}^{-1}(\boldsymbol{\psi}_0). \tag{2.46}$$

The interpretation of the preceding result is that $\widetilde{\boldsymbol{\psi}}$ is approximately normal, with mean $\boldsymbol{\psi}$ and covariance matrix given by the following definition.

Definition 4 *The approximate or asymptotic covariance matrix is*

$$Avar(\widetilde{\boldsymbol{\psi}}) = T^{-1}Var(\widetilde{\boldsymbol{\psi}}). \tag{2.47}$$

The asymptotic standard error (ASE) of an element of $\widetilde{\boldsymbol{\psi}}$ is the square root of the corresponding diagonal element of $Avar(\widetilde{\boldsymbol{\psi}})$.

A formal proof of consistency and asymptotic normality requires the verification of a number of conditions. This matter is addressed in the next sub-section. The nature of the constraints implied by $b < 1$ will be investigated for the various models discussed in the ensuing chapters. On the whole, they do not appear to present practical difficulties, as the two following examples illustrate.

Example 5 *For the Gaussian AR(1) plus noise model described in Section 1.1, it was noted in the discussion below the innovations form, (1.3), that the MA coefficient in the $ARMA(1,1)$ reduced form is $\theta = \phi - \kappa$. Because the Gaussian DCS model is equivalent to the innovations form, with $u_t = v_t$, $\partial u_t/\partial \mu_{t|t-1} = -1$, and consequently, $b = (\phi-\kappa)^2 = \theta^2$. The ARMA model is invertible if $|\theta| < 1$, and invertibility is a standard condition for asymptotic normality of the ML estimators of an ARMA model; see Section 3.3. The* *corresponding parameter space for* κ *is* $0 < \kappa < 1 + \phi$ *and* $1 - \phi < \kappa < 0$. *When* $\phi \leq 0$, $0 < \kappa <$ *and* $0 < \kappa < 1 + \phi$. *(However, it may sometimes be desirable to impose further restrictions coming from the UC form.)*

Example 6 *In a Gaussian scale model with an exponential link function, as in (1.16), the dynamics are driven by* $u_t = y_t^2 / \exp(2\theta_{t|t-1}) - 1$, *and so* $u_t' = -y_t^2 / \exp(2\theta_{t|t-1})$. *Thus* $E(u_t') = E(-y_t^2 / \exp(2\theta_{t|t-1})) = -1$, *and* $E(u_t'^2) = E(y_t^4 / \exp(4\theta_{t|t-1})) = 3$. *In fact, as shown in Sub-section 4.6.2,* $b = \phi^2 - 4\phi\kappa + 12\kappa^2$.

2.3.5 Consistency and Asymptotic Normality*

A proof of the consistency and asymptotic normality of the ML estimator for the first-order model needs a number of regularity conditions to be fulfilled. The first condition is simply a formal statement of the requirement, already noted, that if the model is to be identified, κ must not be zero or take a value such that the constraint $b < 1$ is violated.

Condition 3 *The elements of* $\boldsymbol{\psi}_0$ *are an interior point of the compact parameter space, which for the stationary first-order model will be taken to be* $|\phi| < 1$, $|\omega| < \infty$ *and* $0 < \kappa < \kappa_u$, $\kappa_L < \kappa < 0$, *where* κ_u *and* κ_L *are values determined by the condition* $b < 1$.

Proposition 2 *The model is locally identifiable when Conditions 2 and 3 hold because* $\mathbf{D}(\boldsymbol{\psi}_0)$, *and hence* $\mathbf{I}(\boldsymbol{\psi}_0)$, *is positive definite.*

A set of conditions for consistency and asymptotic normality of ML estimators was given in Sub-section 2.2.4 and shown to hold for IID observations from Student's t and other distributions. The arguments set out there now need to be combined with the results on the stationarity and ergodicity of the derivatives of $\theta_{t|t-1}$. The next condition is a stronger version of Condition 2.

Condition 4 *For the static model, the distributions of the score and its first three derivatives, or equivalently* u_t *and* $\partial^j u_t / \partial\theta^j$, $j = 1, 2, 3$, *are time-invariant and do not depend on* θ. *Furthermore, their expectations exist, as does the expectation of* $u_t \partial u_t / \partial\theta$.

Lemma 8 *When Condition 4 holds,* u_t *in the dynamic model is* $IID(0, \sigma_u^2)$, *and so the process* $\theta_{t+1|t}$ *in (2.30) is strictly stationary when* $\boldsymbol{\psi} = \boldsymbol{\psi}_0$.

Proof. Because u_t is an MD with a time-invariant distribution, it is IID with mean zero. ■

Lemma 9 *The first derivatives of* $\theta_{t+1|t}$ *with respect to* κ, ϕ *and* ω *are stochastic recurrence equations (SREs), and the condition* $|a| < 1$ *is sufficient to ensure that they are strictly stationarity and ergodic at the true parameter value.*

Proof. The first derivatives were given in (2.42). They are stochastic recurrence equations of the form $y_{t+1} = x_t y_t + z_t$, where x_t and z_t are strictly stationarity.

Strict stationarity and ergodicity follow from standard results on SREs; see Brandt (1986) and Straumann and Mikosch (2006, pp. 2450–1). The necessary condition for strict stationarity is $E(\ln|x_t|) < 0$. This condition is satisfied at the true parameter value when $|a| = E(|x_t|) < 1$, because from Jensen's inequality, $E(\ln|x_t|) \leq \ln E(|x_t|) < 0$. ■

Remark 8 *Recall that from Jensen's inequality, $|a| < 1$ is implied by $b < 1$.*

Corollary 6 *The condition $|a| < 1$ is sufficient to ensure that the first derivatives raised to any positive power are strictly stationarity and ergodic at the true parameter value.*

Proof. The proof of Lemma 9 showed that $E(\ln|x_t|) < 0$ when $a < 1$ and so $E(\ln|x_t|^c) = cE(\ln|x_t|) < 0$ for $c > 0$. ■

Corollary 7 *The condition $|a| < 1$ is sufficient to ensure that the second and third derivatives of $\theta_{t+1|t}$ with respect to κ, ϕ and ω are strictly stationarity and ergodic at the true parameter value.*

Proof. Consider the second derivatives. Focussing on ϕ, note that because

$$\frac{\partial\theta_{t+1|t}}{\partial\phi} = \phi\frac{\partial\theta_{t|t-1}}{\partial\phi} + \kappa\frac{\partial u_t}{\partial\phi} + \theta_{t|t-1} - \omega,$$

the second derivative of $\theta_{t+1|t}$ with respect to ϕ is

$$\frac{\partial^2\theta_{t+1|t}}{\partial\phi^2} = \phi\frac{\partial^2\theta_{t|t-1}}{\partial\phi^2} + \frac{\partial\theta_{t|t-1}}{\partial\phi} + \kappa\frac{\partial^2 u_t}{\partial\phi^2} + \frac{\partial\theta_{t|t-1}}{\partial\phi}.$$

Now

$$\frac{\partial^2 u_t}{\partial\phi^2} = \frac{\partial u_t}{\partial\theta_{t|t-1}}\frac{\partial^2\theta_{t|t-1}}{\partial\phi^2} + \frac{\partial^2 u_t}{\partial\theta_{t|t-1}^2}\left(\frac{\partial\theta_{t|t-1}}{\partial\phi}\right)^2,$$

so

$$\begin{aligned}\frac{\partial^2\theta_{t+1|t}}{\partial\phi^2} &= \phi\frac{\partial^2\theta_{t|t-1}}{\partial\phi^2} + 2\frac{\partial\theta_{t|t-1}}{\partial\phi} + \kappa\frac{\partial u_t}{\partial\theta_{t|t-1}}\frac{\partial^2\theta_{t|t-1}}{\partial\phi^2} + \kappa\frac{\partial^2 u_t}{\partial\theta_{t|t-1}}\left(\frac{\partial\theta_{t|t-1}}{\partial\phi}\right)^2\\ &= \left(\phi + \kappa\frac{\partial u_t}{\partial\theta_{t|t-1}}\right)\frac{\partial^2\theta_{t|t-1}}{\partial\phi^2} + 2\frac{\partial\theta_{t|t-1}}{\partial\phi} + \kappa\frac{\partial^2 u_t}{\partial\theta_{t|t-1}}\left(\frac{\partial\theta_{t|t-1}}{\partial\phi}\right)^2.\end{aligned}$$

The first derivative, $\partial\theta_{t+1|t}/\partial\phi$, is strictly stationary when $|a| < 1$, as is its square. Thus the preceding equation for $\partial^2\theta_{t+1|t}/\partial\phi^2$ is an SRE with the same form as the SRE for $\partial\theta_{t+1|t}/\partial\phi$, that is,

$$\frac{\partial^2\theta_{t+1|t}}{\partial\phi^2} = x_t\frac{\partial^2\theta_{t|t-1}}{\partial\phi^2} + \{\textit{strictly stationary process}\}.$$

A similar argument may be employed to show that the derivatives with respect to κ and ω obey SREs of the same form, as do cross-derivatives, such as $\partial^2\theta_{t+1|t}/\partial\phi\partial\kappa$.

The third derivative with respect to ϕ is

$$\frac{\partial^3\theta_{t+1|t}}{\partial\phi^3} = \phi\frac{\partial^3\theta_{t|t-1}}{\partial\phi^3} + \frac{\partial^2\theta_{t|t-1}}{\partial\phi^2} + \kappa\frac{\partial^3 u_t}{\partial\phi^3} + \frac{\partial^2\theta_{t|t-1}}{\partial\phi^2},$$

where

$$\frac{\partial^3 u_t}{\partial\phi^3} = \frac{\partial u_t}{\partial\theta_{t|t-1}}\frac{\partial^3\theta_{t|t-1}}{\partial\phi^3} + \frac{\partial^2 u_t}{\partial\theta^2_{t|t-1}}\frac{\partial\theta_{t|t-1}}{\partial\phi}\frac{\partial^2\theta_{t|t-1}}{\partial\phi^2} + \frac{\partial^3 u_t}{\partial\theta^3_{t|t-1}}\left(\frac{\partial\theta_{t|t-1}}{\partial\phi}\right)^3.$$

The main point to note is the appearance of the third derivative of u_t with respect to ϕ and the cube of the first derivative. However, the argument that $\partial^3\theta_{t+1|t}/\partial\phi^3$ is strictly stationarity follows as before. ■

Lemma 10 *The condition $|a| < 1$ is necessary for the first moments of the first derivatives of $\theta_{t|t-1}$ to be finite, whereas $b < 1$ is necessary for the second derivatives and the squares of the first derivatives to have finite first moments.*

Proof. The existence of first and second moments for the first derivatives of $\theta_{t|t-1}$ was shown when deriving the information matrix. As is apparent from the proof of Corollary 7, the existence of the first moments of the second derivatives requires the existence of the second moment of the first derivatives and $E(\partial^2 u_t/\partial\theta^2) < \infty$. ■

The preceding results can now be used to verify the multivariate versions of (iii) and (iv) in Sub-section 2.2.4.

Proposition 4 *Subject to Conditions 3 and 4,*

$$(1/\sqrt{T})\partial \ln L(\boldsymbol{\psi}_0)/\partial\boldsymbol{\psi} \rightarrow N(0, \mathbf{I}(\boldsymbol{\psi}_0)), \quad as\ T \to \infty,$$

where $\mathbf{I}(\boldsymbol{\psi}_0)$ is positive definite.

Proof. From Lemma 5, the score vector at $\boldsymbol{\psi}_0$ is an MD with conditional covariance matrix, (2.29). For a single element in the conditional score, $\partial \ln f_t/\partial\psi_i$, $i = 1, 2, 3$, where ψ_i is the i-th element of $\boldsymbol{\psi}$, and we may write

$$E_{t-1}\left[\left(\frac{\partial \ln f_t}{\partial\psi_i}\right)^2\right] = I.\left(\frac{\partial\theta_{t|t-1}}{\partial\psi_i}\right)^2, \quad t = 1, \ldots, T.$$

The proof of the central limit theorem for martingale differences in Brown (1971) requires that

$$p\lim T^{-1}\sum I.\left(\frac{\partial\theta_{t|t-1}}{\partial\psi_i}\right)^2$$
$$= I.p\lim T^{-1}\sum\left(\frac{\partial\theta_{t|t-1}}{\partial\psi_i}\right)^2 < \infty, \quad i = 1, 2, 3. \tag{2.48}$$

Because, as noted in Lemma 10, $(\partial\theta_{t|t-1}/\partial\psi_i)^2$ is strictly stationarity and ergodic with finite unconditional mean, it follows from the ergodic theorem that (2.48) holds. Similarly, the existence of second-order moments for the score and $\partial\theta_{t|t-1}/\partial\psi_i$ is enough for the Lindberg condition to hold; see Jensen and Rahbek (2004, p. 1212). ■

Proposition 5 *Subject to Conditions 3 and 4,*

$$(-1/T)\partial^2 \ln L(\boldsymbol{\psi}_0)/\partial\boldsymbol{\psi}\partial\boldsymbol{\psi}' \xrightarrow{P} \mathbf{I}(\boldsymbol{\psi}_0), \quad \textit{as } T \to \infty.$$

Proof. Write

$$\frac{\partial^2 \ln f_t}{\partial\psi^2} = u_t \frac{\partial^2\theta_{t|t-1}}{\partial\psi^2} + \frac{\partial u_t}{\partial\theta_{t|t-1}} \left(\frac{\partial\theta_{t|t-1}}{\partial\psi}\right)^2$$

Thus

$$\frac{1}{T}\frac{\partial^2 \ln L}{\partial\psi^2} = \frac{1}{T}\sum \frac{\partial^2 \ln f_t}{\partial\psi^2} = \frac{1}{T}\sum u_t \frac{\partial^2\theta_{t|t-1}}{\partial\psi^2} + \frac{1}{T}\sum \frac{\partial u_t}{\partial\theta_{t|t-1}} \left(\frac{\partial\theta_{t|t-1}}{\partial\psi}\right)^2.$$

The preceding expression is similar to the one in Jensen and Rahbek (2004, p. 1212). Because u_t and its derivative are independent of $\partial\theta_{t|t-1}/\partial\psi$ and its derivative, the terms on the right-hand side converge, by the ergodic theorem, to

$$E(u_t)E\left(\frac{\partial^2\theta_{t|t-1}}{\partial\psi^2}\right) + E\left(\frac{\partial u_t}{\partial\theta}\right)E\left(\frac{\partial\theta_{t|t-1}}{\partial\psi}\right)^2, \tag{2.49}$$

provided that $E(\partial^2\theta_{t|t-1}/\partial\psi^2)$ and $E[(\partial\theta_{t|t-1}/\partial\psi)^2]$ are finite. The second term in (2.49) is the same as the limit in (2.48). Taking the expectation of $\partial^2\theta_{t|t-1}/\partial\psi^2$ as in Corollary 7 – when ψ is ϕ – shows that $E(\partial^2\theta_{t|t-1}/\partial\psi^2)$ is finite if $E(\partial^2 u_t/\partial\theta^2) < \infty$; see Condition 4. This being the case, the first term in (2.49) is zero. The same is true for the other derivatives and cross-derivatives. ■

The general version of condition (v) in Sub-section 2.2.4 can be stated as

$$\max_{h,i,j=1,\ldots,n} \sup_{\boldsymbol{\psi}\in N(\boldsymbol{\psi}_0)} \left| \frac{\partial^3 \ln L(\boldsymbol{\psi})}{T.\partial\psi_h\partial\psi_i\partial\psi_j} \right| \leq c_T, \tag{2.50}$$

where $\psi_i, i = 1, .., n$ denote the parameters in $\boldsymbol{\psi}$, $N(\boldsymbol{\psi}_0)$ is a neighborhood of the true parameter value and c_T is a random variable such that $0 \leq c_T \xrightarrow{P} c$, $0 < c < \infty$. Finding general conditions under which (2.50) holds is not easy. Instead, theorems are stated for two general classes of scale models of the form

$$y_t = \varepsilon_t \exp(\theta_{t|t-1}), \qquad t = 1, \ldots, T,$$

where the $\varepsilon_t' s$ are IID with zero location and unit scale. Such models are central to Chapters 4 and 5, in which the time-varying scale is denoted by $\lambda_{t|t-1}$ rather than $\theta_{t|t-1}$. The generalized beta and generalized gamma are defined in Sections 5.4 and 5.3, respectively.

Theorem 3 *When ε_t is distributed as t_ν or generalized beta and the true parameters satisfy Condition 3, $\widetilde{\boldsymbol{\psi}}$ is consistent and the limiting distribution of*

$\sqrt{T}(\widetilde{\psi} - \psi_0)$ is multivariate normal, with mean vector zero and covariance matrix, $Var(\widetilde{\psi})$, as in (2.46).

Proof. For the distributions in question, the first three derivatives of $\ln f_t$ consist of linear combinations of the variables $b_t^* = b_t^h(1-b_t)^k$, $h, k = 0, 1, 2, \ldots$, where $b_t = b_t(y_t; \psi)$ is beta distributed at $\psi = \psi_0$. Thus the conditions for Propositions 4 and 5 to be true are satisfied. As regards third derivatives of the log-likelihood function, consider a single parameter (without a subscript) and write

$$\frac{\partial^3 \ln L(\psi)}{\partial \psi^3} = \sum_{t=1}^{T} z_t,$$

where

$$z_t = \frac{\partial^3 \ln f_t(y_t; \psi)}{\partial \psi^3} = \frac{\partial \ln f_t}{\partial \theta_{t|t-1}} \frac{\partial \theta^3_{t|t-1}}{\partial \psi^3} + \frac{\partial^2 \ln f_t}{\partial \theta^2_{t|t-1}} \frac{\partial \theta_{t|t-1}}{\partial \psi} \frac{\partial \theta^2_{t|t-1}}{\partial \psi^2}$$
$$+ \frac{\partial^3 \ln f_t}{\partial \theta^3_{t|t-1}} \left(\frac{\partial \theta_{t|t-1}}{\partial \psi} \right)^3. \tag{2.51}$$

The definition of z_t extends to when there are n parameters, as in (2.50). Write

$$b_t(y_t; \psi) = h(y_t; \psi)/(1 + h(y_t; \psi)), \quad 0 \le h(y_t; \psi) \le \infty.$$

For any admissible ψ, $0 \le b_t(y_t; \psi) \le 1$ and so, generalizing the discussion that follows (2.26), $0 \le b_t^*(y_t; \psi) \le 1$, where $b_t^*(y_t; \psi)$ has the same form as b_t^* at the start of the proof. Thus $\partial^j \ln f_t / \partial \theta^j_{t|t-1}$, $j = 1, 2, 3$ are bounded variables. Furthermore, the derivatives of $\theta_{t|t-1}$ must be bounded at ψ_0, because as shown in Lemma 9, they are stable SREs which are ultimately dependent on $b_t(y_t; \psi)$. They must also be bounded in the neighborhood of ψ_0, because the condition $b < 1$ is more than enough to guarantee the stability condition $E(\ln|x_t|) < 0$. Extending the argument to cover third derivatives with respect to more than one of the parameters in ψ is straightforward. Thus we may conclude that all the third derivatives in (2.50) are bounded. ■

Theorem 4 *When ε_t is distributed as GED or generalized gamma and the true parameters satisfy Condition 3, $\widetilde{\psi}$ is consistent, and the limiting distribution of $\sqrt{T}(\widetilde{\psi} - \psi_0)$ is multivariate normal with mean vector zero and covariance matrix, $Var(\widetilde{\psi})$, as in (2.46).*

Proof. From the last part of Sub-section 2.2.4, we know that the first three derivatives of the log-likelihood function for the GED consist of linear functions of variables, $g_t = g_t(y_t, \psi)$, that are gamma distributed at $\psi = \psi_0$. Thus the conditions for Propositions 4 and 5 to be true are satisfied. The variable g_t takes the form $g_t(y_t, \psi) = \left| y_t \exp(-\theta_{t|t-1}) \right|^{\upsilon}$ in the GED, and in the generalized gamma distribution of Section 5.2, it is $g_t(y_t; \psi) = (y_t \exp(-\theta_{t|t-1}))^{\upsilon}$, so the same arguments hold. Because all moments of the random variable

$g_t(y_t;\boldsymbol{\psi}_0)$ exist, all moments of $g_t(y_t;\boldsymbol{\psi})$ exist in the neighborhood of $\boldsymbol{\psi}_0$ because $g_t(y_t,\boldsymbol{\psi})$ is equal to $g_t(y_t;\boldsymbol{\psi}_0)$ times a scalar that is, independent of y_t and is given by $\exp\theta_{t|t-1}(\boldsymbol{\psi}_0-\boldsymbol{\psi})$, where the notation $\theta_{t|t-1}(\boldsymbol{\psi}_0-\boldsymbol{\psi})$ indicates that $\theta_{t|t-1}$ depends on $\boldsymbol{\psi}_0-\boldsymbol{\psi}$. If a value $\boldsymbol{\psi}^*$ is chosen so that $\theta_{t|t-1}(\boldsymbol{\psi}_0-\boldsymbol{\psi}^*)>\theta_{t|t-1}(\boldsymbol{\psi}_0-\boldsymbol{\psi})$, for all $t=1,\ldots,T$, then $g_t(y_t,\boldsymbol{\psi}^*)$ will uniformly bound $g_t(y_t;\boldsymbol{\psi})$ from above. Let $z_t(\boldsymbol{\psi})$ denote the third derivative, (2.51), generalized so as to be defined with respect to any three elements in $\boldsymbol{\psi}$, that is, $\partial^3\ln f_t(y_t;\psi)/\partial\psi_h\partial\psi_i\partial\psi_j$. Bearing in mind that, as shown earlier, the derivatives of $\theta_{t|t-1}$ must be bounded in the neighborhood of $\boldsymbol{\psi}_0$, it is possible to construct a random variable $z_t(\boldsymbol{\psi}^*)$ from the $g_t(y_t;\boldsymbol{\psi}^*)'s$ that will uniformly bound $z_t(\boldsymbol{\psi})$ from above. Because $g_t(y_t;\boldsymbol{\psi}^*)=g_t(y_t;\boldsymbol{\psi}_0)\exp\theta_{t|t-1}(\boldsymbol{\psi}_0-\boldsymbol{\psi}^*)$, $z_t(\boldsymbol{\psi}^*)$ is a random variable with finite first moment (indeed, all moments are finite), and hence, by the ergodic theorem, $\sum z_t(\boldsymbol{\psi}^*)/T$ converges to a finite quantity, c. ■

Theorems 3 and 4 may be extended to include the estimation of unknown shape parameters, including degrees of freedom. The treatment of third derivatives, including cross-derivatives, entails nothing new in principle.

2.3.6 Nonstationarity

When $\phi=1$, the matrix $\mathbf{D}(\boldsymbol{\psi})$, and hence $\mathbf{I}(\boldsymbol{\psi})$, is no longer positive definite. The usual asymptotic theory does not apply, as the model contains a *unit root*. There is a considerable literature on this topic, starting with the work by Dickey and Fuller on the implications of fitting a first-order autoregressive model to a random walk. However, if the unit root is imposed so that ϕ is set equal to unity, then standard asymptotics do apply. For example, if ϕ is set equal to unity in the Gaussian ARMA(1,1) model, (1.2), the ML estimator of θ is asymptotically normal, provided $|\theta|<1$.

If $\theta_{1|0}$ is fixed and known, the following result is a corollary to Theorems 1 to 4.

Corollary 8 *When ϕ is taken to be unity in (2.31) but $b<1$ and $\omega=\theta_{1|0}$ is known, the information quantity for $\widetilde{\kappa}$ is $\sigma_u^4/k^2(1-b)$, with*

$$b=1-2\kappa\sigma_u^2/k+\kappa^2E[(\partial u_t/\partial\theta)^2], \tag{2.52}$$

assuming that Conditions 3 and 4 hold. If the conditional distribution of the observations is t, GED, generalized gamma or generalized beta, the ML estimator of κ is consistent, and $\sqrt{T}(\widetilde{\kappa}-\kappa)$ has a limiting normal distribution with mean zero and variance $k^2(1-b)/\sigma_u^4$. The introduction of a constant β into the dynamic equation of (2.31) means that it has a (fixed) slope. The information matrix is then

$$\mathbf{I}\begin{pmatrix}\kappa\\ \beta\end{pmatrix}=\frac{\sigma_u^2}{k^2(1-b)}\begin{bmatrix}\sigma_u^2 & \frac{c}{1-a}\\ \frac{c}{1-a} & \frac{1+a}{1-a}\end{bmatrix}, \tag{2.53}$$

where $a = 1 - \kappa\sigma_u^2/k\beta$ and the ML estimators of $\widetilde{\kappa}$ and $\widetilde{\beta}$ are consistent. Furthermore, $\sqrt{T}(\widetilde{\kappa} - \kappa, \widetilde{\beta} - \beta)'$ has a limiting normal distribution with zero mean vector and covariance matrix $\mathbf{I}^{-1}(\kappa, \beta)$.

Proof. Even though $\theta_{t|t-1}$ is nonstationary, the first three derivatives of $\theta_{t|t-1}$ with respect to κ and ω are SREs, which are strictly stationary when $b < 1$. Hence the conditions for consistency and asymptotic normality are satisfied. The information matrix in (2.53) is derived in the same way as (2.44) but with δ replaced by β. ■

Remark 9 *It can be seen from (2.52) that $\kappa > 0$ is a necessary condition for $b < 1$.*

Further issues which arise in connection with the initialization of a nonstationary filter can be found in the chapters on location and scale.

2.3.7 Several Parameters

Lemma 5 and the subsequent corollary may be extended to deal with models in which $\boldsymbol{\theta}$ is a vector of parameters.

Lemma 10 *Consider a static model in which the $n \times 1$ vector of parameters is partitioned as $\boldsymbol{\theta} = (\boldsymbol{\theta}_1', \boldsymbol{\theta}_2')'$, where n_1 and n_2 are the dimensions of $\boldsymbol{\theta}_1$ and $\boldsymbol{\theta}_2$, and the information matrix is similarly partitioned as*

$$\mathbf{I} = \begin{bmatrix} \mathbf{I}_{11} & \mathbf{I}_{12} \\ \mathbf{I}_{21} & \mathbf{I}_{22} \end{bmatrix}.$$

Let $\boldsymbol{\theta}_1$ evolve over time in a dynamic model that depends on the score vector and a vector of parameters, $\boldsymbol{\psi}$. When the information matrix in the static model does not depend on $\boldsymbol{\theta}_1$

$$\mathbf{I}\begin{pmatrix} \boldsymbol{\psi} \\ \boldsymbol{\theta}_2 \end{pmatrix} = \begin{bmatrix} E\left[\frac{\partial \boldsymbol{\theta}_1'}{\partial \boldsymbol{\psi}} \mathbf{I}_{11} \frac{\partial \boldsymbol{\theta}_1}{\partial \boldsymbol{\psi}'}\right] & E\left(\frac{\partial \boldsymbol{\theta}_1'}{\partial \boldsymbol{\psi}}\right) \mathbf{I}_{12} \\ \mathbf{I}_{21} E\left(\frac{\partial \boldsymbol{\theta}_1}{\partial \boldsymbol{\psi}'}\right) & \mathbf{I}_{22} \end{bmatrix}, \tag{2.54}$$

where $\boldsymbol{\theta}_1 = \boldsymbol{\theta}_{1,t|t-1}$.

Proof. Generalizing the transpose of (2.28) gives

$$\frac{\partial \ln f_t(y_t \mid Y_{t-1}; \boldsymbol{\psi})}{\partial \boldsymbol{\psi}'} = \frac{\partial \ln f_t}{\partial \boldsymbol{\theta}_1'} \frac{\partial \boldsymbol{\theta}_1}{\partial \boldsymbol{\psi}'},$$

and so

$$E_{t-1} \frac{\partial \ln f_t}{\partial \boldsymbol{\psi}} \frac{\partial \ln f_t}{\partial \boldsymbol{\psi}'} = \frac{\partial \boldsymbol{\theta}_1'}{\partial \boldsymbol{\psi}} \left[E_{t-1} \left(\frac{\partial \ln f_t}{\partial \boldsymbol{\theta}_1} \frac{\partial \ln f_t}{\partial \boldsymbol{\theta}_1'} \right) \right] \frac{\partial \boldsymbol{\theta}_1}{\partial \boldsymbol{\psi}'} = \frac{\partial \boldsymbol{\theta}_1'}{\partial \boldsymbol{\psi}} \mathbf{I}_{11} \frac{\partial \boldsymbol{\theta}_1}{\partial \boldsymbol{\psi}'}.$$

■

When $n = 1$, the structure of the information matrix simplifies, and a generalization of Theorem 1 follows.

Corollary 9 *Suppose that $\boldsymbol{\theta}_2$ consists of $n-1 \geq 1$ fixed parameters, whereas θ_1 is time-varying and depends on a set of parameters, $\boldsymbol{\psi}$. When the terms in the information matrix of the static model that involve θ_1, including cross-products, do not depend on θ_1,*

$$\mathbf{I}\begin{pmatrix}\boldsymbol{\psi}\\ \boldsymbol{\theta}_2\end{pmatrix} = \begin{bmatrix} E\left(\frac{\partial \ln f_t}{\partial \theta_1}\right)^2 E\left(\frac{\partial \theta_1}{\partial \boldsymbol{\psi}}\frac{\partial \theta_1}{\partial \boldsymbol{\psi}'}\right) & E\left(\frac{\partial \theta_1}{\partial \boldsymbol{\psi}}\right) E\left(\frac{\partial \ln f_t}{\partial \theta_1}\frac{\partial \ln f_t}{\partial \boldsymbol{\theta}_2'}\right) \\ E\left(\frac{\partial \ln f_t}{\partial \theta_1}\frac{\partial \ln f_t}{\partial \boldsymbol{\theta}_2}\right) E\left(\frac{\partial \theta_1}{\partial \boldsymbol{\psi}'}\right) & E\left(\frac{\partial \ln f_t}{\partial \boldsymbol{\theta}_2}\frac{\partial \ln f_t}{\partial \boldsymbol{\theta}_2'}\right) \end{bmatrix}, \tag{2.55}$$

where $\theta_1 = \theta_{1,t|t-1}$. The conditions for asymptotic normality are as in Subsection 2.3.5.

The information matrix for the first-order model is

$$\mathbf{I}\begin{pmatrix}\boldsymbol{\psi}\\ \boldsymbol{\theta}_2\end{pmatrix} = \begin{bmatrix} E\left(\frac{\partial \ln f_t}{\partial \theta_1}\right)^2 \mathbf{D}(\boldsymbol{\psi}) & \begin{pmatrix} 0\\ 0\\ \frac{1-\phi}{1-a}\end{pmatrix} E\left(\frac{\partial \ln f_t}{\partial \theta_1}\frac{\partial \ln f_t}{\partial \boldsymbol{\theta}_2'}\right) \\ E\left(\frac{\partial \ln f_t}{\partial \theta_1}\frac{\partial \ln f_t}{\partial \boldsymbol{\theta}_2}\right)\begin{pmatrix}0 & 0 & \frac{1-\phi}{1-a}\end{pmatrix} & E\left(\frac{\partial \ln f_t}{\partial \boldsymbol{\theta}_2}\frac{\partial \ln f_t}{\partial \boldsymbol{\theta}_2'}\right) \end{bmatrix}, \tag{2.56}$$

where $\mathbf{D}(\boldsymbol{\psi})$ is the matrix in (2.40). When the asymptotic distributions of the ML estimators of θ_1 and $\boldsymbol{\theta}_2$ are independent, the information matrix is block-diagonal, and the top left-hand block is $\mathbf{I}(\boldsymbol{\psi}) = I.\mathbf{D}(\boldsymbol{\psi})$, as in (2.39).

Analytic evaluation of the top left-hand block in (2.55) may not be easy when $n_1 > 1$. For a stationary first-order model,

$$\boldsymbol{\theta}_{1,t+1|t} = (\mathbf{I} - \boldsymbol{\Phi})^{-1}\boldsymbol{\omega} + \boldsymbol{\Phi}\boldsymbol{\theta}_{1,t|t-1} + \mathbf{K}\mathbf{u}_t, \tag{2.57}$$

the parameter vector $\boldsymbol{\psi}$ contains the distinct elements of the vector $\boldsymbol{\omega}$ and the $n \times n$ matrices $\boldsymbol{\Phi}$ and $\mathbf{K}$. A closed-form expression may be obtained in principle, provided that the first two moments of $\mathbf{u}_t$ and $\partial \mathbf{u}_t / \partial \boldsymbol{\theta}_1$ and the associated cross-products do not depend on $\boldsymbol{\theta}_1$. Differentiating the dynamic equations of (2.57) with respect to $\boldsymbol{\psi}'$ yields a matrix stochastic recurrence equation, which will be stable if the roots of the matrix

$$\mathbf{A} = \boldsymbol{\Phi} + \mathbf{K}E(\partial \mathbf{u}_t / \partial \boldsymbol{\theta}')$$

are less than one in absolute value. The existence of the information matrix will depend on a generalization of the condition that $b < 1$ in the univariate model. Restrictions may be needed for identifiability, for example, requiring $\mathbf{K}$ to be symmetric. The issue of whether or not the score vector is to be standardized now becomes more important. The simplest option is $\mathbf{u}_t = \partial \ln f_t / \partial \boldsymbol{\theta}_1$, but there may be a good case for letting $\mathbf{u}_t = \mathbf{I}^{-1}(\boldsymbol{\psi}, \boldsymbol{\theta}_2)\partial \ln f_t / \partial \boldsymbol{\theta}$. Issues of this kind are explored in the chapter on multivariate models.

Some simplification is possible when each time-varying parameter depends on a different set of underlying parameters. The lemma below is for $n = 2$, but this is simply for notational convenience.

Lemma 11 *Suppose that there are two parameters in $\boldsymbol{\theta}$ but that $\theta_{j,t|t-1} = f(\boldsymbol{\psi}_j)$, $j = 1, 2$ with the vectors $\boldsymbol{\psi}_1$ and $\boldsymbol{\psi}_2$ having no elements in common. When the information matrix in the static model depends on neither θ_1 nor θ_2,*

$$\mathbf{I}\begin{pmatrix}\boldsymbol{\psi}_1\\ \boldsymbol{\psi}_2\end{pmatrix} = \begin{bmatrix} I_{11}E\left(\frac{\partial\theta_1}{\partial\boldsymbol{\psi}_1}\frac{\partial\theta_1}{\partial\boldsymbol{\psi}_1'}\right) & I_{12}E\left(\frac{\partial\theta_1}{\partial\boldsymbol{\psi}_1}\frac{\partial\theta_2}{\partial\boldsymbol{\psi}_2'}\right) \\ I_{21}E\left(\frac{\partial\theta_2}{\partial\boldsymbol{\psi}_2}\frac{\partial\theta_1}{\partial\boldsymbol{\psi}_1'}\right) & I_{22}E\left(\frac{\partial\theta_2}{\partial\boldsymbol{\psi}_2}\frac{\partial\theta_2}{\partial\boldsymbol{\psi}_2'}\right) \end{bmatrix}. \tag{2.58}$$

Proof. By straightforward algebra,

$$\mathbf{I}\begin{pmatrix}\boldsymbol{\psi}_1\\ \boldsymbol{\psi}_2\end{pmatrix} = E\left[\begin{pmatrix}\frac{\partial \ln f_t}{\partial\theta_1}\frac{\partial\theta_1}{\partial\boldsymbol{\psi}_1}\\ \frac{\partial \ln f_t}{\partial\theta_2}\frac{\partial\theta_2}{\partial\boldsymbol{\psi}_2}\end{pmatrix}\begin{pmatrix}\frac{\partial \ln f_t}{\partial\theta_1}\frac{\partial\theta_1}{\partial\boldsymbol{\psi}_1}\\ \frac{\partial \ln f_t}{\partial\theta_2}\frac{\partial\theta_2}{\partial\boldsymbol{\psi}_2}\end{pmatrix}'\right]$$

$$= \begin{bmatrix} E\left(\frac{\partial \ln f_t}{\partial\theta_1}\right)^2 E\left(\frac{\partial\theta_1}{\partial\boldsymbol{\psi}_1}\frac{\partial\theta_1}{\partial\boldsymbol{\psi}_1'}\right) & E\left(\frac{\partial \ln f_t}{\partial\theta_1}\frac{\partial \ln f_t}{\partial\theta_2}\right)E\left(\frac{\partial\theta_1}{\partial\boldsymbol{\psi}_1}\frac{\partial\theta_2}{\partial\boldsymbol{\psi}_2'}\right) \\ E\left(\frac{\partial \ln f_t}{\partial\theta_1}\frac{\partial \ln f_t}{\partial\theta_2}\right)E\left(\frac{\partial\theta_2}{\partial\boldsymbol{\psi}_2}\frac{\partial\theta_1}{\partial\boldsymbol{\psi}_1'}\right) & E\left(\frac{\partial \ln f_t}{\partial\theta_2}\right)^2 E\left(\frac{\partial\theta_2}{\partial\boldsymbol{\psi}_2}\frac{\partial\theta_2}{\partial\boldsymbol{\psi}_2'}\right) \end{bmatrix}.$$

■

2.4 HIGHER ORDER MODELS*

Durbin and Koopman (2012, Part II) set out estimation procedures for nonlinear and non-Gaussian state space models in which the nonlinear measurement equation is

$$f(y_t \mid \theta_t; \boldsymbol{\psi}), \qquad \theta_t = \omega + \mathbf{z}_t'\boldsymbol{\alpha}_t, \quad t = 1, \ldots, T, \tag{2.59}$$

where $\mathbf{z}_t$ is a non-stochastic $m \times 1$ vector, ω is a constant and the $m \times 1$ state vector, $\boldsymbol{\alpha}_t$, is generated by a linear transition equation,

$$\boldsymbol{\alpha}_{t+1} = \boldsymbol{\delta} + \mathbf{T}\boldsymbol{\alpha}_t + \boldsymbol{\eta}_t, \quad t = 1, \ldots, T, \tag{2.60}$$

where $\mathbf{T}$ is an $m \times m$ matrix, $\boldsymbol{\delta}$ is an $m \times 1$ vector of constants, and $\boldsymbol{\eta}_t$ is an $m \times 1$ vector of serially uncorrelated disturbances with mean zero and covariance matrix $\mathbf{Q}$. There will typically be contraints on model. For example, if $\boldsymbol{\alpha}_t$ is stationary, $\boldsymbol{\delta}$ is set to zero if ω is non-zero.

The time-varying parameter, θ_t, is the signal. It may depend on a number of different components, including a trend and seasonal, or it may be that the Markov structure for the state vector is a device for allowing θ_t to be a higher-order model, such as an ARMA process. The signal is connected to a set of parameters in the distribution, $f(y_t \mid \theta_t; \boldsymbol{\psi})$, by a link function, a term that originates from the work on generalized linear models by McCullagh and Nelder (1989). When θ_t is location and the conditional distribution is Gaussian, the model takes the standard state space form. Optimal updating of the conditional distribution of the state is by the Kalman filter, and the likelihood function is obtained as a byproduct of the Kalman filer; see Section 3.5. More generally, estimation is carried out by computer-intensive techniques, such as importance sampling or Markov chain Monte Carlo.

The corresponding DCS model is

$$f(y_t \mid \theta_{t|t-1}; \boldsymbol{\psi}), \quad \theta_{t|t-1} = \omega + \mathbf{z}_t'\boldsymbol{\alpha}_{t|t-1}, \quad t = 1, \ldots, T, \tag{2.61}$$
$$\boldsymbol{\alpha}_{t+1|t} = \boldsymbol{\delta} + \mathbf{T}\boldsymbol{\alpha}_{t|t-1} + \boldsymbol{\kappa} u_t,$$

where u_t is the conditional score and $\boldsymbol{\psi}$ denotes unknown parameters in the $m \times 1$ vectors $\boldsymbol{\delta}$ and $\boldsymbol{\kappa}$ and the $m \times m$ matrix $\mathbf{T}$. The filter in (2.61) is stationary provided that the eigenvalues of the matrix $\mathbf{T}$ have modulus less than one. In a conditionally Gaussian model for location, the recursive equation in (2.61) is the steady-state Kalman filter.

The vector $\mathbf{z}_t$ changes over time, in a deterministic fashion, for a certain formulation of the seasonal component, but in other cases of interest, it is time-invariant. For the rest of this sub-section, it will be assumed to be time-invariant, and the t subscript will be dropped. When trend and seasonal components are present, the $\mathbf{T}$ matrix will contain unit roots. Provided that these roots are fixed, rather than estimated, they pose no problem for the asymptotic theory. Further discussion can be found in Section 3.6.

Theorem 5 *When $\boldsymbol{\alpha}_{t+1|t}$ is stationary and Condition 2 holds, a sufficient condition for the existence of the information matrix of the unknown parameters in $\boldsymbol{\psi}$ is that all the roots of the $m^2 \times m^2$ matrix*

$$\mathbf{B} = \mathbf{T} \otimes \mathbf{T} + (\boldsymbol{\kappa}\mathbf{z}' \otimes \mathbf{T} + \mathbf{T} \otimes \boldsymbol{\kappa}\mathbf{z}')E\left(\frac{\partial u_t}{\partial \theta}\right) + \boldsymbol{\kappa}\mathbf{z}' \otimes \boldsymbol{\kappa}\mathbf{z}' E\left(\frac{\partial u_t}{\partial \theta}\right)^2, \tag{2.62}$$

where $\otimes$ is the Kronecker product, have modulus less than one. A necessary condition is that the roots of the $m \times m$ matrix

$$\mathbf{A} = \mathbf{T} + \boldsymbol{\kappa}\mathbf{z}' E\left(\partial u_t / \partial \theta\right) \tag{2.63}$$

have modulus less than one.

Proof. Consider the parameters in $\boldsymbol{\kappa}$. For all $t = 1, \ldots, T$,

$$\frac{\partial \boldsymbol{\alpha}_{t+1|t}}{\partial \kappa_i} = \mathbf{T}\frac{\partial \boldsymbol{\alpha}_{t|t-1}}{\partial \kappa_i} + \boldsymbol{\kappa}\frac{\partial u_t}{\partial \kappa_i} + \mathbf{w}_i u_t, \quad i = 1, \ldots, m,$$

where $\mathbf{w}_i$ is a vector that has one in the i-th position and zeroes elsewhere. Then

$$\frac{\partial u_t}{\partial \kappa_i} = \frac{\partial u_t}{\partial \theta_{t|t-1}} \frac{\partial \theta_{t|t-1}}{\partial \boldsymbol{\alpha}_{t|t-1}'} \frac{\partial \boldsymbol{\alpha}_{t|t-1}}{\partial \kappa_i} = \frac{\partial u_t}{\partial \theta_{t|t-1}} \mathbf{z}' \frac{\partial \boldsymbol{\alpha}_{t|t-1}}{\partial \kappa_i},$$

so

$$\frac{\partial \boldsymbol{\alpha}_{t+1|t}}{\partial \kappa_i} = \left(\mathbf{T} + \boldsymbol{\kappa}\mathbf{z}' \frac{\partial u_t}{\partial \theta_{t|t-1}}\right) \frac{\partial \boldsymbol{\alpha}_{t|t-1}}{\partial \kappa_i} + \mathbf{w}_i u_t,$$

or

$$\frac{\partial \boldsymbol{\alpha}_{t+1|t}}{\partial \kappa_i} = \mathbf{X}_t \frac{\partial \boldsymbol{\alpha}_{t|t-1}}{\partial \kappa_i} + \mathbf{w}_i u_t, \quad i = 1, \ldots, m, \tag{2.64}$$

where

$$\mathbf{X}_t = \mathbf{T} + \frac{\partial u_t}{\partial \theta_{t|t-1}} \boldsymbol{\kappa} \mathbf{z}'. \tag{2.65}$$

Taking conditional expectations of (2.64) gives

$$E_{t-1} \frac{\partial \boldsymbol{\alpha}_{t+1|t}}{\partial \kappa_i} = \mathbf{A} \frac{\partial \boldsymbol{\alpha}_{t|t-1}}{\partial \kappa_i}, \quad i = 1, \ldots, m,$$

where

$$\mathbf{A} = E_{t-1}\mathbf{X}_t = E_{t-1}\left(\mathbf{T} + \boldsymbol{\kappa}\mathbf{z}' \frac{\partial u_t}{\partial \theta_{t|t-1}}\right) = \mathbf{T} + E\left(\frac{\partial u_t}{\partial \theta}\right)\boldsymbol{\kappa}\mathbf{z}'.$$

The unconditional derivative vector is zero if the roots of $\mathbf{A}$ are less than one in absolute value.

The information matrix depends on the $m \times m$ matrix

$$E\left(\frac{\partial \theta_{t+1|t}}{\partial \boldsymbol{\kappa}} \frac{\partial \theta_{t+1|t}}{\partial \boldsymbol{\kappa}'}\right). \tag{2.66}$$

Although only the derivative of $\theta_{t+1|t}$ appears in the formula, it is necessary to evaluate the covariance matrices of the derivatives of the elements of $\boldsymbol{\alpha}_{t+1|t}$ with respect to each element in $\boldsymbol{\kappa}$ in order to find it. From (2.64)

$$\begin{aligned}\frac{\partial \boldsymbol{\alpha}_{t+1|t}}{\partial \kappa_i} \frac{\partial \boldsymbol{\alpha}'_{t+1|t}}{\partial \kappa_j} &= \mathbf{X}_t \frac{\partial \boldsymbol{\alpha}_{t|t-1}}{\partial \kappa_i} \frac{\partial \boldsymbol{\alpha}'_{t|t-1}}{\partial \kappa_j} \mathbf{X}'_t + \mathbf{X}_t \frac{\partial \boldsymbol{\alpha}_{t|t-1}}{\partial \kappa_i} \mathbf{w}'_i u_t \\ &\quad + u_t \mathbf{w}_j \frac{\partial \boldsymbol{\alpha}'_{t|t-1}}{\partial \kappa_j} \mathbf{X}'_t + u_t^2 \mathbf{w}_i \mathbf{w}'_j,\end{aligned}$$

for $i, j = 1, \ldots, m$. We can write

$$\begin{aligned}\mathrm{vec}\left(\frac{\partial \boldsymbol{\alpha}_{t+1|t}}{\partial \kappa_i} \frac{\partial \boldsymbol{\alpha}'_{t+1|t}}{\partial \kappa_j}\right) &= \mathbf{X}_t \otimes \mathbf{X}_t . \mathrm{vec}\left(\frac{\partial \boldsymbol{\alpha}_{t|t-1}}{\partial \kappa_i} \frac{\partial \boldsymbol{\alpha}'_{t|t-1}}{\partial \kappa_j}\right) \\ &\quad + u_t \mathrm{vec}\left(\mathbf{X}_t \frac{\partial \boldsymbol{\alpha}_{t|t-1}}{\partial \kappa_i} \mathbf{w}'_i + \mathbf{w}_j \frac{\partial \boldsymbol{\alpha}'_{t|t-1}}{\partial \kappa_j} \mathbf{X}'_t\right) \\ &\quad + u_t^2 \mathrm{vec}\left(\mathbf{w}_i \mathbf{w}'_j\right),\end{aligned} \tag{2.67}$$

where the vec(.) operator indicates that the columns of the matrix are being stacked one upon the other. Taking conditional expectations

$$E_{t-1}\text{vec}\left(\frac{\partial \boldsymbol{\alpha}_{t+1|t}}{\partial \kappa_i}\frac{\partial \boldsymbol{\alpha}'_{t+1|t}}{\partial \kappa_j}\right)$$

$$= [E_{t-1}(\mathbf{X}_t \otimes \mathbf{X}_t)]\text{vec}\left(\frac{\partial \boldsymbol{\alpha}_{t|t-1}}{\partial \kappa_i}\frac{\partial \boldsymbol{\alpha}'_{t|t-1}}{\partial \kappa_j}\right)$$

$$+ \text{vec}\left([E_{t-1}(u_t\mathbf{X}_t)]\frac{\partial \boldsymbol{\alpha}_{t|t-1}}{\partial \kappa_i}\mathbf{w}'_i + \mathbf{w}_j\frac{\partial \boldsymbol{\alpha}'_{t|t-1}}{\partial \kappa_j}[E_{t-1}(u_t\mathbf{X}_t)]'\right)$$

$$+ [E_{t-1}(u_t^2)]\text{vec}\left(\mathbf{w}_i\mathbf{w}'_j\right).$$

Now

$$\mathbf{X}_t \otimes \mathbf{X}_t = \mathbf{T}\otimes\mathbf{T} + \kappa\mathbf{z}\frac{\partial u_t}{\partial \theta_{t|t-1}}\otimes\mathbf{T} + \mathbf{T}\otimes\kappa\mathbf{z}\frac{\partial u_t}{\partial \theta_{t|t-1}} + \kappa\mathbf{z}\frac{\partial u_t}{\partial \theta_{t|t-1}}\otimes\kappa\mathbf{z}\frac{\partial u_t}{\partial \theta_{t|t-1}}$$

and its unconditional expectation, $E(\mathbf{X}_t \otimes \mathbf{X}_t)$, is $\mathbf{B}$, as in (2.62). Just as Theorem 2 requires $b < 1$, so here the roots of $\mathbf{B}$ need to be less than one in absolute value for the unconditional expectation of (2.67) to exist. This being the case,

$$E\text{vec}\left(\frac{\partial \boldsymbol{\alpha}_{t+1|t}}{\partial \kappa_i}\frac{\partial \boldsymbol{\alpha}'_{t+1|t}}{\partial \kappa_j}\right)$$

$$= (\mathbf{I}-\mathbf{B})^{-1}\left[\text{vec}\left([E(u_t\mathbf{X}_t)]\frac{\partial \boldsymbol{\alpha}_{t|t-1}}{\partial \kappa_i}\boldsymbol{\omega}'_i + \boldsymbol{\omega}_j\frac{\partial \boldsymbol{\alpha}'_{t|t-1}}{\partial \kappa_j}[E(u_t\mathbf{X}_t)]'\right)\right.$$

$$\left. + [E(u_t^2)]\text{vec}\left(\boldsymbol{\omega}_i\boldsymbol{\omega}'_j\right)\right], \qquad (2.68)$$

and once the expectations have been found, the ij-th element, $i, j = 1, \ldots, m$, in (2.66) is given by

$$(\text{vec}\left(\mathbf{z}\mathbf{z}'\right))' E\text{vec}\left(\frac{\partial \boldsymbol{\alpha}_{t+1|t}}{\partial \kappa_i}\frac{\partial \boldsymbol{\alpha}'_{t+1|t}}{\partial \kappa_j}\right) = \left[E\text{vec}\left(\frac{\partial \boldsymbol{\alpha}_{t+1|t}}{\partial \kappa_i}\frac{\partial \boldsymbol{\alpha}'_{t+1|t}}{\partial \kappa_j}\right)\right](\mathbf{z}\otimes\mathbf{z}). \qquad (2.69)$$

When there are unknown parameters in $\mathbf{T}$, the key conditions for ML inference are the same. Let ϕ be a parameter in $\mathbf{T}$. Then

$$\frac{\partial \boldsymbol{\alpha}_{t+1|t}}{\partial \phi} = \mathbf{T}\frac{\partial \boldsymbol{\alpha}_{t|t-1}}{\partial \phi} + \kappa\frac{\partial u_t}{\partial \phi} + \frac{\partial \mathbf{T}}{\partial \phi}\boldsymbol{\alpha}_{t|t-1} = \mathbf{X}_t\frac{\partial \boldsymbol{\alpha}_{t|t-1}}{\partial \phi} + \frac{\partial \mathbf{T}}{\partial \phi}\boldsymbol{\alpha}_{t|t-1}.$$

■

Evaluation of the information matrix may be complicated, but evaluation of $\mathbf{B}$ is straightforward. Once it has been established that the roots of $\mathbf{B}$ have modulus less than one, the information matrix may be computed numerically.

2.5 TESTS

Before fitting a DCS model, it is advisable to test whether time variation is, in fact, present. When a series is random, a first-order DCS model will not be identifiable because, as noted in Corollary 5, the information matrix is singular. Even if a numerical optimization procedure is coaxed into convergence, a Wald test in which the null hypothesis is $\kappa = 0$ should not be carried out.

The Lagrange multiplier principle may be used to construct suitable tests against serial correlation in the feature of interest by taking account of the form of the conditional distribution posited for the dynamic model. Such tests should be able to guard against low power as a consequence of outliers. After a model has been fitted, diagnostics tests may be constructed based on similar principles. These tests may be complemented by procedures for assessing the goodness of fit of the assumed conditional distribution.

2.5.1 Serial Correlation

The standard tests against serial correlation are based on the sample autocorrelations, $r(\tau) = c(\tau)/c(0)$, where

$$c(\tau) = T^{-1} \sum_{t=\tau+1}^{T} (y_t - \overline{y})(y_{t-\tau} - \overline{y}), \quad \tau = 0, 1, 2, \ldots. \tag{2.70}$$

(A divisor of $T - \tau$ can also be used). In particular, the portmanteau test uses the statistic

$$Q(P) = T \sum_{\tau=1}^{P} r^2(\tau), \tag{2.71}$$

where P is a non-zero integer; the Ljung-Box modification is

$$Q^*(P) = T(T+2) \sum_{\tau=1}^{P} (T-\tau)^{-1} r^2(\tau).$$

Both $Q(P)$ and $Q^*(P)$ are asymptotically χ_P^2 when the observations are independent. The weaker assumption that the observations are serially uncorrelated is not sufficient; see the discussion in Sub-section 4.13.2.

The portmanteau test may be derived as a Lagrange multiplier (LM) test against a Gaussian moving average process of order P. Similarly, a DCS test for serial correlation may be developed by considering the $(0, P-1)$ dynamic process

$$\theta_{t+1|t} = \omega + \kappa_0 u_t + \cdots + \kappa_{P-1} u_{t-P+1}, \quad t = 1, \ldots, T, \tag{2.72}$$

where u_t is the score for the t-th observation.

Proposition 6 *Consider a model, as in Corollary 9, where one parameter in θ is time-varying according to (2.72), whereas the other parameters are fixed.*

The LM test statistic for testing the null hypothesis $\kappa_0 = \kappa_1 = \cdots = \kappa_{P-1} = 0$ *is the portmanteau statistic*

$$Q_u(P) = T \sum_{\tau=1}^{P} r_u^2(\tau), \tag{2.73}$$

where $r_u(\tau)$ *is the* τ*-th sample autocorrelation of* u_t*. The asymptotic distribution of* $Q_u(P)$ *under the null hypothesis is* χ_P^2.

Proof. For simplicity, assume that $k = 1$; when $k \neq 1$, it cancels in the final expression. We have

$$\frac{\partial \theta_{t+1|t}}{\partial \kappa_j} = \sum_{i=0}^{P-1} \kappa_i \frac{\partial u_{t-i}}{\partial \kappa_j} + u_{t-j}, \quad j = 0, \ldots, P-1,$$

but under the null hypothesis, when $\boldsymbol{\kappa} = (\kappa_0, .., \kappa_{P-1})' = \mathbf{0}$,

$$\frac{\partial \theta_{t+1|t}}{\partial \kappa_j} = u_{t-j}, \quad j = 0, \ldots, P-1.$$

Hence

$$\mathbf{D}(\boldsymbol{\kappa}) = E\left(\frac{\partial \theta_{t|t-1}}{\partial \boldsymbol{\kappa}} \frac{\partial \theta_{t|t-1}}{\partial \boldsymbol{\kappa}'}\right) = \sigma_u^2 \mathbf{I}_P$$

and so, as in (2.39),

$$\mathbf{I}(\boldsymbol{\kappa}) = \sigma_u^2 \mathbf{D}(\boldsymbol{\kappa}) = \sigma_u^4 \mathbf{I}_P.$$

The result follows from the standard LM formula, that is

$$LM = \frac{\partial \ln L}{\partial \boldsymbol{\kappa}'} \mathbf{I}^{-1}(\boldsymbol{\kappa}) \frac{\partial \ln L}{\partial \boldsymbol{\kappa}},$$

because

$$\frac{\partial \ln f_t}{\partial \kappa_j} = \frac{\partial \ln f_t}{\partial \theta_{t|t-1}} \frac{\partial \theta_{t|t-1}}{\partial \kappa_j} = u_t u_{t-1-j}, \quad j = 0, 1, \ldots, P-1. \tag{2.74}$$

Estimation of fixed parameters, such as degrees of freedom or the unconditional mean, makes no difference to the form of the result, because in (2.55) $\boldsymbol{\psi} = \boldsymbol{\kappa}$ and $E\left(\partial \theta_{t|t-1} / \partial \boldsymbol{\kappa}\right) = \mathbf{0}$. ■

Remark 10 *Under the null hypothesis, the first-order condition,* $\partial \ln L / \partial \omega = 0$*, implies that* $\overline{u} = T^{-1} \sum_{t=1}^{T} u_t = 0$ *because*

$$\frac{\partial \ln L}{\partial \omega} = \sum_{t=1}^{T} \frac{\partial \ln f_t(\theta_{t|t-1})}{\partial \theta_{t|t-1}} \frac{\partial \theta_{t|t-1}}{\partial \omega} = \sum_{t=1}^{T} u_t.$$

Remark 11 *The Ljung-Box statistic*

$$Q_u^*(P) = T(T+2) \sum_{\tau=1}^{P} (T-\tau)^{-1} r_u^2(\tau),$$

may also be used. The asymptotic distribution under the null hypothesis is again χ^2_P.

The degrees of freedom in a t distribution may be estimated without affecting the asymptotic distribution of $Q_u(P)$. Estimation of dynamic parameters, on the other hand, will affect the asymptotic distribution of the portmanteau statistic constructed from residuals. The solution, as in the Box-Pierce test, is to adjust the reference chi-square distribution by reducing the degrees of freedom by the number of dynamic parameters estimated, that is, $p + q$ when an $ARMA(p, q)$ model is fitted. Another possibility might be to develop LM tests.

It is not unusual to be faced with a situation in which the serial correlation in $\theta_{t|t-1}$ is very persistent. In the first-order model, (2.30), persistence means that the parameter ϕ is close to one. In these circumstances, a stationarity test, such as the one proposed by Nyblom and Mäkeläinen (1983) or the more general test of Kwiatkowski et al. (1992) will tend to have higher power than the portmanteau test; see the evidence in Harvey and Streibel (1998). The test statistics could be constructed from conditional score variables.

2.5.2 Goodness of Fit of Distributions

Assessing how well a particular conditional distribution fits the data is an important part of the methodology of DCS models. The goodness of fit of a Gaussian distribution is routinely tested with the Bowman-Shenton (Jarque-Bera) statistic, which is based on sample skewness and kurtosis. The fact that the test statistic consists of two parts is helpful in determining whether a rejection is based primarily on skewness or kurtosis.

More generally, goodness of fit is assessed by reference to the quantiles of the assumed theoretical distribution. There are two approaches. The first is based on the QQ plot, in which the T equally spaced quantiles of the comparison distribution are plotted on the vertical axis, and the order statistics of the sample, $y_{(1)} \leq y_{(2)} \leq \cdots \leq y_{(T)}$, are plotted on the horizontal axis. If the sample comes from the comparison distribution, the plot will approximate a straight 45-degree line. Formally, the plot is of the quantile function $F^{-1}(k/(T+1))$, against $y_{(k)}$, $k = 1, \ldots, T$. Note that, apart from a few exceptions, such as the exponential distribution, uniform, Weibull and log-logistic, closed-form expressions for quantile functions, $F^{-1}(y_t)$, are not generally available, and their evaluation often involves numerical methods.

A second plot, which essentially presents the same information, but in a different way, uses the probability integral transform (PIT). The PIT of a variable is given by its CDF, that is, $PIT(y) = F(y)$. By construction,[6] the PIT has a standard uniform distribution, that is, the range is [0,1]. If the PITs are not uniformly distributed, the shape of the histogram can be informative.

[6] A change of variable from y to $F(y)$ gives the PDF

$$f(F(y)) = f(y) \cdot \partial y/\partial F(y) = 1, \quad 0 \leq F(y) \leq 1.$$

For example, a hump indicates that the forecasts are too narrow and the tails are not adequately represented. The hypothesis that a set of T observations comes from a particular parametric distribution can be tested using the Kolmogorov-Smirnov statistic

$$KS_{PIT} = \max_j \left| PIT_{(j)} - j/T \right|,$$

where $PIT_{(j)}$, $j = 1, \ldots, T$ denotes the ordered $PIT(y_t)'s$; see, for example, Siegal (1956, p. 48). When parameters have been estimated, the distribution of the Kolmogorov-Smirnov statistic will normally have to be found by simulation.

The PITs for most of the distributions employed in this book are readily found.

Example 7 *The PIT of a variable that has an exponential distribution with mean θ is simply*

$$PIT(y_t) = F(y_t) = \int_0^{y_t} \theta^{-1} \exp(-x/\theta)dx = 1 - \exp(-y_t/\theta).$$

Example 8 *The PIT for the standard t_ν distribution is a regularized incomplete beta function, $beta(z_t, \nu/2, \nu/2)$, with $z_t = ((y_t^2 + \nu)^{-1/2} y_t + 1)/2$.*

Berkowitz (2001) suggested transforming the PITs to standard normal variables using an algorithm for computing the inverse of the Gaussian distribution function (the quantile function). This opens up a wide range of tests appropriate for the normal distribution, including the Bowman-Shenton test. Berkowitz argued that such tests tend to have higher power than the nonparametric tests associated with the uniform distribution.

2.5.3 Residuals

Diebold et al. (1998) discuss various ways in which the PITs may be used to assess forecasting schemes. In the present context, this means checking model specification using the PITs of the one-step-ahead prediction errors. For example, plots of the autocorrelation functions of the PITs, and of their powers, may indicate the source of serial dependence. Such plots may be particularly useful for nonparametric modelling, as described in Chapter 6.

Tests based on standardized residuals, their PITs and the normal variates created from PITs offer three alternatives for diagnostic checking. Because the variables are all transformations of each other, it is not clear which will be preferable. Indeed, the answer almost certainly depends on the assumed distribution. The fitting of DCS models also offers a fourth possibility, namely the use of the conditional scores. The conditional scores may be appropriate for testing against serial correlation, and in cases in which they have a known distribution, comparing the empirical and theoretical distributions may be valuable. These matters will be discussed further for particular models.

2.5.4 Model Fit

The overall fit of a model can be assessed in a number of ways. The various criteria which are discussed here are generally applicable and so can be used to compare DCS models with other models. It is assumed that estimation is by maximum likelihood.

The maximized log-likelihood is the basic measure of goodness of fit, but in order to compare different models, an allowance is often made for the number of parameters, n, estimated. The Akaike information criterion (AIC) is defined as

$$AIC = -2\ln L(\widetilde{\psi}) + 2n, \qquad (2.75)$$

while the Bayes information criterion (BIC) has $2n$ replaced by $n \ln T$.

Post-sample predictive testing may also be employed. The predictive likelihood, sometimes called the log-score, is both simple and effective. Looking at the post-sample residuals, scores and PITs may also provide valuable information. Mitchell and Wallis (2011) provided a recent discussion of the issues involved.

2.6 EXPLANATORY VARIABLES

The changing parameter may depend on a set of observable explanatory variables, denoted by the $k \times 1$ vector $\mathbf{w}_t$, as well as on its own past values and the score. The model can be set up as

$$\theta_{t|t-1} = \mathbf{w}_t'\boldsymbol{\gamma} + \theta^{\dagger}_{t|t-1}, \quad t = 1, \ldots, T, \qquad (2.76)$$

where, in the first-order case,

$$\theta^{\dagger}_{t+1|t} = \phi\theta^{\dagger}_{t|t-1} + \kappa u_t, \quad t = 1, \ldots, T,$$

with $\theta^{\dagger}_{1|0} = 0$. The explanatory variables are strictly exogenous in the sense that they are independent of the random variables that enter into the rest of the model in all time periods. For example in a dynamic scale model, $y_t = \varepsilon_t \exp(\theta^{\dagger}_{t|t-1} + \mathbf{w}_t'\boldsymbol{\gamma})$ and strict exogeneity means that $\mathbf{w}_t$ is independent of the standardized IID variables ε_s for all $t, s = 1, \ldots, T$. Nothing more need to be said because u_t is a function of ε_t.

The following result is a relatively straightforward generalization of Theorem 1. A constant mean, ω, is a special case, obtained when $\mathbf{w}_t$ is a scalar equal to unity. If, as in (2.30), the model formulation is

$$\theta_{t+1|t} = \mathbf{w}_t'\boldsymbol{\delta} + \phi\theta_{t|t-1} + \kappa u_t, \qquad (2.77)$$

the information matrix is constructed along the lines of Theorem 2.

Corollary 10 *Assume that the explanatory variables are weakly stationary, with mean $\boldsymbol{\mu}_w$ and second moment Λ_w, and are strictly exogenous. The information matrix for model (2.76) is*

$$\mathbf{I}\begin{pmatrix}\kappa\\ \phi\\ \boldsymbol{\gamma}\end{pmatrix} = \frac{\sigma_u^2}{k^2(1-b)}\begin{bmatrix} A & D & E\boldsymbol{\mu}_w' \\ D & B & F\boldsymbol{\mu}_w' \\ E\boldsymbol{\mu}_w & F\boldsymbol{\mu}_w & \mathbf{C}_w \end{bmatrix}, \tag{2.78}$$

where A, B, C, D, E and F are as in (2.40), and

$$\mathbf{C}_w = (1+\phi^2)\Lambda_w - 2\phi\Lambda_w(1) + \frac{2a(1-\phi)^2}{1-a}\boldsymbol{\mu}_w\boldsymbol{\mu}_w',$$

with $\Lambda_w(1) = E(\mathbf{w}_t\mathbf{w}_{t-1}') = E(\mathbf{w}_{t-1}\mathbf{w}_t')$.

Proof. Model (2.76) may be rewritten in the form of (2.77), that is,

$$\theta_{t+1|t} = (\mathbf{w}_{t+1} - \phi\mathbf{w}_t)'\boldsymbol{\gamma} + \phi\theta_{t|t-1} + \kappa u_t \tag{2.79}$$

Differentiating (2.79) with respect to $\boldsymbol{\gamma}$ gives

$$\frac{\partial\theta_{t+1|t}}{\partial\boldsymbol{\gamma}} = x_t\frac{\partial\theta_{t|t-1}}{\partial\boldsymbol{\gamma}} + \mathbf{w}_{t+1} - \phi\mathbf{w}_t$$

and so

$$E_{t-1}\left(\frac{\partial\theta_{t+1|t}}{\partial\boldsymbol{\gamma}}\right) = a\frac{\partial\theta_{t|t-1}}{\partial\boldsymbol{\gamma}} + E_{t-1}(\mathbf{w}_{t+1} - \phi\mathbf{w}_t).$$

Taking unconditional expectations gives

$$E\left(\frac{\partial\theta_{t+1|t}}{\partial\boldsymbol{\gamma}}\right) = \frac{1-\phi}{1-a}\boldsymbol{\mu}_w.$$

Now

$$\begin{aligned} E_{t-1}\left(\frac{\partial\theta_{t+1|t}}{\partial\boldsymbol{\gamma}}\frac{\partial\theta_{t+1|t}}{\partial\boldsymbol{\gamma}'}\right) &= b\frac{\partial\theta_{t|t-1}}{\partial\boldsymbol{\gamma}}\frac{\partial\theta_{t|t-1}}{\partial\boldsymbol{\gamma}'} \\ &\quad + E_{t-1}((\mathbf{w}_{t+1} - \phi\mathbf{w}_t)(\mathbf{w}_{t+1} - \phi\mathbf{w}_t)') \\ &\quad + \frac{\partial\theta_{t|t-1}}{\partial\boldsymbol{\gamma}}E_{t-1}(x_t(\mathbf{w}_{t+1} - \phi\mathbf{w}_t)') \\ &\quad + E_{t-1}(x_t(\mathbf{w}_{t+1} - \phi\mathbf{w}_t))\frac{\partial\theta_{t|t-1}}{\partial\boldsymbol{\gamma}'}. \end{aligned} \tag{2.80}$$

Because $\mathbf{w}_t$ is assumed to be strictly exogenous,

$$\frac{\partial\theta_{t|t-1}}{\partial\boldsymbol{\gamma}}E_{t-1}(x_t(\mathbf{w}_{t+1} - \phi\mathbf{w}_t)') = a\frac{\partial\theta_{t|t-1}}{\partial\boldsymbol{\gamma}}E_{t-1}(\mathbf{w}_{t+1} - \phi\mathbf{w}_t)'$$

and when unconditional expectations are taken,

$$aE\left[\frac{\partial\theta_{t|t-1}}{\partial\boldsymbol{\gamma}}(\mathbf{w}_{t+1} - \phi\mathbf{w}_t)'\right] = aE\frac{\partial\theta_{t|t-1}}{\partial\boldsymbol{\gamma}}(1-\phi)\boldsymbol{\mu}_w' = \frac{a(1-\phi)^2}{1-a}\boldsymbol{\mu}_w\boldsymbol{\mu}_w'.$$

Taking unconditional expectations in (2.80) then gives $(1-b)^{-1}\mathbf{C}_w$. ∎

Remark 11 *An estimator of the asymptotic covariance matrix is obtained by replacing* Λ_w *and* $\Lambda_w(1)$ *by* $T^{-1}\sum \mathbf{w}_t\mathbf{w}_t'$ *and* $T^{-1}\sum \mathbf{w}_t\mathbf{w}_{t-1}'$*, respectively.*

Remark 12 *The explanatory variables may be fixed. Such variables could include seasonal dummies and trigonometric terms. The asymptotic theory in Corollary 10 applies to fixed variables if*

$$\lim T^{-1}\sum \mathbf{w}_t\mathbf{w}_t' = \Lambda_w.$$

Deterministic time trends may also be included, although the preceding condition needs to be amended slightly. It will be argued later that trends and seasonals are best treated as stochastic, with deterministic components emerging as a special cases.

CHAPTER 3

Location

Linear Gaussian unobserved components models, such as the random walk plus noise of (1.1), play a central role in time series modelling. The Kalman filter and associated smoother provide the basis for a comprehensive statistical treatment. The filtered and smoothed estimators of the signal minimize the MSE of the estimation error, the likelihood is given as a byproduct of one-step prediction errors produced by the Kalman filter and the full multistep predictive distribution has a known Gaussian distribution.

We now want to confront a situation in which the location is buried in noise which is non-Gaussian and which may throw up observations that, when judged by the Gaussian yardstick, are outliers. The aim is to develop an observation-driven model that is tractable and retains some of the desirable features of the linear Gaussian model. Letting the dynamics be driven by the conditional score leads to a model which not only is easy to implement, but also facilitates the development of a comprehensive and relatively straightforward theory for the asymptotic distribution of the ML estimator.

Modelling the additive noise with a Student's t distribution is effective and theoretically straightforward. Indeed, the attractions of using the t distribution to guard against outliers in static models are well-documented; see, for example, Lange, Little and Taylor (1989). The general error distribution is less satisfactory for reasons discussed at the end of the chapter. However, it does point to some interesting connections with dynamic quantiles.

The first four sections describe the DCS-t location model, with Section 3.2 deriving moments and autocorrelations functions, and Section 3.3 presenting the asymptotic distribution of the maximum likelihood estimator. Section 3.5 shows how the state space form enables the first-order model to be generalized, following on from which trend and seasonality are introduced. Smoothing is described in Section 3.7, with the last sub-section offering a further justification for the use of the score to drive the dynamics. The mechanics of forecasting are set out in Section 3.8, whereas Sections 3.9 and 3.11 describe extensions to deal with long memory effects and skewed distributions. Section 3.10 indicates some potential difficulties in adapting the theory for the DCS-t model to the GED.

3.1 DYNAMIC STUDENT'S *t* LOCATION MODEL

When the location changes over time, it may be captured by a model in which $y_t \mid Y_{t-1}$ has a t_ν distribution, (2.1), with conditional median, $\mu_{t|t-1}$, generated by a linear function of

$$u_t = \left(1 + \frac{(y_t - \mu_{t|t-1})^2}{\nu e^{2\lambda}}\right)^{-1} v_t, \quad t = 1, \ldots, T, \tag{3.1}$$

where $v_t = y_t - \mu_{t|t-1}$ is the prediction error and $\varphi = \exp(\lambda)$ is the (time-invariant) scale. Differentiating the log-density, (2.16), shows that u_t is proportional to the conditional score

$$\frac{\partial \ln f_t}{\partial \mu_{t|t-1}} = (\nu + 1)\nu^{-1} \exp(-2\lambda) u_t.$$

No restriction is put on the degrees of freedom, ν, apart from requiring that it be positive: hence the reference to location rather than the mean. The scaling factor, $\exp(2\lambda)$, cancels out if the score is divided by the information quantity for the location, as given in (2.18).

The model can be written in a similar way to the Gaussian innovations form. Thus, in the first-order case, the model corresponds to (1.3) and is

$$\begin{aligned} y_t &= \mu_{t|t-1} + v_t = \mu_{t|t-1} + \exp(\lambda)\varepsilon_t, \quad t = 1, \ldots, T \\ \mu_{t+1|t} &= \delta + \phi\mu_{t|t-1} + \kappa u_t, \end{aligned} \tag{3.2}$$

where ε_t is a serially independent t variate, standardized by setting its scale, φ, to one. For a stationary model, re-parameterization in terms of the unconditional mean, ω, as in (2.31), gives

$$\mu_{t+1|t} = \omega + \mu^{\dagger}_{t+1|t}, \quad \mu^{\dagger}_{t+1|t} = \phi\mu^{\dagger}_{t|t-1} + \kappa u_t, \quad t = 1, \ldots, T, \tag{3.3}$$

where $\mu_{1|0}$ may be set to ω.

Figure 3.1 shows the impact, u, of a standardized ($\lambda = 0$) observation for different degrees of freedom. The Gaussian response is the 45-degree line. For low degrees of freedom, observations that would be seen as outliers for a Gaussian distribution are far less influential. As $|y| \to \infty$, the response tends to zero. Redescending M-estimators, which feature in the robustness literature, have the same property, but the Huber M-estimator has a Gaussian response until a certain point, k, whereupon it is constant; see Maronna et al. (2006, pp. 25–31). M-estimates usually require (robust) estimates of scale to be precomputed.

In a small sample, it may be appropriate to fix ν rather than trying to estimate it. Such a course of action seems to be no less arbitrary than presetting the value of k in an M-estimator. In a moderate-size sample, estimating ν by maximum likelihood offers the possibility of efficient estimation of all the unknown parameters.

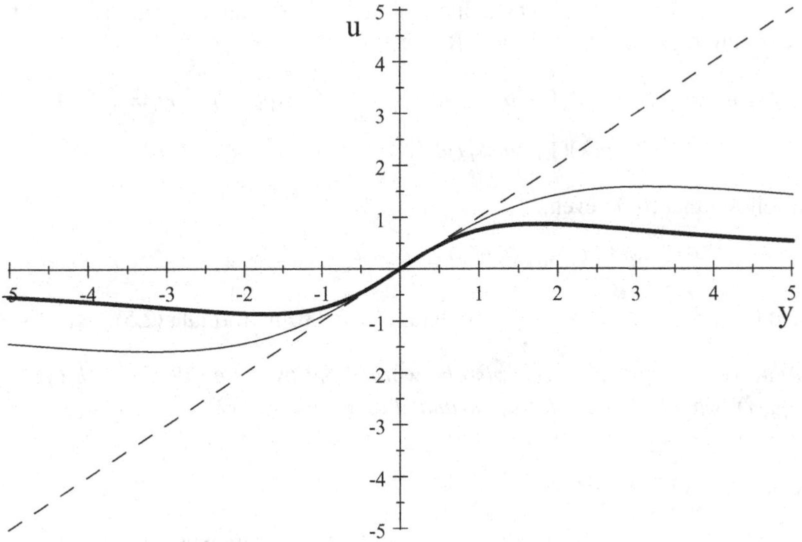

Figure 3.1. Impact of u_t for t_ν (with a scale of one) for $\nu = 3$ (thick), $\nu = 10$ (thin) and $\nu = \infty$ (dashed).

3.2 BASIC PROPERTIES

The prediction errors, v_t, in (3.2) are, by construction, independently and identically distributed as t variates, with mean zero and scale $\exp(\lambda)$. Furthermore, as shown next, the $u_t's$ are also IID. The properties of u_t follow from its the relationship to a beta distribution.

Proposition 7 *The variable u_t can be written*

$$u_t = (1 - b_t)(y_t - \mu_{t|t-1}), \tag{3.4}$$

where

$$b_t = \frac{(y_t - \mu_{t|t-1})^2/\nu \exp(2\lambda)}{1 + (y_t - \mu_{t|t-1})^2/\nu \exp(2\lambda)}, \quad 0 \le b_t \le 1, \quad 0 < \nu < \infty, \tag{3.5}$$

is distributed as beta$(1/2, \nu/2)$. The $u_t's$ are $IID(0, \sigma_u^2)$ and symmetrically distributed. Even moments of all orders exist and are given by

$$E\left(u_t^m\right) = \nu^{m/2}\exp(m\lambda)\frac{B((1+m)/2), (\nu+m)/2))}{B(1/2, \nu/2))}, \quad m = 2, 4, \ldots. \tag{3.6}$$

Proof. The term in brackets in (3.1) is equal to $1 - b_t$, leading to (3.4). Because

$$(y_t - \mu_{t|t-1})/\exp(\lambda) = \varepsilon_t$$

has a standardized t distribution, the distribution of u_t is time-invariant and does not depend on $\mu_{t|t-1}$. Because the distribution of $y_t - \mu_{t|t-1}$ is symmetric, so too is the distribution of u_t, as b_t does not depend on the sign of $y_t - \mu_{t|t-1}$.

The fact that (3.5) has a beta distribution follows from the property of the t distribution given in Corollary 2. Because

$$u_t = \nu^{1/2}\exp(\lambda)(1-b_t)(y_t - \mu_{t|t-1})\nu^{-1/2}\exp(-\lambda), \quad m = 1, 2, 3, \ldots$$
$$= \nu^{1/2}\exp(\lambda)(1-b_t)\varepsilon_t/\nu^{1/2},$$

it follows that for m even,

$$u_t^m = \nu^{m/2}\exp(m\lambda)b_t^{m/2}(1-b_t)^{m/2}, \quad m = 2, 4, \ldots,$$

and (3.6) is obtained by taking expectations and using formula (2.5). ∎

Remark 13 *The theory can also be worked out by noting that* $u_t = \overline{b}_t(y_t - \mu_{t|t-1})$, *where* $\overline{b}_t = 1 - b_t$ *is distributed as* $beta(\nu/2, 1/2)$.

Corollary 11 *The variance of* u_t *is*

$$Var(u_t) = \sigma_u^2 = \nu\exp(2\lambda)E(b_t(1-b_t)) = \frac{\nu^2\exp(2\lambda)}{(\nu+3)(\nu+1)} \tag{3.7}$$

and

$$E\left(u_t^4\right) = \nu^2\exp(4\lambda)E\left(b_t^2(1-b_t)^2\right) = \frac{3\nu^3(\nu+2)\exp(4\lambda)}{(\nu+1)(\nu+3)(\nu+5)(\nu+7)}.$$

Hence the kurtosis of u_t *is*

$$Kurtosis(u_t) = \frac{3(\nu+2)(\nu+3)(\nu+1)}{\nu(\nu+5)(\nu+7)},$$

and so its tails are thinner than those of a normal distribution (unless $\nu < 0.24$*). For example, with* $\nu = 6$*, the kurtosis is 1.76.*

Because the u_t's are $IID(0, \sigma_u^2)$, $\mu_{t|t-1}$ is weakly and strictly stationary so long as $|\phi| < 1$. Although determining the statistical properties of $\mu_{t|t-1}$ requires assuming that it started in the infinite past, the filter needs to be initialized in practice, and this may be done by setting $\mu_{1|0} = \omega = \delta/(1-\phi)$ or $\mu_{1|0}^{\dagger} = 0$ in (3.3).

Remark 14 *The variance of the prediction error in (3.2) is*

$$Var(v_t) = Var(y_t \mid Y_{t-1}) = \nu/(\nu-2)\exp(2\lambda), \quad \nu > 2, \tag{3.8}$$

whereas

$$E(u_t v_t) = \nu\exp(2\lambda)E(b_t) = (\nu/(\nu+1))\exp(2\lambda). \tag{3.9}$$

When $\nu = \infty$, $u_t = v_t$ *and (1.3) is obtained.*

3.2.1 Generalization and Reduced Form

The filter in the first-order model of (3.2) may be generalized to:

$$\mu_{t+1|t} = \delta + \phi_1 \mu_{t|t-1} + \cdots + \phi_p \mu_{t-p+1|t-p} \\ + \kappa_0 u_t + \kappa_1 u_{t-1} + \cdots + \kappa_r u_{t-r}. \tag{3.10}$$

Following the discussion in Sub-section 1.4, such a filter is denoted as *QARMA*(p, r). The full model will be called *DCS-t-QARMA*(p, r). It corresponds to an unobserved component signal plus noise model in which the signal is *ARMA*(p, r).

In the Gaussian case, $u_t = v_t$. If q is defined as $max(p, r + 1)$, we may write

$$y_t = \delta + \phi_1 y_{t-1} + \cdots + \phi_p y_{t-p} \\ + v_t - (\phi_1 - \kappa_0) v_{t-1} - \cdots - (\phi_q - \kappa_q) v_{t-q}, \tag{3.11}$$

which is an *ARMA*(p, q) with MA coefficients $\theta_i = \phi_i - \kappa_{i-1}, i = 1, \ldots, q$. The invertibility conditions apply to $\theta_i = \phi_i - \kappa_{i-1}, i = 1, \ldots, q$ rather than to $\kappa_i, i = 0, \ldots, q$; see also Appendix D. But more generally, for a t_ν distribution with $\nu < \infty$,

$$y_t = \delta + \phi_1 y_{t-1} + \cdots + \phi_p y_{t-p} + \kappa_0 u_{t-1} + \cdots + \kappa_q u_{t-q} \\ + v_t - \phi_1 v_{t-1} - \cdots - \phi_p v_{t-p} \tag{3.12}$$

and the MA disturbances are not identically distributed, as each is a different combination of variables, u_t and v_t, which have different (non-normal) distributions. In fact, they do not all have the same variances. The process is still *ARMA*(p, q), but the MA coefficients are not $\phi_i - \kappa_{i-1}, i = 1, .., q$. (They can, in principle, be found from the autocorrelations).

3.2.2 Moments of the Observations

When (3.10) is stationary, the location can be written as an infinite moving average,

$$\mu_{t|t-1} = \omega + \sum_{j=1}^{\infty} \psi_j u_{t-j}, \qquad \sum_{j=1}^{\infty} \psi_j^2 < \infty, \tag{3.13}$$

where $\omega = \delta/(1 - \phi_1 - \cdots - \phi_p)$, so

$$y_t = \omega + \sum_{j=1}^{\infty} \psi_j u_{t-j} + v_t.$$

The existence of moments of y_t is not affected by the dynamics. The next result follows directly from (3.7) and (3.8).

Proposition 8 *The unconditional variance is*

$$E(y_t - \omega)^2 = E\left(\sum_{j=1}^{\infty} \psi_j u_{t-j} + v_t\right)^2 = \frac{\exp(2\lambda)\nu}{\nu+1}\left[\frac{\nu+1}{\nu-2} + \frac{\nu}{3+\nu}\sum_{j=1}^{\infty}\psi_j^2\right], \tag{3.14}$$

provided that $\nu > 2$.

An expression for the fourth moment may be similarly derived. The introduction of dynamics into the location means that the kurtosis is less than that of the conditional t distribution because the effect of the heavy tails in v_t is diluted by u_t.

3.2.3 Autocorrelation Function

The autocovariances can be found as follows:

$$\begin{aligned} E((y_t - \omega)(y_{t-\tau} - \omega)) &= E(\mu_{t|t-1}(\mu_{t-\tau|t-\tau-1} + v_{t-\tau})), \qquad \tau = 1, 2, 3, \ldots \\ &= E\left(\sum_{j=1}^{\infty} \psi_j u_{t-j}\right)\left(\sum_{j=1}^{\infty} \psi_j u_{t-\tau-j} + v_{t-\tau}\right) \\ &= \psi_\tau E(u_{t-\tau} v_{t-\tau}) + \sum_{j=1} \psi_j \psi_{j+\tau} E\left(u_{t-\tau}^2\right). \end{aligned}$$

Therefore, using (3.7) and (3.9),

$$E((y_t - \omega)(y_{t-\tau} - \omega)) = \frac{\exp(2\lambda)\nu}{\nu+1}\left[\psi_\tau + \frac{\nu}{3+\nu}\sum_{j=1}^{\infty}\psi_j\psi_{j+\tau}\right], \qquad \tau = 1, 2, \ldots .$$

The model is covariance stationary, so long as $\nu > 2$, and the autocorrelation at lag τ is given by the ratio of the term in square brackets in the preceding equation to the term in square brackets in (3.14).

In the first-order model, $\psi_j \psi_{j+\tau} = \kappa^2 \phi^{2j+\tau-2}$ and so $\sum_{j=1}^{\infty} \psi_j \psi_{j+\tau} = \kappa^2 \phi^\tau / (1 - \phi^2)$. Hence

$$\begin{aligned} \rho_\nu(\tau) &= \frac{\psi_\tau + \frac{\nu}{3+\nu}\sum_{j=1}^{\infty}\psi_j\psi_{j+\tau}}{\frac{\nu+1}{\nu-2} + \frac{\nu}{3+\nu}\sum_{j=1}^{\infty}\psi_j^2} \\ &= \frac{\kappa\phi^{\tau-1} + \frac{\nu}{3+\nu}\frac{\kappa^2\phi^\tau}{1-\phi^2}}{\frac{\nu+1}{\nu-2} + \frac{\nu}{3+\nu}\frac{\kappa^2}{1-\phi^2}}, \qquad \nu > 2, \qquad \tau = 1, 2, \ldots . \end{aligned}$$

The form of the ACF is that of an ARMA(1,1) because

$$\rho_\nu(1) = \left[\kappa + \frac{\nu}{3+\nu}\frac{\kappa^2\phi}{1-\phi^2}\right] \Big/ \left[\frac{\nu+1}{\nu-2} + \frac{\nu}{3+\nu}\frac{\kappa^2}{1-\phi^2}\right] \tag{3.15}$$

depends on κ and ϕ, but thereafter, $\rho_\nu(\tau) = \phi\rho_\nu(\tau-1)$, $\tau = 2, 3, \ldots$.

3.3 MAXIMUM LIKELIHOOD ESTIMATION

The log-likelihood function for the DCS-t model is

$$\ln L(\boldsymbol{\psi}, \nu) = T \ln \Gamma\left((\nu+1)/2\right) - \frac{T}{2}\ln\pi - T\ln\Gamma\left(\nu/2\right) \tag{3.16}$$

$$-\frac{T}{2}\ln\nu - T\ln\varphi - \frac{(\nu+1)}{2}\sum_{t=1}^{T}\ln\left(1 + \frac{(y_t - \mu_{t|t-1})^2}{\nu\varphi^2}\right).$$

Maximization of the log-likelihood function with respect to the unknown dynamic parameters in the vector $\boldsymbol{\psi}$ and the scale and shape parameters, λ and ν, can be carried out by numerical optimization.

3.3.1 Asymptotic Distribution of the Maximum Likelihood Estimator

In order to apply the asymptotoc theory of Section 2.3, $\theta_{t|t-1}$ is replaced by $\mu_{t|t-1}$ in Theorem 2, and $\boldsymbol{\theta}_2$ is set to $(\lambda, \nu)'$ in Corollary 9.

Proposition 9 *Let $y_t \mid Y_{t-1}$ have a t_ν distribution with location, $\mu_{t|t-1}$, generated by the first-order model (3.2) or, equivalently, (3.3), with $|\phi| < 1$. Provided that $\kappa \neq 0$ and $b < 1$, $(\widetilde{\boldsymbol{\psi}}', \widetilde{\lambda}, \widetilde{\nu})'$, the ML estimator of $(\boldsymbol{\psi}', \lambda, \nu)'$ is consistent, and the limiting distribution of $\sqrt{T}(\widetilde{\boldsymbol{\psi}}' - \boldsymbol{\psi}', \widetilde{\lambda} - \lambda, \widetilde{\nu} - \nu)'$ is multivariate normal, with mean vector zero and covariance matrix*

$$Var\begin{pmatrix}\widetilde{\boldsymbol{\psi}} \\ \widetilde{\lambda} \\ \widetilde{\nu}\end{pmatrix} = \begin{bmatrix} \frac{\nu+1}{\nu+3}\exp(-2\lambda)\mathbf{D}(\boldsymbol{\psi}) & 0 & 0 \\ 0 & \frac{2\nu}{\nu+3} & \frac{1}{(\nu+3)(\nu+1)} \\ 0 & \frac{1}{(\nu+3)(\nu+1)} & h(\nu)/2 \end{bmatrix}^{-1}, \tag{3.17}$$

evaluated at $\boldsymbol{\psi} = \boldsymbol{\psi}_0$, $\lambda = \lambda_0$ and $\nu = \nu_0$. The matrix $\mathbf{D}(\boldsymbol{\psi})$ is defined as in (2.40) or (2.44), depending on whether $\boldsymbol{\psi} = (\phi, \kappa, \omega)'$ or $\boldsymbol{\psi} = (\phi, \kappa, \delta)'$, the variance σ_u^2 is as in (3.7), $h(\nu)$ is defined in (2.17) and

$$a = \phi - \kappa\frac{\nu}{\nu+3},$$

$$b = \phi^2 - 2\phi\kappa\frac{\nu}{\nu+3} + \kappa^2\frac{\nu\left(\nu^3 + 10\nu^2 + 35\nu + 38\right)}{(\nu+1)(\nu+3)(\nu+5)(\nu+7)},$$

$$c = 0.$$

Proof. The information matrix follows immediately from Theorem 2 and Corollary 9. Note that $\sigma_u^2/k^2 = [(\nu+1)/(\nu+3)]\exp(-2\lambda)$ as $k = \exp(2\lambda)\nu/(\nu+1)$ and that $E(\partial\theta_1/\partial\boldsymbol{\psi}) = \mathbf{0}$ in (2.55) because the asymptotic distribution of μ in the static model is independent of the ML estimators of λ and ν.

As regards, a, b and c in (2.35), the derivative of u_t is

$$\frac{\partial u_t}{\partial \mu} = 2(1-b_t)b_t - (1-b_t).$$

Hence $E(\partial u_t/\partial\mu) = -\nu/(\nu+3)$, which is consistent with σ_u^2 in (3.7). Furthermore,

$$E\left(u_t\frac{\partial u_t}{\partial \mu}\right) = E(2(1-b_t)b_t - (1-b_t))(y_t - \mu_{t|t-1})(1-b_t) = 0$$

as $E((y_t - \mu_{t|t-1}) \mid b_t) = 0$, and

$$\begin{aligned} E\left(\frac{\partial u_t}{\partial \mu}\right)^2 &= E(2(1-b_t)b_t - (1-b_t))^2 = 4E(1-b_t)^2 b_t^2 \\ &\quad - 4E(1-b_t)^2 b_t + E(1-b_t)^2 \\ &= \frac{12\nu(\nu+2)}{(\nu+1)(\nu+3)(\nu+5)(\nu+7)} \\ &\quad - \frac{4\nu(\nu+2)}{(\nu+1)(\nu+3)(\nu+5)} + \frac{(\nu+2)\nu}{(\nu+3)(\nu+1)} \\ &= \frac{\nu\left(\nu^3+10\nu^2+35\nu+38\right)}{(\nu+1)(\nu+3)(\nu+5)(\nu+7)} \le 1. \end{aligned}$$

Consistency and asymptotic normality follow by making a minor amendment to Theorem 3. The first and second derivatives of u_t are linear functions of $b_t^* = b_t^h(1-b_t)^k$, and so $0 \le b_t^* \le 1$ for any admissible $\boldsymbol{\psi}$. As regards u_t itself, because $u_t = (1-b_t)(y_t - \mu_{t|t-1})$, it can be seen that that $u_t = 0$ when $y_t = 0$ and $u_t \to 0$ as $|y_t| \to \infty$. Clearly u_t, like its derivatives, is bounded, and the conditions for (2.50) to hold are fulfilled. ■

Because $c = 0$, there is some simplification in $\mathbf{D}(\boldsymbol{\psi})$ as it appears in (3.17). In particular, for the ω parameterization of (2.40), $E = F = 0$, leading to the following corollary.

Corollary 12 *For the model as set up in (3.3), the ML estimator of ω is distributed independently of the estimators of κ and ϕ in large samples, and its asymptotic variance is*

$$Avar(\widetilde{\omega}) = \frac{1}{T}\frac{\nu+3}{\nu+1}\frac{1-a}{1+a}\frac{1-b}{(1-\phi)^2}\exp(2\lambda). \tag{3.18}$$

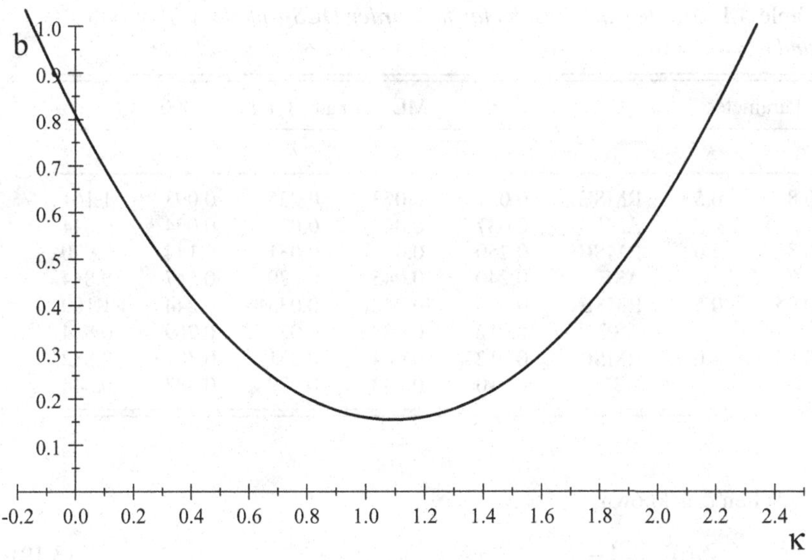

Figure 3.2. Plot of b against κ for $\phi = 0.9$ and $\nu = 6$.

Corollary 13 *When $\mu_{t|t-1}$ depends on a set of exogenous explanatory variables, the asymptotic distribution of the ML estimator is obtained from Corollary 10.*

Remark 15 *The asymptotic theory is even valid for a Cauchy distribution, although care must be taken to ensure a global maximum; see Example 1 in Newey and McFadden (1994, pp. 2119, 2130, 2147).*

Figure 3.2 shows a plot of b against κ for $\phi = 0.9$ and $\nu = 6$. The admissible range is slightly bigger than in the Gaussian case, where, as shown in the next corollary, it is $-0.1 < \kappa < 1.9$.

Corollary 14 *For a Gaussian model, $b < 1$ provided that $\phi - 1 < \kappa < \phi + 1$.*

Proof. Because $u_t = v_t = y_t - \mu_{t|t-1}$, $\partial u_t/\partial \mu_{t|t-1} = -1$ and so $a = \phi - \kappa$, $b = \phi^2 - 2\phi\kappa + \kappa^2 = (\phi - \kappa)^2 = a^2$ and $c = 0$, all of which are consistent with the formulae in Proposition 9. ■

The reduced form for the Gaussian model is the *ARMA*(1, 1) process

$$y_t = \phi y_{t-1} + v_t - \theta v_{t-1}.$$

The condition for strict invertibility in the *ARMA*(1, 1) model is $|\theta| < 1$, and, because $\theta = \phi - \kappa$, invertibility ensures that $b < 1$. The condition $\theta \neq \phi$ is needed for identifiability, and this condition is equivalent to $\kappa \neq 0$.

Table 3.1. *Monte Carlo results for first-order DCS-t model with $\nu = 6$ and $\omega = \lambda = 0$*

Parameter			ML estimates for $T = 1{,}000$				
ϕ	κ		ϕ	κ	λ	ω	ν
0.8	0.5	RMSE	0.037	0.053	0.035	0.093	1.161
		ASE	0.037	0.043	0.029	0.094	0.844
0.8	1.0	RMSE	0.250	0.067	0.031	0.144	0.920
		ASE	0.240	0.045	0.029	0.147	0.844
0.95	0.5	RMSE	0.015	0.048	0.035	0.244	1.100
		ASE	0.012	0.038	0.029	0.269	0.844
0.95	1.0	RMSE	0.012	0.064	0.031	0.387	0.882
		ASE	0.010	0.043	0.029	0.484	0.844

When ϕ is known,

$$Var(\widetilde{\kappa}) = 1 - b = 1 - (\phi - \kappa)^2, \tag{3.19}$$

which is consistent with the standard $MA(1)$ result, $Var(\widetilde{\theta}) = 1 - \theta^2$. When ϕ is estimated, the asymptotic covariance matrix corresponds to that of the *ARMA*(1, 1) model; see Box and Jenkins (1976, p. 246) or Harvey (1993, p. 63).

As regards the ML estimator of ω in a Gaussian *ARMA*(1, 1) model, it follows from (3.18) that

$$Var(\widetilde{\omega}) = \frac{1-\theta}{1+\theta}\frac{1-\theta^2}{(1-\phi)^2}\exp(2\lambda) = \frac{(1-\theta)^2}{(1-\phi)^2}Var(v_t),$$

which is also the variance of the limiting distribution of the sample mean. The sample mean is an efficient estimator of μ for independent Gaussian observations, but, as was shown in Sub-section 2.1.1, it can be very inefficient for a t distribution with small degrees of freedom. The same is true when the observations are serially correlated.

3.3.2 Monte Carlo Experiments

A series of Monte Carlo experiments were carried out by Harvey and Luati (2012) in order to get an indication of how good the asymptotic approximation is for small samples. The figures shown in Table 3.1 are based on computing RMSEs from 1,000 replications for $T = 1{,}000$ observations from a model with $\nu = 6$ and $\omega = \lambda = 0$. In most cases, convergence was rapid, and few computational problems were encountered. The asymptotic standard errors (ASEs) were obtained from the square roots of the diagonal elements of the inverse of (3.17) divided by the sample size. The results show that the empirical RMSEs are somewhat larger than the ASEs, but not by a great deal.

Table 3.2. *ML estimates for first-order DCS-t model*

Parameter	κ	ϕ	λ	ω	ν
Estimate	0.520	0.497	−4.878	0.0079	6.303
Num SE	0.098	0.102	0.073	0.0009	2.310
ASE	0.090	0.140	0.057	0.0009	1.807

3.3.3 Application to U.S. GDP

A Gaussian AR(1) plus noise model, that is, (1.1) with a constant, was fitted to the growth rate of US Real GDP, defined as the first difference of the logarithm, using the STAMP 8 package of Koopman et al. (2009). The data were quarterly, from 1947(2) to 2012(1), and the parameter estimates were as follows:

$$\widetilde{\phi} = 0.501, \quad \widetilde{\sigma}_\eta^2 = 7.62 \times 10^{-5}, \quad \widetilde{\sigma}_\varepsilon^2 = 2.30 \times 10^{-5}, \quad \widetilde{\omega} = 0.0078.$$

There was little indication of residual serial correlation, but the Bowman-Shenton statistic is 30.04, which is clearly significant, as the distribution under the null hypothesis of Gaussianity is χ_2^2. The non-normality clearly comes from excess kurtosis, which is 1.9, rather than from skewness.

Harvey and Luati (2012) fitted a DCS-location-t model and obtained the results shown in Table 3.2. Given that the sample size is only 260, the numerical and analytic standard errors are reasonably close. The estimated degrees of freedom of 6.3 means that the DCS filter is less responsive to more extreme observations, such as the fall of 2009(1), than is the Gaussian filter.

3.4 PARAMETER RESTRICTIONS*

What restrictions on κ might be implied if the DCS location-t model is taken to be an approximation to the first-order UC model,

$$y_t = \mu_t + \varepsilon_t, \quad t = 1, \ldots, T \tag{3.20}$$

$$\mu_{t+1} = \delta + \phi\mu_t + \eta_t, \qquad \eta_t \sim NID(0, \sigma_\eta^2),$$

where ε_t is distributed as t_ν with zero mean and scale φ?

In the Gaussian model, when $\varepsilon_t \sim NID(0, \sigma_\varepsilon^2)$ in (3.20), the invertibility condition on the reduced form implies that the range of κ is $\phi - 1 < \kappa < \phi + 1$. However, in the restricted reduced form, $\phi \leq \kappa \leq 0$ when $-1 < \phi \leq 0$ and $0 \leq \kappa \leq \phi$ for $0 \leq \phi < 1$. The expression for κ in the steady-state innovations form is obtained by equating the autocorrelations at lag one and is

$$\kappa = \phi - \left[\frac{q + 1 + \phi^2 - \sqrt{(q + 1 + \phi^2)^2 - 4\phi^2}}{2\phi} \right]. \tag{3.21}$$

Once away from the Gaussian model, there is no longer a direct relationship between the UC model and the DCS model. Thus exact restrictions corresponding to the UC model cannot be put on the DCS model. An approximation may be obtained by equating the autocorrelations at lag one. The ACF for the UC model with t distributed noise, that is, (3.20), is

$$\rho(\tau) = \frac{q\phi^{\tau}/(1-\phi^2)}{\frac{\nu}{\nu-2} + \frac{q}{1-\phi^2}}, \quad \nu > 2, \qquad \tau = 1, 2, \ldots$$

Setting $\rho_\nu(1) = \rho(1)$, where $\rho_\nu(1)$ was defined in (3.15), gives

$$\frac{\kappa + \frac{\nu}{3+\nu}\frac{\kappa^2\phi}{1-\phi^2}}{\frac{\nu+1}{\nu-2} + \frac{\nu}{3+\nu}\frac{\kappa^2}{1-\phi^2}} = \frac{q\phi/(1-\phi^2)}{\frac{\nu}{\nu-2} + \frac{q}{1-\phi^2}}$$

leading to the quadratic equation

$$\left(\frac{\nu}{\nu-2}\frac{\nu}{3+\nu}\frac{\phi}{1-\phi^2}\right)\kappa^2 + \left(\frac{\nu}{\nu-2} + \frac{q}{1-\phi^2}\right)\kappa - \frac{\nu+1}{\nu-2}\frac{q\phi}{1-\phi^2} = 0.$$

The solution for the Gaussian model was given in (3.21). For finite degrees of freedom, it is more complicated. Nevertheless, it is not difficult to see that the range of κ is wider than in the Gaussian case, because it goes from $\kappa = 0$ when $q = 0$ to

$$\kappa = \frac{\nu+1}{\nu-2}\phi \tag{3.22}$$

when $q = \infty$. When $\nu = 6$, the above upper bound is $\kappa = 1.75\phi$. Thus for $\nu = 6$ and $\phi = 0.9$, the implied range for κ is well within the admissible range, as determined by the condition $b < 1$ required for the asymptotic distribution of the ML estimator; see Figure 3.2. Note, however, that the autocorrelations do not exist when $\nu = 2$, and as $\nu \to 2$ (from above), the upper bound in (3.22) tends to infinity.

3.5 HIGHER ORDER MODELS AND THE STATE SPACE FORM*

The general statistical treatment of unobserved components models is based on the state space form. The corresponding innovations form facilitates the handling of higher-order DCS models.

3.5.1 Linear Gaussian Models and the Kalman Filter

For simplicity, assume a time-invariant univariate time series model and exclude any deterministic components. The general case is set out in Harvey (1989, Chapter 3). The observation in the state space form is related to an $m \times 1$ state vector, $\boldsymbol{\alpha}_t$, through a measurement equation,

$$y_t = \mathbf{z}'\boldsymbol{\alpha}_t + \varepsilon_t, \quad t = 1, \ldots, T, \tag{3.23}$$

where $\mathbf{z}$ is an $m \times 1$ vector and ε_t is a serially uncorrelated disturbance with $E(\varepsilon_t) = \mathbf{0}$ and $Var(\varepsilon_t) = \sigma_\varepsilon^2$. The elements of $\boldsymbol{\alpha}_t$ are usually unobservable but are known to be generated by a transition equation, a special time invariant form of which was given earlier in (2.61). Dropping the $\boldsymbol{\delta}$ vector gives

$$\boldsymbol{\alpha}_{t+1} = \mathbf{T}\boldsymbol{\alpha}_t + \boldsymbol{\eta}_t, \quad t = 1, \ldots, T. \tag{3.24}$$

The specification is completed by assuming that $E(\boldsymbol{\alpha}_1) = \boldsymbol{\alpha}_{1|0}$ and $Var(\boldsymbol{\alpha}_1) = \mathbf{P}_{1|0}$, where $\mathbf{P}_{1|0}$ is a positive semidefinite matrix, and that $E(\varepsilon_t \boldsymbol{\alpha}_0') = \mathbf{0}$ and $E(\boldsymbol{\eta}_t \boldsymbol{\alpha}_0') = \mathbf{0}$ for $t = 1, \ldots, T$. It is usually assumed that the disturbances are uncorrelated with each other in all time periods, that is, $E(\varepsilon_t \boldsymbol{\eta}_s') = \mathbf{0}$ for all $s, t = 1, \ldots, T$, although this assumption may be relaxed.

When the disturbances and initial state are normally distributed, the minimum mean square error estimates of the state and observation at time t, based on information at time $t-1$, are their conditional expectations. The Kalman filter is a recursive procedure for computing these estimates, given $\mathbf{z}, \sigma_\varepsilon^2$, $\mathbf{T}$ and $\mathbf{Q}$ together with the initial conditions, $\boldsymbol{\alpha}_{1|0}$ and $\mathbf{P}_{1|0}$.

The Kalman filter can be written as a single set of recursions going directly from $\boldsymbol{\alpha}_{t|t-1}$ to $\boldsymbol{\alpha}_{t+1|t}$, that is,

$$\boldsymbol{\alpha}_{t+1|t} = \mathbf{T}\boldsymbol{\alpha}_{t|t-1} + \mathbf{k}_t v_t, \quad t = 1, \ldots, T, \tag{3.25}$$

where $v_t = y_t - \mathbf{z}_t'\boldsymbol{\alpha}_{t|t-1}$ is the innovation and $f_t = \mathbf{z}'\mathbf{P}_{t|t-1}\mathbf{z} + \sigma_\varepsilon^2$ is its variance. The gain vector, $\mathbf{k}_t$, is

$$\mathbf{k}_t = (1/f_t)\mathbf{T}\mathbf{P}_{t|t-1}\mathbf{z}, \quad t = 1, \ldots, T, \tag{3.26}$$

and the recursion for the covariance matrix is

$$\mathbf{P}_{t+1|t} = \mathbf{T}(\mathbf{P}_{t|t-1} - (1/f_t)\mathbf{P}_{t|t-1}\mathbf{z}\mathbf{z}'\mathbf{P}_{t|t-1})\mathbf{T}' + \mathbf{Q}. \tag{3.27}$$

Rearranging the preceding equations gives the innovations form representation

$$y_t = \mathbf{z}'\boldsymbol{\alpha}_{t|t-1} + v_t, \quad t = 1, \ldots, T, \tag{3.28}$$

$$\boldsymbol{\alpha}_{t+1|t} = \mathbf{T}\boldsymbol{\alpha}_{t|t-1} + \mathbf{k}_t v_t.$$

As in (1.3), the innovations form, mirrors the original state, space form, except that $\boldsymbol{\alpha}_{t|t-1}$ appears in place of the state and the disturbances in the measurement and transition equations are perfectly correlated. Because the model contains only one disturbance term, it may be regarded as a reduced form, with $\mathbf{k}_t$ subject to restrictions coming from the original structural form.[1]

In a time-invariant model, the covariance matrix $\mathbf{P}_{t+1|t}$ will usually converge to a steady-state, $\mathbf{P}$, given by the solution to the *Riccati* equation (3.27); see Harvey (2006). In the steady-state innovations form, $\mathbf{k}_t$ and f_t are time-invariant.

[1] The single source of error (SSOE) models discussed in Ord et al. (1997) are effectively in innovations form, but if this is the starting point of model formulation, some way of putting constraints on $\mathbf{k}_t$ has to be found.

The filter in (3.25) can be written as

$$\boldsymbol{\alpha}_{t+1|t} = \mathbf{L}_t \boldsymbol{\alpha}_{t|t-1} + \mathbf{k}_t y_t, \qquad t = 1, \ldots, T, \tag{3.29}$$

where $\mathbf{L}_t = \mathbf{T} - \mathbf{k}_t \mathbf{z}_t'$, showing that $\boldsymbol{\alpha}_{t+1|t}$ can be expressed as a linear combination of past observations. In the steady state of a time-invariant model, $\mathbf{L}_t = \mathbf{L}$. When the roots of $\mathbf{L}$ are less than one in absolute value, $\boldsymbol{\alpha}_{t+1|t}$ may be expressed as an infinite moving average of past $y_t's$.

There are a number of ways of initializing the Kalman filter. When the transition equation is stationary, $\boldsymbol{\alpha}_{1|0}$ and $\mathbf{P}_{1|0}$ can be set to the unconditional mean and variance of $\boldsymbol{\alpha}_t$. When the state contains m^* nonstationary elements, a proper prior may be obtained from the first m^* observations, either directly or indirectly, using a diffuse prior, as described in Durbin and Koopman (2012).

Example 9 *Let $p_{t|t-1}$ denote $\sigma_\varepsilon^{-2} MSE(\mu_{t|t-1})$ in the AR(1) plus noise model of (1.1). The Riccati equation is*

$$p_{t+1|t} = \phi^2 p_{t|t-1} - \left[\phi^2 p_{t|t-1}^2 / \left(1 + p_{t|t-1}\right)\right] + q, \quad t = 1, \ldots, T,$$

where $q = \sigma_\eta^2/\sigma_\varepsilon^2 \geq 0$ and $p_{1|0} = q/(1-\phi^2)$. Setting $p_{t+1|t} = p_{t|t-1} = p$ gives

$$p = \left(q + \phi^2 - 1 + \sqrt{(1-q-\phi^2)^2 + 4q}\right)/2, \quad q \geq 0. \tag{3.30}$$

The solution when $q = 0$ is $p = 0$. In this case there is no signal. On the other hand, when $p = \infty$, there is no noise. The steady-state Kalman gain is $\kappa = \phi p/(1+p)$, which on rearranging is seen to be the same as the result in (3.21). The steady-state updating equation,

$$\mu_{t+1|t} = \phi \mu_{t|t-1} + \kappa v_t,$$

can be written as in (3.29), that is

$$\mu_{t+1|t} = (\phi - \kappa)\mu_{t|t-1} + \kappa y_t. \tag{3.31}$$

3.5.2 The DCS Model

A general location DCS model may be set up in the same way as the innovations form of a Gaussian state space model. The model corresponding to the steady-state of (3.28), but with constants included, is

$$\begin{aligned} y_t &= \omega + \mathbf{z}'\boldsymbol{\alpha}_{t|t-1} + v_t, \quad t = 1, \ldots, T, \\ \boldsymbol{\alpha}_{t+1|t} &= \boldsymbol{\delta} + \mathbf{T}\boldsymbol{\alpha}_{t|t-1} + \boldsymbol{\kappa} u_t. \end{aligned} \tag{3.32}$$

The $\mathbf{z}$ vector and $\mathbf{T}$ matrix may be specified in the same way as for the Gaussian UC models. Such models can be found in Harvey (1989) and Koopman et al. (2009), but the canonical trend and seasonal formulations are described in the next section. This leaves the question of how to specify the parameters in the vector $\boldsymbol{\kappa}$. More specifically, what restrictions should be imposed? The issues for the first-order model were discussed in Section 3.4, but even in that case, the answer is not straightforward. In a UC model, the Kalman gain will depend on all components, but the principal determinant in the behavior of a particular element will be the component to which it relates. Thus it may be reasonable to explore the different components in isolation. This is the approach taken in the next section.

The transition equation in (3.32) is stationary, provided that the roots of the transition matrix $\mathbf{T}$ have modulus less than one. When this is the case, $\boldsymbol{\delta}$ is superfluous, and initialization is achieved by setting $\boldsymbol{\alpha}_{1|0} = \mathbf{0}$. When $\boldsymbol{\alpha}_{t|t-1}$ contains nonstationary elements, the best option seems to be to treat their initial values as unknown parameters. Further discussion can be found in the next section.

The asymptotic theory for ML estimation developed for (2.61) may be applied here with $\theta_{t|t-1}$ replaced by $\mu_{t|t-1}$. Let $\mathbf{A}(\nu)$ and $\mathbf{B}(\nu)$ denote $\mathbf{A}$ and $\mathbf{B}$ evaluated for a t_ν distribution. Then

$$\mathbf{A}(\nu) = \mathbf{T} - \{\nu/(\nu+3)\}\boldsymbol{\kappa}\mathbf{z}', \tag{3.33}$$

while $\mathbf{B}(\nu)$ is obtained by substituting the expectations given in the proof of Proposition 9 into expression (2.62). For the (symmetric) t distribution, $E[(\partial u_t/\partial\mu)u_t] = 0$, so $[E(u_t\mathbf{X}_t)] = 0$ and (2.68) becomes

$$E\mathrm{vec}\left(\frac{\partial \boldsymbol{\alpha}_{t+1|t}}{\partial \kappa_i}\frac{\partial \boldsymbol{\alpha}'_{t+1|t}}{\partial \kappa_j}\right) = [\mathbf{I} - \mathbf{B}(\nu)]^{-1}\left[E\left(u_t^2\right)\right]\mathrm{vec}\left(\boldsymbol{\omega}_i\boldsymbol{\omega}'_j\right) \tag{3.34}$$

$$= \frac{\exp(2\lambda)\nu^2}{(\nu+3)(\nu+1)}[\mathbf{I} - \mathbf{B}(\nu)]^{-1}\mathrm{vec}\left(\boldsymbol{\omega}_i\boldsymbol{\omega}'_j\right).$$

The information matrix for the unknown parameters is obtained as in (2.69).

The asymptotic theory requires that the roots of $\mathbf{B}(\nu)$ have modulus less than one. For a Gaussian model, this will be the case if the roots of $\mathbf{A}$ have modulus less than one. This condition on $\mathbf{A}$ is also given in the paper by De Livera, Hyndman and Snyder (2010, pp. 1518–9), in which the state space innovations form is used to model Gaussian time series.

Lemma 12 *In a Gaussian model,* $\mathbf{B} = \mathbf{A} \otimes \mathbf{A}$, *and so the eigenvalues of* $\mathbf{B}$ *are less than one in absolute value if the eigenvalues of* $\mathbf{A}$ *are less than one in absolute value.*

Proof. For $\nu = \infty$, $E(\partial u_t/\partial\mu) = -1$, so $\mathbf{A} = \mathbf{T} - \boldsymbol{\kappa}\mathbf{z}'$. Furthermore, because $E(\partial u_t/\partial\mu)^2 = 1$,

$$\mathbf{B} = \mathbf{T}\otimes\mathbf{T} - \boldsymbol{\kappa}\mathbf{z}'\otimes\mathbf{T} - \mathbf{T}\otimes\boldsymbol{\kappa}\mathbf{z}' + \boldsymbol{\kappa}\mathbf{z}'\otimes\boldsymbol{\kappa}\mathbf{z}' = \mathbf{A}\otimes\mathbf{A}.$$

Hence the N^2 eigenvalues of $\mathbf{B}$ are $\xi_i\xi_j$, $i, j = 1, .., N$, where ξ_i, $i = 1, \ldots, N$ are the eigenvalues of $\mathbf{A}$; see Hamilton (1994, p. 733). ■

3.5.3 QARMA Models

The properties of the *DCS-t-QARMA*(p, r) model were discussed in Subsection 3.2.1. The model may be put in the state space form of (3.32) in a similar way to an *ARMA*(p, r) plus noise unobserved components models. Following the discussion in Section 3.4, it may be possible to develop constraints on the parameters that would be implied by such a UC model. The model will be valid for a wider range of parameters values, but remember that the signal plus noise interpretation lies behind the DCS-t model.

The *QARMA*(p, r) state space form is obtained by letting $m = \max(p, r + 1)$ and defining $\boldsymbol{\alpha}_{t+1|t}$ as an $m \times 1$ vector that satisfies a transition equation in which

$$\mathbf{T} = \begin{bmatrix} \boldsymbol{\phi} & \mathbf{I}_{m-1} \\ & \mathbf{0}'_{m-1} \end{bmatrix},$$

with $\boldsymbol{\phi} = (\phi_1, \ldots, \phi_m)'$ and $\boldsymbol{\kappa} = (\kappa_0, \ldots, \kappa_m)'$. The measurement equation has $\mathbf{z} = (1\ \mathbf{0}'_{m-1})'$, thereby selecting the first element in $\boldsymbol{\alpha}_{t|t-1}$. The matrix in (3.33) is then

$$\mathbf{A} = \begin{bmatrix} \boldsymbol{\phi} + \boldsymbol{\kappa} E(\partial u_t/\partial\lambda) & \mathbf{I}_{m-1} \\ & \mathbf{0}'_{m-1} \end{bmatrix}.$$

Example 10 *For the QARMA*(2, 1) *filter*

$$\mathbf{A} = \begin{bmatrix} \phi_1 - \kappa_0 E(\partial u_t/\partial\lambda) & 1 \\ \phi_2 - \kappa_1 E(\partial u_t/\partial\lambda) & 0 \end{bmatrix}.$$

Proposition 10 *For a Gaussian QARMA*(p, r)*, model, the eigenvalues of* $\mathbf{A}$ *are the same as the roots of the reduced form MA-associated polynomial equation, that is,* $x^m - \theta_1 x^{m-1} - \cdots - \theta_{m-1}x - \theta_m = 0$*, with coefficients* $\theta_i = \phi_i - \kappa_{i-1}, i = 1, \ldots, m$*, where m is the maximum of p and* $r + 1$.

Proof. The structure of $\mathbf{A}$ is the same as the structure of $\mathbf{T}$ for an $AR(p)$ model in which the coefficients are $\theta_i = \phi_i - \kappa_{i-1}, i = 1, .., m$. ■

Example 11 *For the Gaussian ARMA*(2, 1) *filter (as in the previous example but with* $\nu = \infty$*),*

$$\mathbf{A} = \begin{bmatrix} \phi_1 - \kappa_0 & 1 \\ \phi_2 - \kappa_1 & 0 \end{bmatrix} = \begin{bmatrix} \theta_1 & 1 \\ \theta_2 & 0 \end{bmatrix}.$$

The reduced form is ARMA(2, 2) *and the eigenvalues are* $\frac{1}{2}\theta_1 \pm \frac{1}{2}\sqrt{4\theta_2 + \theta_1^2}$ $+ \frac{1}{2}$*, which are the roots of the MA polynomial.*

For the general QARMA filter, the eigenvalues of $\mathbf{A}$ are the same as the roots of a polynomial with coefficients $\phi_i + \kappa_{i-1} E(\partial u_t/\partial\lambda), i = 1, \ldots, p$. These coefficients are not, in general, the same as the coefficients of the MA in the reduced form.

Stationary QARMA models are best estimated with the autoregressive parameters constrained by forcing the roots of the AR polynomial to lie outside the unit circle. The admissibility of the $\kappa_i's$ can be checked by calculating the roots of $\mathbf{B}(\nu)$. The values of p and r may be selected by fitting a range of models and choosing according to an information criterion, such as the AIC or BIC. The correlogram may also be useful, because the reduced form is known to have an ARMA representation. However, the observations should be transformed to the score for the t distribution, as suggested in Section 2.6, because of the masking effects that additive outliers have on the correlation structure; see Li (2004, Chapter 4).

3.6 TREND AND SEASONALITY

Stochastic trend and seasonal components may be introduced into UC models for location. These models, called structural time series models, are described in Harvey (1989) and implemented in the STAMP package of Koopman et al. (2009). The properties of ML estimators in Gaussian models are set out in Harvey (1989, Chapters 3 and 4).

The main elements in the formulation of structural time series models and their statistical treatment are set out next. The way in which the innovations forms of these models lead to corresponding DCS-t models is then explored. A complicating feature is the fact that trend and seasonal components are nonstationary, and this has implications for the initialization of the DCS filters.

3.6.1 Local Level Model

The Gaussian random walk plus noise or *local level* model is

$$\begin{aligned} y_t &= \mu_t + \varepsilon_t, \qquad & \varepsilon_t &\sim NID(0, \sigma_\varepsilon^2), \\ \mu_t &= \mu_{t-1} + \eta_t, \qquad & \eta_t &\sim NID(0, \sigma_\eta^2), \end{aligned} \tag{3.35}$$

where $E(\varepsilon_t \eta_s) = 0$ for all t and s. The signal noise ratio is $q = \sigma_\eta^2/\sigma_\varepsilon^2$, and the parameter θ in the *ARIMA*(0, 1, 1) reduced form representation, obtained as in (1.10), lies in the range $0 \leq \theta < 1$ when $\sigma_\varepsilon^2 > 0$. Because $\theta = 1 - \kappa$, the range of κ in the steady-state innovations form is $0 < \kappa \leq 1$. In this case $\mu_{t+1|t}$ is an exponentially weighted moving average (EWMA) in which the weights on current and past observations are non-negative, because, on setting $\phi = 1$ in (3.31),

$$\mu_{t+1|t} = (1 - \kappa)\mu_{t|t-1} + \kappa y_t. \tag{3.36}$$

For a semi-infinite sample

$$\mu_{t+1|t} = \kappa \sum_{i=0}^{\infty} (1 - \kappa)^i y_{t-i} \tag{3.37}$$

and the weights on past observations sum to one.

For the DCS-t filter, setting $\phi = 1$ and $\delta = 0$ in (3.2) gives

$$\begin{aligned} y_t &= \mu_{t|t-1} + v_t, \\ \mu_{t+1|t} &= \mu_{t|t-1} + \kappa u_t. \end{aligned} \tag{3.38}$$

The initialization of the Kalman filter for (3.35) is best done using a diffuse prior. However, it can be shown that as $p_{1|0} \to \infty$, $\mu_{2|1} \to y_1$ and $p_{2|1} \to 1 + q$; see Harvey (1989, pp. 107–8). Thus using a diffuse prior is effectively the same as initializing the filter with an estimate constructed from the first observation, but with due account taken of the measurement error. A diffuse prior is not an option for a DCS model, but the filter could still be started with $\mu_{2|1} = y_1$. The problem with proceeding in this way is that the filter could be adversely affected if the first observation is an outlier. An alternative way of initializing the DCS filter is to treat $\mu_{1|0}$ as an unknown parameter that must be estimated along with κ and ν. The same approach is used by De Livera, Hyndman and Snyder (2010) to initialize Gaussian single source of error models.

Because $u_t = (1 - b_t)(y_t - \mu_{t|t-1})$, re-arranging the dynamic equation in (3.38) gives

$$\mu_{t+1|t} = (1 - \kappa(1 - b_t))\mu_{t|t-1} + \kappa(1 - b_t)y_t, \quad t = 1, \ldots, T. \tag{3.39}$$

A sufficient condition for the weights on current and past observations to be non-negative is that $\kappa(1 - b_t) < 1$ and, because $0 \leq b_t \leq 1$, this is guaranteed by $0 < \kappa \leq 1$. However, the restriction that $\kappa \leq 1$ is much stricter than is either necessary or desirable. Indeed, the argument based on matching autocorrelations suggests an admissible range of $0 \leq \kappa \leq (\nu + 1)/(\nu - 2)$. As the example that follows shows, estimates of κ greater than one are not unusual and are entirely appropriate when the signal is strong relative to the noise.

As regards asymptotic properties, Corollary 8 applies when $\mu_{1|0}$ is fixed and known or when $\mu_{2|1} = y_1$ and y_1 is fixed. Hence

$$\begin{aligned} Var(\widetilde{\kappa}) &= (1 - b)((\nu + 3)/\nu)^2 \\ &= \left(2\kappa \frac{\nu}{\nu + 3} - \kappa^2 \frac{\nu\left(\nu^3 + 10\nu^2 + 35\nu + 38\right)}{(\nu + 1)(\nu + 3)(\nu + 5)(\nu + 7)}\right)\left(\frac{\nu + 3}{\nu}\right)^2. \end{aligned}$$

The admissible range of κ can easily be gauged from the plot of b in Figure 3.2. In contrast to the case when $|\phi| < 1$, it is necessary that $\kappa > 0$. For finite degrees of freedom, the upper bound will be greater than the value of two that applies to a Gaussian model.

3.6.2 Application to Weekly Hours of Employees in U.S. Manufacturing

Fitting a local level DCS model (initialized with $\mu_{2|1} = y_1$) to seasonally adjusted monthly data on U.S. Average Weekly Hours of Production and Nonsupervisory Employees: Manufacturing[2] from February 1992 to May 2010 (220 observations) gave

$$\widetilde{\kappa} = 1.246 \qquad \widetilde{\lambda} = -3.625 \qquad \widetilde{\nu} = 6.35$$

with numerical (asymptotic) standard errors

$$SE(\widetilde{\kappa}) = 0.161(0.090) \qquad SE(\widetilde{\lambda}) = 0.120(0.062) \qquad SE(\widetilde{\nu}) = 1.630(1.991)$$

A drift term was initially included, but it was statistically insignificant. The value of b is 0.178. Although $\widetilde{\kappa}$ is greater than one, its value is well below the upper bound of 1.690 suggested by (3.22) and the resulting filter is perfectly consistent with the properties of the series. Figure 3.3 shows (part of) the series together with the contemporaneous filter, which for the random walk is $\mu_{t+1|t}$ at time t. As can be seen, the values are very close to the corresponding observations in the majority of cases because $\kappa(1 - b_t)$ is close to one. On the other hand, unusually large prediction errors result in a small value of $\kappa(1 - b_t)$ and most of the weight in (3.39) is assigned to $\mu_{t|t-1}$. When a Gaussian local-level model is fitted, the outliers affect the filtered level more than is desirable.

Estimating the series without imposing the unit root gave

$$\widetilde{\kappa} = 1.229 \qquad \widetilde{\lambda} = -3.652 \qquad \widetilde{\nu} = 6.20 \qquad \widetilde{\phi} = 0.978 \qquad \widetilde{\omega} = 40.18.$$

The estimates of κ, λ and ν are close to those obtained with the local level model. Re-estimating both models with a longer series starting in April 1947 gave very similar results, so the models seem to be stable.

3.6.3 Local Linear Trend

The *local linear trend* model generalises the local level by introducing a stochastic slope, β_t, which itself follows a random walk. Thus

$$\begin{aligned} \mu_t &= \mu_{t-1} + \beta_{t-1} + \eta_t, \qquad & \eta_t &\sim NID(0, \sigma_\eta^2), \\ \beta_t &= \beta_{t-1} + \zeta_t, & \zeta_t &\sim NID(0, \sigma_\zeta^2), \end{aligned} \tag{3.40}$$

where the irregular, level and slope disturbances, ε_t, η_t and ζ_t, respectively, are mutually independent. If both variances σ_η^2 and σ_ζ^2 are zero, the trend is deterministic. When only σ_ζ^2 is zero, the slope is fixed and the trend reduces to a random walk with drift.

Allowing σ_ζ^2 to be positive, but setting σ_η^2 to zero gives an *integrated random walk* (IRW) trend, which when estimated tends to be relatively smooth. It can

[2] Source: U.S. Department of Labor: Bureau of Labor Statistics. The results reported here originally appeared in a working paper by Harvey and Luati (2012).

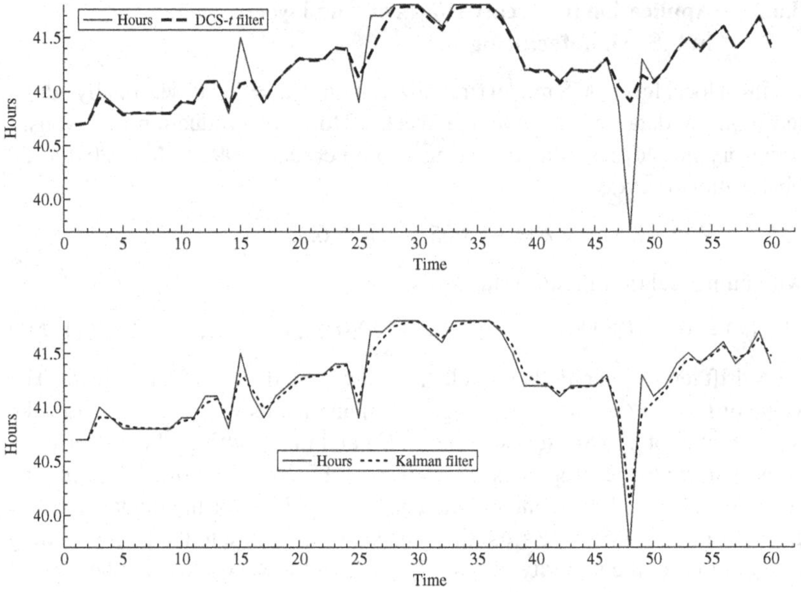

Figure 3.3. DCS and Gaussian (bottom panel) local level models fitted to U.S. average weekly hours of production.

be regarded as an approximation to the fitting of a cubic spline which is the smoothed estimator of the trend from a continuous time model with no level disturbance; see Kohn et al. (1992). The implied discrete time covariance matrix is

$$Var\begin{bmatrix}\eta_t\\ \zeta_t\end{bmatrix} = \begin{bmatrix}\frac{1}{3} & \frac{1}{2}\\ \frac{1}{2} & 1\end{bmatrix}\sigma_\zeta^2.$$

Double exponential smoothing, suggested by the principle of discounted least squares, is obtained by setting $q_\zeta = \sigma_\zeta^2/\sigma_\varepsilon^2 = (q_\eta/2)^2$, where $q_\eta = \sigma_\eta^2/\sigma_\varepsilon^2$; see Harvey (1989, Chapter 2).

The DCS filter corresponding to the steady-state innovations form for (3.40) is

$$\begin{aligned} y_t &= \mu_{t|t-1} + v_t \qquad (3.41)\\ \mu_{t+1|t} &= \mu_{t|t-1} + \beta_{t|t-1} + \kappa_1 u_t\\ \beta_{t+1|t} &= \beta_{t|t-1} + \kappa_2 u_t. \end{aligned}$$

The initialization $\beta_{3|2} = y_2 - y_1$ and $\mu_{3|2} = y_2$ can be used, but, as in the local-level model, initializing in this way is vulnerable to outliers at the beginning. Estimating the fixed starting values, $\mu_{1|0}$ and $\beta_{1|0}$, seems to be a better option.

When the disturbances in the Gaussian UC model, (3.40), are uncorrelated with each other, the restrictions on the innovations form coefficients – which are closely related to the smoothing constants in the Holt-Winters forecasting scheme – are $0 < \kappa_1, \kappa_2 < 1$; see Harvey (1989, p. 177). As with the local level model, the upper bounds on κ_1 and κ_2 can be allowed to increase beyond one as the degrees of freedom decreases. Values of κ_1 and κ_2, which are too big, may put the signal plus noise interpretation in doubt, but the key constraints are those needed for the validity of the asymptotic distributional theory.

An IRW trend in the Gaussian model, (3.40), implies the contraint

$$\kappa_2 = \kappa_1^2/(2 - \kappa_1), \quad 0 < \kappa_1 < 1, \tag{3.42}$$

which may be found using formulae in Harvey (1989, p. 177). The restriction may be imposed on the DCS-t model by treating $\kappa_1 = \kappa$ as the unknown parameter, but without unity imposed as an upper bound.

There may sometimes be a case for imposing a restriction derived from the discounted least squares principle. In this case, $\kappa_1 = 1 - \omega^2$ and $\kappa_2 = (1 - \omega)^2$, where the discount parameter satisfies the restriction $0 \leq \omega < 1$ in the Gaussian model.

3.6.4 Stochastic Seasonal

A fixed seasonal pattern may be modelled as $\gamma_t = \sum_{j=1}^{s} \gamma_j z_{jt}$, where s is the number of seasons and the dummy variable z_{jt} is one in season j and zero otherwise. In order not to confound trend with seasonality, the coefficients, γ_j, $j = 1, \ldots, s$, are constrained to sum to zero. The seasonal pattern may be allowed to change over time by letting the coefficients evolve as random walks. If γ_{jt} denotes the effect of season j at time t and $\boldsymbol{\gamma}_t = (\gamma_{1t}, \ldots, \gamma_{st})'$, then

$$\boldsymbol{\gamma}_t = \boldsymbol{\gamma}_{t-1} + \boldsymbol{\omega}_t, \qquad t = 1, \ldots, T, \tag{3.43}$$

where $\boldsymbol{\omega}_t$ is a normally distributed, zero-mean vector of disturbances. Although all s seasonal components are continually evolving, only one affects the observations at any particular point in time, that is, $\gamma_t = \gamma_{jt}$ when season j is prevailing at time t. The requirement that the seasonal components move in such a way that they always sum to zero, that is, $\sum_{j=1}^{s} \gamma_{jt} = 0$, is enforced by the restriction that the disturbances sum to zero at each point in time. This restriction is implemented by the correlation structure in

$$Var\left(\boldsymbol{\omega}_t\right) = \sigma_\omega^2 \left(\mathbf{I} - s^{-1}\mathbf{ii}'\right), \qquad \sigma_\omega^2 > 0, \tag{3.44}$$

where $\boldsymbol{\omega}_t = (\omega_{1t}, \ldots, \omega_{st})'$ and $\mathbf{i}$ is a vector of ones, coupled with initial conditions requiring that the seasonals sum to zero at $t = 0$. It can be seen from (3.44) that $Var\left(\mathbf{i}'\boldsymbol{\omega}_t\right) = 0$.

In the state space form, the transition matrix is just the identity matrix, but the $\mathbf{z}$ vector must change over time to accommodate the current season. Apart from replacing $\mathbf{z}$ with $\mathbf{z}_t$, the form of the KF remains unchanged. Adapting the innovations form to the DCS observation-driven framework, (2.61), gives

$$y_t = \mathbf{z}_t'\boldsymbol{\alpha}_{t|t-1} + \upsilon_t \tag{3.45}$$

$$\boldsymbol{\alpha}_{t+1|t} = \boldsymbol{\alpha}_{t|t-1} + \boldsymbol{\kappa}_t u_t,$$

where $\mathbf{z}_t$ picks out the current season, $\gamma_{t|t-1}$, that is, $\gamma_{t|t-1} = \mathbf{z}_t'\boldsymbol{\alpha}_{t|t-1}$; compare (3.32). The only question is how to parameterize $\boldsymbol{\kappa}_t$.

The seasonal components in the UC model are constrained to sum to zero, and the same is true of their filtered estimates. Thus $\mathbf{i}'\boldsymbol{\kappa}_t = 0$ in the Kalman filter, and this property should carry across to the DCS filter. If κ_{jt}, $j = 1, \ldots, s$, denotes the j-th element of $\boldsymbol{\kappa}_t$ in (3.45), then in season j we set $\kappa_{jt} = \kappa_s$, where κ_s is a non-negative unknown parameter, whereas $\kappa_{it} = -\kappa_s/(s-1)$ for $i \neq j$. The amounts by which the seasonal effects change therefore sum to zero.

The seasonal recursions can be combined with the trend filtering equations of (3.41) to give a structure similar in form to that of the Kalman filter for the stochastic trend plus seasonal plus noise model, sometimes known as the 'basic structural model'. Thus

$$y_t = \mu_{t|t-1} + \gamma_{t|t-1} + \upsilon_t, \tag{3.46}$$

where $\mu_{t|t-1}$ is as defined in (3.41). The filter can be initialized by regressing the first $s+1$ observations on a constant, time trend and seasonal dummies constrained so that the coefficients sum to zero. Alternatively, the initial conditions at time $t = 0$ are estimated by treating them as parameters; there are $s-1$ seasonal parameters because the remaining initial seasonal state is minus the sum of the others.

3.6.5 Application to Rail Travel

Figure 3.4 shows the logarithm of National Rail Travel, defined as the number of kilometres[3] travelled by passengers in the United Kingdom. In a project carried out for the UK Department for Transport, an unobserved components model was fitted to this series using the STAMP 8 package of Koopman et al. (2009). Trend, seasonal and irregular components were included, but the model was augmented with intervention variables to take out the effects of observations known to be unrepresentative. The intervention dummies were (i) the train driver strikes in 1982(1,3); (ii) the Hatfield crash and its aftermath, 2000(4) and 2001(1); and (iii) the signallers strike in 1994(3).

Harvey and Luati (2012) fitted a DCS-t model of the form (3.46) with a random walk plus drift trend

$$\mu_{t+1|t} = \mu_{t|t-1} + \beta + \kappa_1 u_t, \quad t = 1, \ldots, T.$$

[3] Source: National Rail Trends.

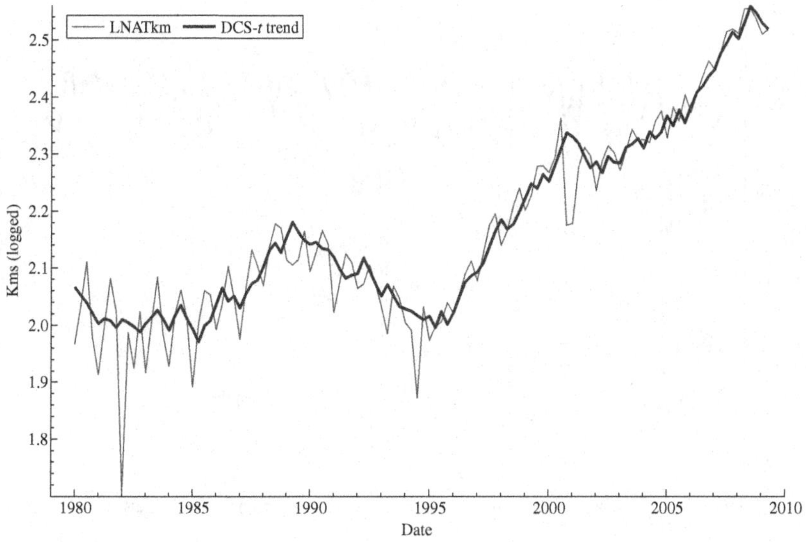

Figure 3.4. Trend from a DCS-*t* model fitted to UK National Rail Travel.

The ML estimates were

$$\widetilde{\kappa}_1 = 1.421(0.161) \qquad \widetilde{\kappa}_s = 0.539\ (0.070) \qquad \widetilde{\lambda} = -3.787\ (0.053)$$

$$\widetilde{\nu} = 2.564\ (0.319) \qquad \widetilde{\beta} = 0.003\ (0.001)$$

where the figures in parentheses are numerical standard errors. The initial value for the level was estimated as $\widetilde{\mu}_{1|0} = 2.066$ and the estimates for the first three initial seasonals were $\widetilde{\gamma}_1 = -0.094$, $\widetilde{\gamma}_2 = -0.010$ and $\widetilde{\gamma}_3 = 0.086$. The last seasonal, $\widetilde{\gamma}_4 = 0.018$, was constructed from the others. In the notation of (3.45), $\widetilde{\gamma}_i$, $i = 1, 2, 3, 4$ is the i-th element of $\boldsymbol{\alpha}_{1|0}$.

The filtered DCS-*t* trend shown in Figure 3.4 appears not to be affected by the outliers, and a graph in Harvey and Luati (2012) indicates that it is very close to the filtered trend obtained from the UC model with interventions. The same is true of the filtered seasonal.

Figure 3.5 shows the residuals, that, is the one-step-ahead prediction errors, and the scores for the DCS model. The outliers (which were removed by dummies in the UC model) show up clearly in the residuals. In the score series, the outliers are downweighted and the autocorrelations are slightly bigger than those of the residuals. The Ljung-Box $Q(3.41)$ statistic is 19.78 for the scores and 12.40 for the residuals. If it can be assumed that only the number of fitted dynamic parameters affects the distribution of the Ljung-Box statistic, its distribution under the null hypothesis of correct model specification is χ^2_{10}, for which the 5% critical value is 18.3. Thus the scores reject the null hypothesis, albeit only marginally, whereas the residuals do not. Having said that, the

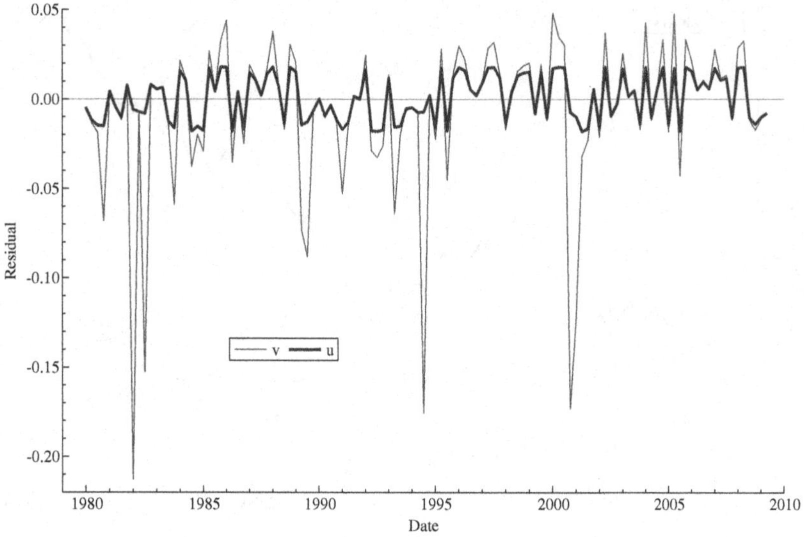

Figure 3.5. Residuals and scores from DCS-t model.

score autocorrelations exhibit no clear pattern, and it is difficult to see how the dynamic specification might be improved.

3.6.6 QARIMA and Seasonal QARIMA Models*

Conditional score models, which in the Gaussian case, give models with a familiar ARIMA or seasonal ARIMA form, may be also be constructed. The key to the asymptotic theory again lies with the state space form. Consider the *ARIMA*(0, 1, 1) model

$$\Delta y_t = \xi_t - \theta \xi_{t-1}, \quad \xi_t \sim NID\big(0, \sigma_\xi^2\big).$$

This model may be rewritten as

$$\begin{aligned} y_t &= \mu_{t|t-1} + v_t \\ \mu_{t+1|t} &= \mu_{t|t-1} + (1-\theta)v_t, \end{aligned}$$

with $\xi_t = v_t$. Replacing v_t by u_t gives the random walk plus noise DCS model.

There need not necessarily be a direct link to a structural time series model. Consider the more general ARIMA model $\varphi_P(L)y_t = \theta_Q(L)\xi_t$. The polynomial $\varphi_P(L)$ may contain unit roots, including seasonal unit roots. For example, $\varphi_P(L) = (1-L)(1-L^4)$. Then

$$y_t = \mu_{t|t-1} + v_t$$

with a $QARMA(\overline{P}, \overline{P}-1)$ equation

$$\mu_{t|t-1} = (1-\varphi(L))\mu_{t|t-1} + [\theta(L) - \varphi(L)]u_t,$$

where $\overline{P} = \max(P, Q-1)$. Although $\mu_{t|t-1}$ and u_t seem to appear on the right hand side of the above equation, their coefficients are, in fact, zero.

Example 12 *The quarterly 'airline' model introduced by Box and Jenkins (1976),*

$$(1-L)(1-L^4)y_t = (1-\theta L)(1-\Theta L^4)\xi_t, \quad \xi_t \sim NID(0, \sigma_\xi^2).$$

can be expressed as

$$y_t = \mu_{t|t-1} + \xi_t,$$

where

$$\begin{aligned}\mu_{t|t-1} &= \mu_{t-1|t-2} + \mu_{t-4|t-5} - \mu_{t-5|t-6} \\ &\quad + (1-\theta)\xi_{t-1} + (1-\Theta)\xi_{t-4} - (1-\theta\Theta)\xi_{t-5}.\end{aligned}$$

The associated QARMA(5, 5) *model is*

$$y_t = \mu_{t|t-1} + v_t,$$

where

$$\begin{aligned}\mu_{t|t-1} &= \mu_{t-1|t-2} + \mu_{t-4|t-5} - \mu_{t-5|t-6} + \kappa u_{t-1} \\ &\quad + K u_{t-4} - (1-(1-\kappa)(1-K))u_{t-5} \\ &= \mu_{t-1|t-2} + \mu_{t-4|t-5} - \mu_{t-5|t-6} + \kappa u_{t-1} \\ &\quad + K u_{t-4} - (\kappa + K - \kappa K)u_{t-5},\end{aligned}$$

with κ *and* K *being non-negative parameters.*

QARIMA model selection is probably best done by using an information criterion, such as AIC or BIC.

3.7 SMOOTHING

The aim of filtering is to find the expected value of the state vector, $\boldsymbol{\alpha}_t$, conditional on the information available at time t. The aim of smoothing is to take account of the information made available after time t. In a linear Gaussian model, the smoothed estimate is $\boldsymbol{\alpha}_{t|T}$, the conditional expectation of $\boldsymbol{\alpha}_t$, and hence its MMSE, based on all the observations in the sample. For a DCS model, the smoothing filter is defined by a symmetry argument rather than being derived as an optimal estimate. However, as we shall see, it can also be rationalized by an argument based on the conditional mode of the posterior distribution of the state. Indeed, this signal extraction interpretation probably provides a more solid foundation for DCS models than the case set out in Chapter 1.

3.7.1 Weights

The filtering equations in a DCS model have the same form as the Kalman filter in a corresponding linear Gaussian unobserved components model. The KF defines an implicit set of weights for current and past observations. Similarly, the backward recursive equations in a fixed interval smoother for a linear Gaussian UC model implicitly define a set of weights for all observations. Smoothing in a DCS model amounts to using a set of smoothing weights that match the weights for the filter. The complications arise because the DCS filter is driven by a nonlinear function of the observations that is itself dependent on the output of the filter.

In a simple linear Gaussian UC model, there are explicit formulae for the filtering and smoothing weights; see Whittle (1983, Chapters 6 and 7). For the AR(1) plus noise model of (1.1), the weights are a function of the parameter, θ, in the reduced form (1.2). To be specific, the weights for the filter in a semi-infinite sample,

$$\mu_{t+1|t} = \sum_{j=0}^{\infty} w_j y_{t-j}, \tag{3.47}$$

are

$$w_j = (\phi - \theta)\theta^j, \qquad j = 0, 1, 2, \ldots. \tag{3.48}$$

The weights for the smoother are two-sided and in a doubly infinite sample,

$$\mu_{t|T} = \sum_{j=-\infty}^{\infty} w_j y_{t-j}, \tag{3.49}$$

where

$$w_j = \frac{(1+\theta^2)\phi - (1+\phi^2)}{(1-\theta^2)\phi}\theta^{|j|}, \qquad j = 0, \pm 1, \pm 2, \ldots, \tag{3.50}$$

simplifying to $w_j = \{(1-\theta)/(1+\theta)\}\theta^{|j|}$, $j = 0, \pm 1, \pm 2, \ldots$, when $\phi = 1$. The expressions for the weights may be modified to take account of a finite sample. Alternatively, and more generally, the weights for finite samples can be computed numerically from the state space form of any linear model by using the algorithm in Koopman and Harvey (2003). There will be a different set of smoothing weights for each value of t from $t = 1$ to T, although those in the middle will typically be very close. Figure 3.6 shows the weights four periods from the end for a random walk plus noise model with signal-noise ratio equal to 0.1.

The DCS-t filter for the first-order model can be written as

$$\mu_{t+1|t} = (\phi - \kappa)\mu_{t|t-1} + \kappa y_t(\mu_{t|t-1}), \tag{3.51}$$

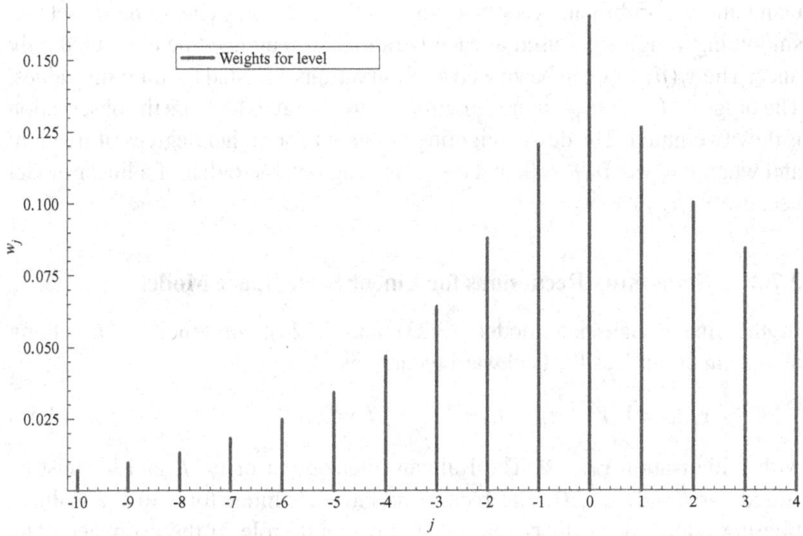

Figure 3.6. Smoothing weights at $t = T - 4$ for a random walk plus noise model with $q = 0.1$.

showing that the weighting of the *pseudo-observations*,

$$y_t(\mu_{t|t-1}) = u_t + \mu_{t|t-1}, \qquad t = 1, \ldots, T, \tag{3.52}$$
$$= (1 - b_t)y_t + b_t\mu_{t|t-1},$$

is the same as in the KF, (3.31), for the corresponding Gaussian UC model. In a semi-infinite sample, these weights are given by formula (3.48), with $\theta = \phi - \kappa$. For smoothing in a doubly infinite sample, the weights are as in (3.50). In the filter, the pseudo-observations depend on b_t, which in turn depends on $\mu_{t|t-1}$: hence the notation $y_t(\mu_{t|t-1})$. For smoothing, the weights are applied to pseudo-observations constructed as

$$y_t(\mu_{t|T}) = (1 - b_{t|T})y_t + b_{t|T}\mu_{t|T}, \quad t = 1, \ldots, T, \tag{3.53}$$

where

$$b_{t|T} = b_{t|T}(\mu_{t|T}) = \frac{(y_t - \mu_{t|T})^2/\nu \exp(2\lambda)}{1 + (y_t - \mu_{t|T})^2/\nu \exp(2\lambda)}. \tag{3.54}$$

Because the $y_t(\mu_{t|T})'s$ depend on the $\mu'_{t|T}s$, the weights need to be applied repeatedly until there is convergence.

Finite sample smoothing weights for the first-order DCS-t model can be obtained by computing them for the UC Gaussian model with signal-noise ratio

$$q = \phi(1 + (\phi - \kappa)^2)/(\phi - \kappa) - 1 - (\phi - \kappa)^2, \tag{3.55}$$

using the algorithm in Koopman and Harvey (2003). The same T sets of smoothing weights are used at each iteration, so they need be computed only once. The $y_t(\mu_{t|T})'s$ can be viewed as observations adjusted for outlying values. The bigger is $(y_t - \mu_{t|T})^2$, the closer $b_{t|T}$ is to one, and the more the observation is downweighted. The downweighting is smaller for higher degrees of freedom and when $\nu = \infty$, $b_{t|T} = 0$, and the weighting reverts to that of a linear model because $y_t(\mu_{t|T}) = y_t$.

3.7.2 Smoothing Recursions for Linear State Space Models

In the linear Gaussian model, (3.23) and (3.24), an efficient smoothing algorithm comprises the backward recursions

$$\mathbf{r}_{t-1} = \mathbf{L}_t'\mathbf{r}_t + \mathbf{z}_t v_t/f_t, \qquad t = T, \dots, 1, \tag{3.56}$$

with initialisation $\mathbf{r}_T = \mathbf{0}$. The Kalman filter output of v_t, f_t and $\mathbf{k}_t$ must be stored for $t = 1, \dots, T$. The recursions have a similar form to the Kalman filtering equations, with $\mathbf{r}_t$ playing an analogous role to the estimated state vector; see Durbin and Koopman (2012, Chapters 4 and 5). The smoothed state vector $\boldsymbol{\alpha}_{t|T}$ can be evaluated by

$$\boldsymbol{\alpha}_{t|T} = \boldsymbol{\alpha}_{t|t-1} + \mathbf{P}_{t|t-1}\mathbf{r}_{t-1}, \qquad t = T, \dots, 1. \tag{3.57}$$

However, the requirement to store $\boldsymbol{\alpha}_{t|t-1}$ and $\mathbf{P}_{t|t-1}$ from the Kalman filter can be avoided by computing $\boldsymbol{\alpha}_{t|T}$ using the forward recursion

$$\boldsymbol{\alpha}_{t+1|T} = \mathbf{T}\boldsymbol{\alpha}_{t|T} + \mathbf{Q}\mathbf{r}_t, \qquad t = 1, \dots, T, \tag{3.58}$$

with $\boldsymbol{\alpha}_{1|T} = \boldsymbol{\alpha}_0 + \mathbf{P}_{1|0}\mathbf{r}_0 = \mathbf{T}^{-1}\boldsymbol{\alpha}_{1|0} + \mathbf{P}_{1|0}\mathbf{r}_0$.

Example 15 *In the AR(1) plus noise model, (1.1), σ_ε^2 can be set to unity without affecting the filter, and so $\mathbf{Q} = q$, which is the signal-noise ratio. The backward smoothing recursion is*

$$r_{t-1} = (\phi - k_t)r_t + (1 - k_t/\phi)v_t, \qquad t = T, \dots, 2, \tag{3.59}$$

whereas (3.57) is

$$\begin{aligned}\mu_{t|T} &= \mu_{t|t-1} + p_{t|t-1}r_{t-1}, \qquad t = 1, \dots T,\\ &= \mu_{t|t-1} + k_t(r_t + v_t/\phi).\end{aligned}$$

The initial values are used in the Kalman filter, namely $\mu_{1|0} = 0$ and $p_{1|0} = q/(1 - \phi^2)$. The alternative forward recursion, (3.58), is

$$\mu_{t+1|T} = \mu_{t|T} + qr_t, \qquad t = 1, \dots, T - 1. \tag{3.60}$$

In the local level model, $\phi = 1$. Because $r_0 = (1 - k_1)r_1 + (1 - k_1)v_1$, initializing with a diffuse prior will give $\mu_{1|T} = (p_{1|0}/(p_{1|0} + 1))(r_1 + y_1)$, which goes to $r_1 + y_1$ as $p_{1|0}$ goes to infinity. Hence $\mu_{1|T} = r_1 + y_1$.

The recursive smoothing algorithms for linear state space models may be adapted to deal with the class of nonlinear UC models described in Section 2.4. Durbin and Koopman (2012, pp. 240–59) provided the details and showed how iterations may be carried out with a Gauss-Newton algorithm.

3.7.3 Smoothing Recursions for DCS Models

The state space smoothing recursions of the previous sub-section may be adapted to give a set smoothed values, $\mu_{t|T}$, $t = 1, \ldots, T$, which are the same as those given by applying the weights from the equivalent UC model to the pseudo-observations of (3.53). These recursions are also based on repeatedly revising the values of the $b'_{t|T}s$ to reflect the latest values of the $\mu'_{t|T}s$.

The DCS filter is first run and then followed by a backward smoother (which will usually have time-invariant system matrices) in which the innovations of (3.56) are replaced by the scores, u_t, $t = 1, \ldots, T$. The forward recursion gives smoothed values of the signal, that is, a set of $\mu'_{t|T}s$. The DCS filter is then run again with the score variable evaluated at $b_{t|T}(\mu_{t|T})$, as in (3.54), that is,

$$u_t(\mu_{t|T}) = (1 - b_{t|T})(y_t - \mu_{t|T}), \quad t = 1, \ldots, T. \tag{3.61}$$

The smoother is then run with the $u_t(\mu_{t|T})'s$ and the whole process of filtering and smoothing repeated until the $\mu'_{t|T}s$ converge.

In the first-order DCS-t model, (3.3), the backward filter in (3.59) becomes

$$r_{t-1} = (\phi - \kappa)r_t + (1 - \kappa/\phi)u_t, \qquad t = T, \ldots, 2,$$

where u_t is repeatedly updated as $u_t(\mu_{t|T})$ after the first iteration. The forward recursion is either

$$\mu_{t|T} = \mu_{t|t-1} + \kappa(r_t + u_t(\mu_{t|T})/\phi), \qquad t = 1, \ldots T,$$

where the smoothed signal in $u_t(\mu_{t|T})$ is from the previous round, or

$$\mu_{t+1|T} = \mu_{t|T} + q r_t, \qquad t = 1, \ldots, T - 1,$$

with q given by (3.55). Because the estimate of the constant, ω, does not change, neither does the initial value, $\mu_{1|0}$. The same is true in the local level when $\mu_{1|0}$ is treated as a fixed parameter.

Generalization of the above recursive method, or indeed the method based on weighting pseudo-observations, appears not to be straightforward. The difficulty lies in finding a UC model which yields the same filter as the DCS model.

3.7.4 Conditional Mode Estimation and the Score

In an unobserved components model, the distribution of the signal conditional on the observations can be written as the joint PDF of the observations and signal divided by the PDF of the observations. Taking logarithms gives

$$\ln f(\boldsymbol{\mu} \mid \mathbf{y}) = \ln f(\boldsymbol{\mu}, \mathbf{y}) - \ln f(\mathbf{y}), \tag{3.62}$$

and maximizing $\ln f(\boldsymbol{\mu} \mid \mathbf{y})$ with respect to $\boldsymbol{\mu}$ gives the conditional modes of the series of signals. For a linear Gaussian state space model, these modes are the same as the conditional expectations of the signals. Hence they are the smoothed estimates. Note that the second term in (3.62), that is, $\ln f(\mathbf{y})$, can be ignored, and so $\ln f(\boldsymbol{\mu} \mid \mathbf{y})$ may be replaced by the more straightforward expression $\ln f(\mathbf{y}, \boldsymbol{\mu}) = \ln f(\mathbf{y} \mid \boldsymbol{\mu}) + \ln f(\boldsymbol{\mu})$.

Consider a model in which the PDF of y_t given μ_t is $f(y_t \mid \mu_t)$ and the dynamic equation for μ_t is a Gaussian AR(1), as in (1.1). The joint log-density of the observations and signals is, ignoring irrelevant constants,

$$\ln f(\mathbf{y}, \boldsymbol{\mu}) = \sum_{t=1}^{T} \ln f(y_t \mid \mu_t) - \frac{1}{2\sigma_\eta^2} \sum_{t=2}^{T} \left(\mu_t - \phi\mu_{t-1}\right)^2 - \frac{1}{2p_{1|0}} \left(\mu_1 - \mu_{1|0}\right)^2 .$$

When μ_t is stationary, $\mu_{1|0} = 0$ and $p_{1|0} = \sigma_\eta^2/(1-\phi^2)$. When μ_t is a random walk initialized with a diffuse prior, $p_{1|0} \to \infty$, and the last term disappears.

For a linear Gaussian model, $f(y_t \mid \mu_t) \propto \exp((y_t - \mu_t)^2/2\sigma_\varepsilon^2)$. Differentiating $\ln f(\mathbf{y}, \boldsymbol{\mu})$ with respect to each element of $\boldsymbol{\mu}$ then gives a set of equations, which, when set to zero and solved, yield the minimum mean square error estimates of the $\mu_t's$. These smoothed estimates may be computed efficiently by the smoothing recursions given in Sub-section 3.7.2.

More generally, for any conditional distribution, $f(y_t \mid \mu_t)$, with a continuous first derivative,

$$\frac{\partial \ln f(\boldsymbol{\mu} \mid \mathbf{y})}{\partial \mu_1} = \frac{\partial f(y_1 \mid \mu_1)}{\partial \mu_1} + \frac{\phi}{\sigma_\eta^2}\left(\mu_2 - \phi\mu_1\right) - \frac{\mu_1}{p_{1|0}}, \tag{3.63}$$

$$\frac{\partial \ln f(\boldsymbol{\mu} \mid \mathbf{y})}{\partial \mu_t} = \frac{\partial f(y_t \mid \mu_t)}{\partial \mu_t} - \frac{1}{\sigma_\eta^2}\left(\mu_t - \phi\mu_{t-1}\right)$$

$$+ \frac{\phi}{\sigma_\eta^2}\left(\mu_{t+1} - \phi\mu_t\right), \quad t = 2, \ldots, T-1,$$

$$\frac{\partial \ln f(\boldsymbol{\mu} \mid \mathbf{y})}{\partial \mu_T} = \frac{\partial f(y_t \mid \mu_T)}{\partial \mu_T} - \frac{1}{\sigma_\eta^2}\left(\mu_T - \phi\mu_{T-1}\right).$$

The conditional modes satisfy the equations obtained by setting these derivatives equal to zero. Durbin and Koopman (2012, pp. 252–3) discuss optimality properties of the conditional modes as estimates of the $\mu_t's$.

The first terms on the right-hand side of the equations in (3.63) are the scores. When evaluated at the conditional modes, they are proportional to the $u_t(\mu_{t|T})'s$ defined in (3.61). Working back to the filter, there is now a rationale for the appearance of the conditional score, $u_t = u(\mu_{t|t-1})$ in place of the innovation, $y_t - \mu_{t|t-1}$.

Summing the equations in (3.63) when they are evaluated at the conditional modes gives the following result when $\phi = 1$, because the terms involving the first differences of the $\mu_t' s$ cancel each other out.

Proposition 11 *When μ_t is a random walk initialized with a diffuse prior, the scores sum to zero when evaluated at the conditional modes, that is,*

$$\sum_{t=1}^{T} u_t(\mu_{t|T}) = 0.$$

De Rossi and Harvey (2009) showed that this result holds generally for stochastic trends, such as the integrated random walk. The formal requirement is that for the transition matrix in (3.24), the first column of $\mathbf{T} - \mathbf{I}$ consists solely of zeroes.

3.8 FORECASTING

The one-step-ahead predictive distribution is given directly by the model. The concern here is with multistep prediction.

3.8.1 QARMA Models

When a DCS model is stationary and $\mu_{t|t-1}$ has a moving average representation in IID variables, as in (3.13), the location at time $T + \ell$ can be written as

$$\mu_{T+\ell|T+\ell-1} = \omega + \sum_{j=1}^{\ell-1} \psi_j u_{T+\ell-j} + \sum_{k=0}^{\infty} \psi_{\ell+k} u_{T-k}, \quad \ell = 2, 3, \ldots.$$

The MMSE estimate of $\mu_{T+\ell|T+\ell-1}$, based on information at time T, is its conditional expectation

$$\mu_{T+\ell|T} = \omega + \sum_{k=0}^{\infty} \psi_{\ell+k} u_{T-k}, \quad \ell = 2, 3, \ldots.$$

The MSE is

$$MSE(\mu_{T+\ell|T}) = \sigma_u^2 \sum_{j=1}^{\ell-1} \psi_j^2, \quad \ell = 2, 3, \ldots.$$

For the t_ν distribution, σ_u^2 is given by (3.7) for any positive ν.

When $\mu_{t+1|t}$ is of the $QARMA(p, r)$ form, (3.10), the predictor, $\mu_{T+\ell|T}$, can be computed recursively, as in an ARMA model. Thus

$$\begin{aligned}\mu_{T+\ell|T} &= \delta + \phi_1 \mu_{T+\ell-1|T} + \cdots + \phi_p \mu_{T+\ell-p|T} \\ &\quad + \kappa_0 u_{T+\ell-1|T} + \cdots + \kappa_r u_{T+\ell-r|T}, \quad \ell = 2, 3, \ldots,\end{aligned}$$

where $\mu_{T+j|T}$ is known for $j \leq 1$, $u_{T+j|T}$ is known for $j \leq 0$ and $u_{T+j|T} = 0$ for $j > 0$. A recursion of this form can be used even if $\mu_{t+1|T}$ is nonstationary.

Example 16 *For the first-order model, (3.2),*

$$\mu_{T+\ell|T} = \delta + \phi\mu_{T+\ell-1|T}, \quad \ell = 2, 3, \ldots,$$

and the recursion is still valid for the local level model, (3.38). When the model is stationary, the recursion can be solved to give $\mu_{T+\ell|T} = \omega(1-\phi^{\ell-1}) + \phi^{\ell-1}\mu_{T+1|T}$, $\ell = 1, 2, 3, \ldots,$ *and when* $\phi = 1$, $\mu_{T+\ell|T} = \delta(\ell-1) + \mu_{T+\ell|T}$.

The predictor of the observation at time $T+\ell$, that is, $y_{T+\ell} = \mu_{T+\ell|T+\ell-1} + v_{T+\ell}$, is

$$y_{T+\ell|T} = \mu_{T+\ell|T}, \quad \ell = 1, 2, 3, \ldots.$$

Provided that $\nu > 1$, $y_{T+\ell|T}$ is the conditional expectation of $y_{T+\ell}$. When $\nu > 2$, $y_{T+\ell|T}$ is the minimum mean square error ℓ – *step* ahead predictor of $y_{T+\ell}$ with

$$MSE(y_{T+\ell|T}) = MSE(\mu_{T+\ell|T}) + Var(v_{T+\ell}), \quad \ell = 1, 2, \ldots, \qquad (3.64)$$

where $MSE(y_{T+1|T}) = 0$.

A formula for the multistep predictive distribution cannot be found unless the model is Gaussian. However, simulation is a viable option. The prediction error associated with $y_{T+\ell|t}$ is

$$\sum_{j=1}^{\ell-1} \psi_j u_{T+\ell-j} + v_{T+\ell}, \quad \ell = 2, 3, \ldots,$$

and u_{T+j}, $j = 1, \ldots, \ell-1$, and $v_{T+\ell}$ can be generated from independent t distributions.

3.8.2 State Space Form*

Multistep predictions can be computed using the state space form of (2.61). The optimal estimator of

$$\boldsymbol{\alpha}_{T+\ell|T+\ell-1} = \sum_{j=0}^{\ell-2} \mathbf{T}^j\boldsymbol{\delta} + \mathbf{T}^{\ell-1}\boldsymbol{\alpha}_{T+1|T} + \sum_{j=0}^{\ell-2} \mathbf{T}^j\boldsymbol{\kappa} u_{T+j+1}, \quad \ell = 2, 3, \ldots,$$

is

$$\boldsymbol{\alpha}_{T+\ell|T} = \left[\sum_{j=0}^{\ell-2} \mathbf{T}^j\right]\boldsymbol{\delta} + \mathbf{T}^{\ell-1}\boldsymbol{\alpha}_{T+1|T}, \quad \ell = 2, 3, \ldots,$$

and the corresponding predictor of $y_{T+\ell}$ is $y_{T+\ell|T} = \mathbf{z}'_{T+\ell}\boldsymbol{\alpha}_{T+\ell|T}$ for $\ell = 1, 2, 3, \ldots,$

The MSE of $y_{T+\ell|T}$ is

$$MSE(y_{T+\ell|T}) = \sigma_u^2 \mathbf{z}'_{T+\ell} \left[\sum_{j=0}^{\ell-2} \mathbf{T}^j \right] \boldsymbol{\kappa}\boldsymbol{\kappa}' \left[\sum_{j=0}^{\ell-2} \mathbf{T}^j \right]' \mathbf{z}_{T+\ell} + Var(\upsilon_{T+\ell}), \quad \ell = 2, 3, \ldots,$$

because the prediction error is $\sum_{j=0}^{\ell-2} \mathbf{T}^j \boldsymbol{\kappa} u_{T+j+1} + \upsilon_{T+\ell}$ for $\ell \geq 2$, and so the full predictive distribution may be simulated as before.

The forecast functions for models containing trends and seasonals take the same form as in the corresponding UC models.

3.9 COMPONENTS AND LONG MEMORY

Fractionally integrated white noise is

$$(1 - L)^d y_t = \varepsilon_t, \quad t = 1, \ldots, T, \tag{3.65}$$

where d need not be an integer, as it would be for a simple differencing operation. The model may be expressed as an infinite autoregression by expanding the operator as

$$(1 - L)^d = 1 - dL - \frac{1}{2} d(1 - d)L^2 - \ldots, \qquad d > -1.$$

Conversely, a moving average is obtained from $(1 - L)^{-d}$.

The model is stationary if $d < 1/2$, in which case the autocorrelations are

$$\rho(\tau) = \frac{\Gamma(1 - d)\Gamma(\tau + d)}{\Gamma(d)\Gamma(\tau + 1 - d)}, \quad \tau = 0, 1, 2, \ldots.$$

When $d > 0$, the observations exhibit long memory. The ACF decays hyperbolically, as illustrated in Figure 3.5, in which the ACF for $d = 0.4$ is contrasted with the ACF of an $AR(1)$ where $\rho(1)$ takes the same value of 0.667; hence, $\phi = 0.667$. The ACF of the $AR(1)$ decays exponentially. The long-memory model may be generalized by letting $(1 - L)^d y_t$ be an $ARMA(p, q)$ process. This model is denoted as $ARFIMA(p, d, q)$.

One interpretation of long memory is as an approximation to a mixture of components. Suppose that the location is the sum of two unobserved first-order autoregressions, that is,

$$y_t = \omega + \mu_{1,t} + \mu_{2,t} + \varepsilon_t, \quad \varepsilon_t \sim NID(0, \sigma_i^2) \tag{3.66}$$

$$\mu_{i,t} = \phi_i \mu_{i,t-1} + \eta_{it}, \quad \eta_{it} \sim NID(0, \sigma_i^2), \quad i = 1, 2,$$

where ε_t, η_{1t} and η_{2t} are mutually independent.

Figure 3.7 shows the ACF of a model in which $\phi_1 = 0.5$ and $\sigma_1^2 = 37.5$, whereas $\phi_2 = 0.99$ with $\sigma_2^2 = 1$. As can be seen, the ACF of this model is close to that of the long memory model.

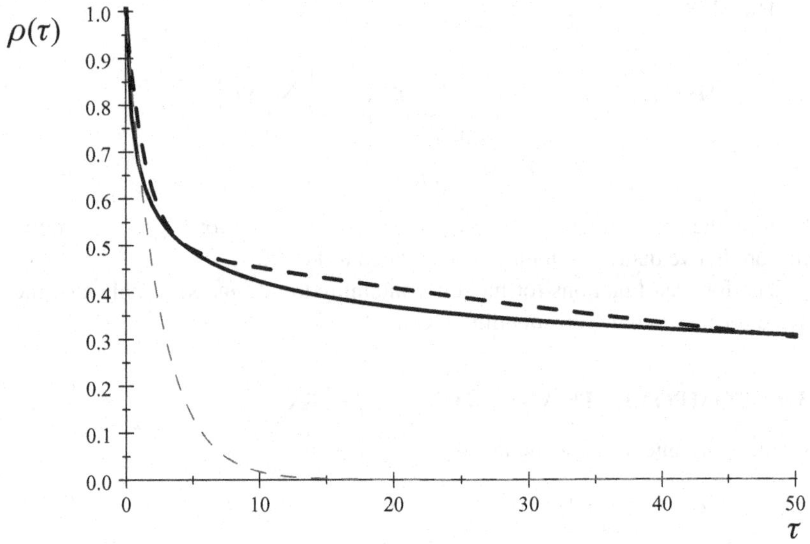

Figure 3.7. Long memory (solid line) and two AR(1)'s. Thin dashed line is an AR(1) with same r(1) as long memory.

The unobserved components model in (3.66) is easily handled by the Kalman filter. The corresponding DCS model is

$$y_t = \omega + \mu_{1,t|t-1} + \mu_{2,t|t-1} + v_t \tag{3.67}$$
$$\mu_{i,t+1|t} = \phi_i \mu_{i,t|t-1} + \kappa_i u_t, \quad i = 1, 2.$$

where $\phi_1 \neq \phi_2$. Note that u_t appears in both dynamic equations, just as the prediction error does in the innovations form.

Remark 16 *Given that the need for at least one component has been established, a Wald test for the presence of a second, that is, a test of significance on $\widetilde{\kappa}_2$, requires that ϕ_2 be fixed (but not at unity), because when $\kappa_2 = 0$, ϕ_2 is not identified. An LM test will set $\phi_2 = 0$; see Harvey (1989, Chapter 5) for a general discussion of such issues. Choosing the number of components may perhaps best be based on a goodness-of-fit criterion, such as the AIC or BIC.*

A long-memory DCS model could be set up directly by letting the level in (3.2) be

$$(1 - L)^d \mu_{t+1|t} = \kappa u_t.$$

However, there are a number of advantages to working with a components model rather than a long-memory model, even though the latter is more parsimonious. The first advantage is that a model with two components, one representing a short-run response and the other capturing the long run, is more readily open to interpretation than is fractionally integrated white noise. Second, on a technical point, it is difficult to combine a long-memory component with other components in a state space form because a long-state vector may be needed for the autoregressive approximation to be satisfactory. Third, the asymptotic theory for a long-memory model appears to be less tractable.

3.10 GENERAL ERROR DISTRIBUTION

Let $y_t = \varepsilon_t \exp(\lambda)$, where ε_t has a general error distribution with positive shape parameter υ and scale $\varphi = \exp(\lambda)$. The conditional log-density of the *t-th* observation is

$$\ln f_t(y_t; \boldsymbol{\psi}, \lambda, \upsilon) = -\left(1+\upsilon^{-1}\right)\ln 2 - \ln\Gamma(1+\upsilon^{-1}) \\ -\lambda - (1/2)\left|y_t - \mu_{t|t-1}\right|^{\upsilon}\exp(-\lambda\upsilon),$$

where $\mu_{t|t-1}$ evolves as a linear function of the score,

$$\frac{\partial \ln f_t}{\partial \mu_{t|t-1}} = \frac{\upsilon}{2\exp(\upsilon\lambda)} sgn(y - \mu_{t|t-1})\left|y_t - \mu_{t|t-1}\right|^{\upsilon-1}, \quad t = 1,\ldots,T. \tag{3.68}$$

It is convenient to define

$$u_t = sgn(y_t - \mu_{t|t-1})\left|\frac{y_t - \mu_{t|t-1}}{\exp(\lambda)}\right|^{\upsilon-1}, \quad \upsilon > 1, \tag{3.69}$$

so the score is $(\upsilon/2)\exp(-\lambda)u_t$. For $\upsilon = 1$, $u_t = sgn(y_t - \mu_{t|t-1})$, except at $y_t = \mu_{t|t-1}$, where it is not defined.

The properties of the model can be obtained in much the same way as for a conditional t distribution. Because

$$u_t^2 = \left|\frac{y_t - \mu_{t|t-1}}{\exp(\lambda)}\right|^{2\upsilon-2}$$

it follows from (2.13) in Chapter 2 that

$$\sigma_u^2 = 2^{2(\upsilon-1)/\upsilon}\Gamma(2-\upsilon^{-1})/\Gamma(1/\upsilon). \tag{3.70}$$

The value of σ_u^2 is unity for both $\upsilon = 2$ and $\upsilon = 1$.

In the static model, the usual asymptotic properties of the ML estimator of μ can be shown to hold, though the proof is non-standard; see Zhu and Zinde-Walsh (2009). However, for the DCS model, Theorem 1 runs into difficulties when $\upsilon < 1.5$, because the higher order moments upon which b depends do not exist.

3.11 SKEW DISTRIBUTIONS

Skewness can be introduced into a t distribution in such a way that most of the theory set out in this chapter for the DCS location model is unchanged.

3.11.1 How to Skew a Distribution

There are a number of ways in which a distribution may be skewed. The method proposed by Fernandez and Steel (1998) provides the ideal solution in the present context. A standardized probability density function, $f(.)$, which is unimodal and symmetric about zero, is used to construct a skewed probability density function

$$f(\varepsilon_t|\gamma) = \frac{2}{\gamma + \gamma^{-1}}\left[f\left(\frac{\varepsilon_t}{\gamma}\right)I_{[0,\infty)}(\varepsilon_t) + f(\varepsilon_t\gamma)I_{(-\infty,0)}(\varepsilon_t)\right], \quad (3.71)$$

where $I_{[0,\infty)}(\varepsilon_t)$ is an indicator variable, taking the value one when $\varepsilon_t \geq 0$ and zero otherwise, and γ is a parameter in the range $0 < \gamma < \infty$. An equivalent but more compact formulation is

$$f(\varepsilon_t|\gamma) = \frac{2}{\gamma + \gamma^{-1}} f\left(\frac{\varepsilon_t}{\gamma^{sgn(\varepsilon_t)}}\right). \quad (3.72)$$

Symmetry is attained when $\gamma = 1$, whereas $\gamma < 1$ and $\gamma > 1$ produce left and right skewness, respectively. In other words, the left-hand tail is heavier when $\gamma < 1$. The median and mean are both negative when $\gamma < 1$, the former because $\Pr(y_t \leq 0) = 1/(1+\gamma^2) > 0.5$ and the latter because, in expression (3.75) below, $(\gamma - 1/\gamma) < 0$.

The uncentered moments of ε_t are

$$E\left(\varepsilon_t^c\right) = M_c \frac{\gamma^{c+1} + (-1)^c/\gamma^{c+1}}{\gamma + \gamma^{-1}}, \quad (3.73)$$

where

$$M_c = 2\int_0^{\infty} z^c f(z)dz = E(|z|^c). \quad (3.74)$$

Hence

$$E(\varepsilon_t) = \mu_\varepsilon = M_1(\gamma - 1/\gamma), \quad (3.75)$$

which is not zero unless $\gamma = 1$, and

$$Var(\varepsilon_t) = \sigma_z^2\left(\gamma^2 - 1 + \gamma^{-2}\right) - M_1^2(\gamma - 1/\gamma)^2, \quad (3.76)$$

where $\sigma_z^2 = Var(z_t) = M_2$. The standard measure of skewness, as given by Fernandez and Steel (1998, eq. 6), is

$$\begin{aligned} E(\varepsilon_t - \mu_\varepsilon)^3 &= E\left(\varepsilon_t^3\right) - 3\mu_\varepsilon E\left(\varepsilon_t^2\right) + 2\mu_\varepsilon^3 \\ &= (\gamma - \gamma^{-1})\left[\left(M_3 + 2M_1^3 - 3M_1M_2\right)\left(\gamma^2 + \gamma^{-2}\right)\right. \\ &\quad \left. + 3M_1M_2 - 4M_1^3\right] \end{aligned}$$

divided by $(Var(\varepsilon_t))^{3/2}$.

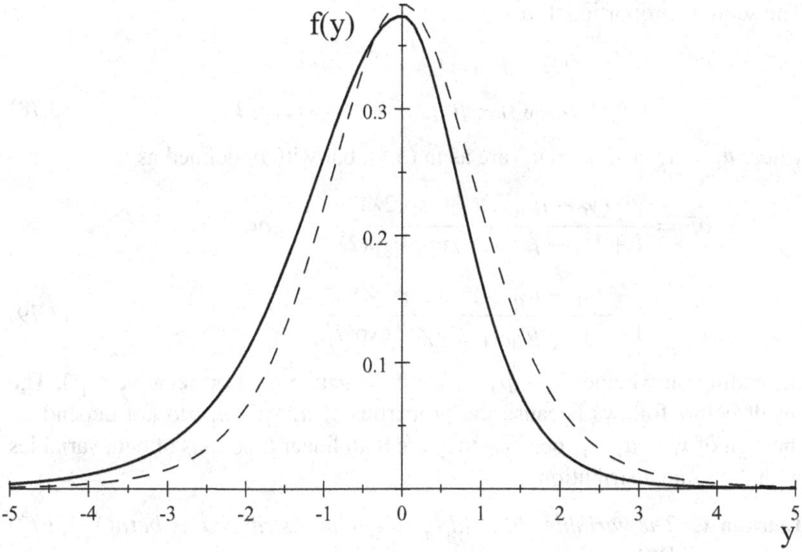

Figure 3.8. Skew t with $\gamma = 0.8$ and normal distribution (dashed).

The introduction of a location parameter, μ, and the logarithm of scale, λ, gives observations

$$y_t = \mu + \varepsilon_t \exp(\lambda), \qquad t = 1, \ldots, T.$$

The formulae for the PDF and the moments may be adapted accordingly. Thus

$$\mu_y = E(y_t) = \mu + \mu_\varepsilon \exp(\lambda),$$

whereas $Var(y_t) = Var(\varepsilon_t)\exp(2\lambda)$, and the third moment about the mean is $E(y_t - \mu_y)^3 = E(\varepsilon_t - \mu_\varepsilon)^3 \exp(3\lambda)$.

3.11.2 Dynamic Skew-*t* Location Model

Figure 3.8 shows the PDF of a skew t constructed from a standardized t_6 distribution with $\gamma = 0.8$. The moments are readily obtained from (3.73) using (2.12).

When the location changes over time, as in (3.2), the log-density of the conditional skew t distribution is

$$\begin{aligned}\ln f_t(\psi, \lambda, \nu, \gamma) = &- \ln((\gamma + \gamma^{-1})/2) + \ln \Gamma\left((\nu+1)/2\right) \\ &- \frac{1}{2}\ln \pi - \ln \Gamma\left(\nu/2\right) - \frac{1}{2}\ln \nu \\ &- \lambda - \frac{(\nu+1)}{2}\ln\left(1 + \frac{(y_t - \mu_{t|t-1})^2}{\gamma^{2\mathrm{sgn}(y_t - \mu_{t|t-1})}\nu e^{2\lambda}}\right). \qquad (3.77)\end{aligned}$$

The score is proportional to

$$u_t = u_t^+ I_{[0,\infty)}(y_t - \mu_{t|t-1}) + u_t^- I_{(-\infty,0)}(y_t - \mu_{t|t-1}), \quad t = 1, \ldots, T, \tag{3.78}$$

where $u_t = u_t^+$ and $u_t = u_t^-$ are as in (3.4), but with b_t defined as

$$b_t^+ = \frac{(y_t - \mu_{t|t-1})^2/\nu \exp(2\lambda)}{1 + (y_t - \mu_{t|t-1})^2/\nu\gamma^2 \exp(2\lambda)} \quad \textit{or}$$

$$b_t^- = \frac{(y_t - \mu_{t|t-1})^2/\nu \exp(2\lambda)}{1 + (y_t - \mu_{t|t-1})^2/\nu\gamma^{-2} \exp(2\lambda)} \tag{3.79}$$

depending on whether $y_t - \mu_{t|t-1}$ is non-negative (b_t^+) or negative (b_t^-). The result below follows because the properties of u_t^+ and u_t^- do not depend on the sign of $y_t - \mu_{t|t-1}$, because they are both linear functions of beta variables with the same distribution.

Lemma 13 *The variables b_t^+ and b_t^- are both distributed as $beta(1/2, \nu/2)$ and u_t is $IID(0, \sigma_u^2)$, where σ_u^2 is as in (3.7).*

The preceding lemma shows that the properties of u_t are exactly as given for a symmetric t distribution in Proposition 7. As a result, the formulae for moments and autocorrelations are the same. Forecasts are as before except that the MMSE predictor of $y_{T+\ell}$ is now

$$y_{T+\ell|t} = \mu_{T+\ell|T} + \mu_\varepsilon \exp(\lambda), \quad \ell = 1, 2, 3, \ldots.$$

Because the predictive distribution is asymmetric, the case for simulating it is even stronger than before.

When γ is known, the information matrix for the skew-t model is exactly as in the symmetric case. The reason is simple: the distribution of the score and its first derivative depend on IID beta variates in exactly the same way as in the symmetric case. When γ is estimated, the asymptotic covariance matrix of the ML estimators of ψ, λ, and ν is unaffected, as these estimators are independent of the ML estimator of γ. In other words, Proposition 9 continues to hold.

Remark 17 *Zhu and Galbraith (2011) give analytic expressions for the covariance matrix, but with a different paramerization for the scale and the skewing parameter. They extend the result to a distribution in which the degrees of freedom take on a different value according to the sign of $y_t - \mu$.*

CHAPTER 4

Scale

An established feature of asset returns is that they exhibit volatility clustering. Another stylized fact about returns is that their distributions typically have heavy tails. Although the Gaussian GARCH structure induces excess kurtosis in the returns, it is not usually enough to match the data. As a result, it is now customary to assume that returns have a conditional Student's t_ν distribution. The GARCH-t model, which was originally proposed by Bollerslev (1987), is widely used in empirical work and as a benchmark for other models.

The t distribution in GARCH-t is employed in the predictive distribution of returns and used as the basis for maximum likelihood estimation of the parameters, but it is not acknowledged in the design of the equation for the conditional variance. The specification of the conditional variance as a linear combination of squared observations is taken for granted, but the consequences are that it responds too much to extreme observations, and the effect is slow to dissipate. These features of GARCH are well-known, and the consequences for testing and forecasting have been explored in a number of papers; see, for example, Franses, van Dijk and Lucas (2004). Other researchers, such as Sakata and White (1998) and Muler and Yohai (2008), have been prompted to develop procedures for robustification; see also Gregory and Reeves (2010).

Letting the dynamic equation for volatility depend on the conditional score of the t distribution yields a model that mitigates the effect of outliers. This model is called Beta-t-GARCH because the conditional score is a linear function of a variable that has a beta distribution. It reduces to the classic Gaussian GARCH specification when the degrees of freedom is infinite.

The Beta-t-GARCH model still suffers from some of the drawbacks of GARCH. Furthermore, the asymptotic distribution of the ML estimators cannot be derived from the theory of Chapter 2. Hence the preference for the Beta-t-EGARCH model, which differs from Beta-t-GARCH in that it employs an exponential link function. In the EGARCH formulation as originally proposed by Nelson (1991), the unconditional moments of the observations typically do not exist for a t_ν distribution with finite degrees of freedom. This is not the case for Beta-t-EGARCH. Indeed, the recognition that the conditional score is a linear function of a beta variable actually enables formulae for the moments and the autocorrelations of absolute values of the observations raised to any positive power to be derived. Furthermore, it is possible to derive closed-form expressions for multistep predictions of the scale and variance, together with the mean square error of these predictions. Hence Beta-t-EGARCH has all the advantages of the standard EGARCH model, but without the disadvantages.

When the conditional distribution of y_t has a generalized error distribution, the DCS approach leads to a complementary class of models in which u_t is a linear function of absolute values of the observations raised to a positive power. These variables can be transformed so as to have a gamma distribution, and the properties of the model, denoted as Gamma-GED-EGARCH, can again be derived. The normal distribution is a special case of the GED, as is the Laplace distribution. The conditional variance equation for the Laplace model has the same form as the conditional variance equation in the EGARCH model adopted by Nelson (1991).

The properties of the Beta-t-EGARCH and Gamma-GED-EGARCH models are derived in Sections 4.2 and 4.4, respectively, with leverage effects introduced in Section 4.3. The results on forecasting are set out in Section 4.5. Section 4.7 investigates the properties of Beta-t-GARCH and compares the model with Beta-t-EGARCH.

The asymptotic theory for Beta-t-EGARCH and Gamma-GED-EGARCH is presented in Section 4.6. It is remarkably transparent and comprehensive. Explicit analytic expressions are given for information matrices, and the modifications needed to deal with additional features such as leverage, components and skew distributions are relatively straightforward. Although the analytic expressions become somewhat elaborate, the conditions needed for the asymptotic distributions to hold are easily verifiable.

The asymptotic theory applies to the leading nonstationary models. The simplicity of the integrated model, in which the logarithm of the scale is a random walk, is particularly appealing. More general models can also be handled. As shown in Section 4.11, smooth trends in volatility can be modelled with cubic splines, and the effects of explanatory variables, including seasonals, can be allowed to change over time.

The performance of the models is illustrated with data on the Dow Jones and Hang Seng stock market indices in Section 4.9. The behavior of the conditional variances produced by the Beta-t-EGARCH model is contrasted with those of the standard EGARCH and GARCH-t models after large shocks, such as the great crash of October 1987. Beta-t-EGARCH gives a better fit. Further evidence on its superior performance is set out in Section 4.14, which extends the model to skewed t distributions.

Section 4.12 discusses a model in which changing scale is combined with changing location. The rate of inflation in the United States provides an illustration. Tests for changing volatility, with and without leverage, are proposed in Section 4.13.

4.1 BETA-t-EGARCH

When the observations have a conditional t distribution,

$$y_t = \varepsilon_t \exp(\lambda_{t|t-1}), \quad t = 1, \dots, T, \tag{4.1}$$

where the serially independent, zero mean variable ε_t has a standard t_ν distribution, that is, $\varphi = 1$ in (2.1). The observations are a martingale difference by construction.

The principal feature of the Beta-t-EGARCH class is that $\lambda_{t|t-1}$ is a linear combination of past values of the MD given by the conditional score

$$u_t = \frac{(\nu + 1)y_t^2}{\nu \exp(2\lambda_{t|t-1}) + y_t^2} - 1, \quad -1 \leq u_t \leq \nu, \quad \nu > 0. \tag{4.2}$$

Figure 1.1 plotted u_t against y_t/σ for t distributions with $\nu = 3$ and 10 and for the normal distribution ($\nu = \infty$).

Proposition 12 *The variable u_t is IID and may be expressed as*

$$u_t = (\nu + 1)b_t - 1, \tag{4.3}$$

where

$$b_t = \frac{y_t^2/\nu \exp(2\lambda_{t|t-1})}{1 + y_t^2/\nu \exp(2\lambda_{t|t-1})}, \quad 0 \leq b_t \leq 1, \quad 0 < \nu < \infty, \tag{4.4}$$

is distributed as $beta(1/2, \nu/2)$, a beta distribution; see Sub-section 2.1.3.

Proof. Because

$$u_t = \frac{(\nu + 1)\varepsilon_t^2}{\nu + \varepsilon_t^2} - 1, \tag{4.5}$$

it depends only on the IID variable, ε_t, and so is itself an IID sequence. The distribution of b_t follows immediately from Corollary 2. ∎

Because $E(b_t) = 1/(\nu + 1)$ and $Var(b_t) = 2\nu/\{(\nu + 3)(\nu + 1)^2\}$, u_t has zero mean and variance

$$\sigma_u^2 = 2\nu/(\nu + 3).$$

In the *Beta-t-EGARCH*(p, r) model, $\lambda_{t|t-1}$ in (4.1) is given by

$$\lambda_{t+1|t} = \delta + \phi_1\lambda_{t|t-1} + \cdots + \phi_p\lambda_{t-p+1|t-p} + \kappa_0 u_t + \kappa_1 u_{t-1} + \cdots + \kappa_q u_{t-r}, \tag{4.6}$$

where $p \geq 0$ and $r \geq 0$ are finite integers. Stationarity (both strict and covariance) of $\lambda_{t|t-1}$ depends on the roots of the autoregressive polynomial lying outside the unit circle, as in (1.17). The implications for stationarity of the observations themselves are determined in Sub-section 4.2.2.

As in earlier chapters, the stationary first-order model,

$$\lambda_{t+1|t} = \delta + \phi\lambda_{t|t-1} + \kappa u_t, \quad |\phi| < 1, \tag{4.7}$$

can be written in terms of the unconditional mean, that is,

$$\lambda_{t+1|t} = \omega(1-\phi) + \phi\lambda_{t|t-1} + \kappa u_t.$$

Leverage effects, which enable $\lambda_{t|t-1}$ to respond asymmetrically to positive and negative values of y_t, will be incorporated into (4.6) in Section 4.3.

4.2 PROPERTIES OF STATIONARY BETA-*t*-EGARCH MODELS

Because the Beta-*t*-EGARCH model belongs to the EGARCH class, we begin by briefly reviewing the classic EGARCH model as introduced by Nelson (1991).

4.2.1 Exponential GARCH

In the EGARCH model

$$y_t = \sigma_{t|t-1}\varepsilon_t, \qquad t = 1, \ldots, T, \tag{4.8}$$

where ε_t is serially independent with unit variance.[1] The logarithm of the conditional variance is given by

$$\ln \sigma^2_{t|t-1} = \omega + \sum_{k=1}^{\infty} \psi_k g(\varepsilon_{t-k}), \quad \psi_1 = 1, \tag{4.9}$$

where ω and ψ_k, $k = 1, \ldots, \infty$, are real and nonstochastic. The $g(\varepsilon_t)'s$ are functions of ε_t, which are IID with zero mean. The model may be generalized by replacing ω by a deterministic function of time, but to do so complicates the exposition unnecessarily. The Beta-*t*-EGARCH model is obtained by equating $g(\varepsilon_t)$ with u_t in (4.5).

The analysis in Nelson (1991), and in almost all subsequent research, focusses on the specification

$$g(\varepsilon_t) = \alpha^*\varepsilon_t + \alpha\left[|\varepsilon_t| - E\,|\varepsilon_t|\right], \tag{4.10}$$

where α and α^* are parameters: the first-order model was given in (1.11). By construction, $g(\varepsilon_t)$ is a zero mean, IID process. Theorem 2.1 in Nelson (1991, p. 351) states that for models (4.8) and (4.9), with $g(\cdot)$ as in (4.10), $\sigma^2_{t|t-1}$, y_t and $\ln \sigma^2_{t|t-1}$ are strictly stationary and ergodic, and $\ln \sigma^2_{t|t-1}$ is covariance stationary if and only if $\sum_{k=1}^{\infty} \psi_k^2 < \infty$. His Theorem 2.2 demonstrates the existence of moments of $\sigma^2_{t|t-1}$ and y_t for the $GED(\upsilon)$ distribution with $\upsilon > 1$. Nelson noted that if ε_t is t_ν distributed, the conditions needed for the existence of the moments of $\sigma^2_{t|t-1}$ and y_t are rarely satisfied in practice.

[1] For a non-normal distribution, ε_t in EGARCH will differ from ε_t in Beta-*t*-EGARCH because in Beta-*t*-EGARCH ε_t is defined to make the scale unity.

Further analysis of the properties of the EGARCH model, including its link to continuous time models, can be found in Nelson and Foster (1994).

4.2.2 Moments

The properties of Beta-*t*-EGARCH may be derived by writing $\lambda_{t|t-1}$ in (4.1) as

$$\lambda_{t|t-1} = \omega + \sum_{k=1}^{\infty} \psi_k u_{t-k}, \tag{4.11}$$

where the $\psi_k' s$ are parameters, as in (4.9), but ψ_1 is not constrained to be unity.

Theorem 6 *For the Beta-t-EGARCH model defined by (4.1) and (4.11) with* $\Sigma\psi_k^2 < \infty$ *and* $0 < \nu < \infty$, $\lambda_{t|t-1}$ *is covariance stationary, the moments of the scale,* $\exp\left(\lambda_{t|t-1}\right)$, *always exist and the m-th moment of* y_t *exists for* $m < \nu$. *Furthermore, for* $\nu > 0$, $\lambda_{t|t-1}$ *and* $\exp\left(\lambda_{t|t-1}\right)$ *are strictly stationary and ergodic, as is* y_t.

Proof. Because u_t has bounded support for finite ν, all its moments exist; see Stuart and Ord (1987 p. 215). Similarly, its exponent has bounded support for $0 < \nu < \infty$ and so $E\left[\exp(au_t)\right] < \infty$ for $|a| < \infty$. Strict stationarity of $\lambda_{t|t-1}$ follows immediately from the fact that the $u_t' s$ are IID. Strict stationarity and ergodicity of y_t hold for the reasons given by Nelson (1991, p. 92) for the EGARCH model. See also He, Teräsvirta and Malmsten (2002). ■

Remark 18 *Long memory may be introduced by premultiplying* $\lambda_{t|t-1}$ *by* $(1-L)^d$, *so providing an alternative to the fractionally integrated EGARCH model of Bollerslev and Mikkelsen (1996). The conditions for Theorem 6 are satisfied by a long-memory model for* $\lambda_{t|t-1}$ *in which* $d < 1/2$.

Remark 19 *It is worth highlighting one of the results of Theorem 6, which is that an unconditional moment of the observations exists whenever the corresponding conditional moment exists. This is not the case for ARCH models in general; see, for example, Sub-section 4.7.1.*

The odd moments of y_t are zero as the distribution of ε_t is symmetric. The next lemma is needed to develop expressions for the even moments and, more generally, for expectations of powers of absolute values.

Theorem 7 *The expectations of powers of absolute values of the observations in the stationary Beta-t-EGARCH model are*

$$E\left(|y_t|^c\right) = \frac{\nu^{c/2}\Gamma(\frac{c}{2}+\frac{1}{2})\Gamma(\frac{-c}{2}+\frac{\nu}{2})}{\Gamma(\frac{1}{2})\Gamma(\frac{\nu}{2})} e^{c\omega} \prod_{j=1}^{\infty} e^{-\psi_j c} \beta_\nu(\psi_j c), \quad -1 < c < \nu. \tag{4.12}$$

where $\beta_\nu(a)$ *is Kummer's (confluent hypergeometric) function,* ${}_1F_1(1/2;$ $(\nu+1)/2; a(\nu+1))$, *that is*

$$\beta_\nu(a) = 1 + \sum_{k=1}^{\infty}\left(\prod_{r=0}^{k-1}\frac{1+2r}{\nu+1+2r}\right)\frac{a^k(\nu+1)^k}{k!}, \qquad 0<\nu<\infty. \tag{4.13}$$

Proof. The first term in

$$E\left(|y_t|^c\right) = E\left(|\varepsilon_t|^c\right) E\left(e^{\lambda_{t|t-1}c}\right), \tag{4.14}$$

is given by (2.12) in Chapter 2 for $-1 < c < \nu$. Because, from (4.11) and (4.3), the last term depends on a linear combination of independent beta variates, it may be written as

$$E\left(e^{\lambda_{t|t-1}m}\right) = e^{m\omega}\prod_{j=1}^{\infty} e^{-\psi_j m} E\left(e^{\psi_j(\nu+1)b_{t-j}m}\right), \tag{4.15}$$

and the expectations evaluated by setting $a = \psi_j m$ in $\beta_\nu(a) = E\left(e^{a(\nu+1)b}\right)$, which is a special case of the MGF of a beta variable, $M_b(a(\nu+1); 1/2,$ $(\nu+1)/2)$ as given by (2.8). ■

Corollary 15 *The even moments of* y_t *in the stationary Beta-t-EGARCH model, that is,* $E(y_t^m)$, $m = 2, 4, \ldots,$ *with* $m < \nu$, *are given by the right-hand side of (4.12) on setting* $c = m$.

Remark 20 *It follows from Jensen's inequality that*

$$E\left(\exp(\lambda_{t|t-1}m)\right) \geq \exp(E(\lambda_{t|t-1}m) = \exp(m\omega). \tag{4.16}$$

Thus the expected value of a time-varying scale, $\exp(\lambda_{t|t-1})$, *is greater than* $\exp(\omega)$. *On comparing each term in the power series expansion of* e^{-a} *with the corresponding term in* $\beta_\nu(a)$, *it can be seen that* $e^{-\psi_j m}\beta_\nu(\psi_j m) \geq 1$ *for finite* ψ_j, *with the equality holding when* $\psi_j = 0$. *For values of* ψ_j *likely to arise in practice,* $e^{-\psi_j m}\beta_\nu(\psi_j m)$ *is close to one. Note also that* $\beta_\nu(-a) < \beta_\nu(a)$ *for* $a \neq 0$.

The serial correlation in scale means that, by Jensen's inequality, the kurtosis in y_t exceeds the kurtosis in ε_t. For a t_ν distribution, the kurtosis is $\kappa_\nu = 3(\nu-2)/(\nu-4)$, $\nu > 4$, and the kurtosis of y_t is given by $\kappa_\nu K_\nu$, where K_ν is obtained as follows.

Corollary 16 *The factor by which the kurtosis increases in the stationary Beta-t-EGARCH model is*

$$K_\nu = \frac{E\left(e^{4\lambda_{t|t-1}}\right)}{\left[E\left(e^{2\lambda_{t|t-1}}\right)\right]^2} = \left(\prod_{j=1}^{\infty}\beta_\nu(2\psi_j)\right)^{-2}\prod_{j=1}^{\infty}\beta_\nu(4\psi_j), \qquad \nu > 4. \tag{4.17}$$

The strength of volatility can be measured by $K_\nu - 1$. For the first-order model, (4.7), where $\psi_k = \kappa\phi^{k-1}$ for $k = 1, 2, \ldots$, typical values of κ and ϕ are 0.03 and 0.98, respectively. In this case, $K_5 = 1.13$, whereas $K_{100} = 1.24$.

Remark 21 *Although the Gaussian distribution corresponds to a t distribution with $\nu = \infty$, the moments of this limiting case of the Beta-t-EGARCH model cannot be obtained from (4.12). However, they are given as a special case of Theorem 9 for the Gamma-GED-EGARCH model of Section 4.4. The $m-th$ even moment of y_t exists if and only if $\psi_j < 1/2m$ for all $j = 1, 2, \ldots$ These restrictions on the ψ_k's are unlikely to be violated for moments up to the fourth. For example, in the first-order model, $\psi_k \leq \kappa$ for all k, and κ is rarely greater than 0.1. Note that this limiting case of the Beta-t-EGARCH model is not the same as Nelson's EGARCH Gaussian model based on (4.10); there the logarithm of the variance depends on the absolute values of standard normal variates rather than their squares.*

4.2.3 Autocorrelation Functions of Squares and Powers of Absolute Values

The ACF of the squared observations and, more generally, their absolute values raised to a positive power is given by the following analytic expression.

Theorem 8 *When $\lambda_{t|t-1}$ is covariance stationary, the ACF of $|y_t|^c$ for $0 < c < \nu/2$ is*

$$\rho(\tau; |y_t|^c) = \frac{G_\nu(\tau, c) - 1}{\kappa_\nu(c)K_\nu(c) - 1}, \quad \tau = 1, 2, \ldots, \tag{4.18}$$

where

$$\begin{aligned}\kappa_\nu(c) &= \frac{E(|\varepsilon_t|^{2c})}{(E(|\varepsilon_t|^c))^2} \\ &= \frac{\Gamma(c+1/2)\Gamma(-c+\nu/2)\Gamma(1/2)\Gamma(\nu/2)}{\{\Gamma(c/2+1/2)\Gamma(-c/2+\nu/2)\}^2}, \quad 0 < c < \nu/2, \end{aligned} \tag{4.19}$$

$$K_\nu(c) = \frac{E\left(e^{2\lambda_{t|t-1}c}\right)}{\left(E\left(e^{\lambda_{t|t-1}c}\right)\right)^2} = \left(\prod_{j=1}^{\infty}\beta_\nu(\psi_j c)\right)^{-2}\prod_{j=1}^{\infty}\beta_\nu(2\psi_j c) \tag{4.20}$$

and, for $\tau = 2, 3, \ldots$,

$$G_\nu(\tau, c) = \beta_{\nu,c}(\psi_\tau c)\left(\prod_{j=1}^{\infty}\beta_\nu(\psi_j c)\right)^{-2}\prod_{j=1}^{\tau-1}\beta_\nu(\psi_j c)\prod_{i=1}^{\infty}\beta_\nu((\psi_{\tau+i}+\psi_i)\,c)$$

or, for $\tau = 1$,

$$G_\nu(1,c) = \beta_{\nu,c}(\psi_1 c)\left(\prod_{j=1}^{\infty}\beta_\nu(\psi_j c)\right)^{-2}\prod_{i=1}^{\infty}\beta_\nu((\psi_{1+i}+\psi_i)\,c),$$

with $\beta_\nu(a)$ *as in (4.13) and*

$$\beta_{\nu,c}(a) = 1+\sum_{k=1}^{\infty}\left(\prod_{r=0}^{k-1}\frac{1+c+2r}{\nu+1+2r}\right)\frac{a^k(\nu+1)^k}{k!}, \qquad 0<\nu<\infty.$$

Proof. See Appendix B.1. ■

Remark 22 *The function* $\beta_{\nu,c}(a)$ *is Kummer's function* ${}_1F_1((1+c)/2;(\nu+1)/2;a(\nu+1))$.

Corollary 17 *When* $c = 2$ *and* $\nu > 4$, *the formula gives the ACF of the squared observations with* $\kappa_\nu(2) = \kappa_\nu = 3\,(\nu-2)\,/\,(\nu-4)$.

The formula for $\rho(\tau;|y_t|^c)$ for the Gaussian model, obtained when $\nu = \infty$, is given is a special case of Theorem 10 for the Gamma-GED-EGARCH model, provided that $\psi_j < 1/2c$, $j = 1, 2, \ldots$.

When $c = 0$, $\rho(\tau;|y_t|^c)$ is indeterminate. However, $c = 0$ corresponds (via the Box-Cox transform) to taking the logarithm of $|y_t|$, and because

$$\ln|y_t| = \lambda_{t|t-1} + \ln|\varepsilon_t|\,, \quad t = 1,\ldots,T, \tag{4.21}$$

it is apparent that the ACF of $\ln|y_t|$ has the same form as that of an ARMA(1,1) process.

4.2.4 Autocorrelations and Kurtosis

The ACF of $\ln|y_t|$ has the form of an $ARMA(p,q)$ process. Thus for the first-order model, $\rho(\tau;\ln|y_t|) = \phi^{\tau-1}\rho(1;\ln|y_t|)$ for $\tau = 1, 2, \ldots$. This relationship holds approximately for $c > 0$. When κ and ϕ are set to 0.03 and 0.98, respectively, in the first-order Gaussian model, the autocorrelations at $\tau = 1, 2$ and 10 for squared observations, that is, $c = 2$, are 0.148, 0.145, and 0.118, respectively. When $c = 1$, that is, absolute values, the corresponding figures are 0.127, 0.124 and 0.104. Heavy tails tend to weaken the autocorrelations. The effect is partly through the kurtosis of $|\varepsilon_t|^{c/2}$, $\kappa_\nu(c)$, which, for a given c, becomes larger as ν decreases. The diminution of the autocorrelations is mitigated by a value of c that is smaller than two. The implications of choosing different values of c are similar to those for the Student's t stochastic volatility model, analyzed in Harvey and Streibel (1998, pp. 180–3). For $\nu = 5$, and κ and ϕ as before, $\rho(1;|y_t|^c)$ is 0.071 for $c = 1$ as opposed to 0.031 for $c = 2$. However, c should not be too small; as $c \to 0$, $\rho(1;|y_t|^c) \to \rho(1;\ln|y_t|) = 0.020$.

He, Teräsvirta and Malmsten (2002) derived expressions for autocorrelations of positive powers of absolute values of the observations in the classic

EGARCH model, (4.8), with first-oder dynamics as in (4.10). The decay of autocorrelations is initially faster than exponential; see Teräsvirta et al. (2010, p. 190). Malmsten and Teräsvirta (2010) showed that the symmetric Gaussian EGARCH is not sufficiently flexible for characterizing series with high kurtosis and slowly changing autocorrelations. See also Teräsvirta et al. (2010, p. 198).

4.3 LEVERAGE EFFECTS

Volatility tends to respond more to falls in stock prices than to rises. One explanation for this phenomenon is that a drop in the share price of a firm will lower the market value and thereby increase the debt-equity ratio. As a result, the risk to investors, as residual claimants, is increased. Hence the term *leverage effect.*

The standard way of incorporating leverage effects into GARCH models is by including a variable in which the squared observations are multiplied by an indicator, $I(y_t < 0)$, taking the value one for $y_t < 0$ and zero otherwise; see Taylor (2005, pp. 220–1). In the Beta-t-EGARCH model, this additional variable is constructed by multiplying $(\nu + 1)b_t = u_t + 1$ by the indicator. Alternatively, the sign of the observation may be used, so the first-order model, (4.7), becomes

$$\lambda_{t+1|t} = \delta + \phi\lambda_{t|t-1} + \kappa u_t + \kappa^* sgn(-y_t)(u_t + 1). \tag{4.22}$$

Taking the sign of *minus* y_t means that the parameter κ^* is normally non-negative for stock returns. With the preceding parameterization, $\lambda_{t+1|t}$ is driven by an MD, as is apparent by writing (4.22) as

$$\lambda_{t+1|t} = \delta + \phi\lambda_{t|t-1} + g(u_t), \tag{4.23}$$

where $g(u_t) = \kappa u_t + \kappa^* sgn(-y_t)(u_t + 1)$. The mean of $\lambda_{t+1|t}$ is as before, that is $\omega = \delta/(1 - \phi)$, but

$$Var(\lambda_{t+1|t}) = \kappa^2\sigma_u^2/(1 - \phi^2) + \kappa^{*2}(\sigma_u^2 + 1)/(1 - \phi^2). \tag{4.24}$$

Although the statistical validity of the model does not require it, the restriction $\kappa \geq \kappa^* \geq 0$ may be imposed to ensure that an increase in the absolute value of a standardized observation does not lead to a decrease in volatility. Figure 4.1 shows the news impact curve of u_t for t_6 with no leverage (thin), moderate leverage (thick) and full leverage (dash). In the case of full leverage, $\kappa = \kappa^*$, and only negative observations affect volatility.

Theorems 6 to 8 may be generalized as follows.

Proposition 13 *When* u_t *in (4.11) is replaced by* $g^\dagger(u_t) = u_t + \kappa^\dagger sgn(-y_t)(u_t + 1)$, *where* $\kappa^\dagger = \kappa^*/\kappa$, *Theorem 6 continues to hold, whereas* $\beta_\nu(\psi_j m)$ *is replaced by*

$$\beta_\nu^*(\psi_j m) = (\beta_\nu(\psi_j(1 + \kappa^\dagger)m)\exp(\kappa^\dagger m) + \beta_\nu(\psi_j(1 - \kappa^\dagger)m)\exp(-\kappa^\dagger m))/2, \quad j = 1, 2, 3, \ldots,$$

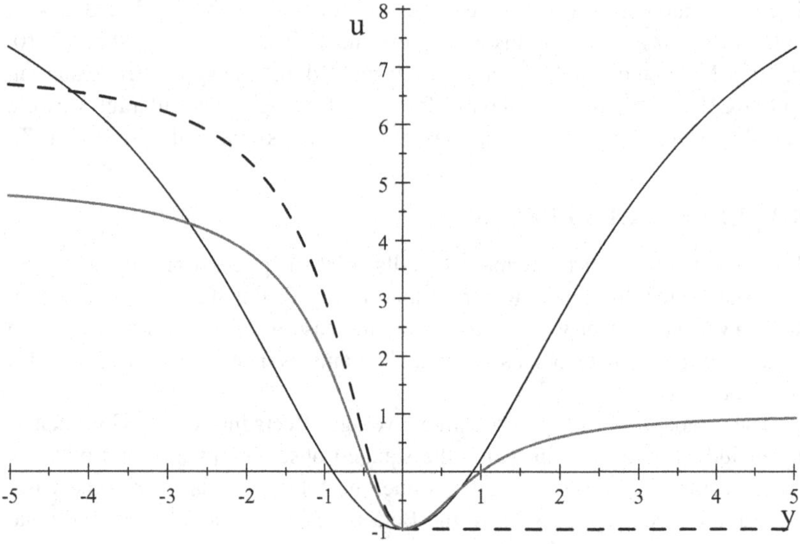

Figure 4.1. Impact of score for t_6 distribution with no leverage (thin), moderate leverage (thick) and full leverage (dash).

in equation (4.15) of Theorem 7. A similar change is made to $\beta_{\nu,c}(\psi_\tau c)$ in the expression for $\rho(\tau; |y_t|^c)$ in Theorem 8.

Proof. The probability that y_t is positive is one-half and b_t is independent of the sign of y_t. Hence replacing $(\nu+1)b_t$ in (4.15) by $g^{\dagger}(u_t) - 1 = (\nu+1)b_t + \kappa^{\dagger} sgn(-y_t)(\nu+1)b_t$ yields (4.12) with $\beta_\nu(\psi_j m/2)$ replaced by $\beta^*_\nu(\psi_j m/2)$. ■

Using the sign rather than the indicator means that the terms within the product in the moment formula, (4.12), remain close to one. When $\psi_j > 0$, $\beta^*_\nu(\psi_j m) > \beta_\nu(\psi_j m)$ so the moments are inflated[1] by a positive κ^*, provided that $\psi_j > 0$ for all j. For the first-order model, (4.22), with $\nu = 5$ together with $\kappa = 0.03$ and $\phi = 0.98$, the factor by which kurtosis increases goes up from $K_5 = 1.129$ to 1.141 when $\kappa^{\dagger} = 0.2$ and to 1.465 when $\kappa^{\dagger} = 1$.

Leverage effects modelled by (4.22) in Beta-t-EGARCH do not induce skewness in the unconditional distribution. However, leverage can increase skewness when it is present in the conditional distribution; see Section 4.14.

A regression of squared observations on the sign of the previous observation is sometimes used as the basis of a simple test for asymmetric effects on conditional volatility; see[2] Engle and Ng (1993). The correlation which leverage induces between $|y_t|^c$ and $sgn(y_{t-1})$ is, therefore, of some interest.

[1] The result follows from applying the inequality $(a+x)^k + (a-x)^k \geq 2a^k$, $a \geq 0$, $|x| \leq a$ and $k > 1$.

[2] Engle and Ng (1993) called this the sign bias test (on raw data). They use the indicator – one if the observation is negative and zero otherwise – rather than the sign.

Proposition 14 *For the Beta-t-EGARCH model of Proposition 13, the correlation between* $|y_t|^c$ *and* $sgn(y_{t-1})$ *for* $0 < c < \nu/2$ *is*

$$\rho(|y_t|^c, sgn(y_{t-1}))$$

$$= \frac{\beta_\nu(\psi_1(1-\kappa^\dagger)c)) - \beta_\nu(\psi_1(1+\kappa^\dagger)c))}{2\left(\left(\kappa_\nu(c)\prod_{j=1}^{\infty}\beta_\nu^*(2\psi_j c) - \left(\prod_{j=1}^{\infty}\beta_\nu^*(\psi_j c)\right)^2\right)\right)^{1/2}} \prod_{j=2}^{\infty}\beta_\nu^*(\psi_j c).$$

This correlation will be negative when $\kappa^\dagger$ is positive. Note that the covariance of $|y_t|^c$ and $sgn(y_{t-1})$ can be interpreted as the difference between the means of $|y_t|^c$ for negative and positive observations. As was shown earlier, the $\rho(\tau; |y_t|^c)'s$ tend to be larger for absolute values than for squares when ν is small. However, this does not seem to be the case for $\rho(|y_t|^c, sgn(y_{t-1}))$. For example, in the first-order model with parameters as in the previous sub-section, the correlations for $c = 2$ and $c = 1$ are -0.0062 and -0.0033, respectively, when $\kappa^\dagger = 0.1$ and -0.050 and -0.031, respectively, when $\kappa^\dagger = 1$.

Engle and Ng (1993) also suggested testing for leverage effects by regressing y_t^2 on y_{t-1} or by a similar regression in which only positive or negative $y_{t-1}'s$ enter the equation. Formulae for the relevant correlations can again be derived.

4.4 GAMMA-GED-EGARCH

In the Gamma-GED-EGARCH model, $y_t \mid Y_{t-1}$ has a general error distribution, (2.3), with time-varying scale parameter $\varphi_{t|t-1} = \exp(\lambda_{t|t-1})$, that is, $\varepsilon_t \sim GED(\upsilon)$ in (4.1), and $\lambda_{t|t-1}$ in (4.6) evolves as a linear function of the conditional score variable

$$u_t = (\upsilon/2)\left|y_t/\exp(\lambda_{t|t-1})\right|^\upsilon - 1, \quad t = 1, \ldots, T. \tag{4.25}$$

The impact curve is shown in Figure 4.2. When $\upsilon = 1$, u_t is a linear function of $|y_t|$. The response is less sensitive to outliers than it is for a normal distribution, but it is far less robust than is Beta-t-EGARCH with small degrees of freedom. More generally, it is clear from (4.25) that u_t is not bounded, although the impact of an extreme observation becomes weaker as υ decreases.

Proposition 15 *The variable* u_t *in (4.25) is IID and may be expressed as*

$$u_t = (\upsilon/2)g_t - 1,$$

where g_t *has a gamma*$(2, 1/\upsilon)$ *distribution; see Lemma 4.*

It follows from the properties of the gamma distribution that the mean of u_t is zero and its variance is υ. When $\lambda_{t|t-1}$ is stationary, the properties of

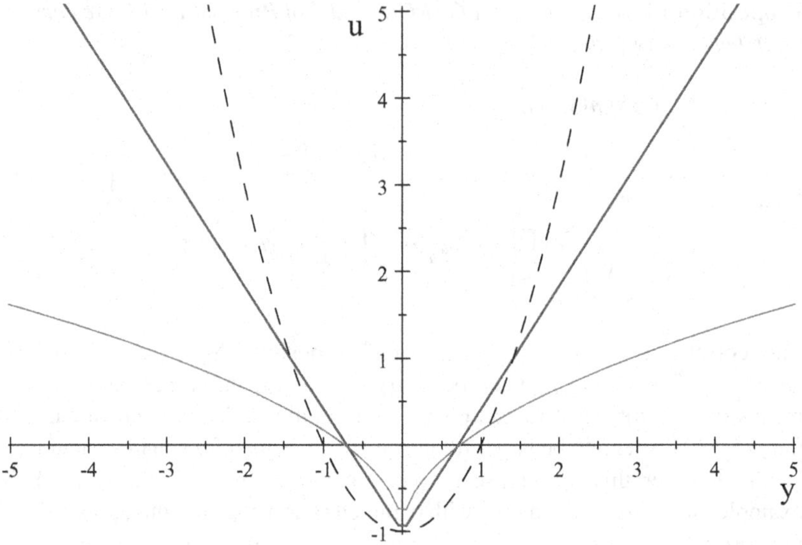

Figure 4.2. Impact of score for GED with $\upsilon = 1$ (thick), $\upsilon = 0.5$ (thin) and $\upsilon = 2$ (dashed).

the Gamma-GED-EGARCH model can be obtained in much the same way as those of Beta-t-EGARCH.

Lemma 14 *Let $\gamma_\upsilon(a) = E(e^{a\upsilon g/2})$, where g has a gamma$(2, 1/\upsilon)$ distribution and a is a constant. Then*

$$\gamma_\upsilon(a) = (1 - a\upsilon)^{-1/\upsilon}, \quad -\infty < a\upsilon < 1, \quad \upsilon > 0. \tag{4.26}$$

Proof. The result follows immediately from the MGF of a gamma variable, (2.11). ∎

Theorem 9 *For the Gamma-GED-EGARCH model defined by (4.1) and (4.11), with u_t as in (4.25), the m-th even moment of y_t exists if and only if $\psi_j < 1/\upsilon m$, for all $j = 1, 2, \ldots$, and is given by the expression*

$$E\left(y_t^m\right) = \frac{2^{m/\upsilon}\Gamma((m+1)/\upsilon)}{\Gamma(1/\upsilon)} e^{m\omega} \prod_{j=1}^{\infty} e^{-m\psi_j}\gamma_\upsilon(m\psi_j), \quad \upsilon > 0. \tag{4.27}$$

Proof. A $GED(\upsilon)$ distributed variable has finite moments. The expression for $E\left(y_t^m\right)$ follows from (4.14) by replacing $(\nu + 1)b_t$ by $(\upsilon/2)g_t$ in (4.15) and using (4.26). ∎

In contrast to the Beta-t-EGARCH model, the changing variance does impose conditions on the existence of moments. It is perhaps surprising that these conditions do not become more stringent as υ becomes smaller, but this is because the heaviness in the tails is offset by the fact that the changing scale depends on the absolute values of observations raised to the υ-th power. In the

EGARCH-GED model analyzed by Nelson (1991), the logarithm of the variance depends on absolute values of the observations for all υ, and the moments for $\upsilon < 1$ can only exist in the unlikely event that residuals that are larger than expected decrease the conditional variance; see Nelson (1991, Appendix 1). On the other hand, the use of absolute values for all υ means that the moments always exist when $\upsilon > 1$; see Theorem 2.2 in Nelson (1991).

The kurtosis for a $GED(\upsilon)$ distribution is $\kappa_\upsilon = \Gamma(5/\upsilon)\Gamma(1/\upsilon)/(\Gamma(3/\upsilon))^2$, and the kurtosis of y_t is $\kappa_\upsilon K_\upsilon$, where K_υ is given below.

Corollary 18 *The factor by which the kurtosis of y_t increases as a result of the changing scale is*

$$K_\upsilon = \left(\prod_{j=1}^{\infty} \gamma_\upsilon(2\psi_j)\right)^{-2} \prod_{j=1}^{\infty} \gamma_\upsilon(4\psi_j), \quad \psi_j < 1/4\upsilon, \quad j = 1, 2, \ldots.$$

The ACFs of powers of absolute values of the observations are given by the following result.

Theorem 10 *When $\lambda_{t|t-1}$ in the Gamma-GED-EGARCH model is covariance stationary, with $\psi_j < 1/\upsilon c$, $j = 1, 2, \ldots$, the expression for $\rho(\tau; |y_t|^c)$ in (4.18) has $\kappa_\upsilon(c)$, $K_\upsilon(c)$ and $G_\upsilon(\tau, c)$ replaced by*

$$\kappa_\upsilon(c) = \frac{\Gamma((2c+1)/\upsilon)\Gamma(1/\upsilon)}{(\Gamma((c+1)/\upsilon))^2}, \qquad 0 < c < \infty,$$

$$K_\upsilon(c) = \left(\prod_{j=1}^{\infty} \gamma_\upsilon(\psi_j c)\right)^{-2} \prod_{j=1}^{\infty} \gamma_\upsilon(2c\psi_j),$$

and, for $\tau = 2, 3, \ldots,$

$$G_\upsilon(\tau, c) = \gamma_{\upsilon,c}(c\psi_\tau)\left(\prod_{j=1}^{\infty} \gamma_\upsilon(\psi_j c)\right)^{-2} \prod_{j=1}^{\tau-1} \gamma_\upsilon(\psi_j c) \prod_{i=1}^{\infty} \gamma_\upsilon((\psi_{\tau+i} + \psi_i)\, c)$$

or, for $\tau = 1$,

$$G_\upsilon(1, c) = \gamma_{\upsilon,c}(c\psi_1)\left(\prod_{j=1}^{\infty} \gamma_\upsilon(\psi_j c)\right)^{-2} \prod_{i=1}^{\infty} \gamma_\upsilon((\psi_{1+i} + \psi_i)\, c),$$

with $\gamma_\upsilon(a)$ as in (4.26) and $\gamma_{\upsilon,c}(a) = E(e^{a\upsilon g/2})$, where g has a gamma(2, $(c+1)/\upsilon$) distribution for $a\upsilon < 1$, so that $\gamma_{\upsilon,c}(a) = (1 - \upsilon a)^{-(c+1)/\upsilon}$ for $\psi_j < 1/\upsilon c$.

Proof. See Appendix B.2. ■

Leverage effects can be introduced as in the Beta-t-EGARCH model. In the first-order case,

$$\lambda_{t+1|t} = \delta + \phi\lambda_{t|t-1} + \kappa u_t + \kappa^* sgn(-y_t)(\upsilon/2)g_t, \qquad (4.28)$$

and the condition for the existence of the m-th even moment is $\kappa + |\kappa^*| < 1/m$. Theorems 9 and 10 generalize as follows.

Proposition 16 *The general Gamma-GED-EGARCH model with leverage has $\lambda_{t|t-1}$ as in (4.11) but with u_t replaced by $g^\dagger(u_t) = u_t + \kappa^\dagger sgn(-y_t)(u_t + 1)$, where $\kappa^\dagger = \kappa^*/\kappa$ and $u_t = (\upsilon/2)g_t - 1$ as in (4.25). The $m-th$ even moment of y_t exists if and only if $\psi_j(1 + |\kappa^\dagger|) < 1/m$, $j = 1, 2, \ldots,$ and expression (4.27) is modified by replacing $\gamma_\upsilon(\psi_j m)$ by*

$$\gamma_\upsilon^*(\psi_j m) = (\gamma_\upsilon(\psi_j(1 + \kappa^\dagger)m) + \gamma_\upsilon(\psi_j(1 - \kappa^\dagger)m))/2, \quad j = 1, 2, 3, \ldots.$$

A similar change is made to $\gamma_{\upsilon,c}(\psi_\tau c)$ in the expression for autocorrelations in Theorem 10.

When $\upsilon = 1$,

$$g(u_t) = \kappa u_t + \kappa^* sgn(-y_t)(\upsilon/2)g_t = (\kappa/2)(|\varepsilon_t| - 2) - (\kappa^*/2)\varepsilon_t$$

has the same form as Nelson's classic (4.10). The condition (A1.7) given by Nelson for the existence of moments when y_t is conditionally $GED(1)$ is the same as in the previous paragraph, although it is framed somewhat differently.[3]

The expression for the correlation between $|y_t|^c$ and the lagged sign, $\rho(|y_t|^c, sgn(y_{t-1}))$, has the same form as for Beta-t-EGARCH.

4.5 FORECASTING

The standard EGARCH model based on (4.10) readily delivers the optimal $\ell-$step ahead forecast – in the sense of minimizing the mean square error – of future logarithmic conditional variance. This forecast is just $E_T(\ln \sigma^2_{T+\ell|T+\ell-1})$, where E_T denotes the expectation based on information at time T. However, as Andersen et al. (2006, pp. 804–5, 810–11) observe, the optimal forecast of the conditional variance, that is $E_T(\sigma^2_{T+\ell|T+\ell-1})$, is difficult to obtain from $E_T(\ln \sigma^2_{T+\ell|T+\ell-1})$. Fortunately, the Beta-$t$-EGARCH and Gamma-GED-EGARCH models are easier to handle: not only can analytic expressions for the conditional scale and variance be found, but so can expressions for higher order moments. The derivations follow along the same lines as those for the moments in Sub-section 4.2.2.

When $\lambda_{t|t-1}$ has a moving average representation, as in (4.11), the independence of the $u_t's$ means that the optimal (MMSE) estimate of

$$\lambda_{T+\ell|T+\ell-1} = \omega + \sum_{j=1}^{\ell-1} \psi_j u_{T+\ell-j} + \sum_{k=0}^{\infty} \psi_{\ell+k} u_{T-k}, \quad \ell = 2, 3, \ldots.$$

[3] In Nelson's model, the logarithm of the variance depends on the observations standardized so as to have unit variance. If these standardized observations are denoted as z, then $\varepsilon = 2\sqrt{2}z$. (The b in Nelson's (A1.7) is a linear function of m.) Hence $g(z)$ in (4.10) is equal to $4\sqrt{2}g(u)$ and so $\alpha = \kappa 2\sqrt{2}$ and $\alpha^* = -\kappa^* 2\sqrt{2}$.

is its conditional expectation

$$\lambda_{T+\ell|T} = \omega + \sum_{k=0}^{\infty} \psi_{\ell+k} u_{T-k}, \quad \ell = 2, 3, \ldots; \tag{4.29}$$

see the discussion in Section 3.9. In the first-order model, (4.7), $\lambda_{T+\ell|T} = \omega + \phi^{\ell-1}(\lambda_{T+1|T} - \omega)$ for $\ell = 1, 2, 3, \ldots$

The median of the predictive distribution of the scale is $\exp(\lambda_{T+\ell|T})$, $\ell = 1, 2, 3, \ldots$. The conditional mean[4] requires an adjustment, the form of which depends on the model.

4.5.1 Beta-*t*-EGARCH

The optimal predictor of volatility, together with its MSE, the volatility of the volatility (VoV), is given by the following result.

Proposition 17 *The MMSE predictor of scale in Beta-t-EGARCH is*

$$E_T\left(e^{\lambda_{T+\ell|T+\ell-1}}\right) = e^{\lambda_{T+\ell|T}} \prod_{j=1}^{\ell-1} e^{-\psi_j} \beta_\nu(\psi_j), \qquad \nu > 0, \quad \ell = 2, 3, \ldots \tag{4.30}$$

where $\lambda_{T+\ell|T}$ is the MMSE predictor of $\lambda_{T+\ell|T+\ell-1}$ and $\beta_\nu(.)$ is Kummer's function. The MSE of the predicted scale is

$$MSE(E_T(e^{\lambda_{T+\ell|T+\ell-1}})) = e^{2\lambda_{T+\ell|T}} \left(\prod_{j=1}^{\ell-1} e^{-2\psi_j} \beta_\nu(2\psi_j) - \left(\prod_{j=1}^{\ell-1} e^{-\psi_j} \beta_\nu(\psi_j) \right)^2 \right).$$

Proof. The conditional expectation of the exponent of $\lambda_{T+\ell|T+\ell-1} m/2$, $m = 1, 2, 3, \ldots$, is

$$E_T\left(e^{\lambda_{T+\ell|T+\ell-1} m}\right) = e^{\lambda_{T+\ell|T} m} \prod_{j=1}^{\ell-1} e^{-\psi_j m} E\left(e^{\psi_j (\nu+1) b_{T+\ell-j} m}\right);$$

compare (4.15). Substituting from (4.13) and setting $m = 1$ gives (4.30). ■

Corollary 19 *The ratio of the root mean square error (RMSE) of the predicted scale to the predicted scale,*

$$R_\nu(\ell) = \left[\left(\prod_{j=1}^{\ell-1} \beta_\nu(\psi_j) \right)^{-2} \left(\prod_{j=1}^{\ell-1} \beta_\nu(2\psi_j) \right) - 1 \right]^{1/2}, \quad \ell = 2, 3, \ldots,$$

is independent of the observations (as is the ratio of the RMSE of the predicted variance to the predicted variance). The limiting value is $R(\infty) = (K_\nu(1) - 1)^{1/2}$, where $K_\nu(1)$ is defined in (4.20), and $R_\nu(\ell) \geq R_\nu(\ell - 1)$.

[4] Although the mean is optimal in the sense of minimizing the predictive MSE, the case for this optimality criterion is weaker when, as here, the predictive distribution is asymmetric.

The inequality $R_\nu(\ell) \geq R_\nu(\ell-1)$ follows from Jensen's inequality, which implies $E_T\left(e^{2\psi_{\ell-1}(\nu+1)b_{T+\ell-1}}\right) \geq (E_T\left(e^{\psi_{\ell-1}(\nu+1)b_{T+\ell-1}}\right))^2$ and hence $\beta_\nu(2\psi_{\ell-1}) \geq (\beta_\nu(\psi_{\ell-1}))^2$. The result is analogous to the property of forecasts in a linear time series model, in which the MSE is monotonically nondecreasing. For $\nu = 5$ and a first-order model with $\kappa = 0.03$ and $\phi = 0.98$, we find $R(2) = 0.034$, $R(3) = 0.048$ and $R(\infty) = 0.172$.

Proposition 18 *The optimal predictor of the variance of* $y_{T+\ell}$ *is*

$$Var_T(y_{T+\ell}) = \frac{\nu}{\nu-2} e^{2\lambda_{T+\ell|T}} \prod_{j=1}^{\ell-1} e^{-2\psi_j} \beta_\nu(2\psi_j), \quad \nu > 2, \quad \ell = 2, 3, \ldots \tag{4.31}$$

and its MSE, assuming $\nu > 4$, *is*

$$Var_T(Var_T(y_{T+\ell})) = \frac{3\nu^2}{(\nu-4)(\nu-2)} e^{4\lambda_{T+\ell|T}} \prod_{j=1}^{\ell-1} e^{-4\psi_j} \beta_\nu(4\psi_j) - (Var_T(y_{T+\ell}))^2. \tag{4.32}$$

When $\ell = 1$, *the terms involving products of* $\beta_\nu(.)$*'s do not appear because* $\lambda_{T+1|T}$ *is known.*

Proof. The conditional variance is $E_T\left(\varepsilon^2_{T+\ell} e^{2\lambda_{T+\ell|T+\ell-1}}\right) = E_T\left(\varepsilon^2_{T+\ell}\right)$ $E_T(e^{2\lambda_{T+\ell|T+\ell-1}})$ and so (4.31) is obtained. The conditional variance of the conditional variance is

$$Var_T(Var_T(y_{T+\ell})) = E_T\left(\varepsilon^4_{T+\ell} e^{4\lambda_{T+\ell|T+\ell-1}}\right) - \left(E_T\left(\varepsilon^2_{T+\ell} e^{2\lambda_{T+\ell|T+\ell-1}}\right)\right)^2.$$

■

When $\lambda_{t|t-1}$ is covariance stationary, $Var_T(y_{T+\ell})$ tends toward the unconditional variance, obtained by setting $m = 2$ in (4.12), as $\ell \to \infty$. The products in (4.30) and (4.31) are typically close to one. It follows from Jensen's inequality that $E_T\left(e^{\lambda_{T+\ell|T+\ell-1}}\right) \geq \exp E_T\left(\lambda_{T+\ell|T+\ell-1}\right) = \exp \lambda_{T+\ell|T}$, so the forecast function will converge to a level greater than $\exp \lambda_{T+\ell|T}$; compare (4.16).

The formulae are modified as indicated in Sub-section 4.4.3 when leverage effects are included. The multistep predictive distributions of $\lambda_{t|t-1}$ and y_t will still be symmetric.

4.5.2 Gamma-GED-EGARCH

Results corresponding to those of the previous sub-section are given next for Gamma-GED-EGARCH. The proposition is stated without proof because the technical details are similar to those of Section 4.4.

Proposition 19 *The optimal predictor of scale, φ, in Gamma-GED-EGARCH is*

$$E_T\left(e^{\lambda_{T+\ell|T+\ell-1}/\upsilon}\right) = e^{\lambda_{T+\ell|T}} \prod_{j=1}^{\ell-1} e^{-\psi_j} \gamma_\upsilon(\upsilon\psi_j), \quad \ell = 2, 3, \ldots.$$

The optimal predictor of the variance of $y_{T+\ell}$ is

$$Var_T(y_{T+\ell}) = \frac{2^{2/\upsilon}\Gamma(3/\upsilon)}{\Gamma(1/\upsilon)} e^{2\lambda_{T+\ell|T}} \prod_{j=1}^{\ell-1} e^{-2\psi_j} \gamma_\upsilon(2\upsilon\psi_j), \quad \ell = 2, 3, \ldots \tag{4.33}$$

and its variance is

$$Var_T(Var_T(y_{T+\ell})) = \frac{2^{4/\upsilon}\Gamma(5/\upsilon)}{\Gamma(1/\upsilon)} e^{4\lambda_{T+\ell|T}} \prod_{j=1}^{\ell-1} e^{-4\psi_j} \gamma_\upsilon(4\upsilon\psi_j) - (Var_T(y_{T+\ell}))^2.$$

Corollary 20 *The ratio of the RMSE of the predicted scale to the predicted scale is*

$$R_\upsilon(\ell) = \left[\left(\prod_{j=1}^{\ell-1} \gamma_\upsilon(2\upsilon\psi_j)\right)\left(\prod_{j=1}^{\ell-1} \gamma_\upsilon(\upsilon\psi_j)\right)^{-2} - 1\right]^{1/2}, \quad \ell = 2, 3, \ldots.$$

For the Gaussian case, $R(2) = 0.045$, $R(3) = 0.063$ and $R(\infty) = 0.225$. For the double exponential (Laplace) distribution, $R(2) = 0.0634$, $R(3) = 0.0$ 90, and $R(\infty) = 0.323$. As before, the fact that $R_\upsilon(\ell) \geq R_\upsilon(\ell - 1)$ follows from Jensen's inequality, but here it can also be verified by taking logarithms and expanding to show that $\gamma_\upsilon(2\psi_{\ell-1}) \geq (\gamma_\upsilon(\psi_{\ell-1}))^2$.

4.5.3 Integrated Exponential Models

When $\phi = 1$, the first-order equation, (4.7), becomes

$$\lambda_{t+1|t} = \delta + \lambda_{t|t-1} + \kappa u_t. \tag{4.34}$$

More generally, $\Delta\lambda_{t|t-1} = \delta + \sum_{k=1}^{\infty} \psi_k u_{t-k}$, as in (4.11). Proposition 17 continues to hold for finite ℓ, but with ψ_j replaced by $\Psi_j = \Sigma_{k=1}^{j} \psi_k$.

For (4.34) $\Psi_j = \kappa$ for all j and because

$$\lambda_{T+\ell|T+\ell-1} = \delta(\ell - 1) + \lambda_{T+1|T} + \kappa \sum_{j=1}^{\ell-1} u_{T+\ell-j}, \quad \ell = 2, 3, \ldots,$$

the multistep forecast is $\lambda_{T+\ell|T} = \delta(\ell - 1) + \lambda_{T+1|T}$. For the Beta-$t$-EGARCH model, the optimal predictor of the scale is

$$E_T\left(e^{\lambda_{T+\ell|T+\ell-1}}\right) = e^{2\lambda_{T+1|T}/2}\prod_{j=1}^{\ell-1} e^{\delta-\kappa}E\left(e^{\kappa(\nu+1)b_{T+\ell-j}}\right) \tag{4.35}$$

$$= e^{\lambda_{T+1|T}}(e^{\delta-\kappa}\beta_\nu(\kappa))^{\ell-1}, \quad \ell = 2, 3, \ldots.$$

Because $\beta_\nu(\kappa)\exp(-\kappa) > 1$ for $\kappa > 0$ – see Remark 7 – the forecasts of the scale will grow exponentially when $\delta = 0$. (The same is true for the forecasts of the variance, where the growth rate, $\ln\beta_\nu(\kappa) - \kappa$, is bigger.) If the preceding predictor of scale is to be constant, then $\exp(\delta - \kappa)\beta_\nu(\kappa)$ must be unity, which requires that

$$\delta = \kappa - \ln\beta_\nu(\kappa) < 0. \tag{4.36}$$

Similarly for Gamma-GED-EGARCH model, $\delta = \kappa - \ln\gamma_\nu(\kappa\upsilon)$.

In contrast to the standard IGARCH model, the random walk in what might be called Beta-t-EIGARCH does not require a (positive) drift term to prevent it converging almost surely to zero; see Nelson (1990). Thus setting $\delta = 0$ is a viable option. The fact that the conditional expectation in (4.35) increases when $\delta = 0$ is not really a cause for concern because the conditional expectation is only optimal in the minimum mean square error sense, and the MSE criterion loses much of its appeal for an asymmetric distribution. The conditional median of the predictive multistep distribution is, of course, constant because it is $\exp(\lambda_{T+1|T})$ for all lead times.

4.5.4 Predictive Distribution

For many purposes, the full predictive distribution of future observations is needed. For example, the quantiles of the predictive distribution are important for assessing risk through the VaR and expected shortfall; see the discussion in Section 1.5. Zhu and Galbraith (2010) provided formulae for quantiles and expected shortfall from a t distribution. The problem of evaluating VaR and expected shortfall more than one step ahead is best approached by simulation.

In the Beta-t-EGARCH model, the distribution of $y_{T+\ell}$, $\ell = 2, 3, \ldots$, conditional on the information at time T, is the distribution of

$$y_{T+\ell} = \varepsilon_{T+\ell}\exp(\lambda_{T+\ell|T+\ell-1}) = \varepsilon_{T+\ell}\left[\prod_{j=1}^{\ell-1} e^{\psi_j((\nu+1)b_{T+\ell-j}-1)}\right]e^{\lambda_{T+\ell|T}}.$$

An analogous expression can be written down for Gamma-GED-EGARCH. Hence it is not difficult to simulate the multistep predictive distribution of the scale and observations; see the discussion in Andersen et al. (2006, pp. 810–11). The term in square brackets is made up of $\ell - 1$ independent beta variates, and this variable can be combined with a draw from a t distribution, $\varepsilon_{T+\ell}$. The composite variable so obtained depends only on the parameters that determine the $\psi'_j s$. Multiplying by $\exp(\lambda_{T+\ell|T})$ gives $y_{T+\ell}$.

The tails of the predictive distribution of $y_{T+\ell}$ become heavier as ℓ increases. The increase in kurtosis for Beta-t-EGARCH, generalizing (4.17), is

$$K_\nu(\ell) = \left(\prod_{j=1}^{\ell-1} \beta_\nu(\psi_j)\right)^{-2} \left(\prod_{j=1}^{\ell-1} \beta_\nu(2\psi_j)\right), \quad \ell = 2, 3, \ldots.$$

Thus ignoring the contribution coming from the variability in the prediction of scale – that is, assuming it is known and just using the conditional t distribution – could be misleading. Note that the existence of moments depends only on the existence of moments of $\varepsilon_{T+\ell}$.

A general discussion of multistep forecasting for nonlinear time series models can be found in Teräsvirta (2006).

4.6 MAXIMUM LIKELIHOOD ESTIMATION AND INFERENCE

The log-likelihood function for the Beta-t-EGARCH model is

$$\ln L(\boldsymbol{\psi}, \nu) = T \ln \Gamma\left((\nu+1)/2\right) - \frac{T}{2}\ln\pi - T\ln\Gamma\left(\nu/2\right) - \frac{T}{2}\ln\nu$$

$$-\sum_{t=1}^{T} \lambda_{t|t-1} - \frac{(\nu+1)}{2}\sum_{t=1}^{T} \ln\left(1 + \frac{y_t^2}{\nu e^{2\lambda_{t|t-1}}}\right).$$

It is assumed that $u_j = 0,\ j \leq 0$ and that $\lambda_{1|0} = \omega$. The ML estimates are obtained by maximizing $\ln L$ with respect to the unknown dynamic parameters, contained in the vector $\boldsymbol{\psi}$, and ν; in the first-order model, $\boldsymbol{\psi}' = (\kappa, \phi, \omega)$. The likelihood function for the Gamma-GED-EGARCH model can be obtained from (2.21) by noting that φ^υ becomes $\exp(\lambda_{t|t-1})$. Andersen et al. (2006, p. 804) observed that a practical drawback to using absolute values, as in (4.10), is that their nondifferentiability at zero makes such EGARCH models 'more difficult to estimate and analyse numerically'. Although this concern might conceivably apply to the estimation of a Gamma-GED-EGARCH model with $\upsilon = 1$, no problems were encountered in the application reported in Section 4.9. For all models, convergence to the maximum was rapid.

Apart from the special case[5] of $EGARCH(0,0)$ analyzed in Straumann (2005, p. 125), no formal theory of the asymptotic properties of ML for EGARCH models has been developed. Nevertheless, ML estimation has been the standard approach to estimation of EGARCH models ever since it was proposed by Nelson (1991).

Straumann and Mikosch (2006) give a definitive treatment of the asymptotic theory for GARCH models. The mathematics are complex. The emphasis is on

[5] In EGARCH(0,0) ϕ is set to zero and so the model is of little or no practical value.

quasi-maximum likelihood, and on page 2452 they state 'A final treatment of the QMLE in EGARCH is not possible at the time being, and one may regard this open problem as one of the limitations of this model.' As will be shown next, the problem lies with the classic formulation of the EGARCH model.

Straumann and Mikosch (2006, p. 2490) also noted the difficulty of deriving analytic formulae for asymptotic standard errors: 'In general, it seems impossible to find a tractable expression for the asymptotic covariance matrix . . . even for $GARCH(1,1)$'. They suggested the use of numerical expressions for the first and second derivatives, as computed by recursions.[6] Further discussion can be found in Francq and Zakoïan (2009, 2010).

4.6.1 Asymptotic Theory for Beta-*t*-EGARCH

It was noted below (4.11) that the $u_t's$ for Beta-t-EGARCH are IID. Differentiating (4.2) gives

$$\begin{aligned}\frac{\partial u_t}{\partial \lambda_{t|t-1}} &= \frac{-2(\nu+1)y_t^2\nu\exp(2\lambda_{t|t-1})}{(\nu\exp(2\lambda_{t|t-1})+y_t^2)^2} \\ &= \frac{-2(\nu+1)y_t^2/\nu\exp(2\lambda_{t|t-1})}{(1+y_t^2/\nu\exp(2\lambda_{t|t-1}))^2} = -2(\nu+1)b_t(1-b_t),\end{aligned}$$

and because, like u_t, this depends only on a beta variable, it is also IID at the true parameter values. All moments of u_t and $\partial u_t/\partial\lambda$ exist, and this is more than enough to satisfy Condition 2.

Proposition 20 *For first-order Beta-t-EGARCH model, (4.7), set*

$$\begin{aligned}a &= \phi - \kappa\frac{2\nu}{\nu+3} \\ b &= \phi^2 - \phi\kappa\frac{4\nu}{\nu+3} + \kappa^2\frac{12\nu(\nu+1)(\nu+2)}{(\nu+7)(\nu+5)(\nu+3)} \\ c &= \kappa\frac{4\nu(1-\nu)}{(\nu+5)(\nu+3)}, \qquad \nu > 0.\end{aligned}$$

Provided that $b < 1$, $\widetilde{\boldsymbol{\psi}}$ *is consistent, and the limiting distribution of* $\sqrt{T}(\widetilde{\boldsymbol{\psi}}' - \boldsymbol{\psi}', \widetilde{\nu} - \nu)'$ *is multivariate normal, with mean vector zero and covariance matrix*

$$Var\begin{pmatrix}\widetilde{\boldsymbol{\psi}} \\ \widetilde{\nu}\end{pmatrix} = \begin{bmatrix} \frac{2\nu}{\nu+3}\mathbf{D}(\boldsymbol{\psi}) & \frac{1}{(\nu+3)(\nu+1)}\begin{pmatrix}0 \\ 0 \\ \frac{1-\phi}{1-a}\end{pmatrix} \\ \frac{1}{(\nu+3)(\nu+1)}\begin{pmatrix}0 & 0 & \frac{1-\phi}{1-a}\end{pmatrix} & h(\nu)/2 \end{bmatrix}^{-1},$$

[6] QML also requires that an estimate of the fourth moment of the standardized disturbances be computed.

where $\mathbf{D}(\psi)$ *is the matrix given in (2.44) or, when the model is parameterized in terms of* ω, *(2.40).*

Proof. Consistency and asymptotic normality follow from Theorem 3. As regards the details, evaluating $E(b^h(1-b)^k)$ from (2.5) gives

$$E_{t-1}\left[\left(\frac{\partial u_t}{\partial \lambda_{t|t-1}}\right)\right] = -2(\nu+1)E(b_t(1-b_t)) = \frac{-2\nu}{\nu+3},$$

which is $-\sigma_u^2$. For b and c,

$$E_{t-1}\left[\left(\frac{\partial u_t}{\partial \lambda_{t|t-1}}\right)^2\right] = 4(\nu+1)^2 E(b_t^2(1-b_t)^2) = \frac{12\nu(\nu+1)(\nu+2)}{(\nu+7)(\nu+5)(\nu+3)}$$

and

$$\begin{aligned} E_{t-1}\left[u_t\left(\frac{\partial u_t}{\partial \lambda_{t|t-1}}\right)\right] &= -2E_{t-1}\left[((\nu+1)b_t-1)(\nu+1)b_t(1-b_t)\right] \\ &= -2(\nu+1)^2E_{t-1}(b_t^2(1-b_t))+2(\nu+1)E_{t-1}(b_t(1-b_t)) \\ &= \frac{-6\nu(\nu+1)}{(\nu+5)(\nu+3)} + \frac{2\nu}{\nu+3} = \frac{4\nu(1-\nu)}{(\nu+5)(\nu+3)}. \end{aligned}$$

These formulae are then substituted in (2.35). The ML estimators of ν and λ are not asymptotically independent in the static model; see the information matrix in (2.18). Hence expression (2.55) is used with $\lambda = \theta_1$ and $\theta_2 = \nu$. ∎

The preceding result does not require the existence of moments of the conditional t distribution. However, a model with $\nu \leq 1$ has no mean and so would probably be of little practical value.

Corollary 21 *When* $\lambda_{t+1|t} = \beta + \lambda_{t|t-1} + \kappa u_t, t = 1, \ldots, T$ *and* $\lambda_{1|0}$ *is fixed and known, it follows from Corollary 8 that, provided that* $b < 1$, *the limiting distribution of* $\sqrt{T}(\widetilde{\kappa} - \kappa, \widetilde{\beta} - \beta)'$ *is multivariate normal with mean zero and covariance matrix* $\mathbf{I}^{-1}(\widetilde{\kappa}, \widetilde{\beta})$, *as in (2.53), with* $a = 1 - 2\kappa\nu/(\nu+3)$ *and*

$$b = 1 - \kappa\frac{4\nu}{\nu+3} + \kappa^2\frac{12\nu(\nu+1)(\nu+2)}{(\nu+7)(\nu+5)(\nu+3)}.$$

When β *is set to zero,*

$$I(\widetilde{\kappa}) = \frac{\sigma_u^4}{2\kappa\sigma_u^2 - \kappa^2 E[(\partial u_t/\partial\lambda)^2]}.$$

In both cases the limiting distribution of $\sqrt{T}(\widetilde{\nu} - \nu)$ is $N(0, 2/h(\nu))$.

Remark 23 *For small* κ, $I(\widetilde{\kappa}) \simeq \sigma_u^2/2\kappa$. *Thus for a* t_ν *distribution, the approximate standard error of* $\widetilde{\kappa}$ *is*

$$SE(\widetilde{\kappa}) \simeq \sqrt{\kappa(\nu+3)/\nu T}, \qquad \kappa > 0. \tag{4.37}$$

The state space forms for higher order models and models with trends and seasonals were given in Section 3.6. For the Beta-t-EGARCH model, $\mathbf{A}(\nu)$ is as in (3.33) and

$$\mathbf{B}(\nu) = \mathbf{T} \otimes \mathbf{T} - \left(\kappa \mathbf{z}' \otimes \mathbf{T} + \mathbf{T} \otimes \kappa \mathbf{z}'\right) \frac{2\nu}{\nu+3} + \kappa \mathbf{z}' \otimes \kappa \mathbf{z}' \frac{12\nu(\nu+1)(\nu+2)}{(\nu+7)(\nu+5)(\nu+3)}.$$

4.6.2 Monte Carlo Experiments

Table 4.1 reports Monte Carlo results, adapted from Harvey and Sucarrat (2012), for the first-order Beta-t-EGARCH model with κ, ϕ, ω, and ν all unknown. The expression for the information matrix indicates that the asymptotic distribution of these parameters does not depend on the value of ω, and this is supported by simulation evidence. For each experiment, which consisted of 1000 replications, the tables show the asymptotic standard error (ASE) for each parameter, together with the numerical root mean square error. The means for each parameter were also computed, but because these are all close to the true values, they are not reported.

For $T = 1000$, the ASE underestimates the RMSE for all parameters except ω. For κ the underestimation is rather small, at most 10%. For ω the bias seems to be in the other direction for ϕ close to one. Again, the difference is rarely more than 10%. For ϕ the ASE can be half the RMSE when ϕ is 0.95 or 0.99, though the underestimation is less serious when κ is bigger. The ASE for ν is not very sensitive to the other parameters, and the ratio of the ASE to the RMSE is around 0.65.

For $T = 10{,}000$, the ASE's and RMSE's for ω, ϕ and κ are all very close. For ν the ratio of the ASE to the RMSE is around 0.8, so convergence to the asymptotic distribution is much slower. However, a zero mean static model gives similar results, so the DCS model is not displaying anything unusual. The empirical distributions of the estimates for $T = 10{,}000$ showed no substantial deviations from normality.

When, in the random walk model, the initial value, $\lambda_{1|0}$, is treated as parameter, ω, to be estimated, it appears from the simulation evidence in Table 4.2 that the asymptotic distribution of the ML estimator of κ is unchanged from that in Corollary 21. The asymptotic standard errors for $\kappa = 0.05$ and 0.10 are 0.0027 and 0.0039, respectively, and these are almost exactly the same as the figures in Table 4.2.

If ϕ is estimated unrestrictedly, it will have a nonstandard distribution. (A reasonable conjecture is that the limiting distribution of $T\widetilde{\phi}$ can be expressed in terms of functionals of Brownian motion, as is the case when a series is a random walk and observations are regressed on their lagged values.) The simulations reported in Table 4.3, where ω, ϕ and κ are all unknown parameters, indicate that the distribution of $\widetilde{\kappa}$ is unchanged, which is to be expected because, unlike $\widetilde{\phi}$, $\widetilde{\kappa}$ is not superconsistent. The parameter ω is not estimated consistently, but this should not affect the asymptotic distribution of $\widetilde{\phi}$ and $\widetilde{\kappa}$.

Table 4.1. *Monte Carlo results based on 1000 replications for first order Beta-t-EGARCH with $\nu = 6$*

Parameter		(a) ML estimates for T = 1000							
ϕ	κ	RMSE(ϕ)	ASE(ϕ)	RMSE(κ)	ASE(κ)	RMSE(ω)	ASE(ω)	RMSE(ν)	ASE(ν)
0.90	0.05	0.075	0.052	0.016	0.016	0.053	0.049	1.357	0.844
	0.10	0.038	0.032	0.018	0.017	0.065	0.069	1.406	0.845
0.95	0.05	0.058	0.024	0.014	0.013	0.069	0.069	1.334	0.844
	0.10	0.019	0.017	0.016	0.015	0.098	0.109	1.332	0.846
0.99	0.05	0.010	0.006	0.010	0.010	0.198	0.226	1.371	0.845
	0.10	0.008	0.005	0.013	0.013	0.312	0.428	1.356	0.846

Parameter		(b) ML estimates for T = 10,000							
ϕ	κ	RMSE(ϕ)	ASE(ϕ)	RMSE(κ)	ASE(κ)	RMSE(ω)	ASE(ω)	RMSE(ν)	ASE(ν)
0.90	0.05	0.0172	0.0163	0.0051	0.0050	0.017	0.015	0.354	0.267
	0.10	0.0104	0.0101	0.0058	0.0055	0.022	0.022	0.336	0.267
0.95	0.05	0.0080	0.0075	0.0041	0.0041	0.021	0.022	0.345	0.267
	0.10	0.0053	0.0052	0.0048	0.0048	0.032	0.034	0.325	0.267
0.99	0.05	0.0018	0.0018	0.0030	0.0031	0.065	0.071	0.343	0.267
	0.10	0.0016	0.0016	0.0041	0.0041	0.118	0.135	0.317	0.268

Table 4.2. *Monte Carlo results based on 1000 replications for Beta-t-EGARCH with ϕ known to be unity and ν known to be* 6

Parameter		Mean and SD for T = 10,000			
ω	κ	Mean (ω)	SD (ω)	Mean (κ)	SD (κ)
0	0.05	0.014	0.309	0.050	0.0027
0	0.10	0.011	0.435	0.100	0.0038

Table 4.3. *Monte Carlo results for Beta-t-EGARCH with $\phi = 1$, but estimated, and ν known to be* 6

Parameter		Mean and SD for T = 10,000					
ω	κ	Mean (ω)	SD (ω)	Mean (κ)	SD (κ)	Mean (ϕ)	SD (ϕ)
0	0.05	0.012	0.313	0.050	0.0027	1.000	0.00033
0	0.10	0.020	0.435	0.100	0.0038	1.000	0.00031

4.6.3 Gamma-GED-EGARCH

The log-likelihood function for a Gamma-GED-EGARCH model with zero mean is

$$\ln L(\mu, \lambda, \upsilon) = -T\left(1+\upsilon^{-1}\right)\ln 2 - T\ln\Gamma(1+\upsilon^{-1}) - \sum_{t=1}^{T}\lambda_{t|t-1} - \frac{1}{2}\sum_{t=1}^{T}\left|y_t\exp(-\lambda_{t|t-1})\right|^{\upsilon}.$$

The distribution of u_t, defined in (4.25), is gamma, as is that of its derivative,

$$\frac{\partial u_t}{\partial \lambda_{t|t-1}} = -(\upsilon^2/2)\left|y_t\right|^{\upsilon} / \exp(\lambda_{t|t-1}\upsilon) = -(\upsilon^2/2)g,$$

and the asymptotic distribution of the ML estimators can be obtained from the results of Chapter 2.

Proposition 21 *For the stationary first-order Gamma-GED-EGARCH model, (4.25), define*

$$a = \phi - \kappa\upsilon$$
$$b = \phi^2 - 2\phi\kappa\upsilon + \kappa^2\upsilon^2(\upsilon+1)$$
$$c = -\kappa\upsilon^2.$$

For a given value of υ and provided that $b < 1$, $\widetilde{\psi}$ is consistent, and the limiting distribution of $\sqrt{T}(\widetilde{\psi} - \psi)'$ is multivariate normal, with zero mean and covariance matrix as in (2.46), with $k = 1$ and $\sigma_u^2 = \upsilon$.

Proof. Taking conditional expectations and using Corollary 3, that is, $E(g^k) = 2^k\Gamma(k+\upsilon^{-1})/\Gamma(\upsilon^{-1})$. the derivative of u_t gives $-\upsilon$, which is $-\sigma_u^2$. In addition,

$$E_{t-1}\left[\left(\frac{\partial u_t}{\partial \lambda_{t|t-1}}\right)^2\right] = (\upsilon^2/2)^2 E_{t-1}\left(g_t^2\right) = \upsilon^2(\upsilon+1)$$

and

$$E_{t-1}\left[u_t\left(\frac{\partial u_t}{\partial \lambda_{t|t-1}}\right)\right] = -\frac{\upsilon^3}{4}E(g_t^2) + \frac{\upsilon^2}{2}E(g_t) = -\upsilon^2.$$

Consistency and asymptotic normality follow from Theorem 4. ■

Remark 24 *As with the Beta-t-EGARCH model, the asymptotic distribution of the dynamic parameters changes when υ is estimated because the ML estimators of υ and λ are not asymptotically independent in the static model; see Sub-section 2.2.2.*

For a Gaussian conditional distribution, $\upsilon = 2$ and so $b = \phi^2 - 4\phi\kappa + 12\kappa^2$ and $a = \phi - 2\kappa$. Hence $b > a^2$, whereas for the Gaussian location model $b = a^2$; see Corollary 14. These expressions for a and b are also given by letting $\nu \to \infty$ in Proposition 20. For the Laplace, $\upsilon = 1$ and $b = \phi^2 - 2\phi\kappa + 2\kappa^2$, which, perhaps surprisingly, permits a wider range for κ than does the normal, even though (or perhaps because) the Laplace distribution has heavier tails.

Figure 4.3 shows b plotted against κ for $\phi = 0.98$ and t_6, normal and Laplace distributions. Because κ is typically less than 0.1, the constraint imposed by b is unlikely ever to be violated. Indeed, the measure of volatility based on the increase in kurtosis, (4.17), would be unreasonably high if κ were too large. Note that, as the degrees of freedom falls, the t distribution can accommodate a wider range of values for κ.

Remark 25 *When the constant term in the dynamic equation is taken to be ω rather than δ, it may be concentrated out of the likelihood function because, from (2.22),*

$$\widetilde{\omega}(\phi,\kappa,\upsilon) = \frac{1}{\upsilon}\ln\left(\frac{\upsilon}{2}\frac{\sum\left|y_t\exp(-\lambda^{\dagger}_{t|t-1})\right|^{\upsilon}}{T}\right),$$

where $\lambda^{\dagger}_{t+1|t} = \phi\lambda^{\dagger}_{t|t-1} + \kappa u_t$, *with* $\lambda^{\dagger}_{1|0} = 0$, *and* $\lambda_{t|t-1} = \omega + \lambda^{\dagger}_{t|t-1}$.

4.6.4 Leverage

When leverage effects are present, the asymptotic theory for Beta-t-EGARCH and Gamma-GED-EGARCH continues to hold, but with some additional

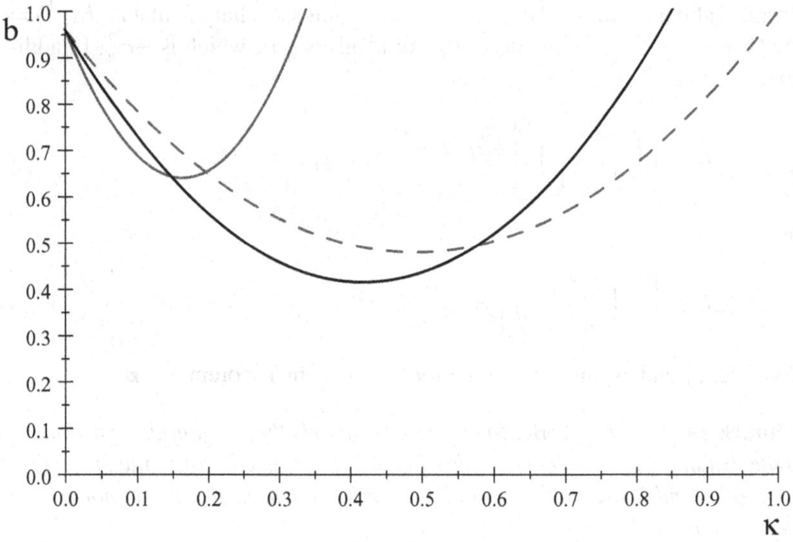

Figure 4.3. b against κ for $\phi = 0.98$ and (i) *t distribution* with $\nu = 6$ (solid), (ii) normal (upper line), and (iii) Laplace (thick dash).

complexity for the information matrix expression. The formula for b is modified by replacing κ^2 by $\kappa^2 + \kappa^{*2}$ to give

$$b^* = \phi^2 + 2\phi\kappa E\left(\frac{\partial u_t}{\partial \lambda}\right) + (\kappa^2 + \kappa^{*2})E\left(\frac{\partial u_t}{\partial \lambda}\right)^2. \tag{4.38}$$

Consistency and asymptotic normality follow from the general results in Section 2.3.5.

Proposition 22 *Provided that $b^* < 1$ and that there are no unknown parameters apart from those in the dynamic equation, (4.22), parameterized in terms of $\omega = \delta/(1-\phi)$, the covariance matrix of the limiting distribution of $\sqrt{T}(\widetilde{\psi} - \psi)$ is*

$$Var\begin{pmatrix}\widetilde{\kappa}\\ \widetilde{\phi}\\ \widetilde{\omega}\\ \widetilde{\kappa}^*\end{pmatrix} = \frac{1-b^*}{\sigma_u^2}\begin{bmatrix} A & D & E & 0\\ D & B^* & F^* & D^*\\ E & F^* & C & E^*\\ 0 & D^* & E^* & A^*\end{bmatrix}^{-1}, \tag{4.39}$$

where A, C, D and E are as in (2.40), F^* is F with κc expanded to become $\kappa c + \kappa^* c^*$,

$$A^* = \sigma_u^2 + 1$$

$$B^* = \frac{\left(\kappa^2\sigma_u^2 + \kappa^{*2}(\sigma_u^2 + 1)\right)(1 + a\phi)}{(1 - \phi^2)(1 - a\phi)}$$

$$E^* = c^*(1 - \phi)/(1 - a)$$

$$D^* = \frac{a\kappa^*(\sigma_u^2 + 1)}{1 - a\phi},$$

with a as in (2.35), but b and c modified to become (4.38) and

$$c^* = \kappa^* E\left(u_t \frac{\partial u_t}{\partial \lambda}\right) + \kappa^* E\left(\frac{\partial u_t}{\partial \lambda}\right).$$

Proof. The derivative with respect to the leverage parameter is

$$\frac{\partial \lambda_{t+1|t}}{\partial \kappa^*} = \phi \frac{\partial \lambda_{t|t-1}}{\partial \kappa^*} + \kappa \frac{\partial u_t}{\partial \kappa^*} + \kappa^* sgn(-y_t) \frac{\partial u_t}{\partial \kappa^*} + sgn(-y_t)(u_t + 1)$$

$$= x_t^* \frac{\partial \lambda_{t|t-1}}{\partial \kappa^*} + sgn(-y_t)(u_t + 1), \tag{4.40}$$

where

$$x_t^* = \phi + \left(\kappa + \kappa^* sgn(-y_t)\right) \frac{\partial u_t}{\partial \lambda_{t|t-1}}.$$

The derivatives in (2.32) are similarly modified by the addition of the derivatives of the leverage term, so x_t^* replaces x_t in all cases. However, because y_t is symmetric and u_t depends only on y_t^2,

$$E_{t-1}(x_t^*) = \phi + E_{t-1}\left((\kappa + \kappa^* sgn(-y_t)) \frac{\partial u_t}{\partial \lambda_{t|t-1}}\right) = a$$

and the formulae for the expectations in (2.36) are unchanged. As regards (4.40), $E(sgn(-y_t)(u_t + 1)) = 0$ so

$$E\left(\frac{\partial \lambda_{t+1|t}}{\partial \kappa^*}\right) = 0.$$

The expected values of the squares and cross-products in the extended information matrix are obtained in much the same way as in Appendix A.1. Note that

$$x_t^* sgn(-y_t)(u_t + 1) = (\phi + ((\kappa + \kappa^* sgn(-y_t)) \frac{\partial u_t}{\partial \lambda_{t|t-1}})(sgn(-y_t)(u_t + 1))$$

$$= \left(\phi + \kappa \frac{\partial u_t}{\partial \lambda_{t|t-1}}\right)(sgn(-y_t)(u_t + 1) + \kappa^* \frac{\partial u_t}{\partial \lambda_{t|t-1}}(u_t + 1),$$

so

$$c^* = E_{t-1}(x_t^* sgn(-y_t)(u_t+1)) = \kappa^* E_{t-1}\left(\frac{\partial u_t}{\partial \lambda_{t|t-1}}(u_t+1)\right).$$

The formula for b^* is similarly derived. The derivation of B^* is sketched out in Appendix A.3. ■

For the Beta-t-EGARCH model

$$b^* = \phi^2 - \kappa\phi\frac{4\nu}{\nu+3} + (\kappa^2+\kappa^{*2})\frac{12\nu(\nu+1)(\nu+2)}{(\nu+7)(\nu+5)(\nu+3)},$$

and

$$c^* = \kappa^*\frac{4\nu(1-\nu)}{(\nu+5)(\nu+3)} + \kappa^*\frac{2\nu}{\nu+3}$$

When ν is estimated, the asymptotic covariance matrix of the full set of parameters can be found by modifying the covariance matrix as in Proposition 20. The formulae for Gamma-GED-EGARCH may be similarly adapted.

Remark 26 *When there is no leverage effect, $\kappa^* = 0$ and so $c^* = D^* = E^* = 0$. Hence*

$$Var\left(\widetilde{\kappa}^*\right) = (1-b)(\sigma_u^2+1)/\sigma_u^2. \tag{4.41}$$

A Wald test of the null hypothesis that $\kappa^* = 0$ can be constructed from (4.41) or from the estimated covariance matrix in the fitted model. Either way, the alternative hypothesis will usually be $\kappa^* > 0$, so the test will be one-sided. If a likelihood ratio (LR) test is to be carried out, it should be noted that, for a one-sided alternative of this kind, the asymptotic distribution of the LR statistic is not χ_1^2, but rather a mixture of χ_1^2 and χ_0^2 leading to a test at the α% level of significance being based on the 2α% significance points. The construction of a Lagrange multiplier test is discussed briefly in Sub-section 4.13.3.

Remark 27 *If $\kappa = \kappa^*$, the only dynamic volatility effects are from negative returns. A Wald or LR test of this hypothesis against $\kappa \neq \kappa^*$ can be carried out in the usual way. If the constraint $\kappa = \kappa^*$ is imposed, the asymptotic covariance of the ML estimator of $(\widetilde{\phi}, \widetilde{\omega}, \widetilde{\kappa}^*)$ is as in (4.39), but with $\sigma_u^2 + 1$ replaced by $2\sigma_u^2 + 1$ in A^* and E^*.*

Finally, note that the asymptotic distributional theory for the δ parameterization can be developed in a similar way. The main result is stated below.

Proposition 23 *For the first-order model with leverage, (4.22), the covariance matrix of the limiting distribution of $\sqrt{T}(\widetilde{\psi} - \psi)$ is*

$$Var\begin{pmatrix}\widetilde{\kappa}\\ \widetilde{\phi}\\ \widetilde{\delta}\\ \widetilde{\kappa}^*\end{pmatrix} = \frac{k^2(1-b^*)}{\sigma_u^2}\begin{bmatrix} A & D & E & 0\\ D & B^* & F^* & D^*\\ E & F^* & C & E^*\\ 0 & D^* & E^* & A^*\end{bmatrix}^{-1}, \qquad b^* < 1,$$

where A, C, D *and* E *are as in (2.44),* F^* *is* F *with* κc *expanded to become* $\kappa c + \kappa^* c^*$*, and*

$$A^* = \sigma_u^2 + 1$$

$$B^* = \frac{2a\delta(\delta + \kappa c)}{(1-\phi)(1-a)(1-a\phi)} + \frac{1+a\phi}{(1-a\phi)(1-\phi)}\left(\frac{\delta^2}{1-\phi} + \frac{\kappa^2\sigma_u^2}{1+\phi} + \frac{\kappa^{*2}(\sigma_u^2+1)}{1+\phi}\right)$$

$$E^* = c^*/(1-a)$$

$$D^* = \frac{\delta c^*}{(1-\phi)(1-a)} + \frac{a\kappa^*(\sigma_u^2+1)}{1-a\phi}.$$

with a, b^* *and* c^* *as in Proposition 22.*

4.7 BETA-*t*-GARCH

If an exponential link function is not used, then

$$y_t = \sigma_{t|t-1} z_t, \quad \nu > 2, \quad t = 1, \ldots, T, \tag{4.42}$$

where $z_t = ((\nu-2)/\nu)^{1/2}\varepsilon_t$ has a t_ν distribution, but standardized so as to have unit variance. For $\nu > 2$, the *Beta-t-GARCH*(1, 1) model is

$$\sigma_{t+1|t}^2 = \delta + \phi\sigma_{t|t-1}^2 + \kappa\sigma_{t|t-1}^2 u_t, \quad \delta > 0,\ \phi \geq 0,\ \kappa \geq 0, \tag{4.43}$$

where u_t is as in (1.15). The model can be rewritten as

$$\sigma_{t+1|t}^2 = \delta + \beta\sigma_{t|t-1}^2 + \alpha\sigma_{t|t-1}^2(\nu+1)b_t, \quad \delta > 0, \beta \geq 0,\ \alpha \geq 0,$$

where $(\nu+1)b_t = u_t + 1$, $\alpha = \kappa$ and $\beta = \phi - \kappa$. In the limit as $\nu \to \infty$, $\sigma_{t|t-1}^2(\nu+1)b_t = y_t^2$ leading to the standard *GARCH*(1, 1) specification.

Some properties of the *Beta-t-GARCH*(1, 1) model are given in the next subsection. There is nothing fundamentally new in these results: known formulae are simply adapted to take account of the moments of u_t. The properties of the Gamma-GED-GARCH model can be derived in a similar way. Generalization to higher order models is less straightforward than it is for the exponential models of the previous sections.

4.7.1 Properties of First-Order Model

Proposition 24 *If* $Ez_t^j < \infty$*, a necessary and sufficient condition for the existence of the j-th moment of* y_t *is*

$$E(\phi + \kappa u_t)^{j/2} < 1, \quad j = 2, 4, \ldots.$$

Proof. The model is a member of the class of models defined by He and Teräsvirta (1999) in which $\sigma_{t|t-1}$ in (4.42) is given by

$$\sigma_{t|t-1}^d = a(z_{t-1}) + c(z_{t-1})\sigma_{t-1|t-2}^d. \tag{4.44}$$

He and Teräsvirta (1999) stated the condition for the existence of moments in terms of $c(z_t)$, that is, $E[c(z_t)]^{j/2} < 1,\ j = 2, 4, \ldots$. In (4.43), $d = 2$, $a(z_t) = \delta$ and $c(z_t) = \phi + \kappa u_t$. ■

From He and Teräsvirta (1999), y_t is strictly stationary and ergodic if $E(\phi + \kappa u_t) = \phi < 1$; see also Theorem 1 in Ling and McAleer (2002). Furthermore, y_t is second-order stationary if $\nu > 2$.

The condition for the existence of the fourth moment is

$$\phi^2 + \kappa^2 E(u_t^2) = \phi^2 + \kappa^2 \frac{2\nu}{\nu + 3} < 1, \quad \nu > 4, \tag{4.45}$$

or, if we let $c(z_t) = \beta + \alpha(\nu + 1)b_t$,

$$\beta^2 + 2\alpha\beta + \frac{3\alpha^2(\nu + 1)}{\nu + 3} < 1, \quad \nu > 4.$$

The corresponding condition for GARCH-t is

$$\phi^2 + \kappa^2 \left(\frac{3(\nu - 2)}{\nu - 4} - 1 \right) = \phi^2 + \kappa^2 \frac{2(\nu - 1)}{\nu - 4} < 1, \quad \nu > 4. \tag{4.46}$$

In the limit as $\nu \to \infty$, the preceding expressions all tend to the standard Gaussian $GARCH(1, 1)$ condition for the existence of fourth moments. The difference is that for Beta-t-GARCH, the coefficient of κ^2 is less than two for finite ν, whereas in (4.46), it is greater than two.

Proposition 25 *When the fourth moment of y_t exists, the factor by which the kurtosis of y_t exceeds that of z_t, or equivalently ε_t, is*

$$K_\nu^* = \frac{E\left(\sigma_{t|t-1}^4\right)}{\left(E\sigma_{t|t-1}^2\right)^2} = \frac{1 - \phi^2}{1 - \phi^2 - \kappa^2 2\nu/(\nu + 3)}.$$

The values of K_ν^* for $\nu = 5$ and $\nu = 100$ are 1.13 and 1.21, respectively. These figures are close to the figures quoted for K_ν in Sub-section 4.2.2. The kurtosis in y_t is $\kappa_\nu(2)K_\nu^*$, where $\kappa_\nu(2)$ is as defined in (4.19). For a normal distribution, subtracting three from κ_y yields the formula, given by Bollerslev (1986), for the excess kurtosis in a Gaussian model.

As in the standard GARCH(1,1) model, the autocorrelation function of *Beta-t-GARCH*(1, 1) is of the form $\rho(\tau; y_t^2) = \phi^{\tau-1}\rho(1; y_t^2)$ for $\tau \geq 1$, but $\rho(1; y_t^2)$ now depends on ν as well as ϕ and κ.

Proposition 26 *The autocorrelation function of the squared observations in the Beta-t-GARCH*(1, 1) *model with $0 < \phi < 1$ is*

$$\rho(\tau; y_t^2) = \frac{\phi^{\tau-1}(\phi + 2\kappa)K_\nu^* - \phi^\tau}{\kappa_\nu(2) - 1}, \quad \tau = 1, 2, \ldots. \tag{4.47}$$

The formula reduces to that of the standard GARCH(1, 1) *model in the limit as $\nu \to \infty$.*

Proof. See Appendix B.3. ■

Forecasts of the conditional variance more than one step ahead can be made for Beta-*t*-GARCH models, as in standard GARCH case, by using the law of iterated expectations. However, in contrast to Beta-*t*-EGARCH, the variables driving the dynamics, the $\sigma^2_{t|t-1}u_t's$ in (4.43), are not IID.

4.7.2 Leverage Effects

The Beta-*t*-GARCH model may be extended to include leverage effects by adding the indicator variable $I(y_t < 0)(\nu + 1)b_t$. When (4.43) is modified in this way, the model is still a special case of (4.44) with

$$\begin{aligned} c(z_t) &= \beta + \alpha(\nu + 1)b_t + \alpha^* I(y_t < 0)(\nu + 1)b_t \\ &= \beta + \{\alpha + \alpha^* I(y_t < 0)\}(\nu + 1)b_t. \end{aligned}$$

Hence the condition for the existence of the second moment, assuming $\nu > 2$, is now $\alpha + \beta + \alpha^*/2 < 1$, whereas the fourth moment exists if

$$\beta^2 + 2\alpha\beta + \frac{3(\alpha^2 + \alpha\alpha^* + \alpha^{*2}/2)(\nu + 1)}{\nu + 3} < 1, \quad \nu > 4. \tag{4.48}$$

Modelling leverage effects with an equivalent specification in terms of the sign of y_{t-1}, as in (4.22), is not a good option here, as there is nothing to prevent the conditional variance from becoming negative.

4.7.3 Link with Beta-*t*-EGARCH

A Taylor series expansion of the conditional variance in the Beta-*t*-EGARCH model gives

$$\begin{aligned} \sigma^2_{t|t-1} &= \{\nu/(\nu - 2)\}e^{2\lambda_{t|t-1}} = \{\nu/(\nu - 2)\}e^{2\omega}e^{2\lambda_{t|t-1}-2\omega} \\ &= \{\nu/(\nu - 2)\}e^{2\omega}(1 + 2(\lambda_{t|t-1} - \omega) + 2(\lambda_{t|t-1} - \omega)^2 + \ldots). \end{aligned} \tag{4.49}$$

If higher order terms are negligible,

$$\sigma^2_{t|t-1} \simeq \{\nu/(\nu - 2)\}e^{2\omega}(1 + 2\sum_{i=1}^{\infty} \psi_i u_{t-i}).$$

Because $E(\sigma^2_{t|t-1}) \simeq \{\nu/(\nu - 2)\}e^{2\omega}$, it follows that, if the variation around $E(\sigma^2_{t|t-1})$ is relatively small,

$$\sigma^2_{t|t-1} \simeq \{\nu/(\nu - 2)\}e^{2\omega} + 2\sum_{i=1}^{\infty} \psi_i \sigma^2_{t-i|t-1-i} u_{t-i}.$$

In the Beta-*t*-EGARCH(1, 0) model $\psi_i = \kappa\phi^{i-1}$ so

$$\sigma^2_{t|t-1} \simeq \{\nu/(\nu - 2)\}e^{2\omega}(1 - \phi) + \phi\sigma^2_{t-1|t-2} + 2\kappa\sigma^2_{t-1|t-2}u_{t-1}. \tag{4.50}$$

The preceding expression suggests that a *Beta-t-GARCH*$(1,1)$ model, with $\delta = \{\nu/(\nu-2)\}e^{2\omega}(1-\phi)$, can be regarded as approximating a *Beta*-t-*EGARCH*$(1,0)$ model with similar values of ϕ and ν, but δ (or ω) and κ roughly twice the size. Similarly, if a leverage term is added, κ^* will be approximately double the value in Beta-t-EGARCH. These expectations are borne out by the results reported in the next section.

The closeness of Beta-t-GARCH and Beta-t-EGARCH models is a point in favour of the exponential formulation. The Beta-t-EGARCH parameters do not need to be constrained to ensure that the variance is positive, and whether or not particular moments exist is immediately apparent from the degrees of freedom of the fitted t distribution.

The fact that $E(\lambda_{t|t-1}-\omega)^2$ is proportional to $2\nu/(\nu+3)$ suggests that the quadratic term in (4.49) will be smaller for smaller ν, thereby leading to a closer approximation. On a related point, it might be thought that the Gaussian exponential model is ruled out by the exponentiation of large squared (standardized) observations. However, as was noted after Proposition 25, the strength of volatility in a *Beta-t-GARCH*$(1,1)$ model with high ν is only slightly less than it is for a *Beta-t-EGARCH*$(1,0)$ model with the same ϕ and κ. Presumably, if the true model really is (close to) Gaussian, the chance of an extreme observation arising and causing a big increase in volatility is rather small.

4.7.4 Estimation and Inference

For recent discussions of the asymptotics of the Gaussian *GARCH*$(1,1)$ model, see Fiorentina et al. (1996) and, more generally, the paper by Straumann and Mikosch (2006) and the book by Francq and Zakoïan (2010). As observed earlier, analytic expressions for the information matrix of GARCH models cannot be obtained. Note that it is usually necessary for the fourth moment of the conditional distribution to exist if the ML estimators are to have the standard asymptotic properties.

The asymptotic result in Chapter 2 does not apply to Beta-t-GARCH models, as the information matrix in the static model depends on σ^2. Hence the condition for Lemma 5 does not hold. However, it should be possible to find the conditions under which the ML estimators are asymptotically normal by adapting the argument in Straumann and Mikosch (2006). Analytic standard errors could be computed numerically.

4.7.5 Gamma-GED-GARCH

The Gamma-GED-GARCH model is as in (4.42), with the dynamic equation, corresponding to (4.43) in the first-order case, driven by

$$u_t = (\upsilon/2)\left|y_t/\sigma_{t|t-1}\right|^{\upsilon} - 1.$$

The model specification is completed by taking $y_t \mid Y_{t-1}$ to have a *GED*(υ) distribution with conditional variance $\sigma^2_{t|t-1}$. Setting $\upsilon = 2$ gives the GARCH model (1.14). Note that $\sigma^2_{t|t-1}u_t$ in the dynamic equation is the standardized score. The model is similar to models within the *asymmetric power ARCH* class (APARCH) of Ding, Granger and Engle (1993), but with the difference that the conditional distribution of the observations is GED rather than normal. (Leverage effects are also handled differently). Setting $\upsilon = 1$ gives the conditional variance equation proposed by Taylor (1986).

4.8 SMOOTHING

Smoothed volatilities for the first-order Beta-t-EGARCH model may be computed using weights obtained from the Gaussian UC model corresponding to the dynamic equation, (4.7). The weights are computed for each point in time, with a signal-noise ratio obtained from expression (3.55). They are then applied repeatedly to the pseudo-observations,

$$y_t(\lambda_{t|T}) = (\nu+1)b_{t|T} - 1 + \lambda_{t|T}, \qquad t = 1, \dots, T,$$
$$= \frac{(\nu+1)y_t{}^2/\nu \exp(2\lambda_{t|T})}{1 + y_t{}^2/\nu \exp(2\lambda_{t|T})} - 1 + \lambda_{t|T},$$

until convergence. A smoothed set of time-varying scales is given by $\varphi_{t|T} = \exp(\lambda_{t|T})$, $t = 1, \dots, T$. For Gamma-GED-EGARCH,

$$y_t(\lambda_{t|T}) = (\upsilon/2)\left|y_t \exp(-\lambda_{t|T})\right|^{\upsilon} - 1 + \lambda_{t|T}, \qquad t = 1, \dots, T.$$

When the conditional distribution is Gaussian, both the above formulae reduce to $y_t(\lambda_{t|T}) = y_t^2 \exp(-2\lambda_{t|T}) - 1 + \lambda_{t|T}$.

4.9 APPLICATION TO HANG SENG AND DOW JONES

First-order models, with and without leverage, were estimated by ML for the daily de-meaned returns (times 100) of two stock market indices, the Dow Jones Industrial Average and the Hang Seng. The series were obtained from `Yahoo!Finance`; see http://uk.finance.yahoo.com. The Dow Jones data run from 1st October 1975 to 13th August 2009, giving $T = 8548$ returns. The Hang Seng runs from 31st December 1986 to 10th September 2009, giving $T = 5630$. As expected, the returns have heavy tails, and their absolute values and squares show strong serial correlation.

The estimation procedures were programmed in `Ox 5`, and the sequential quadratic programming maximization algorithm for nonlinear functions subject to nonlinear constraints, `MaxSQP` in Doornik (2007), was used throughout. The parameter estimates are presented in Tables 1 to 5, together with the maximized log-likelihood and the AIC, defined as in (2.75) but divided by the sample size. Bayes (Schwartz) information criteria were also calculated, but they are very similar to the AICs and so are not reported.

Table 4.4. *Parameter estimates for Beta-t-EGARCH models with leverage*

	Hang Seng		Dow Jones	
Parameter	Estimates (num. SE)	Asy. SE	Estimates (num. SE)	Asy. SE
δ	0.003 (0.0010)	0.0009	−0.0025 (0.0005)	0.0013
ϕ	0.993 (0.003)	0.0017	0.989 (0.002)	0.0028
κ	0.047 (0.004)	0.0037	0.030 (0.003)	0.0026
κ^*	0.021 (0.003)	0.0027	0.016 (0.002)	0.0019
ν	5.98 (0.45)	0.355	7.64 (0.56)	0.475
a, b	0.931	0.876	0.946	0.898
$\ln L$	−9747.6		−11180.3	
AIC	3.474		2.629	

Table 4.4 reports estimates for *Beta-t-EGARCH*(1, 0), with leverage. The ML estimates and associated numerical standard errors (SEs), obtained from the inverse of the Hessian matrix, were reported in Harvey and Chakravarty (2009). The asymptotic SEs are close to the numerical SEs. For both series, the leverage parameter, κ^*, has the expected (positive) sign. The likelihood ratio statistic is large in both cases, and it easily rejects the null hypothesis that $\kappa^* = 0$ against the alternative that $\kappa^* > 0$; see Sub-section 4.13.3. The same conclusion is reached if the standard errors are used to construct (one-sided) Wald tests based on the standard normal distribution; see Remark 26. The values of b are also given in Table 4.4: for both series b is well below unity.

Table 4.5 shows the results for Gamma-GED-EGARCH. The conclusions with regard to the leverage effect are much the same as for Beta-t-EGARCH. For both series, the log-likelihoods are smaller than for the corresponding Beta-t-EGARCH models.

Table 4.5. *Parameter estimates for Gamma-GED-EGARCH models with and without leverage*

	Hang Seng		Dow Jones	
Parameter	Leverage	No leverage	Leverage	No leverage
δ	−0.008	−0.006	−0.010	−0.007
ϕ	0.974	0.981	0.988	0.990
κ	0.035	0.038	0.019	0.023
κ^*	0.014	–	0.010	–
υ	1.23	1.23	1.31	1.33
$\ln L$	−9773.8	−9801.6	−11230.5	−11258.2
AIC	3.474	3.481	2.629	2.634

Table 4.6. *Parameter estimates for standard EGARCH models*

	Hang Seng		Dow Jones	
Parameter	Gaussian	GED	Gaussian	GED
$\delta^{\dagger}$	0.8039	0.8268	0.8030	0.8002
ϕ	0.963	0.975	0.982	0.987
α	0.244	0.199	0.133	0.115
α^{*}	−0.103	−0.076	−0.068	−0.054
υ	2 (fixed)	1.25	2 (fixed)	1.37
$\ln L$	−9979.8	−9770.7	−11430.6	−11219.5
AIC	3.547	3.472	2.675	2.626

Table 4.6 reports parameter estimates for the standard $EGARCH(1,0)$ model in which $\sigma^2_{t|t-1}$ in (4.8) is given by (1.11). The maximized log-likelihoods are much smaller than they are for Beta-t-EGARCH, but for a GED distribution, they are close to those obtained with Gamma-GED-EGARCH. The estimates of υ are also close: 1.25 and 1.37 for Hang Seng and Dow Jones, respectively, as opposed to 1.23 and 1.32. Recall from the end of Section 4.4 that the models are equivalent when $\upsilon = 1$, but the parameterization differs.

Table 4.7 presents the results for the Beta-t-GARCH model. The results are consistent with those obtained for the Beta-t-EGARCH models, in that the estimates of ϕ and ν are similar while those of δ, κ and κ^* are roughly double, but the maximized log-likelihoods are slightly smaller.

Table 4.8 gives the estimates and standard errors for the benchmark GARCH-t model obtained with the G@RCH program of Laurent (2007). The leverage is captured by the indicator variable, but using the sign gives essentially the same result. If it is acknowledged that the conditional distribution is not Gaussian, the estimates computed under the assumption that it is conditionally Gaussian – denoted in Table 4.8 simply as GARCH – are

Table 4.7. *Parameter estimates for Beta-t-GARCH models with and without leverage*

	Hang Seng		Dow Jones	
Parameter	Estimate	No leverage	Estimate	No leverage
δ	0.035 (0.007)	0.018	0.010 (0.002)	0.006
ϕ	0.988 (0.004)	0.995	0.991 (0.002)	0.994
κ	0.104 (0.010)	0.110	0.067 (0.006)	0.067
κ^{*}	0.054 (0.008)	–	0.038 (0.005)	–
ν	5.97 (0.45)	5.55	7.64 (0.57)	7.29
$\ln L$	−9748.6	−9785.0	−11182.4	−11222.3
AIC	3.465	3.477	2.618	2.627

Table 4.8. *Parameter estimates for GARCH-t and GARCH with leverage, together with transformed Beta-t-GARCH parameters from Table 4.6*

	Hang Seng			Dow Jones		
Parameter	GARCH-t	GARCH	B-t-G	GARCH-t	GARCH	B-t-G
δ	0.048 (0.011)	0.081	0.035	0.011 (0.002)	0.017	0.010
β	0.888 (0.014)	0.845	0.884	0.936 (0.007)	0.919	0.927
α	0.051 (0.008)	0.053	0.050	0.027 (0.004)	0.027	0.050
α^*	0.087 (0.021)	0.151	0.108	0.052 (0.010)	0.076	0.076
ν	5.87 (0.54)	–	5.97	7.21 (0.62)	–	7.64
$\ln L$	−9770.1	−9991.0	−9748.6	−11192.8	−11428.8	−11182.4
AIC	3.473	3.548	3.465	2.620	2.673	2.618

best described as quasi-maximum likelihood. The columns at the end show the estimates for Beta-t-GARCH converted from the parameterization in Table 4.6. The estimates are close. However, although the condition for covariance stationarity of the GARCH-t fitted to Hang Seng is satisfied, as the estimate of $\beta + \alpha + \alpha^*/2 = \phi$ is 0.982, the condition for the existence of the fourth moment is violated because the relevant statistic takes a value of 1.021 and so is greater than one. On the other hand, the fourth moment condition for the Beta-t-GARCH model, (4.45), is satisfied, as the statistic is 0.997. The maximized log-likelihoods for Beta-t-GARCH are greater than those for GARCH-t.

Plots of the conditional standard deviations (SDs) produced by the Beta-t-GARCH and Beta-t-EGARCH models are difficult to distinguish, and the only marked differences between their conditional standard deviations and those obtained from conventional EGARCH and GARCH-t models are after extreme values. Figure 4.4 shows the SDs of Dow Jones produced by Beta-t-EGARCH and GARCH-t, both with leverage effects, around the 'great crash' of 1987. (The largest value is 22.5, but the y axis has been truncated). Figure 4.5 shows the corresponding graph for Hang Seng SDs, but for a different period, the second half of 1989. The two graphs are similar, in that the GARCH-t filter reacts strongly to the extreme observations and then returns slowly to the same level as Beta-t-EGARCH.

A consequence of the behavior of standard GARCH models is that the standardized residuals, $e_t = y_t/\widetilde{\sigma}_{t|t-1}, t = 1, \ldots T$, are abnormally small for some time after an extreme observation. For the period of the Dow Jones index covered by Figure 4.4, the medians of the $|e_t|$'s – which correspond to half the interquartile range of the e_t's – are 0.607 and 0.457 for Beta-t-EGARCH and GARCH-t, respectively. The corresponding numbers for the period of the Hang Seng index covered by Figure 4.5 are 0.546 and 0.448, respectively. The median of the absolute value of a t-variable with unit variance is 0.580 for seven degrees of freedom and 0.586 for six degrees of freedom.

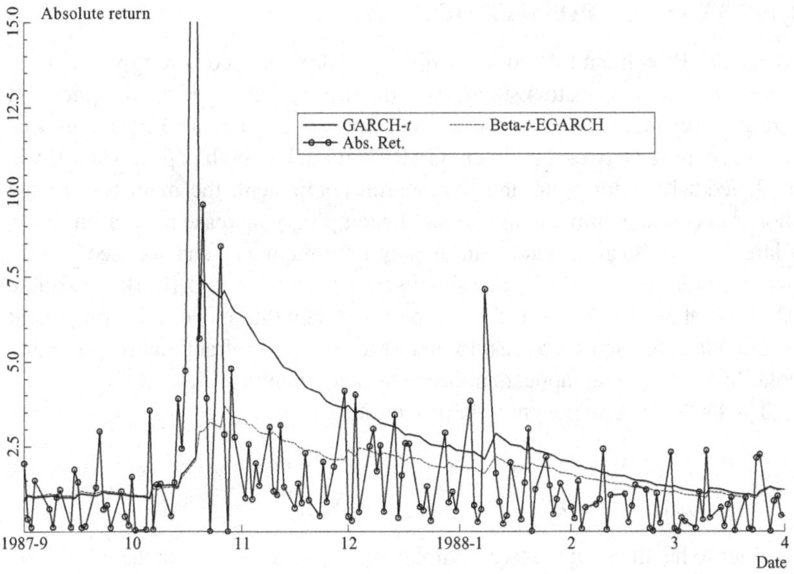

Figure 4.4. Dow Jones absolute (de-meaned) returns around the great crash of October 1987, together with estimated conditional standard deviations for Beta-t-EGARCH and GARCH-t, both with leverage. The horizontal axis gives the year and month.

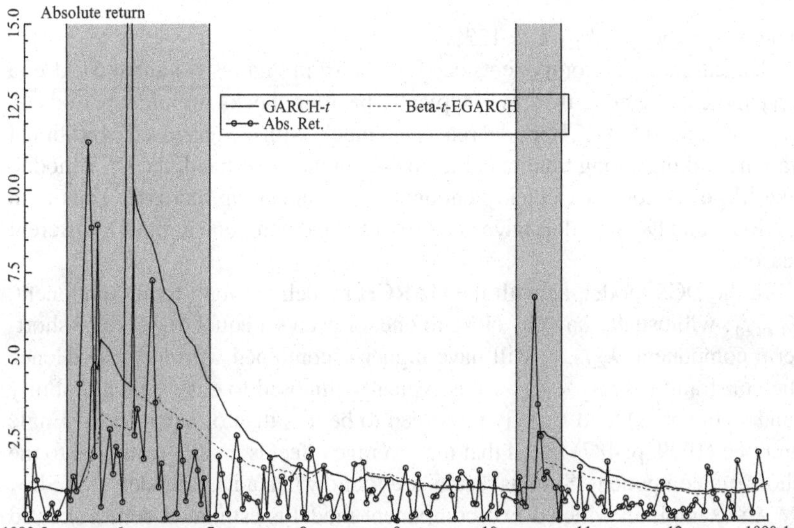

Figure 4.5. Hang Seng absolute returns in 1989, together with estimated conditional standard deviations for Beta-t-EGARCH and GARCH-t, both with leverage.

4.10 TWO COMPONENT MODELS

Alizadeh, Brandt and Diebold (2002, p. 1088) argued strongly for two-component (or two-factor) stochastic volatility dynamics, in both equity and foreign exchange. They adopt a SV framework, whereas Engle and Lee (1999) proposed a two-component GARCH model. In both papers, volatility is modelled with a long-run and a short-run component, the main role of the short-run component being to pick up the temporary increase in volatility after a large shock. Such a model can display long memory behavior; see Andersen et al. (2006, pp. 806–7) and the discussion in Section 3.10. But, to quote Alizadeh et al. (2002, pp. 1087–8), the interpretability of the two component model 'stands in sharp contrast to that of long memory fractionally integrated volatility, which often appears mysterious and nonintuitive'.

The DCS two-component volatility model,

$$\lambda_{t|t-1} = \omega + \lambda_{1,t|t-1} + \lambda_{2,t|t-1}, \qquad with$$

$$\lambda_{i,t+1|t} = \phi_i \lambda_{i,t|t-1} + \kappa_i u_t, \quad i = 1, 2,$$

is easier to handle than the two-component GARCH model; see the discussion on the non-negativity constraints in Engle and Lee (1999, p. 480). The formulae for moments and ACFs can be obtained directly from the earlier results because the MA representation is

$$\lambda_{t|t-1} = \omega + \sum_{k=1}^{\infty} \psi_{1,k} u_{t-k} + \sum_{k=1}^{\infty} \psi_{2,k} u_{t-k} = \omega + \sum_{k=1}^{\infty} \psi_k u_{t-k},$$

where $\psi_k = \psi_{1k} + \psi_{2k}$, $k = 1, 2, \ldots$.

The case for two components can be seen from Figures 4.4 and 4.5. After a very large movement, there will typically be after-shocks for a few periods. A one-component GARCH model reacts too much, with the increased conditional variance taking a long time to come down. On the other hand, the DCS model, like SV, does not react quickly enough to the short-term increase. Thus both GARCH and DCS models have need for a second component, but for different reasons.

In the DCS model, as with the GARCH model, the long-term component, $\lambda_{1,t|t-1}$, will usually have ϕ_1 close to one, or even set equal to one. The short-term component, $\lambda_{2,t|t-1}$, will have higher κ combined with lower ϕ. Hence the constraint $0 < \phi_2 < \phi_1 < 1$ is typically imposed to ensure identifiability (and stationarity), and κ_1 may be forced to be less than or equal to κ_2. Engle and Lee (1999, p. 487) found that the leverage effect is mainly restricted to the short-run component. Similar results are found when a DCS model is fitted.

An example in which a two-component model is estimated with a skewed t distribution is given later in Section 4.14.

Example 17 *Figure 1.2 highlighted the robust response of a Beta-t-EGARCH, with leverage, to an outlier in Apple returns. The model gives a much bigger likelihood than the GARCH-t model, with leverage captured by an indicator,* *as in Glosten et al. (1993). A two-component model fits even better, giving parameter estimates of*

$$\widetilde{\omega} = 0.791 \qquad \widetilde{\phi}_1 = 0.998 \qquad \widetilde{\phi}_2 = 0.862$$
$$\widetilde{\kappa}_1 = 0.014 \qquad \widetilde{\kappa}_2 = 0.041 \qquad \widetilde{\kappa}^* = 0.020 \qquad \widetilde{\nu} = 5.42.$$

The leverage effect is confined to the short-term component. The Ljung-Box statistic for the first 20 squared residual autocorrelations was 12.88, whereas the corresponding statistic for the scores was 19.29; see Sub-section 4.13.4 for a brief discussion of volatility diagnostics.

4.11 TRENDS, SEASONALS AND EXPLANATORY VARIABLES IN VOLATILITY EQUATIONS

It is straightforward to introduce trends, seasonals and explanatory variables into EGARCH models. The local level model is easily handled, and it was shown in Corollary 21 that the asymptotic distribution of the ML estimator can be established. Another possibility is to follow Engle and Rangel (2008), who propose the use of cubic splines for capturing slowly changing movements in volatility. These movements may be due to macroeconomic variables. The approach in Engle and Rangel (2008, p. 1192) is to fit the splines nonparametrically. However, as was pointed out in Sub-section 3.7.2, the smoothed estimates of trend in an integrated random walk are known to be closely related to a cubic spline, and models of this kind were proposed for estimating location in the presence of heavy-tailed additive error. The same approach may be adapted for volatility. The same restriction on the κ vector may be used, that is, if κ is the (positive) level parameter, then $\kappa^2/(\kappa + 2)$ is used for the slope. The only theoretical problem concerns the restrictions needed for the derivation of the asymptotic distribution of the ML estimators.

There is strong case for requiring that volatility be stationary, and this would seem to rule out the use of trends. Fortunately, setting up a cubic spline as signal extraction from an unobserved components model makes it straightforward to produce a stationary component with the smoothness of a cubic spline. All that needs to be done is to introduce a damping factor, ϕ, into the equations. Thus the integrated random walk trend is modified to

$$\mu_t = \phi\mu_{t-1} + \beta_{t-1}, \qquad \eta_t \sim NID(0, \sigma_\eta^2),$$
$$\beta_t = \phi\beta_{t-1} + \zeta_t, \qquad \zeta_t \sim NID(0, \sigma_\zeta^2),$$

and a corresponding change is made to the DCS filter. In principle, ϕ could be estimated, but it may be more practical to set it to a value close to one. Filters of this kind are widely used in engineering; see Harvey and Trimbur (2003).

The availability of intra-day data provides an impetus for developing methods for capturing the 'seasonal' patterns that arise from the changes in volatility within the day. Such patterns are sometimes called periodicity or diurnal effects; see Martens et al. (2002), Laurent (2013, Chapter 7) and Engle and Sokalska

(2012). The intra-day periodic pattern is related to the activity in the various markets around the world.

Andersen and Bollerslev (1998) were among the first to fit intra-day GARCH models to returns constructed from short time intervals within the day. They introduced a diurnal component, s_t, into the standard GARCH setup, (4.42), so that $y_t = \sigma_{t|t-1}s_t z_t$, $t = 1, \ldots, T$, where y_t is the demeaned return. Andersen and Bollerslev (1998) dealt with the multiplicative diurnal effects by a two-step procedure in which the long-run movements were first estimated by a daily GARCH model, and then the logarithms of absolute values of standardized intra-day (five-minute) returns were regressed on a limited number of sines and cosines to capture the intra-day pattern. Such a device is sometimes called a Fourier flexible form; see Gallant (1984).

An EGARCH model provides a natural, and far simpler, way of dealing with multiplicative seasonality and diurnal effects. Furthermore, it opens the way to a more general model in which the pattern is allowed to evolve over time. The case for a changing diurnal pattern can be found in Deo et al. (2005), especially their Figure 4. A limited number of trigonometric terms can be used, as in the Fourier flexible form. Alternatively, time-varying splines can be fitted, as in Harvey and Koopman (1993) and Bowsher and Meeks (2008). The asymptotic theory follows from the discussion in Section 2.6.

The correlograms of the absolute values of adjusted intra-day returns shown in Figure 11 of Andersen and Bollerslev (1998, p. 256) are consistent with a two-component model in which the long-run component changes relatively slowly. Thus volatility may depend on an integrated random walk trend, a stochastic diurnal component and a short-term AR(1) process.

Fixed explanatory variables may be introduced into volatility, so

$$\lambda_{t|t-1} = \mathbf{w}_t'\boldsymbol{\gamma} + \lambda_{t|t-1}^{\dagger}, \quad t = 1, \ldots, T,$$

where $\lambda_{t|t-1}^{\dagger}$ includes trend, seasonal components and short-term components. The asymptotic theory for the ML estimators of the coefficients, $\boldsymbol{\gamma}$, of the explanatory variables, $\mathbf{w}_t$, follows immediately from Proposition 20 and Corollary 10. Because scale is given by the exponent of $\lambda_{t|t-1}$, the multiplicative nature of the model should be transparent.

Dummy variables for news announcements were included by Andersen and Bollerslev (1998), as these can be expected to affect volatility. A specific form was assumed for the dynamic pattern following an announcement. Dummy variables of this kind are a special case of explanatory variables and can be handled as discussed in the previous paragraph. Alternatively, the dynamics of the news shock can be assumed to be the same as for any other shock by formulating the model as in (2.77).

News announcements may not always be anticipated, and so it is important that models are resistant to sudden jumps in prices. Jumps appear as outliers in returns. Figure 4.6 shows one-minute returns for the FTSE on a day in February 2012. The effect of a news announcement (on U.S. unemployment figures) is

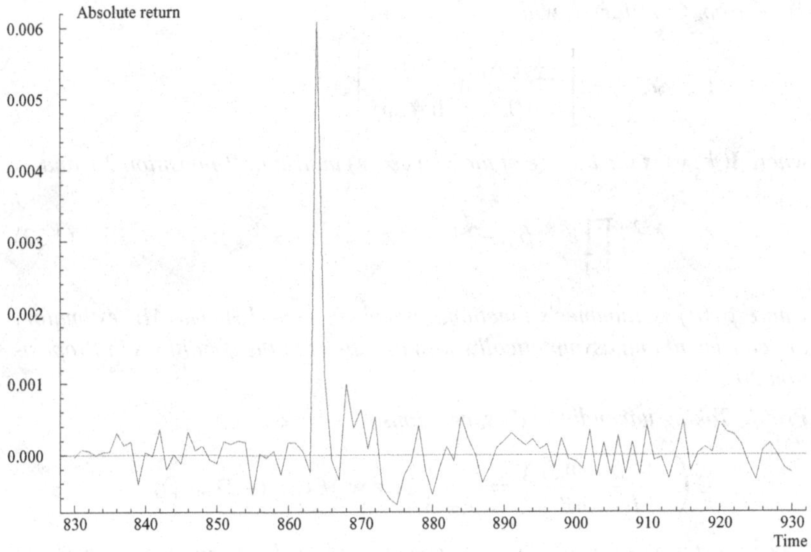

Figure 4.6. One-minute FTSE returns for a day in February 2012.

striking. The advantage of the Beta-t-EGARCH model is that the effect on the estimate of the underlying level of volatility can be expected to be rather small.

4.12 CHANGING LOCATION

Up to now the discussion has been simplified by assuming that the location of the series is zero. The first sub-section that follows shows that introducing explanatory variables for the location is straightforward. The second sub-section examines what happens when a stochastic location is combined with a stochastic scale.

4.12.1 Explanatory Variables

A non-zero location parameter can be introduced into the conditional t distribution without complicating the asymptotic theory for the estimation of the parameters in Beta-t-EGARCH models. More generally, the location may depend linearly on a set of strictly exogenous variables, $\mathbf{w}_t$, that is

$$y_t = \mathbf{w}_t'\boldsymbol{\beta} + \varepsilon_t \exp(\lambda_{t|t-1}), \quad t = 1, \dots, T, \tag{4.51}$$

in which case the ML estimators of the associated parameters are asymptotically independent of the estimators of $\boldsymbol{\psi}$ and ν; see the information matrix, (2.18).

Proposition 27 *Assume that the explanatory variables in (4.51) are weakly stationary with mean $\boldsymbol{\mu}_w$ and second moment Λ_w and are strictly exogenous.*

Then, from Corollary 9, with $\boldsymbol{\theta}_2 = (\boldsymbol{\beta}', \nu)'$,

$$\mathbf{I}(\boldsymbol{\beta}, \boldsymbol{\psi}, \nu) = \begin{bmatrix} \frac{\nu+1}{\nu+3}\zeta\Lambda_w & 0 \\ 0 & \mathbf{I}(\boldsymbol{\psi}, \nu) \end{bmatrix},$$

where $\mathbf{I}(\boldsymbol{\psi}, \nu)$ *is the inverse of the* $Var(\boldsymbol{\psi}, \nu)$ *matrix in Proposition 20, and*

$$\zeta = e^{-2\omega}\prod_{j=1}^{\infty} e^{2\psi_j}\beta_\nu(-2\psi_j) \tag{4.52}$$

where $\beta_\nu(a)$ *is Kummer's function, as defined in (4.13). The ML estimators are consistent and asymptotically normal subject to the conditions in Proposition 20.*

Proof. *Taking unconditional expectations gives*

$$E\left(\frac{\partial \ln f_t}{\partial \boldsymbol{\beta}}\frac{\partial \ln f_t}{\partial \boldsymbol{\beta}'}\right) = \frac{\nu+1}{\nu+3}E(\mathbf{w}_t\mathbf{w}_t')E(\exp(-2\lambda_{t|t-1})).$$

The expectation of $\exp(-2\lambda_{t|t-1})$ *is evaluated in the same way as (4.15) to give* ζ. ■

Remark 28 *The expected value of* $\exp(-2\lambda_{t|t-1})$ *is greater than, or equal to,* $\exp(-2\omega)$, *because, by Jensen's inequality,* $E\left(\exp(-2\lambda_{t|t-1})\right) \geq \exp(E(-2\lambda_{t|t-1})) = \exp(-2\omega)$. *When there is no heteroscedasticity,* $\zeta = \exp(-2\omega)$.

When location is just a constant, so $\mathbf{w}_t = 1$ and $\beta = \mu$, the asymptotic variance of the ML estimator of μ is

$$Avar(\widetilde{\mu}) = T^{-1}(\nu+3)/\zeta(\nu+1).$$

When there is no heteroscedasticity, the sample mean can be quite inefficient for small degrees of freedom, as was shown in Figure 2.2. Changing volatility only makes matters worse.

Corollary 22 *For the Beta-t-EGARCH model of (4.51) with* $\mathbf{w}_t'\boldsymbol{\beta} = \mu$, *the inefficiency of the sample mean increases by a factor of* $\prod_{j=1}^{\infty}\beta_\nu(2\psi_j)\beta_\nu(-2\psi_j)$.

Proof. Because $Var(\overline{y}) = E\left[\sum \varepsilon_t \exp(\lambda_{t|t-1})\right]^2$, we have, provided that $\nu > 2$,

$$Var(\overline{y}) = \frac{1}{T}\left(\frac{\nu}{\nu-2}\right)E\left(e^{2\lambda_{t|t-1}}\right) = \frac{1}{T}\left(\frac{\nu}{\nu-2}\right)e^{2\omega}\prod_{j=1}^{\infty}e^{-2\psi_j}\beta_\nu(2\psi_j), \tag{4.53}$$

because $E(\varepsilon_t^2) = \nu/(\nu - 2)$, and it follows from the LIE that all cross-products in the unconditional expectation of $\left[\sum \varepsilon_t \exp(\lambda_{t|t-1})\right]^2$ are zero. When the variance is constant over time, $Var(\overline{y}) = T^{-1}\exp(2\omega)\nu/(\nu - 2)$, while $Avar(\widetilde{\mu}) = T^{-1}\exp(2\omega)(\nu+3)/(\nu+1)$. The changing variance causes the inefficiency of $\overline{y}$ to increase, because the asymptotic variance of $\overline{y}$ increases by a factor of $\exp(2\omega)E\left(e^{2\lambda_{t|t-1}}\right)$, whereas that of $\widetilde{\mu}$ increases by $\exp(2\omega)/E\left(e^{-2\lambda_{t|t-1}}\right)$ and, by Jensen's inequality, $E(\exp 2\lambda_{t|t-1}) \geq 1/E(\exp(-2\lambda_{t|t-1}))$. The expression for the factor by which inefficiency increases can be derived from $E(\exp 2\lambda_{t|t-1})E(\exp(-2\lambda_{t|t-1}))$ using (4.52) and (4.53). ■

For Gamma-GED-EGARCH, it follows from Zhu and Zinde-Walsh (2009) that, for $\upsilon \geq 1$, the information matrix in Proposition 27 above becomes

$$\mathbf{I}(\boldsymbol{\beta}, \boldsymbol{\psi}, \upsilon) = \begin{bmatrix} \frac{\upsilon^2 2^{-2/\upsilon}\Gamma(2-\upsilon^{-1})}{\Gamma(\upsilon^{-1})}\zeta\Lambda_w & 0 \\ 0 & \mathbf{I}(\boldsymbol{\psi}, \upsilon) \end{bmatrix},$$

where

$$\zeta = e^{-2\omega}\prod_{j=1}^{\infty} e^{2\psi_j}\gamma_\upsilon(-2\upsilon\psi_j).$$

The result can be derived by first observing that the score with respect to $\boldsymbol{\beta}$ is $\mathbf{w}_t(\upsilon/2)\exp(-\lambda)u_t$, with u_t as in (3.68), and that the formula for σ_u^2 was given in (3.69). Then $\zeta = E\left(e^{-2\lambda_{t|t-1}}\right)$ follows as in (4.27).

A result similar to the one in Corollary 22 holds, in that the presence of Gamma-GED-EGARCH causes the inefficiency of the sample mean to increase by a factor of $\prod_{j=1}^{\infty}\gamma_\upsilon(2\upsilon\psi_j)\gamma_\upsilon(-2\upsilon\psi_j)$.

4.12.2 Stochastic Location and Stochastic Scale

The Student's t model for time-varying location described in Chapter 3 may be combined with Beta-t-EGARCH. In other words, $y_t \mid Y_{t-1}$ has a t_ν distribution with mean $\mu_{t|t-1}$ and scale $\exp(\lambda_{t|t-1})$, that is,

$$y_t = \mu_{t|t-1} + \varepsilon_t \exp(\lambda_{t|t-1}), \qquad t = 1, \ldots, T.$$

The structure of the information matrix in the static model is such that the forms of the dynamic equations for $\mu_{t|t-1}$ and $\lambda_{t|t-1}$ are essentially unchanged. Thus λ in (3.1) of Chapter 3 becomes $\lambda_{t|t-1}$ and u_t in (4.6) is modified to take account of $\mu_{t|t-1}$ so becoming

$$u_t = \frac{(\nu+1)(y_t - \mu_{t|t-1})^2}{\nu\exp(2\lambda_{t|t-1}) + (y_t - \mu_{t|t-1})^2} - 1, \qquad t = 1, \ldots, T.$$

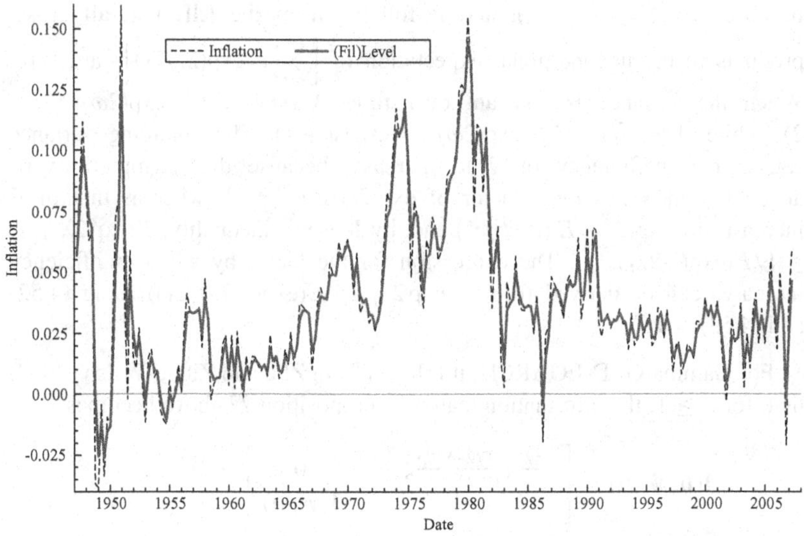

Figure 4.7. Filtered estimates of level from a Gaussian random walk plus noise fitted to U.S. inflation.

Estimation by ML is straightforward. Unfortunately, the presence of $\lambda_{t|t-1}$ in the part of the information matrix associated with $\mu_{t|t-1}$ means that Theorem 2 cannot be applied.[7] Some other route is needed to establish consistency and asymptotically normality of the ML estimators.

As an example, consider the seasonally adjusted rate of inflation in the United States. The data[8] used is the annualized rate of inflation as measured by the first differences of the logarithm of the quarterly Consumer Prices Index (CPI), from 1947(1) to 2007(2), multiplied by four. The rate of inflation is often taken to follow a random walk plus noise, and so the estimator of the level is an exponentially weighted moving average of current and past observations. Thus for the DCS-t model

$$\mu_{t+1|t} = \mu_{t|t-1} + \kappa^{\dagger} u_t, \tag{4.54}$$

where u_t is as in (3.1) and the dagger serves to differentiate $\kappa^{\dagger}$ from the κ parameter in the dynamic scale equation. For the Gaussian unobserved components model, u_t is the prediction error and $\kappa^{\dagger}$ is the Kalman gain. Fitting such a model using the STAMP package gave an estimate of 0.579 for $\kappa^{\dagger}$. The plot of the filtered level, $\mu_{t+1|t}$, in Figure 4.7 shows it to be sensitive to extreme values, while the correlogram of the absolute values of the residuals provides strong evidence of serial correlation in variance.

7 Asymptotic results are similarly difficult to prove for the ARMA-GARCH model; see Francq and Zakoian (2004, 2010) and Lange et al. (2010).

8 Source: U.S. Bureau of Labor Statistics, www.bls.gov.

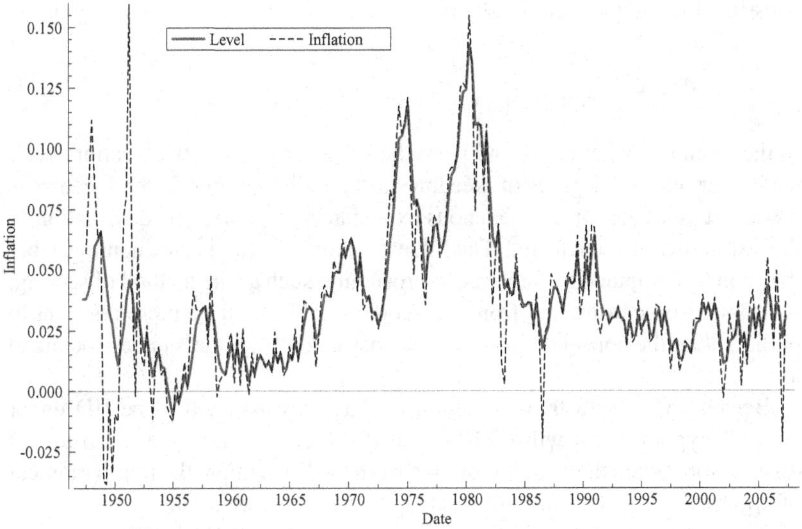

Figure 4.8. Filtered U.S. inflation from a DCS-t model with scale modelled as Beta-t-EGARCH.

Estimating a model in which filtered location is a random walk, (4.54), and scale evolves as a first-order Beta-t-EGARCH process, (4.7), gives the following ML estimates (with standard errors in parentheses): for location, $\widetilde{\kappa}^{\dagger} = 0.699(0.097)$, and for scale, $\widetilde{\delta} = -0.370(0.214)$, $\widetilde{\phi} = 0.912(0.051)$ and $\widetilde{\kappa} = 0.\ 118(0.041)$, with $\widetilde{\nu} = 11.71(4.58)$. Figure 4.8 shows that the filtered level responds less to extreme values than does the level in the homoscedastic Gaussian model.

4.13 TESTING FOR CHANGING VOLATILITY AND LEVERAGE

Tests for changing volatility may be developed by following the general principles laid out for DCS models in Section 2.6. However, the possibility of leverage does raise some new issues.

The standard test for changing volatility is the portmanteau test, or the Box-Ljung modification, based on squared observations. As was demonstrated in Sub-section 4.2.4, the autocorrelations of absolute values will tend to be bigger for a heavy-tailed distributions, but a transformation that reflects the properties of the distribution may be even better. Furthermore there is a need to avoid sample autocorrelations being adversely affected by outliers.

4.13.1 Portmanteau Test for Changing Volatility

A Lagrange multiplier test for changing volatility in a Beta-t-EGARCH model can be carried out with the $Q_u(P)$ statistic, (2.73). The variables used to construct the sample autocorrelations, $r_u(j)$, $j = 1, 2, \ldots,$ will be written as

$$\widetilde{y}_t(\lambda) = \frac{(\widetilde{\nu}+1)(y_t-\widetilde{\mu})^2}{\widetilde{\nu}\exp(2\widetilde{\lambda})+(y_t-\widetilde{\mu})^2} - 1, \qquad t = 1, \ldots, T, \qquad (4.55)$$

(rather than u_t), where $\widetilde{\mu}$, $\widetilde{\lambda}$ and $\widetilde{\nu}$ are the ML estimators of the location, scale parameter and the degrees of freedom in the t distribution. If the location is modelled as a function of exogenous explanatory variables, the distribution of the test statistic is not affected. The ML estimators, $\widetilde{\mu}$, $\widetilde{\lambda}$ and $\widetilde{\nu}$, are nonlinear, but they can be computed by an iterative procedure, such as the method of scoring. A test statistic constructed from the score variables will be more resistant to outliers than the conventional statistic constructed from the squares (obtained as $\nu \to \infty$).

Because $\widetilde{y}_t(\lambda)$ is a transformation of variables assumed to be IID under the null hypothesis, it will be IID even if the observations are not from a t distribution. When the observations are from a t distribution, the fourth moment of $\widetilde{y}_t(\lambda)$ will always exist,[9] and this may be true more generally.

Tests against heteroscedasticity from a Gamma-GED-EGARCH model can be constructed in a similar way. The $\widetilde{y}_t(\lambda)$ variables will be the absolute value of $y_t - \widetilde{\mu}$ raised to the power $\widetilde{\upsilon}$, the estimated shape parameter.

Remark 29 *For the GARCH-t model of Bollerslev (1987), the LM test is as in (2.73), but with $r_u^2(j)$ replaced by the cross-correlation between u_t and $(y_{t-j} - \overline{y})^2/\widetilde{\sigma}^2$, $j = 1, \ldots, P$. This statistic will be affected by outliers. Of course, for the Gaussian model, it is just the standard portmanteau statistic formed from squared autocorrelations.*

The serial correlation in $\lambda_{t|t-1}$ is often very persistent, so that in the first-order model, the parameter ϕ is close to one. As noted in Sub-section 2.5.1, a stationarity test, such as the one proposed by Nyblom and Mäkeläinen (1983) or the more general test of Kwiatkowski et al. (1992), will tend to have higher power than the portmanteau test. Harvey and Streibel (1998) explored the powers of various transformations of the observations in the context of an SV model. Taking absolute values is a good compromise, but using the conditional score variables $\widetilde{y}_t(\lambda)'s$ of (4.55) may be even better.

4.13.2 Martingale Difference Test

The null hypothesis of the preceding tests against changing volatility is that the observations are IID. In order to be confident that a rejection is not a consequence of serial correlation in the level of y_t, it is prudent to first test the null hypothesis that the returns series is a martingale difference. If this hypothesis cannot be rejected, it can be concluded that there is no significant serial correlation in returns. A rejection with the $Q_u(P)$ statistic can then be

[9] McLeod and Li (1983) stated the conditions needed for the test statistic to be χ^2_P.

taken as an indication of nonlinear effects, the most likely of which stem from changing volatility.

The portmanteau statistic may be robustified so that the null hypothesis is an MD, and consequently, the size and power of the test are not adversely affected by conditional heteroscedasticity. The test statistic in Lobato et al. (2001) takes the form

$$Q^*(P) = T\sum_{\tau=1}^{P}\frac{c^2(\tau)}{w(\tau)},$$

where $c(\tau)$ is the sample autocovariance, (2.70), and

$$w(\tau) = \frac{1}{T-\tau}\sum_{\tau=1}^{P}\sum_{t=\tau+1}^{T}(y_t-\overline{y})^2(y_{t-\tau}-\overline{y})^2, \qquad \tau = 1, 2, \ldots.$$

Under the MD hypothesis, $Q^*(P)$ is asymptotically distributed as χ^2_P. Escanciano and Lobato (2009) described an automatic data-driven procedure for selecting the number of lags, P.

The preceding test could be made robust to heavy tails by replacing $y_t - \overline{y}$ in the formula for $c(\tau)$ by a variable derived from the score in (3.4), that is,

$$\widetilde{y}_t(\mu) = \frac{y_t-\widetilde{\mu}}{1+(y_t-\widetilde{\mu})^2/\widetilde{\nu}\exp(2\widetilde{\lambda})}, \qquad t = 1, \ldots, T, \tag{4.56}$$

As in (4.55), $\widetilde{\lambda}$ and $\widetilde{\nu}$ are ML estimators, as is $\widetilde{\mu}$. The formula for $w(\tau)$ may be best amended by replacing $(y_t - \overline{y})^2$ by (4.55)

4.13.3 Leverage

A Lagrange multiplier test against changing volatility with leverage may be carried out with a Q_u-statistic in which the autocorrelations of the $\widetilde{y}_t(\lambda)$ variables, defined as in (4.55) for a Beta-t-EGARCH model, are added to the cross-correlations between $\widetilde{y}_t(\lambda)$ and $(1+\widetilde{y}_{t-h}(\lambda))sgn(-y_{t-h})$ for $h = 1, \ldots, P^*$. This test statistic is distributed as a chi-square variate with $P + P^*$ degrees of freedom under the null hypothesis of constant volatility.

The above test is based on the dynamic equation

$$\lambda_{t|t-1} = \omega + \sum_{j=1}^{P}\kappa_{j-1}u_{t-j} + \sum_{h=1}^{P^*}\kappa^*_{h-1}sgn(-y_{t-h})(u_{t-h}+1),$$

where a zero mean for returns has been assumed for simplicity; see the discussion surrounding (4.22). Differentiating the log-likelihood function with respect to the κ_j's gives the expression in (2.74), whereas differentiating with respect to the κ^*_h's gives

$$\frac{\partial \ln L}{\partial \kappa^*_h} = \sum_{t=h+1}^{T} u_t(1+u_{t-h})sgn(-y_{t-h}), \qquad h = 1, \ldots, P^*-1. \tag{4.57}$$

Hence the information matrix is

$$\mathbf{I}\begin{pmatrix}\widetilde{\kappa}\\ \widetilde{\kappa}^*\end{pmatrix} = \sigma_u^2\begin{bmatrix}\sigma_u^2\mathbf{I}_{P-1} & \mathbf{0}\\ \mathbf{0} & (1+\sigma_u^2)\mathbf{I}_{P^*-1}\end{bmatrix}.$$

A test solely against leverage effects can be carried out by constructing an LM test when a volatility model has been fitted without leverage. For a first-order model, the information matrix leading to (4.39) is block diagonal when $\kappa^* = 0$, so the test is not complicated and only requires that the score be constructed by programming a recursion based on (4.40). However, if a volatility model is being estimated, the additional computational effort of including a leverage variable is small, and a Wald test is then possible; see Remark 26.

4.13.4 Diagnostics

A Box-Pierce test can be carried out on the residuals obtained from fitting Beta-t-EGARCH models. These residuals are

$$\widetilde{u}_t(\lambda) = \frac{(\widetilde{\nu}+1)(y_t-\widetilde{\mu})^2}{\widetilde{\nu}\exp(2\lambda_{t|t-1}) + (y_t-\widetilde{\mu})^2} - 1, \quad t = 1,\ldots,T.$$

The expectation is that the portmanteau statistic formed from the above residuals will have an asymptotic distribution, which is χ^2_{P-n} when a dynamic model with n parameters is correctly fitted. For a first-order model, as in (4.7), n is two.

Diagnostic tests may also be carried out with other transformations, such as absolute values or PITs. Computing PITs also offers the possibility of checking how well the assumed condititional distribution fits the data. A more detailed discussion of such issues may be found in the next chapter.

4.14 SKEW DISTRIBUTIONS

The case for introducing skewed conditional distributions into GARCH models is set out in Giot and Laurent (2003). When the conditional distribution of a Beta-t-EGARCH model, $y_t = \mu + \varepsilon_t \exp(\lambda_{t|t-1})$, is skewed by the method described in Section 3.12, the log-density is as in (3.77) but with λ and $\mu_{t|t-1}$ replaced by $\lambda_{t|t-1}$ and μ, respectively. The variable,

$$u_t = \frac{(\nu+1)(y_t-\mu)^2}{\nu\gamma^{2\text{sgn}(y_t-\mu)}\exp(2\lambda_{t|t-1}) + (y_t-\mu)^2} - 1, \qquad (4.58)$$

obtained from the score, depends on the sign of $y_t - \mu$, but, as in the skew location model of Sub-section 3.12.2, the distribution of u_t is independent of the sign; it is a linear function of a $beta(1/2, \nu/2)$ variable, as in (4.3). As a result, many of the analytic expressions for Beta-t-EGARCH extend quite straightforwardly.

Provided that the m-th unconditional moment of y_t around μ exists, it may be written as

$$E\left(y_t-\mu\right)^m=E\left(\varepsilon_t^m\right)E\left(e^{\lambda_{t|t-1}m}\right),\quad m=1,2,3,\ldots, \tag{4.59}$$

where $E\left(\varepsilon_t^m\right)$ is now given by (3.73), with expression (2.12) being be used to evaluate M_c. The formula for $E\left(e^{\lambda_{t|t-1}m}\right)$ is the same as in the symmetric case, that is (4.15). Hence the mean is

$$\mu_y=\mu+\frac{\nu^{1/2}\Gamma((\nu-1)/2)}{\Gamma(\nu/2)\sqrt{\pi}}(\gamma-1/\gamma)\left[e^{\omega}\prod_{j=1}^{\infty}e^{-\psi_j}\beta_\nu(\psi_j)\right],\quad \nu>1, \tag{4.60}$$

and expression for other moments are similarly obtained. The ACF of $(y_t-\mu_y)^2$ can be derived as in Section 4.3, whereas the multistep predictor of the variance of $y_{T+\ell}$, $\ell=2,3,\ldots,$ given in (4.31) needs to be modified to

$$Var_T(y_{T+\ell})=\frac{\nu}{\nu-2}\left(\gamma^2-1+\gamma^{-2}\right)e^{2\lambda_{T+\ell|T}}\prod_{j=1}^{\ell-1}e^{-2\psi_j}\beta_\nu(2\psi_j)$$
$$-\left(\mu_y-\mu\right)^2,\quad \nu>2.$$

When γ is known and there is no leverage, the information matrix is exactly as in the symmetric case because the distribution of the score and its first derivative depend on IID beta variates with the same distribution. However, the asymptotic distribution of the ML estimators of the dynamic parameters is affected when γ is also estimated by ML. Zhu and Galbraith (2010) give an analytic expression for the information matrix, but with a different parameterization for the scale and the skewing parameter.[10] The full information matrix for the dynamic model can be constructed as in Proposition 20.

The Gamma-GED-EGARCH model extends to the skew case in the same way as does Beta-t-EGARCH, and its properties may be similarly derived.

There is a problem with using the preceding skewing method for modelling returns because the conditional expectation,

$$E_{t-1}y_t=\mu+\mu_\varepsilon\exp(\lambda_{t|t-1}),$$

[10] The skewing parameter is $\alpha=1/(1+\gamma^2)$. Thus α is in the range 0 to 1 and symmetry is $\alpha=0.5$. The scale measure is

$$\sigma=(\gamma+1/\gamma)\sigma'/2=(\gamma+1/\gamma)\exp(\lambda)\sqrt{\nu/4(\nu-2)},$$

where σ' is the standard deviation in the Fernandez-Steel model; see Zhu and Galbraith (2010, equation 4). Our formulae for the information matrix may be adapted quite easily by redefining λ as $\ln\sigma$.

is not constant. Therefore, y_t cannot be a martingale difference. The solution is to let μ be time-varying. The model is reformulated as

$$y_t = \mu^S_{t|t-1} + \varepsilon_t \exp(\lambda_{t|t-1}), \quad t = 1, \ldots, T \tag{4.61}$$
$$\mu^S_{t|t-1} = \mu_y - \mu_\varepsilon \exp(\lambda_{t|t-1}),$$

where μ_y is a constant parameter, which is both the conditional and the unconditional mean.[11] The time-varying parameter $\mu^S_{t|t-1}$ replaces μ in the likelihood function.

The score in the model with the MD modification is

$$u_t = \frac{(\nu+1)((y_t - \mu_y + \mu_\varepsilon \exp(\lambda_{t|t-1}))(y_t - \mu_y)}{\nu\gamma^{2\mathrm{sgn}(y_t - \mu_y + \mu_\varepsilon \exp(\lambda_{t|t-1}))} \exp(2\lambda_{t|t-1}) + (y_t - \mu_y + \mu_\varepsilon \exp(\lambda_{t|t-1}))^2} - 1. \tag{4.62}$$

Unfortunately, unlike (4.58), u_t does not have the simple beta distribution of (4.3). Thus analytic evaluation of unconditional moments is difficult. The same is true for the information matrix. However, the distribution of u_t does not depend on $\lambda_{t|t-1}$ and neither do the distributions of its derivatives. Thus the conditions for the ML estimator to be consistent and asymptotically normal hold, just as they do in the symmetric case.

The model in (4.61) can also be expressed as

$$y_t = \mu_y + (\varepsilon_t - \mu_\varepsilon)\exp(\lambda_{t|t-1}). \tag{4.63}$$

As noted, analytic evaluation of moments about μ_y using (4.15) is difficult. However, the skewness is

$$S(\nu, \gamma) = \frac{E[(\varepsilon_t - \mu_\varepsilon)^3]E\exp(3\lambda_{t|t-1})}{\left[E[(\varepsilon_t - \mu_\varepsilon)^2]E(\exp(2\lambda_{t|t-1}))\right]^{3/2}}$$

and so the factor by which it changes because of changing volatility is just

$$S_\nu = \frac{E\exp(3\lambda_{t|t-1})}{\left[E(\exp(2\lambda_{t|t-1}))\right]^{3/2}}, \qquad \nu > 3. \tag{4.64}$$

It follows from Hölder's inequality[12] that S_ν is greater than, or equal to, one. Thus changing volatility increases skewness.

If leverage depends on the sign of ε_t, the dynamic equation is now

$$\lambda_{t+1|t} = \delta + \phi\lambda_{t|t-1} + \kappa u_t + \kappa^* sgn(-y_t + \mu_y - \mu_\varepsilon \exp(\lambda_{t|t-1}))(u_t + 1). \tag{4.65}$$

[11] The same problem arises with other GARCH models, and Giot and Laurent (2003) transformed their Skew-t GARCH model to make it an MD. They also standardize to make the variance one, but in the above skew-t model, this is not necessary.

[12] $E|x|^r \leq \left[E|x|^s\right]^{r/s}$. Here $x = \exp(\lambda) \geq 0$, and r and s can be set to 2 and 3, respectively.

There is also a case for letting the leverage depend on $sgn(y_t - \mu_y)$, the rationale being that leverage should depend on whether the return is above or below the mean. Leverage in itself does not induce skewness in the multi-step and unconditional distributions of Beta-t-EGARCH models. However, as was noted in below (4.64), volatility will tend to increase the skewness in the unconditional distribution when the conditional distribution is skewed. The question then arises as to whether leverage exacerbates this increase.

The quantile function of a skew t distribution is given by expression (9) in Giot and Laurent (2003). Formulae for VaR and expected shortfall in a skew t are given in Zhu and Galbraith (2010, p. 300). These formulae may be used in one-step ahead prediction. Multistep conditional distributions can be computed by simulation, simply by generating beta variates and combining them with an observation generated from a skew t.

Harvey and Sucarrat (2012) reported results of fitting the MD model with two components and leverage, set up to depend on $sgn(y_t - \mu_y)$, to a range of returns series. Estimation was carried out using the program in Sucarrat (2012). Leverage and negative skewness were found to be particularly pronounced among stock market indices, such as SP 500, FTSE, DAX and Nikkei. The skewness parameter estimate ranges from 0.86 to 0.91, which means that the risk of a large negative (demeaned) return is higher than a large positive return. Interestingly, but perhaps not surprisingly, large stocks with relatively regular earnings payouts, including Apple, Boeing, Sony and McDonald's, do not exhibit as much negative skewness as do the indices.

Example 18 *Fitting Beta-t-EGARCH with leverage to daily returns on Merck, a global pharmaceutical and chemical company, for the period January 1999 to October 2011, gave the following estimates:*

$$\widetilde{\omega} = 0.326 \qquad \widetilde{\phi} = 0.987 \qquad \widetilde{\kappa} = 0.039$$

$$\widetilde{\kappa}^* = 0.024 \qquad \widetilde{\nu} = 4.66 \qquad \widetilde{\gamma} = 0.949$$

The (numerical) t value for $\widetilde{\gamma} - 1$ *is 2.25. There is no evidence of residual serial correlation since value of the score-based Ljung-Box statistic was* $Q_u(20) = 17.04$, *and the probability of a* χ^2_{17} *variable exceeding* 17.04 *is 0.45.*

Returns sometimes exhibit mild serial correlation. Such effects may be removed prior to fitting a volatility model as was done in the previous section. However, rather than simply using a standard procedure for estimating an ARMA model, a DCS model may be fitted, thereby providing protection against outliers. Indeed a DCS model with a skew distribution may be fitted with location and volatility estimated jointly, as described in Sub-section 4.12.2. The case for adopting the MD modification of (4.61) may not be so strong when there is serial correlation in the level.

4.15 TIME-VARYING SKEWNESS AND KURTOSIS*

The DCS approach also suggests a way of capturing time-varying skewness. Let γ of the preceding sub-section change over time, but set μ to zero to simplify the discussion. Suppose that an exponential link function is used to model a changing γ, that is $\gamma_{t|t-1} = \exp(\xi_{t|t-1})$. There is no reason to assume stationarity, so the parameter can be allowed to evolve as a random walk, that is $\xi_{t+1|t} = \xi_{t|t-1} + \kappa u_t$, where the score with respect to $\xi_{t|t-1}$ is

$$u_t = \frac{(\nu+1)(y_t-\mu)^2/\nu e^{2\xi_{t|t-1}sgn(y_t-\mu)}\exp(2\lambda_{t|t-1})}{1+(y_t-\mu)^2/\nu e^{2\xi_{t|t-1}sgn(y_t-\mu)}\exp(2\lambda_{t|t-1})}sgn(y_t-\mu)+\frac{1-e^{2\xi_{t|t-1}}}{1+e^{2\xi_{t|t-1}}}.$$

A slight modification is needed for the MD model of Sub-section 4.14.3.

Kurtosis should be similarly allowed to evolve by letting the degrees of freedom change over time. This was done in Creal et al. (2008), and some of their results indicate that it may sometimes be possible to track changing kurtosis using the DCS approach. However, an asymptotic theory for the ML estimators of the parameters in dynamic equations for kurtosis or skewness is not easy to establish, as it does not seem possible to find a link function that makes the variance of the score independent of the changing parameter. Overall, attempting to track changing skewness or kurtosis may be asking too much of the data unless the sample size is very large.

CHAPTER 5

Location/Scale Models for Non-negative Variables

Many variables, particularly those associated with intra-day financial data, are intrinsically non-negative. Examples include the time between trades; realized volatility, which is the estimator of daily variance obtained from a set of returns within the day; and the range of a price over a day.

Distributions appropriate for non-negative variables include the gamma, Weibull, Burr and F. As a rule, the location and scale for such distributions are closely connected, usually depending on the same parameter. If the location/scale is to change over time, the use of an exponential link function ensures that it remains positive. The unobserved components model is then

$$y_t = \varepsilon_t \exp(\lambda_t), \qquad 0 \leq y_t < \infty, \quad t = 1, \ldots, T,$$

where $\lambda_t = \ln \mu_t$ depends on a disturbance term, η_t, which may or may not be correlated with the standardized IID variable, ε_t. In the first-order model,

$$\lambda_{t+1} = \delta + \phi\lambda_t + \eta_t, \quad \eta_t \sim NID\left(0, \sigma_\eta^2\right); \tag{5.1}$$

see, for example, Bauwens and Veredas (2004) and Bauwens and Hautsch (2009, p 964–5). As with the stochastic volatility model, taking logarithms, that is,

$$\ln y_t = \lambda_t + \ln \varepsilon_t, \quad t = 1, \ldots, T, \tag{5.2}$$

gives a linear state space form. For some variables, like the logarithm of range, quasi-maximum likelihood estimation using the Kalman filter may be more satisfactory than it is for the SV model because $\ln \varepsilon_t$ is likely to be reasonably close to a normal distribution. Nevertheless, efficient estimation usually requires the use of simulation-based methods, as in Koopman et al. (2012).

Multiplicative error models (MEMs) provide an observation-driven approach for dynamic non-negative variables; see Russell and Engle (2010) for a recent survey. MEMs are GARCH-type models in which the conditional mean, $\mu_{t|t-1}$, and hence the conditional scale, is a linear function of past observations. In the context of modelling duration, they are called *autoregressive conditional duration* (ACD) models. The first-order model can be written

$$y_t = \varepsilon_t \mu_{t|t-1}, \qquad 0 \leq y_t < \infty, \quad t = 1, \dots, T, \tag{5.3}$$

$$\mu_{t+1|t} = \delta + \beta \mu_{t|t-1} + \alpha y_t, \qquad \delta > 0,\ \alpha, \beta \geq 0, \tag{5.4}$$

where ε_t has a distribution with mean one. Thus the mean is a weighted average of past observations; when $\alpha + \beta = 1$, it is an EWMA. Rearranging the dynamic equation shows that the mean can be written in terms of the prediction error, that is,

$$\mu_{t+1|t} = \delta + (\alpha + \beta)\mu_{t|t-1} + \alpha(y_t - \mu_{t|t-1}), \qquad t = 1, \dots, T.$$

In much of the MEM literature, the emphasis has been on the gamma and Weibull distributions, both of which include the exponential distribution as a special case.

An exponential link function, $\mu_{t|t-1} = \exp(\lambda_{t|t-1})$, has been used by Brandt and Jones (2006) and others. However, it is the combination of the exponential link function with the conditional score that facilitates the development of an asymptotic distribution theory and enables comprehensive expressions for the moments, autocorrelations and forecasts to be derived. The practical implication is that the conditional score for a heavy-tailed distribution will give extreme observations less weight than they would receive in the standard MEM framework.

It is not always convenient to define ε_t so that its mean is one. For many purposes, it is better to work with a measure of scale. Because scale and location differ only by a factor of proportionality, the statistical properties of parameters estimated with an exponential link function are essentially unchanged. The dynamic conditional score model can be written

$$y_t = \varepsilon_t \exp(\lambda_{t|t-1}), \quad t = 1, \dots, T, \tag{5.5}$$

$$\lambda_{t+1|t} = (1 - \phi)\omega + \phi\lambda_{t|t-1} + \kappa u_t, \qquad |\phi| < 1, \tag{5.6}$$

where ω is the unconditional mean of $\lambda_{t|t-1}$ and $\exp(\lambda_{t|t-1})$ is equal to a measure of scale, with the distribution of ε_t standardized accordingly. The dynamics are driven by the (standardized) score, u_t.

The statistical theory of DCS models for non-negative variables is simplified by the fact that for the gamma and Weibull distributions, the score and its derivatives are dependent on a gamma variate, whereas for the Burr, log-logistic and F distributions, the dependence is on a beta variate. In fact, the theory can be rationalized by regarding the gamma and Weibull distributions as special cases of the generalized gamma distribution, whereas the Burr and log-logistic distributions are special cases of the generalized beta distribution. The F distribution is related to the generalized beta distribution in that the special case when the degrees of freedom are the same is equivalent to a special case of the generalized beta. Members of the generalized beta class are particularly useful in situations in which there is evidence of heavy tails.

The first-order model of (5.6) may be generalized as in (4.6). Consistency of terminology for dynamic scale models suggests that the various specifications be called by names such as *Beta-Burr-EGARCH*(p, r) or *Gamma-Weibull-EGARCH*(p, r). Generalizations to include trends and seasonals follow as in the previous chapter.

The first section that follows sets out some generic properties of DCS models for non-negative distributions, and this is followed by a detailed treatment of generalized gamma and generalized beta distributions. Section 5.4 discusses the log-normal model, and it is noted that because $\ln y_t$ is the sum of volatility and noise, the model can be treated as parameter-driven or observation-driven. Section 5.5 reports the results of Monte Carlo experiments. A discussion on how to extend the models to include changing diurnal patterns can be found in Section 5.6, as can a description of techniques for capturing leverage and long-memory effects. After a section on tests and model selection, models are fitted to intra-day data on range and duration.

The last section discusses how to formulate DCS models to handle count data and qualitative observations.

5.1 GENERAL PROPERTIES

The maximum likelihood estimators of mean and variance in samples of IID observations from a Gaussian distribution are linear combinations of the observations and their squares, respectively. The ML estimator of location/scale for a gamma distribution is likewise a linear combination of the observations. For more complex dynamic models, estimation procedures associated with the gamma distribution provide a simple benchmark against which to assess other methods, just as methods associated with the normal do. However, Gaussian models are vulnerable to outliers, and the same is true of a MEM model or any other model, including a DCS model, which assumes a gamma conditional distribution; see, for example, Kleiber and Kotz (2003, p. 165). Using a different conditional distribution does not solve the problem within the MEM framework, but it does when the DCS approach is adopted.

This section sets out the general approach to formulating DCS models for non-negative variables and explains how to derive their properties. An exponential link function yields a score, the conditional distribution of which is independent of $\lambda_{t|t-1}$. The dynamic equation for $\lambda_{t|t-1}$ is a linear function of IID variables, which in turn depend on the standardized variables, ε_t.

5.1.1 Heavy Tails

The coefficient of variation (CV), which is defined as the ratio of the standard deviation to the mean, is a useful measure for characterizing distributions of non-negative variables; see, for example, Bauwens et al. (2004, table 2). An exponential distribution has a CV, of one and a distribution is said to exhibit *overdispersion* if the CV exceeds one. However, as will become apparent later, overdispersion is neither necessary nor sufficient for a distribution to be heavy-tailed.

The most widely accepted criterion for classifying a distribution as heavy-tailed is by reference to the survival function of an exponential distribution; see Asmussen (2003).

Definition 5 *A distribution is said to be heavy-tailed if*

$$\lim_{y\to\infty} \exp(y/\alpha)\overline{F}(y) = \infty \qquad \textit{for all } \alpha > 0, \tag{5.7}$$

where $\overline{F}(y) = \Pr(Y > y) = 1 - F(y)$ *is the survival function.*

When y has an exponential distribution, $\overline{F}(y) = \exp(-y/\alpha)$, so $\exp(y/\alpha)\overline{F}(y) = 1$ for all y.

Definition 6 *A distribution is said to be long-tailed if, for a fixed positive value of* x,

$$\lim_{y\to\infty} \Pr(Y > y + x \mid y) = 1, \qquad x > 0.$$

When a distribution is long-tailed, the probability of an observation being bigger than a value at some point beyond y, given that it is known to be at least y, is close to one. In other words, for large y, $\overline{F}(y + x) \simeq \overline{F}(y)$. All long-tailed distributions are heavy-tailed, but the converse is not true.

The preceding criteria are related to the behavior of the conditional score and whether or not it discounts large observations.

5.1.2 Moments and Autocorrelations

When $\lambda_{t|t-1}$ is generated by a stationary process with mean ω, that is,

$$\lambda_{t|t-1} = \omega + \sum_{j=1}^{\infty} \psi_j u_{t-j}, \tag{5.8}$$

where ψ_j, $j = 1, 2, \ldots$, are fixed coefficients,

$$E\left(y_t^m\right) = E\left(\varepsilon_t^m\right) E(e^{m\lambda_{t|t-1}}) = E\left(\varepsilon_t^m\right) e^{m\omega} \prod_{j=1}^{\infty} E(e^{m\psi_j u_{t-j}}), \qquad m = 1, 2, \ldots \tag{5.9}$$

For all the models considered here, the $u_t's$ are linear functions of independent gamma, beta or normal variates, so the terms $E(\exp m\psi_j u_{t-j})$, $j = 1, 2, \ldots$, are all moment generating functions with a known analytic form. When u_t is beta distributed, the existence of moments of y_t depends solely on the existence of moments for the conditional distribution, just as it does in Beta-t-EGARCH. For models in which u_t is gamma distributed, conditions need to be placed on the parameters of the dynamic scale process.

The effect of volatility is to inflate the moments. In other words, the unconditional moments are greater than, or equal to, the conditional ones. Specifically, $E\left(y_t^m\right) \geq E\left(\varepsilon_t^m\right)$ because, from Jensen's inequality, $E\left(e^{m\lambda_{t|t-1}}\right) \geq \exp E\left(m\lambda_{t|t-1}\right)$. Just as in (4.17), where the increase in kurtosis minus one can be taken as a measure of volatility in a GARCH model, so one subtracted from the increase in second moment divided by the squared mean, that is,

$$V = \frac{\prod_{j=1}^{\infty} E(e^{2\psi_j u_{t-j}})}{\left(\prod_{j=1}^{\infty} E(e^{\psi_j u_{t-j}})\right)^2} - 1, \tag{5.10}$$

can be taken as a measure of volatility here. Note that this measure can also be interpreted as the increase in variance divided by the squared mean.

Expressions for the autocorrelations of the observations raised to a positive power, that is,

$$\rho\left(\tau; y_t^c\right) = \frac{E\left(y_t^c y_{t-\tau}^c\right) - E\left(y_t^c\right) E\left(y_{t-\tau}^c\right)}{E\left(y_t^{2c}\right) - E\left(y_t^c\right) E\left(y_{t-\tau}^c\right)}. \quad \tau = 1, 2, \ldots, \quad c > 0,$$

are given by

$$\rho\left(\tau; y_t^c\right) = \frac{G(\tau) - 1}{\kappa(c)V(c) - 1}, \quad \tau = 1, 2, \ldots, \tag{5.11}$$

where

$$\kappa(c) = \left(E\left(\varepsilon_t^c\right)\right)^{-2} E\left(\varepsilon_t^{2c}\right), \quad c > 0,$$

$$V(c) = \left(\prod_{j=1}^{\infty} E(e^{c\psi_j u_{t-j}})\right)^{-2} \prod_{j=1}^{\infty} E(e^{2c\psi_j u_{t-j}}),$$

and $G(\tau, c)$, $\tau = 2, \ldots,$ is

$$G(\tau, c) = \frac{E\left(\varepsilon_{t-\tau}^c e^{c\psi_\tau u_{t-\tau}}\right)}{E\left(\varepsilon_t^c\right)} \left(\prod_{j=1}^{\infty} E(e^{c\psi_j u_{t-j}})\right)^{-2}$$

$$\times \prod_{j=1}^{\tau-1} E(e^{c\psi_j u_{t-j}}) \prod_{i=1}^{\infty} E(e^{c(\psi_{\tau+i}+\psi_i)u_{t-j}}),$$

or, for $\tau = 1$,

$$G(1, c) = \frac{E\left(\varepsilon_{t-1}^c e^{c\psi_1 u_{t-1}}\right)}{E\left(\varepsilon_t^c\right)} \left(\prod_{j=1}^{\infty} E(e^{c\psi_j u_{t-j}})\right)^{-2} \prod_{i=1}^{\infty} E\left(e^{c(\psi_{1+i}+\psi_i)u_{t-j}}\right).$$

Most of the terms are obtained directly from formulae for MGFs. It is only the evaluation of $E(\varepsilon_{t-\tau}^c e^{c\psi_\tau u_{t-\tau}})$ that requires a little work, but the solution is along the same lines as was set out for Beta-t-EGARCH in Appendix B.1.

The formulae simplify in the leading case when $c = 1$. Other transformations, such as the square root and logarithmic, may be worth exploring. In the logarithmic case, which corresponds to $c = 0$, the formula is derived directly by writing an equation for $\ln y_t$ as in (4.21).

Remark 30 *The MEM in (5.3) is strictly stationary when $\alpha + \beta < 1$, in which case the unconditional mean is $\omega = \delta/(1 - \alpha - \beta)$. The unconditional variance*

$$\sigma_y^2 = \frac{\omega^2(1 - \beta^2 - 2\alpha\beta)Var(\varepsilon_t)}{1 - (\alpha + \beta)^2 - \alpha^2 Var(\varepsilon_t)}$$

requires $(\alpha + \beta)^2 + \alpha^2 Var(\varepsilon_t) < 1$. This condition is somewhat analogous to the fourth moment condition in GARCH(1,1). Because the filter weights the observations directly, the ACF for the observations is easily obtained. Finding expressions for the ACF of y_t^c is difficult for $c \neq 1$.

5.1.3 Forecasts

The optimal estimator of $\lambda_{T+\ell|T+\ell-1}$ in a stationary model is

$$\lambda_{T+\ell|T} = \omega + \sum_{k=0}^{\infty} \psi_{\ell+k} u_{T-k}, \quad \ell = 2, 3, \ldots,$$

with prediction error is $\sum_{j=1}^{\ell-1} \psi_j u_{T+\ell-j}$. Expressions for the forecasts of volatility and its RMSE can be found as in Section 4.5. It is straightforward to simulate the multistep predictive distributions because

$$y_{T+\ell} = \varepsilon_{T+\ell} \exp\left(\sum_{j=1}^{\ell-1} \psi_j u_{T+\ell-j}\right) [\exp(\lambda_{T+\ell|T})] \qquad (5.12)$$

and, as already, noted u_t is a linear function of gamma or beta variates.

5.1.4 Asymptotic Distribution of Maximum Likelihood Estimators

When only the scale is time-varying and an exponential link function is adopted, the information matrices for distributions that belong to the generalized gamma and generalized beta families are given by (2.55). For the first-order model, (5.6), the information matrix is (2.56), with $\boldsymbol{\psi} = (\kappa, \phi, \omega)'$. This matrix may be evaluated quite easily because $\mathbf{D}(\boldsymbol{\psi})$ is as in (2.40) and all that needs to be done is to combine this matrix with the static information matrix for the distribution in question. Proof of consistency and asymptotic normality of ML estimators, together with the associated conditions on the parameters, follows as in Chapter 4.

Remark 31 *MEM models are sometimes estimated by treating the conditional distribution as though it were exponential; see Engle and Russell (2010, p. 401). The attraction of this simple QML estimator is that it is consistent for conditional distributions with finite variance, and valid standard errors can be computed numerically from the usual sandwich formula. (No analytic expressions can be derived.) However, the QML estimator is predicated on the notion that obtaining consistent estimators of the parameters in (5.4) is what is required. The linearity of this dynamic equation is not questioned, but when the conditional distribution is not gamma, the dynamic equation in the DCS model is driven by a nonlinear function of the observations. In any case, the whole conditional distribution is often of interest for forecasting.*

5.2 GENERALIZED GAMMA DISTRIBUTION

The PDF of a gamma variable, $gamma(\alpha, \gamma)$, was given in (2.9). When the conditional distribution of y_t in (5.5) is $gamma(\alpha, \gamma)$, with ε_t standardized by setting its scale equal to one, the exponential link function $\alpha_{t|t-1} = \exp(\lambda_{t|t-1}) = \mu_{t|t-1}/\gamma$, $t = 1, \ldots, T$, yields the log-density for the $t-th$ observation as

$$\ln f_t(\psi, \gamma) = -\gamma\lambda_{t|t-1} + (\gamma - 1)\ln y_t - y_t \exp(-\lambda_{t|t-1}) - \ln\Gamma(\gamma), \quad t = 1, \ldots, T.$$

The conditional score is then

$$u_t = y_t/\exp(\lambda_{t|t-1}) - \gamma = \varepsilon_t - \gamma, \quad t = 1, \ldots, T,$$

with $\sigma_u^2 = \gamma$. Thus the score variables are just the centered IID standardized gamma variables of (5.5), and the effect of an observation on the scale is linear.

The PDF of the Weibull distribution is

$$f(y; \alpha, \upsilon) = \frac{\upsilon}{\alpha}\left(\frac{y}{\alpha}\right)^{\upsilon-1} \exp\left(-(y/\alpha)^{\upsilon}\right), \quad 0 \leq y < \infty, \quad \alpha, \upsilon > 0,$$

where α is the scale and υ is the shape parameter. The mean is $\mu = \alpha\Gamma(1 + 1/\upsilon)$ and the variance is $\alpha^2\Gamma(1 + 2/\upsilon) - \mu^2$. Because $\overline{F}(y) = \exp[-(y/\alpha)^{\upsilon}]$, the expression in Definition 5 is $\exp[y/\alpha - (y/\alpha)^{\upsilon}]$. Hence the Weibull distribution has a heavy tail when $\upsilon < 1$.

Figure 5.1 contrasts the PDF of a standardized (that is $\alpha = 1$) Weibull variate with $\upsilon = 0.5$ and the PDFs when $\upsilon = 1$, an exponential, and $\upsilon = 2$. Figure 5.2 plots the corresponding scores, $\upsilon y^{\upsilon} - \upsilon$. As can be seen, large observations are discounted when $\upsilon = 0.5$.

The properties of the gamma model are relatively easy to derive. However, most of them are given by specializing results for the generalized gamma distribution. The same is true for the properties of the Weibull distribution. The generalized gamma (GG) distribution is

$$f(y; \alpha, \gamma, \upsilon) = \frac{\upsilon}{\alpha\Gamma(\gamma)}\left(\frac{y}{\alpha}\right)^{\upsilon\gamma-1} \exp\left(-(y/\alpha)^{\upsilon}\right), \quad 0 \leq y < \infty, \quad \alpha, \gamma, \upsilon > 0.$$

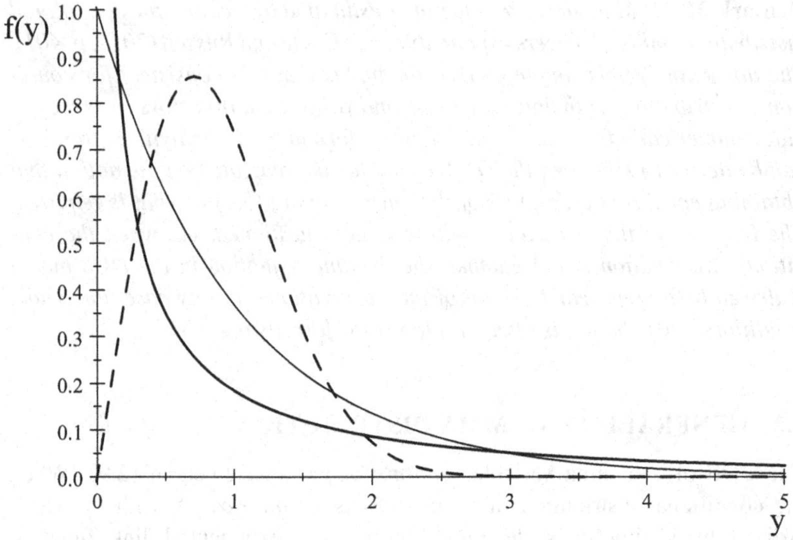

Figure 5.1. Weibull density functions for $\upsilon = 0.5$, exponential ($\upsilon = 1$, thin line) and $\upsilon = 2$ (dashes).

The mean is $\alpha\Gamma(\gamma + 1/\upsilon)/\Gamma(\gamma)$. A full description is given in Kleiber and Kotz (2003, Chapter 5). The gamma distribution is obtained when $\upsilon = 1$, whereas setting $\gamma = 1$ with $\upsilon > 0$ yields the Weibull distribution. The exponential distribution has $\upsilon = \gamma = 1$.

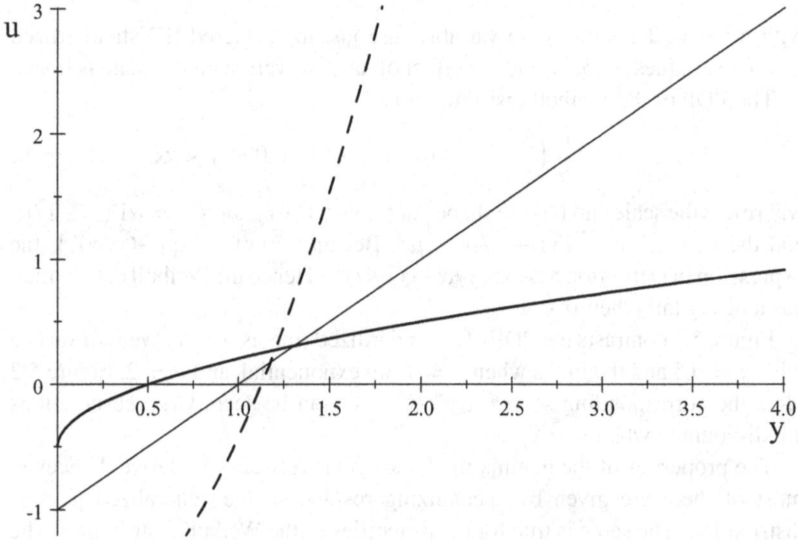

Figure 5.2. Weibull score functions (impact curves) for $\upsilon = 0.5$, exponential ($\upsilon = 1$, thin straight line) and $\upsilon = 2$ (dashes).

Remark 32 *For a gamma distribution, the coefficient of variation is $1/\gamma$. Thus there is overdispersion for $\gamma < 1$. The Weibull distribution displays overdispersion when $\upsilon < 1$, and as shown earlier, it has a heavy tail when $\upsilon < 1$. However, a gamma distribution never has a heavy tail, and this feature is consistent with its linear score function.*

The log-density for the t-th observation from the GG distribution when $\alpha_{t|t-1}$ is time-varying with an exponential link function is

$$\ln f_t(\lambda, \gamma, \upsilon) = \ln \upsilon - \lambda_{t|t-1} + (\upsilon\gamma - 1)\ln(y_t e^{-\lambda_{t|t-1}}) - (y_t e^{-\lambda_{t|t-1}})^{\upsilon} - \ln \Gamma(\gamma),$$

giving a score of

$$\frac{\partial \ln f_t}{\partial \lambda_{t|t-1}} = u_t = \upsilon(y_t e^{-\lambda_{t|t-1}})^{\upsilon} - \upsilon\gamma = \upsilon\left(\varepsilon_t^{\upsilon} - \gamma\right). \tag{5.13}$$

The following result, which can be proved directly by change of variable, enables the properties of the model to be obtained relatively easily.

Proposition 28 *For the generalized gamma distribution, the variables $g_t = \varepsilon_t^{\upsilon} = (y_t e^{-\lambda_{t|t-1}})^{\upsilon}$ are IID as $gamma(1, \gamma)$ at the true parameter values.*

5.2.1 Moments

The expressions given in Sub-section 5.1.2 may be easily specialized to the generalized gamma case.

Proposition 29 *For the generalized gamma model defined by (5.5) and (5.8), and u_t as in (5.13), the m-th moment exists if and only if $\psi_j < 1/\upsilon m$, for all $j = 1, 2, \ldots$, and is given by the expression*

$$E\left(y_t^m\right) = \frac{\Gamma(\gamma + m/\upsilon)}{\Gamma(\gamma)} e^{m(\omega - \gamma\upsilon\Sigma\psi_j)} \prod_{j=1}^{\infty}(1 - \upsilon m\psi_j)^{-\gamma}, \quad \psi_j < 1/\upsilon m, \quad m > 0.$$

Proof. In (5.9) $u_t = \upsilon(\varepsilon_t^{\upsilon} - \gamma)$, and the formula for the moment-generating function of a standardized gamma variate is $\gamma_{\gamma}(c) = E(e^{cg}) = (1-c)^{-1/\gamma}$, the result follows because $c = \upsilon m\psi_j$. ■

Corollary 23 *The unconditional mean – for example, the expected time between trades in a duration model – is*

$$E(y_t) = \frac{\Gamma(\gamma + 1/\upsilon)}{\Gamma(\gamma)} e^{\omega - \gamma\upsilon\Sigma\psi_j} \prod_{j=1}^{\infty}(1 - \upsilon\psi_j)^{-\gamma}, \qquad \psi_j < 1/\upsilon.$$

Corollary 24 *The volatility measure, (5.10), is*

$$V = \frac{\Pi_{j=1}^{\infty}(1 - 2\upsilon\psi_j)^{-\gamma}}{\left(\Pi_{j=1}^{\infty}(1 - \upsilon\psi_j)^{-\gamma}\right)^2} - 1.$$

Proposition 30 *When $\lambda_{t|t-1}$ is covariance stationary and $\psi_j < 1/2\upsilon c$, $j = 1, 2, \ldots$, the ACF of the observations raised to a positive power, c, is given by (5.11) with*

$$\kappa(c) = \frac{E\left(\varepsilon_t^{2c}\right)}{\left(E\left(\varepsilon_t^c\right)\right)^2} = \frac{\Gamma(\gamma + 2c/\upsilon)\Gamma(\gamma)}{(\Gamma(\gamma + c/\upsilon))^2}, \qquad c > 0, \tag{5.14}$$

$$V(c) = \left(\prod_{j=1}^{\infty}(1 - c\upsilon\psi_j)^{-\gamma}\right)^{-2} \prod_{j=1}^{\infty}(1 - 2c\upsilon\psi_j)^{-\gamma},$$

and $G(\tau, c)$, $\tau = 1, 2, \ldots$, equal to

$$(1 - c\upsilon\psi_\tau)^{-(c+1)\gamma}\left(\prod_{j=1}^{\infty}(1 - c\upsilon\psi_j)^{-\gamma}\right)^{-2}$$
$$\times\left[\prod_{j=1}^{\tau-1}(1 - c\upsilon\psi_j)^{-\gamma}\right]\prod_{i=1}^{\infty}(1 - c\upsilon(\psi_{\tau+i} + \psi_i))^{-\gamma},$$

with the term in square brackets absent for $\tau = 1$.

Proof. Using (2.11) to evaluate (5.11) gives all the terms except $E\left(y_t^c y_{t-\tau}^c\right)$. Evaluating this expression is not straightforward because of the dependence between $e^{\lambda_{t|t-1}}$ and $\varepsilon_{t-\tau}^c$. Following the argument in Appendix B gives the result. ■

Corollary 25 *When the ACF is for the untransformed observations, that is, $c = 1$, (5.14) is simply*

$$\kappa(1) = \frac{\Gamma(\gamma + 2/\upsilon)\Gamma(\gamma)}{(\Gamma(\gamma + 1/\upsilon))^2}.$$

For the classic gamma distribution, it reduces to $(1 + \gamma)/\gamma$.

Corollary 26 *The ACF for the score of the GG distribution is obtained by setting $\upsilon = c$ in Proposition 30.*

5.2.2 Forecasts

The formulae for forecasts of scale and observations take a similar form to those derived for the Gamma-GED-EGARCH model in Sub-section 4.5.2.

Proposition 31 *The optimal (MMSE) predictor of the scale, assuming that $\psi_j < \upsilon$, $j = 1, 2, \ldots$, is*

$$\alpha_{T+\ell|T} = E_T\left(e^{\lambda_{T+\ell|T+\ell-1}}\right) = e^{\lambda_{T+\ell|T}}\prod_{j=1}^{\ell-1} e^{-\gamma\upsilon\psi_j}(1 - \upsilon\psi_j)^{-\gamma}, \quad \ell = 2, 3, \ldots.$$

Provided that $\psi_j < \upsilon/2$ for $j = 1, 2, \ldots$, the volatility of the volatility is

$$VoV(\ell) = e^{2\lambda_{T+\ell|T}} \prod_{j=1}^{\ell-1} e^{-2\gamma\upsilon\psi_j}(1 - 2\upsilon\psi_j)^{-\gamma} - \alpha^2_{T+\ell|T}, \quad \ell = 2, 3, \ldots.$$

The predictor of level is $\mu_{T+\ell|T} = (\Gamma(\gamma + 1/\upsilon)/\Gamma(\gamma))\alpha_{T+\ell|T}$. The optimal predictor of the observation at $T + \ell$, that is, $E_T(y_{T+\ell})$, is the same as $\mu_{T+\ell|T}$. The optimal predictor of the variance of $y_{T+\ell}$ for $\ell = 2, 3, \ldots$, is

$$Var_T(y_{T+\ell}) = \frac{\Gamma(\gamma + 2/\upsilon)}{\Gamma(\gamma)} e^{2\lambda_{T+\ell|T}} \prod_{j=1}^{\ell-1} e^{-2\gamma\upsilon\psi_j}(1 - 2\upsilon\psi_j)^{-\gamma} - (E_T(y_{T+\ell}))^2.$$

As noted in Sub-section 5.1.3, it is easy to simulate the multistep predictive distribution from (5.12) by generating independent gamma variates. For one-step-ahead prediction, it is worth noting that for the Weibull distribution, the CDF is

$$F_T(y_{T+1}) = 1 - \exp[-(y_{T+1}e^{-\lambda_{T+1|T}})^{\upsilon}],$$

and so an expression for the quantile function can be obtained without difficulty.

5.2.3 Maximum Likelihood Estimation

The information matrix for a GG distribution is given in Kleiber and Kotz (2003, p. 157). When the scale parameter is replaced by its logarithm, λ, the information matrix is independent of λ. Differentiating the score in (5.13) yields

$$\frac{\partial^2 \ln f_t}{\partial \lambda^2_{t|t-1}} = \frac{\partial u_t}{\partial \lambda_{t|t-1}} = -\upsilon^2(y_t e^{-\lambda_{t|t-1}})^{\upsilon} = -\upsilon^2 g_t, \qquad t = 1, \ldots, T, \qquad (5.15)$$

so both the score and its derivative depend on the gamma variate, g_t. Hence the quantities needed to derive the asymptotic distribution of the ML estimators of parameters in a DCS model are easily found.

Proposition 32 *Consider the first-order model, (5.6), with unknown parameters $\boldsymbol{\psi} = (\kappa, \phi, \omega)'$. Provided that $|\phi| < 1$ and $b < 1$, the limiting distribution of $\sqrt{T}(\widetilde{\boldsymbol{\psi}}' - \boldsymbol{\psi}', \widetilde{\gamma} - \gamma, \widetilde{\upsilon} - \upsilon)'$ is multivariate normal, with zero mean and covariance matrix given by the inverse of*

$$\begin{bmatrix} \upsilon^2\gamma\mathbf{D}(\boldsymbol{\psi}) & \upsilon E(\partial\lambda/\partial\boldsymbol{\psi}) & -(1 + \gamma\psi(\gamma))E(\partial\lambda/\partial\boldsymbol{\psi}) \\ \upsilon E(\partial\lambda/\partial\boldsymbol{\psi}') & \psi'(\gamma) & -\psi(\gamma)/\upsilon \\ -(1 + \gamma\psi(\gamma))E(\partial\lambda/\partial\boldsymbol{\psi}') & -\psi(\gamma)/\upsilon & \{1 + \psi(\gamma)[2 + \psi(\gamma)] + \gamma\psi'(\gamma)\}/\upsilon^2 \end{bmatrix},$$

where $\mathbf{D}(\boldsymbol{\psi})$ is as in (2.40) with $\sigma^2_u = \upsilon^2\gamma$,

$$a = \phi - \gamma\upsilon^2\kappa,$$

$$b = \phi^2 - 2\phi\kappa\upsilon^2\gamma + \kappa^2\upsilon^4(1 + \gamma)\gamma,$$

$$c = -\kappa\upsilon^3\gamma$$

and $E(\partial\lambda/\partial\boldsymbol{\psi}) = (0\; 0\; (1 - \phi)/(1 - a))'$.

Proof. Because $g_t \sim gamma(1, \gamma)$, the first and second moments of (5.15) can be evaluated from (2.10). Thus

$$E\left[\left(\frac{\partial u_t}{\partial \lambda}\right)^k\right] = (-1)^k \upsilon^{2k}\frac{\Gamma(k+\gamma)}{\Gamma(\gamma)}, \quad k = 1, 2, \ldots,$$

leading to $E(\partial u_t/\partial \lambda) = -\upsilon^2\gamma$ and $E\left[(\partial u_t/\partial \lambda)^2\right] = \upsilon^4(1+\gamma)\gamma$. For c,

$$E\left[u_t\left(\frac{\partial u_t}{\partial \lambda}\right)\right] = \upsilon^3 E\left[g_t^2 - \gamma g_t\right] = -\upsilon^3\gamma.$$

The derivatives depend on gamma variables and so Theorem 4 can be applied.

■

Kleiber and Kotz (2003, p. 157) observe that the generalized gamma distribution is difficult to estimate and, when plausible estimates are obtained, their asymptotic covariance matrix is often close to being singular, with highly correlated υ and γ. Hence the gamma ($\upsilon = 1$) and Weibull ($\gamma = 1$) distributions are more practical. Specializing the formulae in Proposition 32 gives the following results.

Corollary 27 *The covariance matrix of the limiting distribution of the ML estimators for a conditional gamma distribution is*

$$Var\begin{pmatrix}\tilde{\boldsymbol{\psi}}\\ \tilde{\gamma}\end{pmatrix} = \begin{bmatrix}\gamma\mathbf{D}(\boldsymbol{\psi}) & (0\,0\,(1-\phi)/(1-a))'\\ (0\,0\,(1-\phi)/(1-a)) & \psi'(\gamma)\end{bmatrix}^{-1}.$$

Corollary 28 *For the Weibull distribution*

$$Var\begin{pmatrix}\tilde{\boldsymbol{\psi}}\\ \tilde{\upsilon}\end{pmatrix} = \begin{bmatrix}\upsilon^2\mathbf{D}(\boldsymbol{\psi}) & -0.423(0\,0\,(1-\phi)/(1-a))'\\ -0.423(0\,0\,(1-\phi)/(1-a)) & 1.824/\upsilon^2\end{bmatrix}^{-1}.$$

Corollary 29 *The exponential distribution is obtained by setting $\gamma = \upsilon = 1$, so $Var(\tilde{\boldsymbol{\psi}}) = \mathbf{D}^{-1}(\boldsymbol{\psi})$ with $b = \phi^2 - 2\phi\kappa + 2\kappa^2$.*

The constraint $b < 1$ permits a wide range of admissible values of κ. Figure 5.3 shows a plot of b for the exponential distribution with $\phi = 0.98$. Plots for gamma and Weibull distributions tell a similar story: the dashed line shows b against κ for a Weibull distribution with $\upsilon = 0.8$. As will be seen later, estimates of κ obtained in practice are typically quite small.

5.3 GENERALIZED BETA DISTRIBUTION

The generalized beta distribution (of the second kind) has PDF

$$f(y) = \frac{\nu(y/\alpha)^{\nu\xi-1}}{\alpha B(\xi,\varsigma)\left[(y/\alpha)^\nu + 1\right]^{\xi+\varsigma}}, \qquad \alpha, \nu, \xi, \varsigma > 0, \tag{5.16}$$

where α is the scale parameter, ν, ξ and ς are shape parameters, and $B(\xi, \varsigma)$ is the beta function. If all three shape parameters are unrestricted, the model is

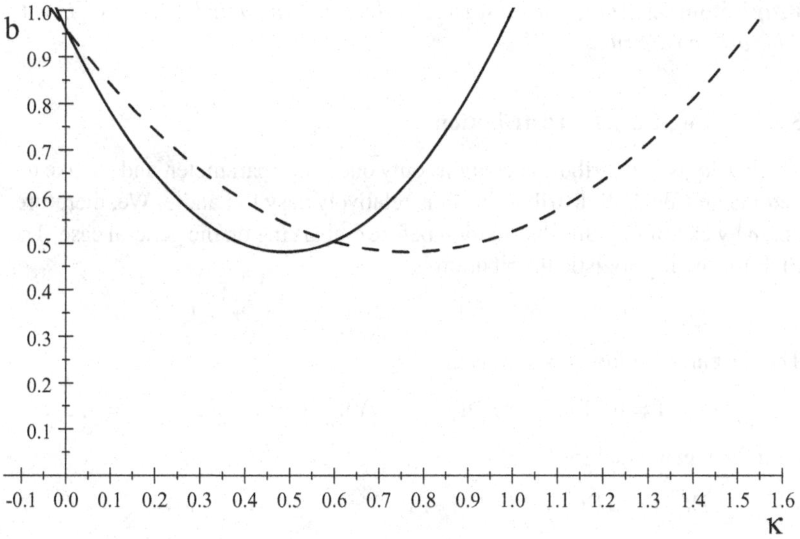

Figure 5.3. Plot of b, when $\phi = 0.98$, for the exponential distribution and a Weibull distribution with $\upsilon = 0.8$.

difficult to estimate. However, the generalized beta (GB2) distribution is very useful from the theoretical point of view because it contains many important distributions as special cases. These include the log-logistic and Burr distributions. The F distribution is closely related. Many of these distributions have been found useful as models of income and wealth and losses in insurance; see Kleiber and Kotz (2003, Chapter 6). All have potential in financial econometrics.

The log-density for the GB2 distribution with an exponential link function for the scale is

$$\ln f_t(\nu, \xi, \varsigma) = \ln \nu + \nu\xi\lambda_{t|t-1} + (\nu\xi - 1)\ln y_t \\ - (\xi + \varsigma)\ln((y_t e^{-\lambda_{t|t-1}})^{\nu} + 1) - \ln B(\xi, \varsigma),$$

and so

$$\frac{\partial \ln f_t}{\partial \lambda_{t|t-1}} = u_t = \nu(\xi + \varsigma)b_t(\xi, \varsigma) - \nu\xi, \tag{5.17}$$

where

$$b_t(\xi, \varsigma) = \frac{(y_t e^{-\lambda_{t|t-1}})^{\nu}}{(y_t e^{-\lambda_{t|t-1}})^{\nu} + 1}. \qquad t = 1, \ldots, T.$$

Because $0 \le b_t(\xi, \varsigma) \le 1$, it follows that as $y_t \to \infty$, the score approaches an upper bound of $\nu\varsigma$.

The following result can be proved directly.

Proposition 33 *At the true parameter values, the variable $b_t(\xi, \varsigma)$ is IID with a $beta(\xi, \varsigma)$ distribution.*

5.3.1 Log-Logistic Distribution

The log-logistic distribution contains only one shape parameter, and so, like the gamma and Weibull distributions, it is relatively easy to handle. We, therefore, begin by examining this distribution before embarking on the general case. The PDF for the log-logistic distribution is

$$f(y) = (\nu/\alpha)(y/\alpha)^{\nu-1}(1 + (y/\alpha)^{\nu})^{-2}, \qquad \nu, \alpha > 0.$$

The uncentered moments are given by

$$E(y_t^m) = \alpha^m \Gamma(1 + m/\nu)\Gamma(1 - m/\nu), \quad 0 < m < \nu, \quad m = 1, 2, \ldots,$$

with the mean equal to

$$E(y_t) = \alpha\Gamma(1 + 1/\nu)\Gamma(1 - 1/\nu) = \alpha\pi/(\nu \sin(\pi/\nu)), \qquad \nu > 1.$$

The quantile function formula is

$$F^{-1}(\tau) = \alpha\left(\frac{\tau}{1-\tau}\right)^{1/\nu}, \qquad 0 < \tau < 1,$$

and so the median is just α.

A time-varying scale with an exponential link function gives a log-density of

$$\ln f_t(\psi, \nu) = \ln \nu - \nu\lambda_{t|t-1} + (\nu - 1)\ln y_t - 2\ln(1 + (y_t e^{-\lambda_{t|t-1}})^{\nu}),$$
$$t = 1, \ldots, T,$$

and so

$$\frac{\partial \ln f_t}{\partial \lambda_{t|t-1}} = u_t = \frac{2\nu(y_t e^{-\lambda_{t|t-1}})^{\nu}}{1 + (y_t e^{-\lambda_{t|t-1}})^{\nu}} - \nu = 2\nu b_t(1, 1) - \nu, \tag{5.18}$$

where

$$b_t(1, 1) = \frac{(y_t e^{-\lambda_{t|t-1}})^{\nu}}{1 + (y_t e^{-\lambda_{t|t-1}})^{\nu}}$$

is distributed as $beta(1, 1)$. Because a $beta(1, 1)$ distribution is a standard uniform distribution, it is immediately apparent that the expectation of u_t is zero, and its variance is $\nu^2/3$. The fact that $b_t(1, 1)$ has a uniform distribution suggests that it might be the same as the PIT and indeed this turns out to be the case.

The asymptotic theory is not complicated. Differentiating the score gives

$$\frac{\partial u_t}{\partial \lambda_{t|t-1}} = -2\nu^2 b_t(1 - b_t)$$

and the following result is a special case of Proposition 36 of Sub-section 5.3.3.

Proposition 34 *Consider a conditional log-logistic distribution with a stationary first-order dynamic equation, (5.6). Provided that $b < 1$, the limiting distribution of $\sqrt{T}(\widetilde{\boldsymbol{\psi}}' - \boldsymbol{\psi}', \widetilde{\nu} - \nu)'$ is multivariate normal, with zero mean and covariance matrix*

$$Var\begin{pmatrix}\widetilde{\boldsymbol{\psi}} \\ \widetilde{\nu}\end{pmatrix} = \begin{bmatrix}(3/\nu^2)\mathbf{D}^{-1}(\boldsymbol{\psi}) & \mathbf{0} \\ \mathbf{0}' & 0.699\nu^2\end{bmatrix}, \tag{5.19}$$

where $\mathbf{0}$ is a vector of zeroes and $\mathbf{D}(\boldsymbol{\psi})$ is as in (2.40) with

$$\begin{aligned} a &= \phi - \kappa\nu^2/3 \\ b &= \phi^2 - (2/3)\nu^2\phi\kappa + 2\kappa^2\nu^4/15 \\ c &= 0. \end{aligned} \tag{5.20}$$

5.3.2 Moments, Autocorrelations and Forecasts

As with the Beta-t-EGARCH model, the boundedness of the score means that the existence of moments is not affected by the changing volatility.

Proposition 35 *For the generalized beta model defined by (5.5) and (5.8), and u_t as in (5.17), the m-th moment exists if and only if $\psi_j < 1/\nu m$, for all $j = 1, 2, \ldots$, and is given by the expression*

$$E(y_t^m) = E(\varepsilon_t^m) E\exp(m\lambda_{t|t-1}), \quad -\nu\xi < m < \nu\varsigma,$$

where the moments of the standardized variable are

$$E(\varepsilon_t^m) = \frac{\Gamma(\xi + m/\nu)\Gamma(\varsigma - m/\nu)}{\Gamma(\xi)\Gamma(\varsigma)}, \quad -\nu\xi < m < \nu\varsigma,$$

and

$$E\exp(m\lambda_{t|t-1}) = e^{m(\omega - \nu\xi\Sigma\psi_j)} \prod_{j=1}^{\infty} M_\beta(\nu(\xi + \varsigma)m\psi_j; \xi, \varsigma), \tag{5.21}$$

with $M_\beta(c; \alpha, \beta)$ denoting the MGF of a standardized beta variate, (2.8).

Proof. In (5.9), $u_t = \nu(\xi + \varsigma)b_t - \nu\xi$. ■

Corollary 30 *The volatility measure, (5.10), is*

$$V = \frac{\Pi_{j=1}^{\infty} M_\beta(\nu(\xi + \varsigma)2\psi_j; \xi, \varsigma)}{\left(\Pi_{j=1}^{\infty} M_\beta(\nu(\xi + \varsigma)\psi_j; \xi, \varsigma)\right)^2} - 1.$$

The formulae for the autocorrelations of powers of y_t follow from the formulae in Sub-section 5.2.2 in a similar way to those of Beta-t-EGARCH.

The optimal predictor of the scale is

$$\alpha_{T+\ell|T} = E_T\left(e^{\lambda_{T+\ell|T+\ell-1}}\right)$$
$$= e^{\lambda_{T+\ell|T}} e^{m(\omega - \nu\xi\Sigma\psi_j)} \prod_{j=1}^{\infty} e^{\nu(\xi+\varsigma)m\Sigma\psi_j} M_\beta(\nu(\xi+\varsigma)m\psi_j; \xi, \varsigma),$$

whereas the predictor of level, and hence the observations, $y_{T+\ell}$, is

$$\mu_{T+\ell|T} = \frac{\Gamma(\xi+1/\nu)\Gamma(\varsigma-1/\nu)}{\Gamma(\xi)\Gamma(\varsigma)}\alpha_{T+\ell|T}, \quad \ell = 2, 3, \ldots. \qquad \nu\varsigma > 1.$$

The volatility of the volatility can be similarly found, as can the predictor of the variance of $y_{T+\ell}$. The multistep predictive distribution can be simulated by generating independent beta variates in (5.12).

5.3.3 Maximum Likelihood Estimation

The static information matrix can be found in Kleiber and Kotz (2003, p. 194). Adapting it to the exponential link function gives

$$\mathbf{I}\begin{pmatrix}\lambda\\ \nu\\ \xi\\ \varsigma\end{pmatrix} = \begin{bmatrix} \frac{\nu^2\xi\varsigma}{1+\xi+\varsigma} & I_{12} & \frac{\nu\varsigma}{\xi+\varsigma} & \frac{-\nu\xi}{\xi+\varsigma} \\ I_{21} & I_{22} & I_{23} & I_{24} \\ \frac{\nu\varsigma}{\xi+\varsigma} & I_{23} & \psi'(\xi)-\psi'(\xi+\varsigma) & -\psi'(\xi+\varsigma) \\ \frac{-\nu\xi}{\xi+\varsigma} & I_{24} & -\psi'(\xi+\varsigma) & \psi'(\varsigma)-\psi'(\xi+\varsigma) \end{bmatrix}, \tag{5.22}$$

where

$$I_{21} = I_{12} = \frac{\xi-\varsigma-\xi\varsigma\,(\psi(\xi)-\psi(\varsigma))}{1+\xi+\varsigma}, \qquad I_{23} = I_{32} = -\frac{\varsigma\,(\psi(\xi)-\psi(\varsigma))-1}{\nu(\xi+\varsigma)},$$

$$I_{24} = I_{42} = -\frac{\xi\,(\psi(\varsigma)-\psi(\xi))-1}{\nu(\xi+\varsigma)},$$

and I_{22} is

$$\frac{1+\xi+\varsigma+\xi\varsigma\left(\psi'(\xi)+\psi'(\varsigma)+(\psi(\varsigma)-\psi(\xi)+(\xi-\varsigma)/\xi\varsigma)^2\right)-(\xi\varsigma)^{-1}\left(\xi^2+\varsigma^2\right)}{\nu^2(1+\xi+\varsigma)}.$$

The proposition below follows from the fact that the score and its derivative,

$$\frac{\partial u_t}{\partial\lambda_{t|t-1}} = \frac{-\nu^2(\xi+\varsigma)(y_t e^{-\lambda_{t|t-1}})^\nu}{((y_t e^{-\lambda_{t|t-1}})^\nu+1)^2} = -\nu^2(\xi+\varsigma)b_t(1-b_t), \tag{5.23}$$

depend on a beta distribution, as shown in Proposition 33.

Proposition 36 *For a conditional GB2 distribution with a first-order stationary dynamic model with* $b < 1$, *the limiting distribution of* $\sqrt{T}(\widetilde{\psi}' - \psi',$

$\widetilde{\nu}-\nu,\ \widetilde{\xi}-\xi,\ \widetilde{\varsigma}-\varsigma)'$ is multivariate normal, with covariance matrix given by combining the inverse of (2.56) with the appropriate elements of (5.22) and the quantities a, b and c, evaluated from

$$E\left[\frac{\partial u_t}{\partial \lambda}\right] = \frac{-\nu^2\xi\varsigma}{\xi+\varsigma+1},$$

$$E\left[\left(\frac{\partial u_t}{\partial \lambda}\right)^2\right] = \frac{\nu^4(\xi+\varsigma)\xi\varsigma\,(\varsigma+1)(\xi+1)}{(\varsigma+\xi+3)(\varsigma+\xi+2)(\varsigma+\xi+1)}$$

and

$$E\left[u_t\frac{\partial u_t}{\partial \lambda}\right] = \frac{\nu^3\xi\varsigma(\xi+\varsigma)(\xi+1)}{(\varsigma+\xi+2)(\varsigma+\xi+1)} - \frac{\nu^3\xi\varsigma}{(\xi+\varsigma+1)}.$$

Proof. The formula in (2.5) gives the expectation of (5.23) as

$$E\left[\frac{\partial u_t}{\partial \lambda}\right] = -\nu^2(\xi+\varsigma)E(b_t(1-b_t)) = \frac{-\nu^2\xi\varsigma}{\xi+\varsigma+1}.$$

The same formula is used to evaluate

$$E\left[\left(\frac{\partial u_t}{\partial \lambda}\right)^2\right] = \nu^4(\xi+\varsigma)^2E\left[b_t^2(1-b_t)^2\right]$$

and

$$E\left[u_t\frac{\partial u_t}{\partial \lambda}\right] = \nu^3(\xi+\varsigma)^2E\left[b_t^2(1-b_t)\right] - \nu^3(\xi+\varsigma)E[b_t(1-b_t)].$$

A formal proof of consistency and asymptotic normality follows directly from Theorem 3 because the preceding functions of the score and its derivative depend only on variables of the form $b_t^h(1-b_t)^k$, $h, k = 1, 2, \ldots$. ■

Corollary 31 *For the log-logistic distribution, the result in (5.19) follows because $\xi = \varsigma = 1$ and so*

$$I_{11} = \nu^2/3, \qquad I_{12} = 0 \qquad \textit{and}$$

$$I_{22} = \frac{1}{3\nu^2}\left[3+\psi'(1)+\psi'(1)-2\right] = \frac{1}{3\nu^2}\left[\frac{\pi^2}{3}+1\right] = \frac{1.430}{\nu^2}.$$

5.3.4 Burr Distribution

The generalized (Type XII) Burr distribution, also known as the Singh-Maddala distribution, is obtained by setting $\xi = 1$ in (5.16) so

$$f(y) = \frac{\varsigma\nu(y/\alpha)^{\nu-1}}{\alpha\left[(y/\alpha)^{\nu}+1\right]^{1+\varsigma}}, \qquad \alpha, \nu, \varsigma > 0,$$

because $B(1, \varsigma) = 1/\varsigma$. There are a number of different parameterizations, for example those in Tadikamalla (1980) and Grammig and Maurier (2000), but the one based on the GB2 distribution is the most convenient. The Weibull distribution can be obtained by letting $\varsigma \to \infty$. Indeed, the Burr distribution is sometimes called the compound Weibull. The Weibull, in turn, becomes an exponential distribution when $\nu = 1$.

The log-logistic distribution is a special case of the Burr distribution obtained by setting $\varsigma = 1$. When a Burr distribution is fitted, a Wald test of $\varsigma = 1$ is straightforward.

The CDF, and hence the PIT, of a Burr variate has, as Kleiber and Kotz (2003, p. 198) put it, the 'pleasantly simple form'

$$F(y) = 1 - \left[\left(ye^{-\lambda_{t|t-1}}\right)^{\nu} + 1\right]^{-\varsigma}. \tag{5.24}$$

The quantile function is equally simple, namely,

$$F^{-1}(\tau) = \exp \lambda_{t|t-1}[(1-\tau)^{-1/\varsigma} - 1]^{1/\nu}, \qquad 0 < \tau < 1.$$

The PIT for the unrestricted GB2 distribution is more complicated; see Kleiber and Kotz (2003, p. 188).

The fact that the survival function, $\overline{F}(y)$, is $\left[(y/\alpha)^{\nu} + 1\right]^{-\varsigma}$ makes it easy to see that the Burr distribution is long-tailed, and therefore heavy-tailed, because in Definition 6

$$\frac{\overline{F}(y+x)}{\overline{F}(y)} = \left[\frac{(y/\alpha)^{\nu} + 1}{(y+x)/\alpha)^{\nu} + 1}\right]^{\varsigma} \to 1 \qquad as \quad y \to \infty.$$

As noted after (33), the score for all GB2 distributions discounts large observations because it approaches an upper bound of $\nu\varsigma$ as $y \to \infty$; see Figure 1.3.

The coefficient of variation can indicate overdispersion or underdispersion. For a Burr distribution, the variance, and hence the CV, goes to zero, as $\nu\varsigma \to \infty$. It only exceeds one if $\nu\varsigma$ is sufficiently small, but recall that when $\nu\varsigma \leq 2$, the variance does not exist because $\Gamma(\varsigma - 2/\nu) \to \infty$ as $\nu\varsigma \to 2$. Figure 5.4 shows the coefficient of variation plotted against ν for a log-logistic distribution, that is, $\varsigma = 1$. There is overdispersion only when ν is close to two, at which point the variance does not exist.

The score in (5.17) simplifies a little for the Burr distribution and has a $beta(1, \varsigma)$ distribution. In the information matrix, the element for ς, that is, $\psi'(\varsigma) - \psi'(\xi + \varsigma)$, becomes $\psi'(\varsigma) - \psi'(1 + \varsigma) = 1/\varsigma^2$.

5.3.5 Generalized Pareto Distribution

Extreme value distributions are employed in a number of ways. For example, they may be used to model the maximum or minimum value of a daily return in a month. Alternatively, they may model the distribution of a variable, given that the value is above or below a certain predefined threshold. The generalized Pareto distribution is sometimes used for this purpose; see Tsay

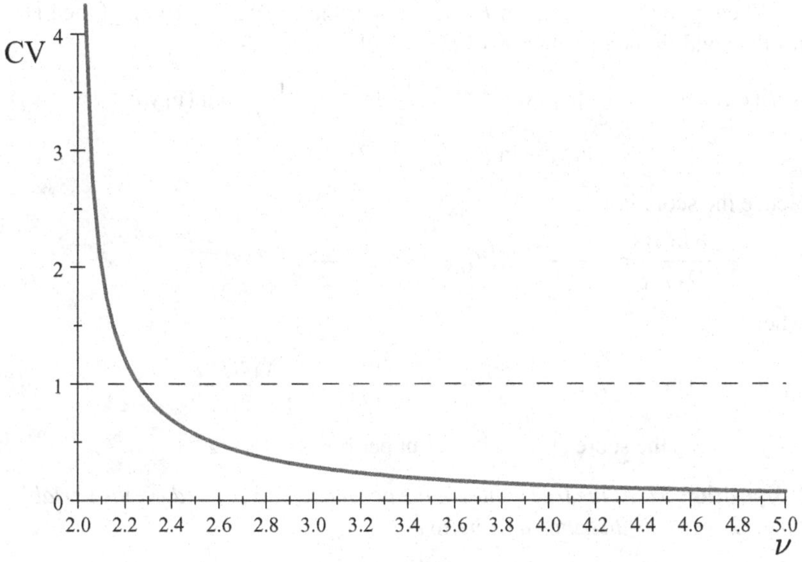

Figure 5.4. Coefficient of variation for log-logistic distribution.

(2010, p. 360–377). Its PDF, for $y \geq y_0$, where y_0 is a lower bound, is

$$f(y) = \eta^{-1}\left[1 + ky/\eta\right]^{-1/k-1}, \quad \eta > 0, \ k > 0,$$

where η and k are scale and shape parameters. Letting k be zero gives the exponential distribution.

If the generalized Pareto distribution is reparameterized by defining $\alpha = \eta/k$ and $\varsigma = 1/k$, it is readily seen to be a special case of the Burr distribution in which $\nu = 1$. The scale parameter may, therefore, be allowed to evolve over time, according to $\alpha_{t|t-1} = \exp(\lambda_{t|t-1})$, and the moments, forecasts and asymptotic distribution can be found from the general results for the GB2 distribution.

5.3.6 *F* Distribution

If centered returns have a t_ν distribution, their squares will be distributed as $F(1, \nu)$. This observation suggests the F distribution as a candidate for modelling various measures of daily volatility. More generally, the two shape parameters (degrees of freedom) in the $F(\nu_1, \nu_2)$ distribution give it considerable versatility.

The F distribution with $\nu_1 = \nu_2$ is a special case of the GB2 distribution obtained by setting $\xi = \varsigma = \nu_1/2 = \nu_2/2$ and $\nu = 1$. Even though F distributions with different degrees of freedom do not fall within the GB2 class, the score has a beta distribution and the properties of the model may be derived along similar lines.

When ε_t in (5.5) is from an $F(\nu_1, \nu_2)$ distribution, the logarithm of the PDF for the conditional distribution of the t-th observation is

$$\ln f_t(\psi, \nu_1, \nu_2) = \frac{\nu_1}{2} \ln \nu_1 y_t e^{-\lambda_{t|t-1}} + \frac{\nu_2}{2} \ln \nu_2 - \frac{\nu_1 + \nu_2}{2} \ln(\nu_1 y_t e^{-\lambda_{t|t-1}} + \nu_2)$$
$$- \ln y_t - \ln B(\nu_1/2, \nu_2/2).$$

Hence the score is

$$\frac{\partial \ln f_t}{\partial \lambda_{t|t-1}} = \frac{\nu_1 + \nu_2}{2} b_t(\nu_1/2, \nu_2/2) - \frac{\nu_1}{2},$$

where

$$b_t(\nu_1/2, \nu_2/2) = \frac{\nu_1 y_t e^{-\lambda_{t|t-1}}/\nu_2}{1 + \nu_1 y_t e^{-\lambda_{t|t-1}}/\nu_2} = \frac{\nu_1 \varepsilon_t/\nu_2}{1 + \nu_1 \varepsilon_t/\nu_2}.$$

As $y_t \to \infty$, the score approaches its upper bound of $\nu_2/2$.

Proposition 37 *At the true values of the parameters,* ψ, ν_1 *and* ν_2, *the variable* $b_t(\nu_1/2, \nu_2/2)$ *is distributed as* $beta(\nu_1/2, \nu_2/2)$.

Proof. Because ε_t depends on the ratio of independent chi-square variables, the result follows from Lemma 3. ■

Taking expectations of the score confirms that it has zero mean because $E(b_t(\nu_1/2, \nu_2/2)) = \nu_1/(\nu_1 + \nu_2)$.

The moments and ACF of the observations in the DCS-F model can be found from the properties of the beta distribution and the moments of the F distribution. The mean of an $F(\nu_1, \nu_2)$ distribution is $\nu_2/(\nu_2 - 2)$, $\nu_2 > 2$ and the variance is $2\nu_2^2(\nu_1 + \nu_2 - 2)/(\nu_1(\nu_2 - 2)^2(\nu_2 - 4))$, $\nu_2 > 4$.

As regards the asymptotic distribution, differentiating the score gives

$$\frac{\partial u_t}{\partial \lambda_{t|t-1}} = -\frac{\nu_1 + \nu_2}{2} b_t(1 - b_t).$$

Hence its expectation is easily found using (2.5), as are the expectations of

$$\left(\frac{\partial u_t}{\partial \lambda_{t|t-1}}\right)^2 = \left(\frac{\nu_1 + \nu_2}{2}\right)^2 b_t^2(1 - b_t)^2$$

and

$$u_t \frac{\partial u_t}{\partial \lambda_{t|t-1}} = -\left(\frac{\nu_1 + \nu_2}{2}\right) b_t^2(1 - b_t) + \frac{\nu_1}{2} b_t(1 - b_t).$$

The formulae for a, b and c are similar to those for the Burr distribution; see Andres (2012).

5.4 LOG-NORMAL DISTRIBUTION

If, in the unobserved components model (5.2) and (5.1), the disturbance term, $\ln \varepsilon_t$, and the disturbance driving λ_t are both Gaussian, the model is linear. It can be handled efficiently by the Kalman filter, with the log-likelihood function constructed from the prediction error decomposition. The log-density is

$$\ln f_t(\ln y_t) = -\frac{1}{2}\ln 2\pi - \frac{1}{2}\ln \sigma_t^2 - \frac{1}{2\sigma_t^2}(\ln y_t - \lambda_{t|t-1})^2, \qquad t = 1, \ldots, T,$$

where σ_t^2 is the prediction error variance at time t. The parameters are the variance of $\ln \varepsilon_t$, denoted $\sigma^2_{\ln \varepsilon}$, together with δ, ϕ and σ^2_η (or alternatively, the signal–noise ratio, $q = \sigma^2_\eta / \sigma^2_{\ln \varepsilon}$). However, the parameters could also be taken to be as in the steady-state Kalman filter, so they become[1] σ^2, δ (or ω), ϕ and κ. These are the parameters of the innovations form. They are also the parameters for the model when it is adapted so as to be within the DCS class for non-negative variables with the distribution of y_t lognormal.[2] Instead of $\lambda_{t|t-1}$ being a time-varying conditional mean for $\ln y_t$, it is the logarithm of a conditional scale[3] for y_t, as in (5.5). Note that σ^2 is now a shape parameter as witnessed by the fact that the CV is $\exp(\sigma^2) - 1$. The log-density is

$$\ln f_t(y_t) = -\frac{1}{2}\ln 2\pi - \frac{1}{2}\ln \sigma^2 - \frac{1}{2\sigma^2}(\ln y_t e^{-\lambda_{t|t-1}})^2 - \ln y_t, \quad t = 1, \ldots, T.$$

Hence the conditional score for $\lambda_{t|t-1}$ is

$$\frac{\partial \ln f_t}{\partial \lambda_{t|t-1}} = \frac{\ln(y_t e^{-\lambda_{t|t-1}})}{\sigma^2}. \tag{5.25}$$

Dividing the score by the information quantity gives

$$u_t = \ln(y_t \exp(-\lambda_{t|t-1})) = \ln \varepsilon_t, \qquad t = 1, \ldots, T,$$

as the most convenient disturbance for the dynamic equation.

ML estimation of the DCS model is helped by the fact that σ^2 can be concentrated out of the likelihood function because, for given values of ω, ϕ and κ,

$$\widetilde{\sigma}^2 = T^{-1}\sum_{t=1}^{T}(\ln y_t e^{-\lambda_{t|t-1}})^2.$$

The asymptotic distribution of the ML estimators is easily deduced because the score, (5.25), is normal. In fact, the theory is essentially the same as in Section 3.3. The covariance matrix of the limiting distribution of $\sqrt{T}(\widetilde{\boldsymbol{\psi}}' - \boldsymbol{\psi}', \widetilde{\sigma}^2 - \sigma^2)'$ is

$$Var\begin{pmatrix}\widetilde{\boldsymbol{\psi}} \\ \widetilde{\sigma}^2\end{pmatrix} = \begin{bmatrix}\sigma^2 \mathbf{D}^{-1}(\boldsymbol{\psi}) & \mathbf{0} \\ \mathbf{0}' & 2\sigma^4\end{bmatrix},$$

[1] When the KF is run, σ_t^2 will normally be time-varying because of the initialization, but will tend towards a constant, σ^2, as $t \to \infty$.

[2] The log-normal can be obtained as a limiting case of the GG distribution; see Kleiber and Kotz (2003, p. 149).

[3] The two $\lambda'_{t|t-1}s$ may not be identical because of different initializations, but they will converge.

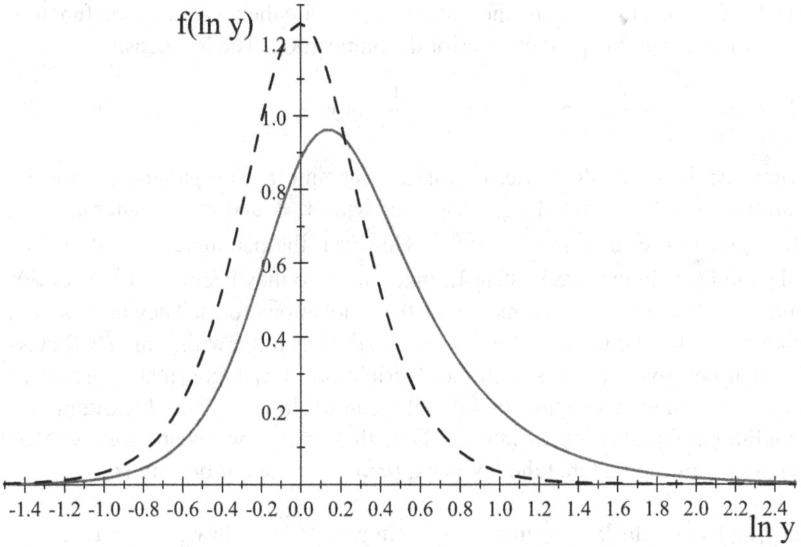

Figure 5.5. Logarithm of variable with Burr distribution with $\nu = 5$ and $\varsigma = 0.5$ and logarithm of variable with log-logistic distribution (i.e. logistic distribution) with $\nu = 5$ (dashed).

where the matrix $\mathbf{D}(\psi)$ is as in (2.40) with $a = \phi - \kappa$, $b = a^2$ and $c = 0$. As shown in Corollary 14, the condition $b < 1$ holds provided $\phi - 1 < \kappa < \phi + 1$.

Predictions of volatility, its variance and other moments can be made using the formula for the MGF of a normal distribution. Thus

$$E_T\big(\exp(m\lambda_{T+\ell|T+\ell-1})\big) = \exp(m\lambda_{T+1|T}).\prod_{j=1}^{\ell-1}\exp\big(0.5\sigma^2 m^2\psi_j^2\big), \quad \ell = 2, 3, \ldots.$$

It is straightforward to simulate the multistep predictive distribution by generating independent normal variates. However, this is not really necessary as the quantiles of y_t may be obtained directly from those of $\ln y_t$ by taking the exponent.

It is instructive to contrast the log-normal distribution with the log-logistic. The log-logistic distribution has a similar shape to the log-normal, and both have heavy tails, but the tail of the log-logistic is heavier. This difference is reflected in the respective score functions: as can be seen from (5.25), the score of the log-normal is unbounded, whereas that of the log-logistic has an upper bound of ν. Hence the log-logistic is more resistant to extreme observations.

If the distribution of $\ln y$ is taken to be the point of reference, the scale in the log-normal and log-logistic distributions translates into location for the normal and logistic distributions. Figure 5.5 shows the PDF of the logistic. It is remarkably similar to the PDF for a normal distribution, but there is excess kurtosis of 6/5. The PDF for the logarithm of a Burr variate with ς set to 0.5, but

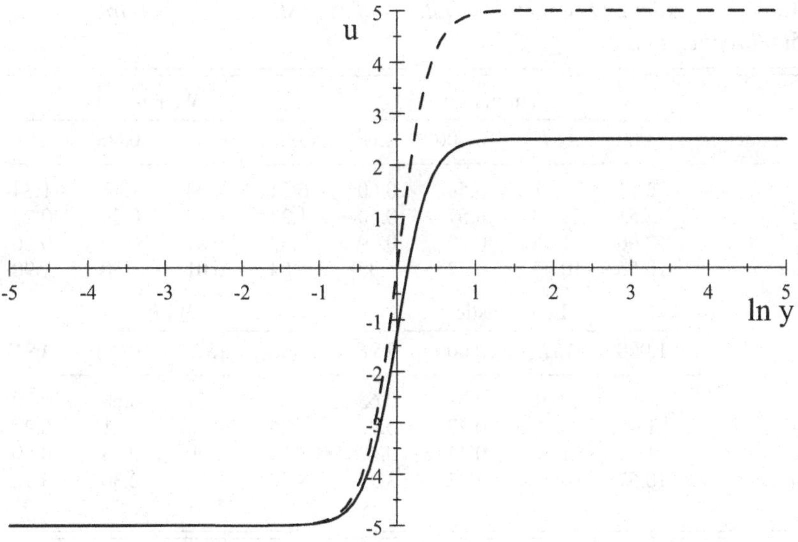

Figure 5.6. Score functions for logarithm of variable with Burr distribution with $\nu = 5$ and $\varsigma = 0.5$ and variable with logistic distribution with $\nu = 5$ (dashed).

with the same value of ν as for the logistic, is also shown. (Both distributions are standardized by setting λ to zero.) The flexibility given by the extra parameter is noticeable in the skewness and heavier upper tail, a feature that is of some practical importance in modelling range and realized volatility.

The score function for the normal distribution is, of course, linear, as in Figure 3.1, but the score for the logistic[4] goes towards an upper bound of ν as $\ln y \to \infty$ and a lower bound of minus ν as $\ln y \to -\infty$. Figure 5.6 shows the scores for the logarithms of variables with the Burr and log-logistic distributions, with the same parameters as in Figure 5.5.

5.5 MONTE CARLO EXPERIMENTS

A set of Monte Carlo experiments was carried out to determine the small sample properties of ML estimators; see Andres and Harvey (2012). For samples of size 1000 and 10,000, the means and standard deviations of the estimates from 5000 replications were obtained for gamma ($\gamma = 6$), Weibull ($\upsilon = 2$), log-logistic ($\nu = 4$) and Burr ($\nu = 4$, $\varsigma = 0.75$). The dynamic parameters were set to $\phi = 0.98$ and $\kappa = 0.1$, both of which are typical of what might be expected in practice. According to the asymptotic theory, the large sample distribution of all estimators is independent of ω, which was therefore set to zero.

[4] The formula for the score of $x = \ln y$ is the same as the formula for the score of y, but with y replaced by $\exp(x)$.

Table 5.1. *Estimated standard deviations of ML estimates* ($\times 100$) *from 5000 replications*

	Gamma				Weibull			
Parameters	1,000	ASE	10,000	ASE	1,000	ASE	10,000	ASE
ω	2.51	1.91	0.58	0.60	6.21	4.24	1.40	1.34
ϕ	2.51	1.89	0.57	0.60	1.24	0.85	0.28	0.27
κ	2.00	1.86	0.59	0.59	0.83	0.81	0.25	0.26
ν or υ	10.56	10.53	3.27	3.33	5.04	6.01	1.50	1.90
	Log-logistic				Burr			
	1,000	ASE	10,000	ASE	1,000	ASE	10,000	ASE
ω	2.69	2.01	0.66	0.63	3.10	2.21	0.68	0.70
ϕ	1.10	0.80	0.27	0.25	1.26	0.84	0.31	0.27
κ	1.31	1.32	0.43	0.42	1.50	1.60	0.58	0.50
ν	10.57	10.58	3.43	3.35	8.88	9.86	2.36	3.12
ς					20.96	22.31	6.22	7.05

The averages of the ML estimates were close to the true values. The standard deviations for ω, ϕ and κ shown in Table 5.1 tend to be slightly bigger than the asymptotic standard errors ($ASEs$). In almost all cases, the figures are closer for $T = 10{,}000$ than for $T = 1{,}000$. No problems were encountered in maximizing the log-likelihood functions.

5.6 LEVERAGE, LONG MEMORY AND DIURNAL VARIATION

Leverage effects are likely to play a prominent role in modelling variables associated with stock returns; see Engle and Gallo (2006). Information on the direction of the market is readily available, and so leverage may be introduced into DCS models for non-negative variables in the same way as was done for the Beta-t-EGARCH and Gamma-GED-EGARCH models. The results on ACFs may be similarly derived and the asymptotic distribution of the ML estimators is given by Proposition 23.

A plot of the score for a standardised Burr distribution is shown as the dashed line in Figure 5.7. (The second moment does not exist for these particular parameter values, but this does not affect the viability of the model.) The Burr score function, or impact curve, is less sensitive to large observations than is the gamma score. Indeed, as already shown, the score for a Burr distribution, and for GB distributions in general, converges to an upper bound as $y_t \to \infty$. When a leverage effect is to be modelled, the variable $u_t + E(u_t)$ is multiplied by an indicator taking the value one or minus one according to whether the market has moved up or down in the current period. If a negative value of the

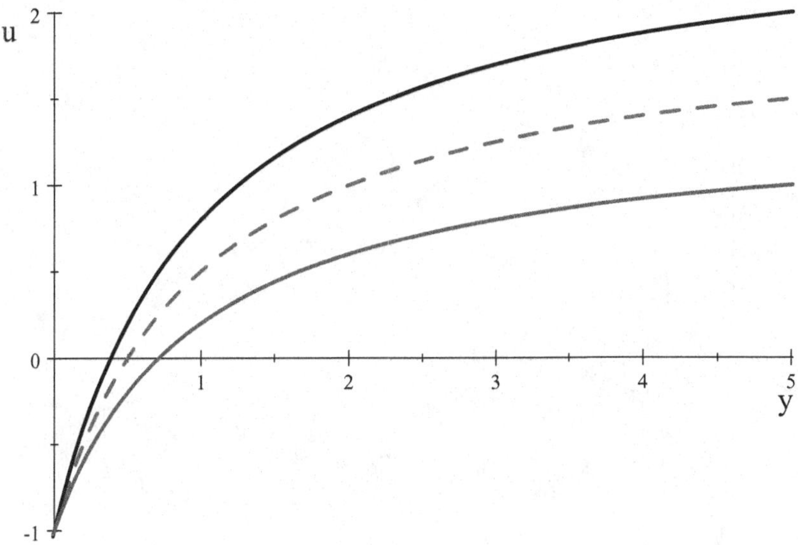

Figure 5.7. Plot of conditional score against a standardized observation for Burr distribution with $\nu = 2$ and $\gamma = 1$ (dashed). Leverage effect response for negative (positive) returns is given by the upper (lower) line.

indicator increases volatility, the effect on the score of a negative (positive) value is as shown by the upper (lower) line in Figure 5.7.

Two component models are likely to prove useful for modelling series that seem to exhibit long memory; see the discussion in Section 4.10. A typical correlogram is shown in the next section in Figure 5.8.

Explanatory variables can be included in the equation for $\lambda_{t|t-1}$ as in Section 2.6, and time variation can be modelled as in Section 4.11. There are no new technical issues of any substance. A component is needed to capture the diurnal pattern; see, for example, Brownlees et al. (2011). The structure is similar to that adopted for intra-day returns by Andersen and Bollerslev (1998), but the DCS approach allows the diurnal pattern, which may be time-varying, to be estimated as part of the model. A time-varying diurnal component can be made more parsimonious by using a limited number of trigonometric terms or by a time-varying periodic spline as in Harvey and Koopman (1993). An overnight effect, to allow for a jump at the beginning of trading, may also be included. The overnight effect is modelled by a dummy variable, which is unity for the first observation of the day and zero otherwise, but it too may be allowed to evolve slowly over time.

The use of an exponential link function means that the various components enter the model a multiplicative fashion. The model is as in (5.5), with

$$\lambda_{t|t-1} = \lambda_{1,t|t-1} + \lambda_{2,t|t-1} + \gamma_{t|t-1} + \varkappa_{t|t-1}, \quad t = 1, \ldots, T,$$

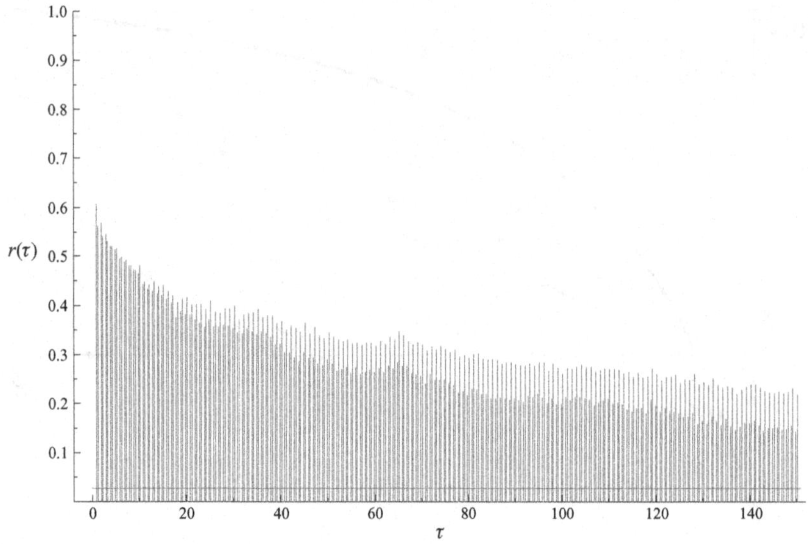

Figure 5.8. Sample ACFs of Range and LogRange for CAC index.

where $\lambda_{1,t|t-1}$ is a long-term component, which may be a persistent AR(1), a random walk or an integrated random walk, a short-term component, $\lambda_{2,t|t-1}$, a diurnal component, $\gamma_{t|t-1}$, and an overnight effect, $\varkappa_{t|t-1}$. There is already a good deal of evidence in favour of the exponential formulation; see Martens et al. (2002) and Brownlees et al. (2011).

5.7 TESTS AND MODEL SELECTION

Model selection requires decisions to be made about the distribution and the form of the dynamic equation for the scale. The starting point is testing against serial correlation in the observations. However, just as squared observations may be unduly influenced by outliers in returns, so the observations themselves may not be robust here. A square root or logarithmic transformation may be better. The correlograms for the daily range of the Paris CAC index[5] and its logarithm are shown in Figure 5.8. The first few sample autocorrelations for the raw observations are bigger than those given by the logarithmic transformation, but at higher lags the autocorrelations of the logarithms are bigger and die away more slowly. A similar pattern occurs with the daily Dow Jones range where there are more significant outliers.

Tests for changing scale can be carried out using the Box-Ljung statistic. Under the null hypothesis the observations are independent, so any transformation can be used. If a distribution is specified at the outset, Lagrange multiplier

[5] See Sub-section 5.8.1 for details.

tests can be carried out with the $Q_u(P)$ statistic, (2.73), based on the score. For example, with the F distribution,

$$\widetilde{u}_t = \frac{\widetilde{\nu}_1 + \widetilde{\nu}_2}{2} \frac{\widetilde{\nu}_1 y_t \exp(-\widetilde{\lambda})/\widetilde{\nu}_2}{1 + \widetilde{\nu}_1 y_t \exp(-\widetilde{\lambda})/\widetilde{\nu}_2} - \frac{\widetilde{\nu}_1}{2}, \qquad t = 1, \ldots, T,$$

where $\widetilde{\lambda}$, $\widetilde{\nu}_1$ and $\widetilde{\nu}_2$ are the ML estimators of the location/scale parameter and the degrees-of-freedom parameters in the static distribution. When the distribution is gamma, the LM test simply uses the untransformed observations. For other distributions from the generalized gamma family, the LM test will use the autocorrelations for y_t^{υ}, where the shape parameter, υ, is estimated.

When there is no prior guidance regarding the form of the conditional distribution, it may be useful to fit an unobserved components dynamic model to the logarithm of the observations. The measurement equation is (5.2), and this is combined with a suitable transition equation. The simplicity of the estimation procedure, which assumes a linear model, offers the opportunity to experiment with various dynamic specifications. Examining the distribution of the residuals may suggest which distributions are likely to prove most useful; see Figure 5.5. Indeed, a test of normality may indicate that the log-normal model fits the data, in which case there is no need to proceed any further.

When a DCS model is fitted, diagnostic tests of serial correlation and distribution can be based on the scores; the residuals, that is, $y_t \exp(-\lambda_{t|t-1})$; the PITs of the residuals and the normalized PITs. As with the exponential distribution, the PITs for a Weibull distribution are given by a simple formula, namely,

$$PIT(y_t) = 1 - \exp[-(y_t e^{-\lambda_{t|t-1}})^{\upsilon}], \qquad t = 1, \ldots, T.$$

Computing the PIT for an observation from a gamma or generalized gamma distribution is a little more complicated in that it requires the evaluation of an incomplete gamma function. Similarly, for some members of the generalized beta family, including the F distribution, finding the PIT requires a routine for computing a regularized incomplete beta function. However, there is a closed form expression, (5.24), for the PIT of a Burr distribution, and hence for the log-logistic as well.

The Lagrange multiplier test principle suggests that the scores be used to test against serial correlation. However, a test based on the residuals may also be informative. An attraction of making the probability integral transformation to the residuals is that it may yield serial correlation tests which are more robust. Furthermore, the PITs are comparable for different conditional distributions, and their histograms are very useful for assessing goodness of fit. Figure 5.9 shows the PIT residuals from fitting a DCS gamma model to the duration data for Boeing described in Section 5.9. The gamma distribution is clearly unsatisfactory: the fit near the origin is poor, and the high values close to one indicate that a heavy tail is not being captured. The parallel lines on the graph

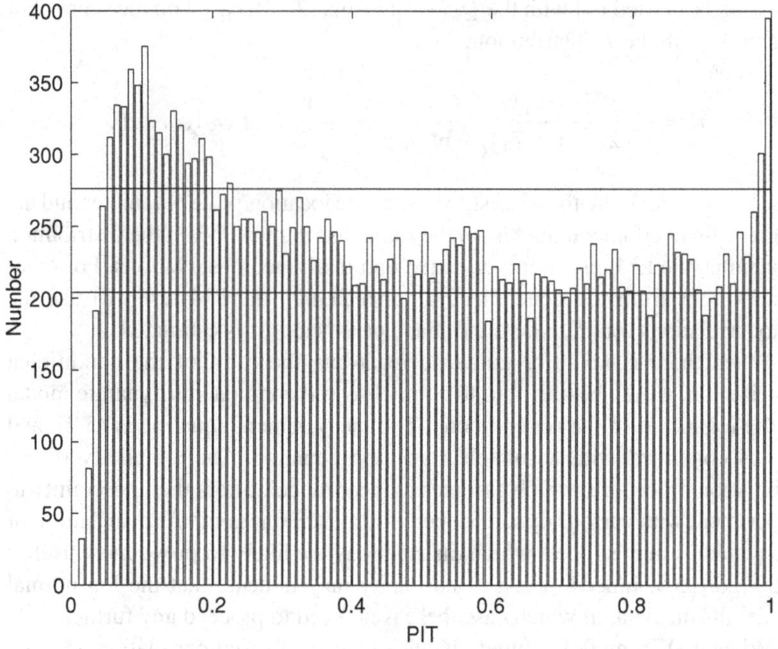

Figure 5.9. PITs from fitting a DCS gamma model to data on duration of trades for Boeing.

are such that, if the PITs were independent and uniformly distributed,[6] only 1% of them would lie outside the range.

Although an inspection of the histogram of PITs or normalized PITs is often sufficient to eliminate a distribution from further consideration, the choice between competing candidates is best made by goodness-of-fit criteria. As was noted in Sub-section 2.5.4, the AIC or BIC may be used within the sample, whereas outside the sample, the predictive likelihood is simple and effective. Post-sample residuals, scores and PITs may also be usefully examined.

5.8 ESTIMATING VOLATILITY FROM THE RANGE

Although it requires monitoring the price throughout the day, the range, that is, the difference between the highest and lowest logged prices in a day, is very easy to obtain and has long been reported. When price movements within the day can be represented by Brownian motion, the distribution of the logarithm of the range can be shown to be approximately normal. The mean of the logarithm of the range is a linear function of volatility – as measured by scale – and so

[6] Even if the model is correct, this assumption does not hold when parameters are estimated. Thus the lines serve to indicate goodness of fit rather than providing the basis for a formal test.

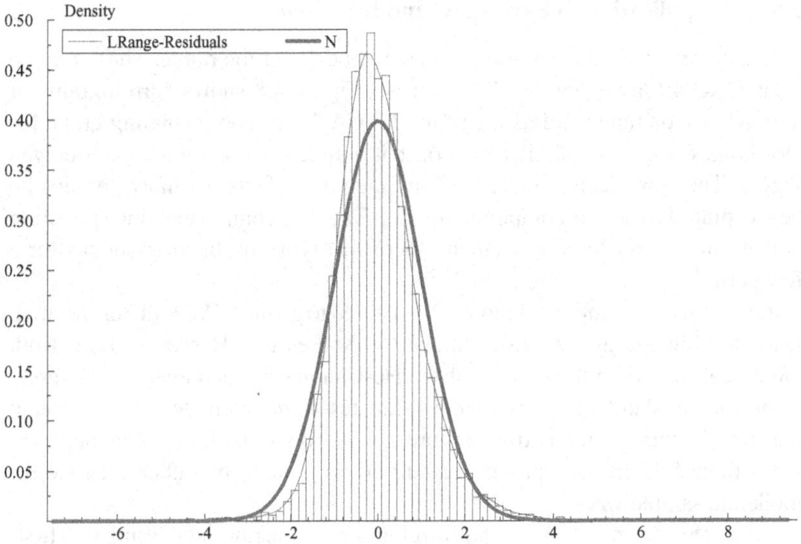

Figure 5.10. Standardized residuals from a two-component Gaussian model fitted to the logarithm of Dow Jones daily range.

when volatility changes over time, it can be extracted using the Kalman filter. Alizadeh, Brandt and Diebold (2002) studied this estimator in some detail and make a convincing case for its use. To be more specific,

$$\ln R_t = \lambda_t + v_t, \quad t = 1, \ldots, T, \tag{5.26}$$

where R_t is the range in day t and λ_t follows an unobserved components volatility model, such as (5.6).

There is a weakness in the case for using a Gaussian UC model to extract volatility from the range, and this stems from the fact that intra-day price movements may not be well-approximated by Brownian motion because of occasional jumps. Consequently, the Gaussian approximation to the logarithm of range may not always be satisfactory. The favourable evidence for Gaussianity reported in Alizadeh, Brandt and Diebold (2002) is for exchange rates. The case for equities may be less convincing, as witnessed in Figure 5.10, which shows the histogram of residuals from fitting a two-component UC model to the logarithm of the daily range for the Dow Jones index. The DCS approach offers a wide variety of distributional options for modelling the range itself (rather than its logarithm). Just as there is no theory leading from intra-day models of price movements to t distributions for daily returns, so there is no theory for suggesting what distributions for the range might arise when intra-day movements are not fully described by Brownian motion. Thus the choice between candidate distributions such as gamma, Weibull, lognormal, Burr and F is a matter for empirical investigation.

5.8.1 Application to Paris CAC and Dow Jones

Two data sets were used to estimate DCS models for the range. These are the Paris CAC 40 index and the Dow Jones.[7] Figure 5.8 shows correlograms of the raw data on range and its logarithm for CAC. The corresponding graph for Dow Jones displays a similar pattern, but with autocorrelations that are even bigger. The slow decline indicates long memory effects that may perhaps be best captured by a two-component model. The two-components interpretation is that after a very large movement, there will typically be after-shocks for a few periods.

One- and two-component models were fitted to gamma, Weibull, log-normal, Burr, log-logistic and F distributions by Andres and Harvey (2012). Both numerical (based on the inverse of the Hessian matrix) and analytical expressions for the standard errors of the estimates were calculated. It was found that the numerical standard errors are not always reliable. As was apparent from Table 5.1, the asymptotic standard errors seem to be rather accurate for moderate sample sizes.

As might be expected from the correlograms of the raw data, fitting two first-order components, with the short-run component containing a leverage term, gave a much better fit than a simple one-component model. The fit with the Weibull distribution was particularly bad. The reason is clear from Figure 5.1: in order to have a long tail, the Weibull must have considerable mass near the origin, and the range has near zero mass at the origin.

It is instructive to discuss some of the models in detail. The log-logistic model fitted to CAC gave the following estimates, with numerical SEs in parentheses:

$$\underset{(0.054)}{\widetilde{\omega} = -4.828} \quad \underset{(0.002)}{\widetilde{\phi}_1 = 0.998} \quad \underset{(0.009)}{\widetilde{\phi}_2 = 0.962}$$

$$\underset{(0.010)}{\widetilde{\kappa}_1 = 0.025} \quad \underset{(0.009)}{\widetilde{\kappa}_2 = 0.066} \quad \underset{(0.031)}{\widetilde{\kappa}_L = 0.040} \quad \underset{(0.034)}{\widetilde{\nu} = 4.546}$$

The values of the coefficients show a pattern that is not unusual for volatility data. The first component is highly persistent, and little would be lost by simply setting ϕ_1 to unity. As regards the short-term component, the effect of leverage is that the overall response, $\widetilde{\kappa}_2 + \widetilde{\kappa}_L$, is 0.026 for positive returns and 0.106 for negative returns. The PITs, and hence the scores, indicate very little serial correlation, but this is not the case with the standardized residuals, in which some positive serial correlation remains.

[7] The data were taken from the Yahoo finance webpage. First, the range was constructed for the CAC40 index between 1 March 1990 and 17 August 2011 (approximately 5400 observations). The in-sample estimation period runs until 1st of January 2008. Similarly, the daily high-low range is constructed for the Dow Jones index between the 1st of October 1975 and the 17th of August 2011. The out-of-sample period starts on the 1st of January 2009.

The log-normal distribution gives the best fit for both one- and two-component models. The two-component estimates are:

$$\widetilde{\omega} = -4.818 \qquad \widetilde{\phi}_1 = 0.998 \qquad \widetilde{\phi}_2 = 0.953$$

$$\widetilde{\kappa}_1 = 0.046 \qquad \widetilde{\kappa}_2 = 0.103 \qquad \widetilde{\kappa}_L = 0.039 \qquad \widetilde{\sigma}^2 = 0.146$$

The estimates for Burr and log-logistic are not very different, but the maximized log-likelihoods are smaller at 17350.01 and 17349.97, respectively, as opposed to 17409.07 for the log-normal. The closeness of the maximized log-likelihoods for Burr and log-logistic models is reflected in the estimate of ς, which is 1.018, with a standard error of 0.011. Neither the likelihood ratio test nor the Wald test would reject the null hypotheses of a log-logistic distribution, that is, $\varsigma = 1$, at any conventional level of significance.

Although the log-normal model gave the best fit to the CAC series, it does not fit the Dow Jones data well. For the two-component Burr model,

$$\underset{(0.085)}{\widetilde{\omega} = -3.998} \qquad \underset{(0.002)}{\widetilde{\phi}_1 = 0.998} \qquad \underset{(0.005)}{\widetilde{\phi}_2 = 0.885}$$

$$\underset{(0.010)}{\widetilde{\kappa}_1 = 0.036} \qquad \underset{(0.070)}{\widetilde{\kappa}_2 = 0.062} \qquad \underset{(0.029)}{\widetilde{\kappa}_L = 0.028} \qquad \underset{(0.718)}{\widetilde{\nu} = 9.952} \qquad \underset{(0.192)}{\widetilde{\varsigma} = 0.760}$$

The log-logistic estimates of the dynamic parameters were similar, and the shape parameter was $\widetilde{\nu} = 8.922$. However, the maximized log-likelihood is 34,697.76 as against 34,727.61. Thus an LR or Wald test of $\varsigma = 1$ would clearly reject the log-logistic. The log-normal likelihood was much smaller at 34,345.07. The PITs of the log-normal are far from uniform, and the score residuals (comparable with the residuals from fitting a Gaussian UC model to the logarithm of the range) are far from normality. The extra parameter in the Burr gives it the flexibility to capture some of the skewness and excess kurtosis that is apparent in these residuals from Figure 5.10. The log-logistic is able to capture some of the excess kurtosis, but not the skewness.

The maximized log-likelihood for the one-component Burr model was 34,624.3. The AIC and BIC, which allow for the three additional parameters, are both smaller (and hence better) for the two-component model, being −69439.21 and −69381.53, respectively, as opposed to −69240.46 and −69245.69. The two-component model removes some, but not all, of the serial correlation in the PITs and scores, as well as in the residuals. Although the autocorrelations are rather small when set against those for the raw data, there may be a case for adding AR and/or MA component to the long-run and/or short-run equations. In the short-run equation, there is the additional possibility of augmenting the MA term by a lagged leverage variable.

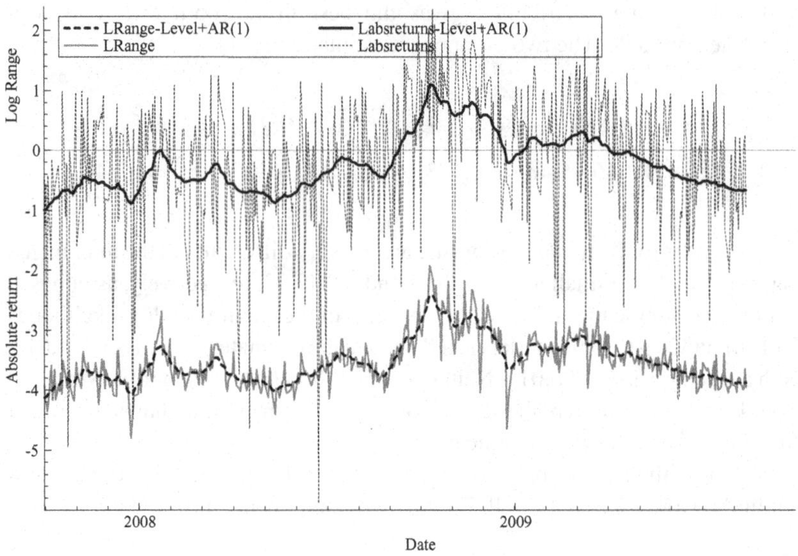

Figure 5.11. Smoothed volatility extracted from logarithm of absolute returns (top) and logarithm of range.

5.8.2 The Range-EGARCH Model

The implicit assumption in using the range to estimate volatility is that the time path of estimated volatility is essentially the same as that of the volatility measured by a daily GARCH model. Evidence is presented in this section to show that this is indeed the case, and a suggestion is made regarding how the volatility extracted from range can be calibrated so as to be comparable with the volatility in a Beta-t-EGARCH model. If desired, it can be incorporated into a Beta-t-EGARCH model.

Equation (5.26) is the measurement equation in an unobserved components model for estimating volatility from range. Volatility can also be extracted from a stochastic volatility model by applying the Kalman filter to the state space form obtained by combining the dynamic equation in (1.6) with the measurement equation, (1.7), obtained by taking logarithms of absolute values of returns. However, as was noted in Sub-section 1.3.1, $\ln|\varepsilon_t|$ is far from normal when ε_t is normal, and its standard deviation is roughly four times that of v_t in (5.26). Nevertheless, the case for using range to extract volatility in returns is immediately apparent from Figure 5.11, which shows the smoothed volatilities extracted from the logarithm of absolute returns and the logarithm of the range for the Dow Jones index over the same period as was used in the application reported in Section 4.9. The volatility from the range displays movements that are close to those from absolute returns, but the smaller variability in the range is clearly evident. Estimation was carried out for a bivariate model with first-order dynamics using STAMP 8, but without imposing any cross-equation restrictions. The two autoregressive coefficients were close, and the correlation between the disturbances in the autoregressive processes is quite high, at 0.95.

If a suitable range model can be found, it may be estimated and inference carried out on the estimates of the dynamic parameters, ϕ and κ in the first-order case, and on parameters governing the shape of the distribution. Estimation of the constant, ω^d, is then effected simply by estimating the scale in a static t or GED model applied to the returns, divided by $\exp(\lambda_{t|t-1})$, where $\lambda_{t|t-1}$ is constructed with the constant set to zero. Thus the daily volatility measure is just $\lambda^d_{t|t-1} = \widetilde{\omega}^d + \lambda_{t|t-1}$.

In the combined model, the conditional distribution is t or GED, but $\lambda_{t|t-1}$ is driven by the score of the range model. Hence the name Range-EGARCH model. If leverage effects are included,

$$\lambda_{t+1|t} = (1-\phi)\widetilde{\omega}^d + \widetilde{\phi}\lambda_{t|t-1} + \widetilde{\kappa}u_t^R + \widetilde{\kappa}^* sgn(returns_t)\left(u_t^R + E(u_t^R)\right),$$

where u_t^R denotes the score of the range model, tildes on ϕ and κ denote estimation from the range model and $sgn(\text{returns}_t)$ is the sign of de-meaned returns.

The predictions of volatility and its RMSE can be obtained directly from the properties of the range model. All that needs to be done is to adjust with $\widetilde{\omega}^d$. Estimating the full predictive distribution requires that the range volatility be simulated and then combined with a simulation of the conditional distribution.

5.9 DURATION

Duration models are widely used in financial econometrics to capture the changing intensity governing the time between events. Thus they may be used to model the times between trades of an asset. In this context, here is a relationship with volatility in that higher volatility tends to be associated with more trades. Duration models are also used in other areas. For example, actuaries and insurance companies are interested in the time taken to settle claims; see, for example, Ozkok et al. (2012).

Bauwens et al. (2004) investigated a wide range of autoregressive conditional duration models for price, volume and trade duration data.[8] In their conclusion, they argued that price durations are perhaps the most interesting duration processes due to their close links to market microstructure and options pricing.[9] They found that employing the basic MEM specifications with the

[8] Diurnal effects are removed prior to estimation.

[9] A trade duration is given by the time interval between two consecutive trade events. A price duration is measured by the time interval between two bid-ask quotes during which a cumulative change in the mid-price of at least \$0.125 is observed. A volume duration denotes the time interval between two bid-ask quotes during which the cumulative traded volume amounts to at least 25,000 shares.

Table 5.2. *ML estimates for Boeing volume duration*

	Gamma		Weibull		Log-normal	
	Estimate	ASE	Estimate	ASE	Estimate	ASE
ω	−0.001	0.003	0.002	0.003	−0.011	0.005
ϕ	0.966	0.013	0.971	0.010	0.961	0.015
κ	0.118	0.019	0.067	0.011	0.102	0.016
ν, υ or σ^2	2.133	0.082	1.551	0.034	0.590	0.024
LogL	−1012.78		−1014.34		−1092.65	
AIC/BIC	2033.6	2028.3	2036.7	2031.46	2193.30	2188.07
	Log-logistic		**Burr**		**F**	
	Estimate	ASE	Estimate	ASE	Estimate	ASE
ω	−0.010	0.013	0.036	0.013	−0.001	0.004
ϕ	0.952	0.017	0.971	0.010	0.967	0.005
κ	0.162	0.028	0.082	0.012	0.055	0.013
ν, ν or ν_1	2.316	0.057	1.680	0.044	4.256	0.016
ς or ν_2	–	–	8.006	0.751	1000.0	7.607
LogL	−1064.35		−1010.35		−1012.93	
AIC/BIC	2136.7	2131.46	2030.7	2023.9	2035.86	2029.08

exponential and Weibull distributions is not advisable. An exponential link function gives much better results for the Weibull distribution. However, their preference is for the generalized gamma and Burr distributions, again with exponential link functions. Their 'log-ACD' specification has the conditional mean in (5.4) set to $\mu_{t|t-1} = \exp(\lambda^*_{t|t-1})$, where

$$\lambda^*_{t+1|t} = \delta + \beta\lambda^*_{t|t-1} + \alpha \ln y_t \qquad or$$

$$\lambda^*_{t+1|t} = \delta + \beta\lambda^*_{t|t-1} + \alpha y_t \exp(-\lambda^*_{t|t-1}).$$

The first of the above dynamic equations corresponds to the DCS model for a log-normal distribution, whereas the second is the DCS model for a gamma distribution. Neither resembles the DCS equation for any member of the generalized beta family, where the conditional score takes the form (5.17).

Bauwens et al. (2004) reached similar conclusions regarding the best models when volume duration data are used. Table 5.2, adapted from Andres and Harvey (2012), shows the results of fitting various DCS models to the Boeing volume duration data used by Bauwens et al. (2004). The first 1200 observations were used for estimation, with the remaining reserved for post-sample evaluation. The Burr distribution gives the best fit, followed closely by Weibull. The Weibull shape parameter is greater than one, meaning that the distribution has the humped shape shown in Figure 5.1. The log-logistic distribution does not give a good fit, and the hypothesis that the second shape parameter in the

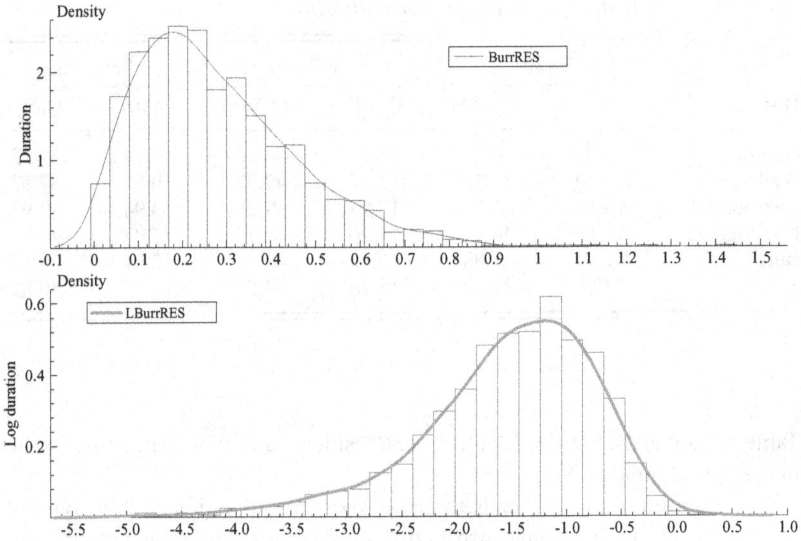

Figure 5.12. Histograms of Burr residuals and their logarithms for Boeing volume duration data.

Burr, ς, is unity is easily rejected using a LR test. The gamma and F distributions[10] are only marginally worse than the Weibull, but the log-normal fit is very bad. The results are consistent with those reported by Bauwens et al. (2004) for a range of companies.

One particularly interesting feature of the results is that although the maximized likelihood function for the Weibull distribution is only marginally worse than that of the Burr distribution, its shape parameter of 1.57 means that, in contrast to the Burr distribution, it does not have a heavy tail. The QQ plots indicate that there are six or seven observations that are outliers for the Weibull, but not for the Burr. The corresponding graphs for the scores tell the same story, but the outlying Weibull observations do not show up in the histogram of the PITs.

Although all Burr distributions have a heavy tail, a value of less than one for the ς scale parameter means that the distribution of the logarithm of the variable is skewed to the left. Figure 5.12 shows the histogram of the residuals from the fitted Burr model, together with the histogram of their logarithms; compare Figure 5.5, where $\varsigma > 1$.

The diagnostics give little indication of residual serial correlation. In contrast to the Q-statistics for the Dow Jones range data, the Q-statistics shown in

[10] The fitted gamma and F distributions are quite close, as a gamma distribution with $\gamma = \nu_1/2$ is obtained from an F distribution in which $\nu_2 \to \infty$.

Table 5.3. *Q-statistics for Boeing volume duration*

	Scores		PITs		Residuals	
Distribution	Q(10)	Q(50)	Q(10)	Q(50)	Q(10)	Q(50)
Gamma	12.74	39.77	15.47	44.96	12.74	39.77
Weibull	8.20	32.78	17.32	47.97	10.59	37.52
Log-normal	16.13	46.00	17.05	47.28	14.94	42.92
Log-logistic	15.13	46.52	15.26	46.76	14.07	43.23
Burr	11.58	38.08	15.72	44.53	12.67	39.12
F	12.81	39.97	15.46	44.97	12.77	39.81

Table 5.3 are all rather similar for scores, residuals and PITs. The same is true in the post-sample period.

The duration literature tends to emphasize the estimation of location, but because the full conditional distribution may be very different for different types of data, this is unwise. Furthermore, the evidence showing a poor fit for the exponential distribution cautions against the use of QML.

5.10 REALIZED VOLATILITY

Brownlees and Gallo (2010) describe various intra-day volatility measures, including realized volatility, which is the estimator of daily variance obtained from a set of N returns within the day. To be specific, if $r_{t,j}$ is the return in period j of day t, so the daily return is $\sum_{j=1}^{N} r_{t,j}$, the realized volatility is computed as $\widehat{\sigma}_{t,N}^2 = \sum_{j=1}^{N} r_{t,j}^2, \quad t = 1, \ldots, T$. Although realized volatility is a fairly accurate estimator of volatility, it still requires some smoothing to produce a good estimator of the underlying movements in volatility; see Taylor (2005, Chapter 12). One possibility is to take logarithms and apply the Kalman filter on the assumption that $\ln \widehat{\sigma}_{t,N}$ is approximately normal. However, Taylor (2005, pp. 327–42) notes that there is often significant skewness and kurtosis. Some of the DCS models described in this chapter are therefore likely to prove useful. As with range and duration, it will be necessary to take account of diurnal patterns, long memory characteristics and overnight effects.

5.11 COUNT DATA AND QUALITATIVE OBSERVATIONS

Time series methods for modelling count data and qualitative observations are described in Harvey (1989, Chapters 6 and 7) and Durbin and Koopman (2012). DCS models offer an alternative way forward, but a comprehensive theory is yet to be developed. This section sketches out some of the issues involved.

The mean and variance in the Poisson distribution

$$f(y) = \mu^y e^{-\mu}/y! \qquad y = 0, 1, 2, \ldots,$$

are both μ. The ML estimator of μ is the sample mean, $\overline{y}$, and its variance is μ/T.

When the mean changes over time, an exponential link function, $\mu_{t|t-1} = \exp\theta_{t|t-1}$, ensures that it remains positive, even though $\theta_{t|t-1}$ is unconstrained. The conditional score of $\theta_{t|t-1}$ is $y_t - \exp\theta_{t|t-1}$, which, when divided by the information quantity, gives

$$u_t = (y_t - \exp\theta_{t|t-1})/\exp\theta_{t|t-1} = y_t \exp(-\theta_{t|t-1}) - 1, \qquad t = 1, \ldots, T.$$

Unfortunately, the conditions for Theorem 1 do not hold for this transformation, nor do they appear to hold for any other transformation.

Davis, Dunsmuir and Streett (2003) showed that when

$$\theta_{t+1|t} = \omega + \kappa u_t,$$

which corresponds to $p = r = 0$ in (1.17), the process generating $\theta_{t|t-1}$ is uniformly ergodic, and hence there exists a unique stationary distribution for $\theta_{t|t-1}$ and its logarithm. If u_t were simply set to $y - \exp\theta_{t|t-1}$, they demonstrated that the conditional mean would evolve in an unstable fashion. They further showed that if $\theta_{t|t-1}$ is started with its stationary distribution, the y_t process will also be stationary and ergodic. As a result they were able to prove that $\sqrt{T}$ times the ML estimator of the unknown dynamic parameters, $\boldsymbol{\psi}$, has a limiting distribution in which the asymptotic covariance matrix is the inverse of

$$\mathbf{I}(\boldsymbol{\psi}) = \lim \frac{1}{T}\sum_{t=1}^{T} I_t(\theta_{t|t-1})\left(\frac{\partial\theta_{t|t-1}}{\partial\boldsymbol{\psi}}\frac{\partial\theta_{t|t-1}}{\partial\boldsymbol{\psi}'}\right) = \lim \frac{1}{T}\sum_{t=1}^{T} e^{\theta_{t|t-1}}\left(\frac{\partial\theta_{t|t-1}}{\partial\boldsymbol{\psi}}\frac{\partial\theta_{t|t-1}}{\partial\boldsymbol{\psi}'}\right).$$

In contrast to the DCS models covered by Lemma 5, the information matrix does not decompose nicely into two parts. As already observed, a model with $p = r = 0$ is like $ARCH(1)$ and so is of limited value. Davis, Dunsmuir and Streett (2003, p. 782) stated that the result on the stationarity of the observations readily extends to the case when $r > 0$, but note that a central limit theorem for the ML estimator is currently unavailable.

In the binomial model where the probability of $y_t = 1$ is π and the probability of $y_t = 0$ is $1 - \pi$, the usual link function is the logistic. Thus with time-variation

$$\pi_{t|t-1} = 1/(1 + \exp(-\theta_{t|t-1})), \qquad t = 1, \ldots, T.$$

The score for the t-th observation is $y_t - \pi_{t|t-1} = y_t - 1/(1 + \exp(-\theta_{t|t-1}))$. The information quantity is $\pi_{t|t-1}(1 - \pi_{t|t-1})$, and so the standardized score is

$$u_t = \frac{y_t - \pi_{t|t-1}}{\pi_{t|t-1}(1 - \pi_{t|t-1})}.$$

Again, the conditions for Theorem 1 do not hold for the score or any transformation of it.

Despite the lack of a general asymptotic theory for ML estimation of the dynamic parameters in models with discrete conditional distributions, such evidence as there is lends support to the use of the standardized score from a link function chosen to keep the time-varying parameter within the appropriate range.

CHAPTER 6

Dynamic Kernel Density Estimation and Time-Varying Quantiles

A GARCH filter weights squared observations to produce a measure of variance, but variance is of limited utility when the conditional distribution is not Gaussian. Letting the score drive the dynamics reflects the full conditional distribution, and this was the approach adopted for the models described in Chapters 3, 4 and 5. However, if a parametric model is felt to be too restrictive, the question arises regarding whether a distribution-free filter is possible.

When observations are independent, a probability density function, or the corresponding cumulative distribution function, may be estimated nonparametrically by using a kernel. There is an enormous literature on this topic, but relatively little has been written on applying kernel estimation to time series; see, for example, Markovich (2007). However, if the distribution is thought to change over time, observations may be weighted by adapting the filters described in the preceding chapters. Not only can updating be carried out recursively,[1] but a likelihood function can be constructed from the predictive distributions, as in an observation-driven model. Hence dynamic parameters may be estimated by maximum likelihood. Furthermore, the dynamic specification may be checked using the residuals given by the predictive cumulative distribution function. The methods are those appropriate for the probability integral transform.

There has been considerable interest in recent years in estimating changing quantiles. Engle and Manganelli (2004) defined a general class of nonlinear dynamic models in which the quantiles depend on functions of past observations, but De Rossi and Harvey (2009) argued that only indicator variables should be used in this context. The indicator variables can be obtained as the first derivatives of the quantile criterion function, and so when used to construct a filter, they are, in a sense, similar to conditional scores. Indeed, the indicator function for the median of a Laplace distribution is the conditional score. The signal extraction argument used in Sub-section 3.7.3 to motivate DCS models extends to time-varying quantiles and makes it possible to show

[1] Although it has long been known that updating can be carried out recursively – see the discussion in Markovich (2007, pp. 73–4) – there has been little or no exploration of the kind of weighting typically used in filtering for the mean or variance.

that, when estimated by smoothing, a time-varying quantile satisfies a property that generalizes the basic definition of a quantile.

Time-varying quantiles may also be extracted from the cumulative distribution function. In the time-invariant case, there are efficiency gains, albeit small ones, in estimating quantiles this way as compared with simply using the sample quantiles calculated from the order statistics; see Sheather and Marron (1990). The final section illustrates the technique with an application to financial returns.

The first section develops filters for estimating time-varying densities. Attention is focussed on the exponentially weighted moving average and a stable filter, analogous to that of the first-order model which featured extensively in earlier chapters. The ways in which bandwidth selection methods designed for time-invariant distributions may be adapted to deal with changing distributions are explored, and estimation by maximum likelihood and cross-validation is discussed. Section 6.2 discusses time-varying quantiles and includes a final sub-section which shows how the signal extraction approach to formulating dynamic quantile models can be applied to dynamic kernels. Section 6.3 briefly considers forecasting, whereas Section 6.4 applies the methods to the NASDAQ index.

6.1 KERNEL DENSITY ESTIMATION FOR TIME SERIES

Using a sample of T observations drawn from a distribution with probability density function $f(y)$, a kernel estimator of $f(y)$ at a particular point y is given by

$$\overline{f}_T(y) = \frac{1}{Th}\sum_{i=1}^{T} K\left(\frac{y - y_i}{h}\right), \tag{6.1}$$

where $K(.)$ is the kernel and h is the bandwidth. The kernel, $K(\cdot)$, is symmetric about the origin and everywhere non-negative. It integrates to one when divided by h. The Epanechnikov (quadratic) kernel is 'optimal' if the choice is restricted to non-negative kernels, and the criterion is taken to be the asymptotic minimum integrated squared error for a fixed density. The Epanechnikov kernel is

$$K(z) = \begin{cases} \frac{3}{4\sqrt{5}}(1 - \frac{z^2}{25}), & |z| < \sqrt{5} \\ 0, & |z| \geq \sqrt{5} \end{cases}. \tag{6.2}$$

The efficiency loss from using suboptimal kernels is typically small, and the Gaussian kernel, whose relative efficiency is 0.95, is often used in practice.

The choice of bandwidth is more important than the choice of kernel. One possibility is to use cross-validation, but rule-of-thumb methods are common in applied work, and they usually deliver satisfactory results. A popular choice is the suggestion in Silverman (1986) of

$$h_{opt} = T^{-1/5} 1.06 \min\{\hat{\sigma}, \widehat{IQR}/1.34\}, \tag{6.3}$$

where $\hat{\sigma}$ is the sample standard deviation and $\widehat{IQR}$ is the sample interquartile range. However, there may be a case for having a wider bandwidth in regions where the PDF is smaller.

The kernel estimator of the cumulative distribution function, $F(y)$, is given by

$$\overline{F}_T(y) = \frac{1}{T}\sum_{i=1}^{T} H\left(\frac{y - y_i}{h}\right), \tag{6.4}$$

where $H(.)$ is a kernel which has properties like those of a CDF rather than a PDF. A kernel of this form may be obtained by integrating the kernel in (6.1). Integrating the Epanechnikov kernel gives

$$H(z) = \begin{cases} 0, & z \leq -\sqrt{5} \\ \frac{1}{2} + \frac{3z}{4\sqrt{5}}(1 - \frac{z^2}{25}), & |z| < \sqrt{5} \\ 1, & z \geq \sqrt{5} \end{cases}.$$

6.1.1 Filtering and Smoothing

A weighting scheme may be introduced into the kernel estimator so as to make predictions of the density at time $t+1$, based on information at time t. Thus

$$f_{t+1|t}(y) = \frac{1}{h}\sum_{i=1}^{t} K\left(\frac{y - y_i}{h}\right) w_{t,i}, \quad t = 1, \ldots, T, \tag{6.5}$$

whereas, for the distribution function,

$$F_{t+1|t}(y) = \sum_{i=1}^{t} H\left(\frac{y - y_i}{h}\right) w_{t,i}. \tag{6.6}$$

The weights, $w_{t,i}$, $i = 1, \ldots, t$, $t = 1, \ldots, T$, may change over time, although in the steady-state, $w_{t,i} = w_{t-i}$. For an EWMA scheme, the weights sum to unity. The expressions for smoothing are similar except that the summations run from $t = 1$ to T.

Filters may be constructed for the predictive density for a given value of y. The first-order filter is

$$f_{t+1|t}(y) = \delta_y + \beta f_{t|t-1}(y) + \alpha\frac{1}{h}K\left(\frac{y - y_t}{h}\right), \quad t = 1, \ldots, T,$$

where $\alpha \geq 0$, $\beta \geq 0$ and $\delta_y > 0$. Alternatively,

$$f_{t+1|t}(y) = \delta_y + \phi f_{t|t-1}(y) + \kappa u_t, \quad t = 1, \ldots, T, \tag{6.7}$$

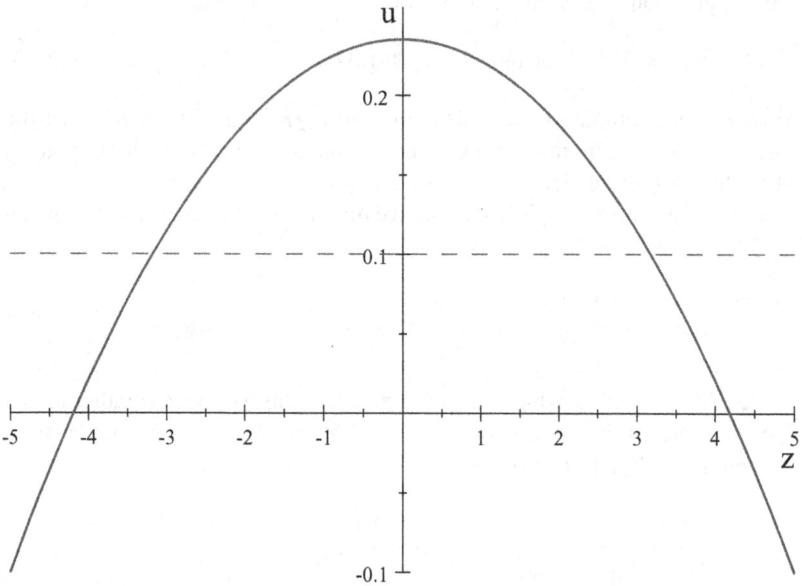

Figure 6.1. Impact of Epanechnikov kernel when $f_{t|t-1}(y) = 0.1$.

where $\phi = \alpha + \beta$, $\kappa = \alpha$, and the innovation for the density is

$$u_t(y) = \frac{1}{h} K\left(\frac{y - y_t}{h}\right) - f_{t|t-1}(y), \tag{6.8}$$

which is similar in form to the conditional score in a DCS model.

As before, the condition for stationarity is $\phi < 1$ and so $\delta_y = (1 - \phi) f(y)$, where $f(y)$ is the unconditional PDF at y. Rather than introduce a large number of additional parameters into an optimization procedure, it is best to set each δ_y to $(1 - \phi)\overline{f}_T(y)$, where $\overline{f}_T(y)$ is the corresponding unconditional estimator in (6.1). Thus

$$f_{t+1|t}(y) = (1 - \phi)\overline{f}_T(y) + \phi f_{t|t-1}(y) + \kappa u_t, \quad t = 1, \dots, T. \tag{6.9}$$

The filter updates the estimate of the PDF at y. The maximum impact is when there is a direct hit, that is, the observation coincides with y. In this case $h^{-1}K(0) - f_{t|t-1}(y)$ must be positive. On the other hand, an observation far from y will have little or no effect, and so $u_t(y)$ is close to $-f_{t|t-1}(y)$. Figure 6.1 shows the impact of an observation, standardized as $z_t = (y - y_t)/h$, for an Epanechnikov kernel, (6.2), and $f_{t|t-1}(y)$ (arbitrarily) set to 0.1.

Remark 33 *The variable u_t plays a similar role to the score in a parametric model. Is it then an MD? Taking conditional expectations gives*

$$E_{t-1}u_t(y) = \frac{1}{h}E_{t-1}K\left(\frac{y-y_t}{h}\right) - E_{t-1}f_{t|t-1}(y)$$

$$= \frac{1}{h}\int_{-\infty}^{\infty} K\left(\frac{y-y_t}{h}\right) f_{t|t-1}(y_t)dy_t - f_{t|t-1}(y)$$

If $f_{t|t-1}(y)$ is locally uniform, then

$$E_{t-1}u_t(y) \simeq f_{t|t-1}(y) - f_{t|t-1}(y) = 0.$$

A scheme similar to that in (6.9) may be employed for the CDF. Thus

$$F_{t+1|t}(y) = (1-\phi)\overline{F}_T(y) + \phi F_{t|t-1}(y) + \kappa U_t(y), \quad t = 1, \ldots, T,$$

where $\overline{F}_T(y)$ is the unconditional kernel estimator of the CDF and

$$U_t(y) = H\left(\frac{y-y_t}{h}\right) - F_{t|t-1}(y) \tag{6.10}$$

is the innovation. Note that $-F_{t|t-1}(y) \leq V_t(y) \leq 1 - F_{t|t-1}(y)$.

Simple exponential weighting gives recursions similar to those for IGARCH. Thus for the PDF,

$$f_{t+1|t}(y) = f_{t|t-1}(y) + \kappa u_t(y), \quad 0 < \kappa \leq 1, \quad t = 1, \ldots, T, \tag{6.11}$$

and similarly for the CDF. Schemes of this kind are not new; see, for example, Wegman and Davies (1979).

The EWMA filters are best initialized from the first m observations, where m is chosen to be sufficiently large. Thus for the PDF, $f_{m+1|m}(y)$ is computed directly from (6.5). The CDF recursion for $F_{t+1|t}(y)$ may be initialized similarly.

The filters for $F_{t+1|t}(y)$ and $f_{t+1|t}(y)$ may be run by defining a grid of N points in the range $[y_{\min}, y_{\max}]$. Backward recursions for smoothing may also be developed. Alternatively, we can compute the weights for a given t, $t = 1, \ldots, T$, with the algorithm in Koopman and Harvey (2003), and use these to construct filtered estimates of the PDF or CDF directly from (6.5) and (6.6). Smoothed estimates can be similarly obtained. When the aim is to compute estimation criteria, residuals and a limited number of quantiles, algorithms based on this direct approach seem to be more computationally efficient. A full set of filtering and smoothing recursions for a grid is not necessary unless an estimate of the density is required for each time period.

6.1.2 Estimation

The recursive nature of the filter leads naturally, but perhaps surprisingly, to a maximum likelihood procedure for estimating unknown parameters, as contained in a vector denoted ψ. These parameters include the bandwidth, h, as well as any parameters governing the dynamics, such as κ and ϕ in (6.9). The log-likelihood function is

$$\ln L(\boldsymbol{\psi}) = \sum_{t=m}^{T-1} \ln f_{t+1|t}(y_{t+1}) \tag{6.12}$$

$$= \sum_{t=m}^{T-1} \ln \left[\frac{1}{h} \sum_{i=1}^{t} K \left(\frac{y_{t+1} - y_i}{h} \right) w_{t,i} \right],$$

where, for a nonstationary filter like (6.11), m is some preset number of observations used to initialize the procedure. The value of m will depend on the sample at hand, but it may not be unreasonable to set it to 50 or 100 if the sample size is big; the main consideration is that the predictions be meaningful. When a non-negative kernel with unbounded support, such as a Gaussian kernel, is used, $f_{t|t-1}(y_t) > 0$ for all $t = m+1, \ldots, T$. The computational requirement for the likelihood is not very burdensome because, at each point in time, the kernel density only needs to be evaluated at $y = y_t$. From the theoretical point of view, it is interesting to note that the likelihood can be written in terms of the innovations because, from (3.1), $\widehat{f}_{t|t-1}(y_t) = h^{-1} K(0) - v_t(y_t)$ for $t = m+1, \ldots, T$.

For smoothing, there is a case for estimating the parameters by maximizing the likelihood cross-validation criterion

$$CV(\boldsymbol{\psi}) = \prod_{t=1}^{T} f_{(-t)|T}(y_t),$$

where

$$f_{(-t)|T}(y_t) = \frac{1}{h} \sum_{i \neq t}^{T} K \left(\frac{y_t - y_i}{h} \right) w_{t,T,i}$$

is given by a two-sided smoothing filter.

Kohn, Ansley and Wong (1992) compared ML and cross-validation as methods for estimating the parameters in unobserved components models and found a slight advantage for ML. However, in the present context, there is no model as such, and the interaction between the bandwidth and the dynamic parameters means that the choice of criterion function may be governed, at least partially, by whether filtering or smoothing is being carried out. Thus cross-validation may be preferred to ML for smoothing.

The number of parameters to be estimated could be reduced by setting the bandwidth according to a rule of thumb, such as (6.3), with T set equal to the effective sample size. In the steady-state of the Gaussian local level model, the MSE of the contemporaneous filtered estimator of the level is $\sigma_\varepsilon^2 \kappa$. If the level were fixed, the MSE of the sample mean would be σ_ε^2 / T. This suggests an effective sample size for the filtering of $T(\kappa) = 1/\kappa$. For smoothing, the suggestion is $T(\beta) = (2 - \kappa)/\kappa \simeq 2/\kappa$, provided that t is not too close to the beginning or end of the sample. Therefore, when the bandwidth selection criterion is proportional to $T^{-1/5}$, the bandwidth for filtering will be bigger by a factor of approximately $2^{1/5} = 1.15$.

The estimation procedure thus involves first maximizing the likelihood function or the cross-validation criterion, thereby obtaining estimates of the parameters and the bandwidth h. These estimates are then used to compute the estimates of the PDF, CDF and quantiles. The CDF (filtered or smoothed) can be computed directly, as in (6.6). Quantile functions can be obtained by inverting estimated CDFs, as described in Section 6.2 below.

6.1.3 Correcting for Changing Mean and Variance

If the series displays trending movements, there is clearly a problem with implementing the preceding algorithms for estimating time-varying distributions. A possible solution is to model the level separately, for example, by a random walk plus noise and then to adjust the observations so that the dynamic kernel estimation is applied to the innovations. Thus $H(.)$ in (6.10), or $K(.)$, is redefined by replacing y_t by $y_t - \mu_{t|t-1}$. Serial correlation may be handled similarly by fitting an ARMA model.

A straightforward option for dealing with short-term movements in the variance is to fit a model for the conditional variance so that $H(.)$ becomes

$$H\left(\frac{y - (y_t - \mu_{t|t-1})}{h\sigma_{t|t-1}}\right) = H\left(\frac{y - y_t + \mu_{t|t-1}}{h\sigma_{t|t-1}}\right).$$

A Beta-t-EGARCH with stochastic location, as in Sub-section 4.12.2, could be used to produce $\sigma_{t|t-1}$ and $\mu_{t|t-1}$. Proceeding in this way has the advantage that the residuals are not subject to distortion from outlying observations.

The disadvantage of prefiltering, irrespective of how it is implemented, is that the treatment of the scale and mean becomes decoupled from the estimation of the distribution as a whole.

6.1.4 Specification and Diagnostic Checking

The use of the probability integral transform for checking the specification of a given parametric distribution was described in Sub-section 2.5.1. Here the PIT is given directly by the predictive kernel CDF, that is, the PIT of the t-th observation is $F_{t|t-1}(y_t)$. As with the evaluation of the $f_{t|t-1}(y_t)'s$ in the likelihood function, the calculation at each point in time need only be done for $y = y_t$.

6.2 TIME-VARYING QUANTILES

A plot showing how the quantiles have evolved over time provides a good visual impression of the changing distribution. The first sub-section that follows explains how quantiles can be computed from the kernel estimates. The second sub-section describes models for estimating individual time-varying quantiles directly.

As the tails of the distribution are approached, there is less information on which estimation may be based. Similarly, the precision with which a quantile may be estimated tends to be low. When the distribution is constant, the τ quantile, $\xi(\tau)$, $0 < \tau < 1$, can be estimated by the sample quantile, $\widehat{\xi}(\tau)$, and it can be shown that $\sqrt{T}(\widehat{\xi}(\tau) - \xi(\tau))$ has a limiting normal distribution with mean zero and variance

$$Var(\widehat{\xi}(\tau)) = \tau(1-\tau)/f^2(\xi(\tau)), \quad 0 < \tau < 1.$$

For the sample median from a standard normal distribution, $Var(\widehat{\xi}(0.5))$ is $\pi/2 = 1.57$, whereas for $\tau = 0.025$ or 0.975 the figure is 7.25.

Tests against changing quantiles are studied in Busetti and Harvey (2010).

6.2.1 Kernel-Based Estimation

The τ quantile can be estimated from the distribution function by solving $\widehat{F}(y) = \tau$, that is, $\widehat{\xi}(\tau) = \widehat{F}^{-1}(\tau)$. Nadaraya (1964) showed that $\widehat{\xi}(\tau)$ is consistent and asymptotically normal with the same asymptotic distribution as the sample quantile. Azzalini (1981) proposed the use of a Newton-Raphson procedure for finding $\widehat{\xi}(\tau)$.

Filtered and smoothed estimators of changing quantiles can be similarly computed from time-varying CDFs. Thus, for filtering, $\xi_{t|t-1}(\tau) = F_{t|t-1}^{-1}(\tau)$, for $t = m+1, \ldots, T$. The iterative procedure to calculate $\xi_{t|t-1}(\tau)$ is based on the direct evaluation of $F_{t|t-1}(y)$ in the vicinity of the quantile. The estimate in the previous time period may be used as a starting value.

The estimates of bandwidth obtained by ML or CV suffer from the drawback that the asymptotically optimal choice of bandwidth for a kernel estimator of a CDF is proportional to $T^{-1/3}$, whilst the optimal bandwidth for a PDF is proportional to $T^{-1/5}$; see, for example, Azzalini (1981). A bandwidth for a kernel estimator of a CDF can be found by cross-validation, as in Bowman et al. (1998), or by a rule of thumb approach, as in Altman and Léger (1995). It may be worth experimenting with these bandwidth selection criteria for quantile estimation.

6.2.2 Direct Estimation of Individual Quantiles

The signal extraction framework of Sub-section 3.7.4 may be generalized by replacing the conditional distribution of the observations, $f(y_t|\mu_t)$, by some function, $\rho(y_t \mid \mu_t)$. Doing so leads to the following criterion function replacing $\ln f(\boldsymbol{\mu} \mid \mathbf{y})$:

$$J(\boldsymbol{\mu}) = -\sum_{t=1}^{T} \frac{1}{h}\rho(y_t|\mu_t) - \frac{1}{2\sigma_\eta^2}\sum_{t=2}^{T}(\mu_t - \phi\mu_{t-1})^2 - \frac{1}{2p_{1|0}}(\mu_1 - \phi\mu_{1|0})^2. \quad (6.13)$$

The assumption that μ_t follows a stochastic process can be regarded as a device for inducing local weighting of the observations. The parameter σ_η^2 then plays the role of a smoothing constant which determines how rapidly μ_t changes. Recall that when μ_t is an integrated random walk, signal extraction essentially amounts to fitting a cubic spline.

If $\rho(.)$ is differentiable, $J(\boldsymbol{\mu})$ is maximized with respect to the elements of $\boldsymbol{\mu}$ by solving a set of equations with the same form as those in (3.63). As a simple example, setting $\rho(y_t|\mu_t) = (y_t - \mu_t)^2/2\sigma^2$ leads to a QML estimator for a time-varying location. More generally, we may wish to consider aspects of location other than central tendency, such as quantiles.

The τ-th quantile for a set of T observations, $\widetilde{\xi}(\tau)$, can be obtained as the solution to the minimization of

$$S_\tau(\xi) = \sum_{t=1}^{T} \rho_\tau(y_t - \xi) = \sum_{y_t<\xi} (\tau - 1)(y_t - \xi) + \sum_{y_t \geq \xi} \tau(y_t - \xi) \tag{6.14}$$

with respect to $\xi = \xi(\tau)$, where $\rho_\tau(.)$ is the *check function* for quantiles. The check function is defined as

$$\rho_\tau(y_t - \xi) = (\tau - I(y_t - \xi < 0))\,(y_t - \xi)\,, \tag{6.15}$$

where $I(.)$ is one when $y_t < 0$ and zero otherwise, and using it in (6.13), with μ_t replaced by $\xi_t = \xi_t(\tau)$, provides a criterion function for estimating time-varying quantiles. The first term in each of the equations corresponding to those in (3.63) is given by $h^{-1} IQ(y_t - \xi_t(\tau))$, where

$$IQ(y_t - \xi_t(\tau)) = \begin{cases} \tau - 1, & \text{if} \quad y_t < \xi_t(\tau) \\ \tau, & \text{if} \quad y_t > \xi_t(\tau) \end{cases}, \qquad t = 1, \ldots, T, \tag{6.16}$$

is the *quantile indicator function*; $IQ(0)$ is not determined but can be set to zero. The values of the quantiles which satisfy the equations will be denoted $\xi_{t|T}(\tau)$. The possibility of a solution in which the estimated quantile passes through an observation has to be taken into account when designing an algorithm for computing them. Note that in terms of the notation of (3.61), the indicator could be written as $u_t(\xi_{t|T}(\tau))$.

De Rossi and Harvey (2006, 2009) estimated time-varying quantiles with weighting patterns derived from linear models for signal extraction, as in (6.13). The weighting scheme derived from the local level model yields

$$\xi_{t|T} = \frac{\kappa}{2-\kappa} \sum_{j=-\infty}^{\infty} (1-\kappa)^{|j|} [\xi_{t|T} + IQ(y_{t+j} - \xi_{t+j|T})]. \tag{6.17}$$

Yu and Jones (1998) adopted a nonparametric approach to constructing time-varying quantiles based on local weighting of quantile indicators by a kernel. In (6.17), the kernel is replaced by $(1-\kappa)^{|j|}$, so giving an exponential decay. The time series model determines the shape of the kernel, and the signal–noise ratio plays a role similar to that of the bandwidth.

The model-based approach to estimating time-varying quantiles results in their having the following important property when the dynamic equation is a stochastic level or trend.

Proposition 38 *When the conditions of Proposition 11 hold, the estimated time-varying quantiles satisfy the fundamental property of sample quantiles in that the number of observations which are less than the corresponding quantile, that is, the number of occasions on which* $y_t < \xi_{t|T}$ *for* $t = 1, \ldots, T$, *is no more than* $[T\tau]$, *whereas the number greater is no more than* $[T(1-\tau)]$.

When the trend reverts to a constant, the usual defining feature of quantiles is satisfied.

Remark 34 *Expectiles, denoted* $\mu(\omega), 0 < \omega < 1$, *are similar to quantiles, but they are determined by tail expectations rather than tail probabilities. For a given value of* ω, *the sample expectile,* $\widetilde{\mu}(\omega)$, *is obtained by minimizing the asymmetric least squares function,*

$$S_\omega(\mu) = \sum \rho_\omega(y_t - \mu) = \sum |\omega - I(y_t - \mu < 0)| \, (y_t - \mu)^2, \quad (6.18)$$

with respect to μ. *Differentiating* S_ω *and dividing by* -2 *gives*

$$\sum_{t=1}^{T} |\omega - I(y_t - \mu < 0)| \; (y_t - \mu). \quad (6.19)$$

The sample expectile, $\widetilde{\mu}(\omega)$, *is the value of* μ *that makes (6.19) equal to zero. Setting* $\omega = 0.5$ *gives the mean, that is* $\widetilde{\mu}(0.5) = \overline{y}$. *For other* ω*'s, it is necessary to iterate. The continuity of the derivative of* $\rho_\omega(y_t - \mu)$ *makes time-varying expectiles easier to handle than quantiles. However, under certain conditions they can be shown to coincide; see De Rossi and Harvey (2009).*

The smoothed estimate of a quantile at the end of the sample is the filtered estimate. The model-based approach automatically determines a weighting pattern at the end of the sample. For the EWMA scheme derived from the local level model, the filtered estimator must satisfy

$$\xi_{t+1|t} = \kappa \sum_{j=0}^{\infty} (1-\kappa)^j [\xi_{t-j|t} + IQ(y_{t-j} - \xi_{t-j|t})];$$

compare (3.37). Thus $\xi_{t+1|t}$ is an EWMA of the pseudo-observations, $\xi_{t-j|t} + IQ(y_{t-j} - \xi_{t-j|t})$. As new observations become available, the smoothed estimates need to be revised. However, filtered estimates could be used instead, so

$$\xi_{t+1|t}(\tau) = \xi_{t|t-1}(\tau) + \kappa u_t(\tau), \quad (6.20)$$

where $u_t(\tau) = IQ(y_t - \xi_{t|t-1}(\tau))$ is an indicator which plays a similar role to that of the conditional score in a DCS model.

The filter in (6.20) belongs to the class of CAViaR models[2] proposed by Engle and Manganelli (2004) in the context of tracking value at risk. In CAViaR, the first-order conditional quantile is a GARCH-type filter of the form

$$\widehat{\xi}_{t+1|t}(\tau) = \delta + \beta\widehat{\xi}_{t|t-1}(\tau) + \alpha q(y_t), \tag{6.21}$$

where $q(y_t)$ is a function of y_t. Suggested specifications include an adaptive model, which in a limiting case has the same form as (6.20) with $\alpha = \kappa$ and, in the more general first-order model, $\beta = \phi - \kappa$. Other CAViaR specifications, which are based on actual values, rather than indicators, may suffer from a lack of robustness to additive outliers. That this is the case is clear from an examination of Figure 1 in Engle and Manganelli (2004, p. 373). More generally, the evidence on predictive performance in Kuester et al. (2006, pp. 80–1) indicates a preference for the adaptive specification.

The dynamic parameters, such as κ in (6.17), may be estimated by minimizing the sum of the predictive indicators or by cross-validation. The functions to be minimized are, respectively,

$$P_\tau = \sum_{t=1}^{T} \rho_\tau(y_t - \xi_{t|t-1}(\tau)) \qquad \text{or} \qquad CV_\tau = \sum_{t=1}^{T} \rho_\tau(y_t - \widetilde{\xi}_{t|T}^{(-t)}), \tag{6.22}$$

where $\widetilde{\xi}_{t|T}^{(-t)})$ is the smoothed value at time t when y_t is dropped.

The advantage of fitting individual quantiles is that different parameters may be estimated for different quantiles. The disadvantage is that the quantiles may cross; see Gourieroux and Jasiek (2008). If the parameters across quantiles have to be the same to prevent them crossing, the ability to have different models for different quantiles loses much of its appeal.

Remark 35 *The conditional mode signal extraction argument used to derive the quantiles may be adapted to the dynamic kernel by replacing μ_t by $f_t(y)$ in (6.13) and defining*

$$\rho(y_t | f_t(y)) = -\frac{1}{2}\left[\frac{1}{h}K\left(\frac{y_t - y}{h}\right) - f_t(y)\right]^2$$

for all admissible values of y. For a given value of y, differentiating this new criterion function, $J(\mathbf{f})$, with respect to $f_t(y)$ for all t, setting the derivatives to zero and solving, gives the smoothed estimate, $f_{t|T}(y)$. The residuals, expressed using the notation of (3.61), are

$$u_t(f_{t|T}(y)) = \frac{1}{h}K\left(\frac{y_t - y}{h}\right) - f_{t|T}(y), \qquad t = 1, \ldots, T.$$

For all y, Proposition 11 shows that $\sum_{t=1}^{T} u_t(f_{t|T}(y)) = 0$. The variable driving the filter, that is $u_t(y)$ in (6.8), is of the same form as $u_t(f_{t|T}(y))$.

[2] CAViaR: conditional autoregressive value at risk by regression quantiles.

6.3 FORECASTS

For exponential weighting, the multistep forecast of the distribution is the same as the one-step ahead forecast, that is $f_{T+\ell|T}(y) = f_{T+1|T}(y)$, $\ell = 2, 3, \ldots$. For the stable model

$$f_{T+\ell|T}(y) = \overline{f}_T(y) + \phi(f_{T+\ell-1|T}(y) - \overline{f}_T(y)), \quad \ell = 2, 3, \ldots.$$

Similar schemes can be used to forecast the quantiles. For the stable first-order model

$$\xi_{T+\ell|T}(\tau) = \widetilde{\xi}_T(\tau) + \phi(\xi_{T+\ell-1|T}(\tau) - \widetilde{\xi}_T(\tau)), \quad \ell = 2, 3, \ldots,$$

and so, assuming ϕ is positive, predictions converge from above or below to the long-run (unconditional) quantile, $\widetilde{\xi}_T(\tau)$.

6.4 APPLICATION TO NASDAQ RETURNS

Harvey and Oryshchenko (2011) fitted a dynamic kernel density to NASDAQ returns. The sample starts on 5th February 1971 and ends on 20th February 2009, thus covering 13,896 days. Once weekends and holidays are excluded, there are 9,597 observations. As is usually the case with financial series, there is clear volatility clustering, and the correlograms of the absolute values and squares of de-meaned returns are large and slowly decaying. The distribution of returns is heavy-tailed and asymmetric.

6.4.1 Direct Modelling of Returns

Figure 6.2 shows filtered and smoothed time-varying quantiles of NASDAQ returns for $\tau = 0.05, 0.25, 0.50, 0.75$, and 0.95. Exponential weights and an Epanechnikov kernel were used throughout. The discount parameters for filtering and smoothing were estimated by maximising the log-likelihood function and likelihood cross-validation criterion, respectively. The filtering estimates for the discount parameter and bandwidth were, respectively, $\widetilde{\beta} = 0.993$ and $\widetilde{h} = 0.429$. The estimates for smoothing were $\widehat{\beta} = 0.993$ and $\widehat{h} = 0.262$. In the notation of (6.11), $\beta = 1 - \kappa$.

The quantiles seem to track the changing distribution well. However, as Figure 6.3 shows, there is still some residual serial correlation in the absolute values and squares of the PITs. The histogram of PITs, shown in the same figure,[3] is too high in the middle and too low at the ends, indicating departures from uniformity and hence imperfections in the forecasting scheme. The hump-shaped distribution indicates difficulties in capturing tail behaviour. The problems could be caused by the bandwidth being too wide, resulting in a degree of oversmoothing. Such a phenomenon is not unusual in kernel density

[3] For the ACFs, the lines parallel to the horizontal axis are for two standard deviations, i.e., $\pm 2/\sqrt{T}$. For the histogram of PITs, the dashed lines are similarly for two standard deviations, i.e., $\pm 2\sqrt{(k-1)/T}$, where k is the number of bins.

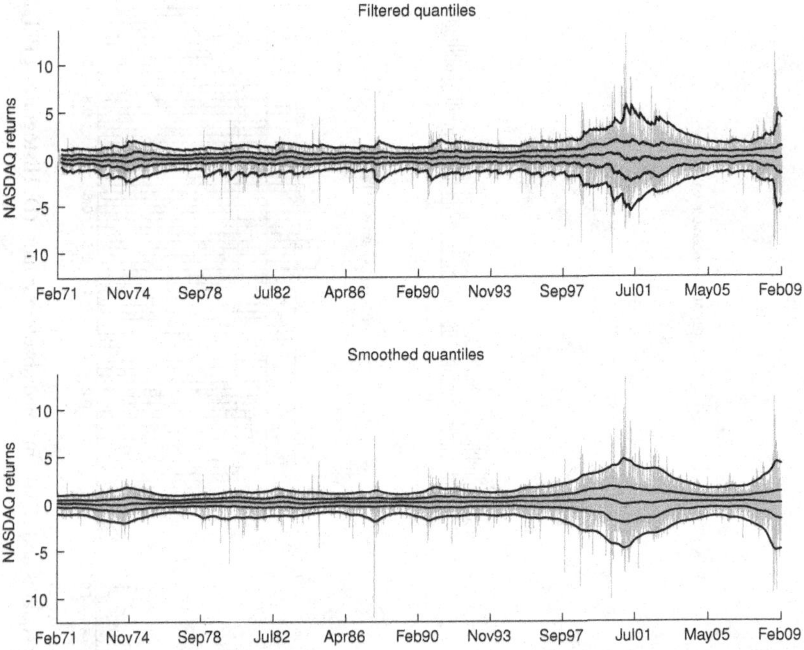

Figure 6.2. Filtered (upper panel) and smoothed (lower panel) time-varying quantiles of NASDAQ returns.

estimation. Forecasting performance might be improved by allowing the bandwidth to vary with time or by using different bandwidths to estimate the tails and the middle of the distribution.

Changing the basis for bandwidth selection is unlikely to correct the failure to pick up short-term serial correlation (at lag one) or to remove all the movements in volatility. The reason is that a time-varying kernel can only realistically track long-term movements. Hence there may be a case for prefiltering.

6.4.2 ARMA-GARCH Residuals

To prefilter the NASDAQ data, Harvey and Oryshchenko (2011) fitted an $MA(1)$ model with a first-order GARCH-t conditional variance equation. The estimates of α and β in the GARCH model were 0.098 and 0.901, respectively, so the sum is close to the IGARCH boundary. The estimated $MA(1)$ parameter was 0.210 and the degree of freedom of the t distibution was estimated to be 7.04.

Fitting a time-varying kernel to the GARCH residuals gave the following results. For filtering: $\widetilde{\beta} = 0.9996$ and $\widetilde{h} = 0.359$. For smoothing: $\widehat{\beta} = 0.9991$ and $\widehat{h} = 0.334$. The smoothing constants are bigger than those estimated for the raw data and, because they are closer to one, there is less scope for tracking

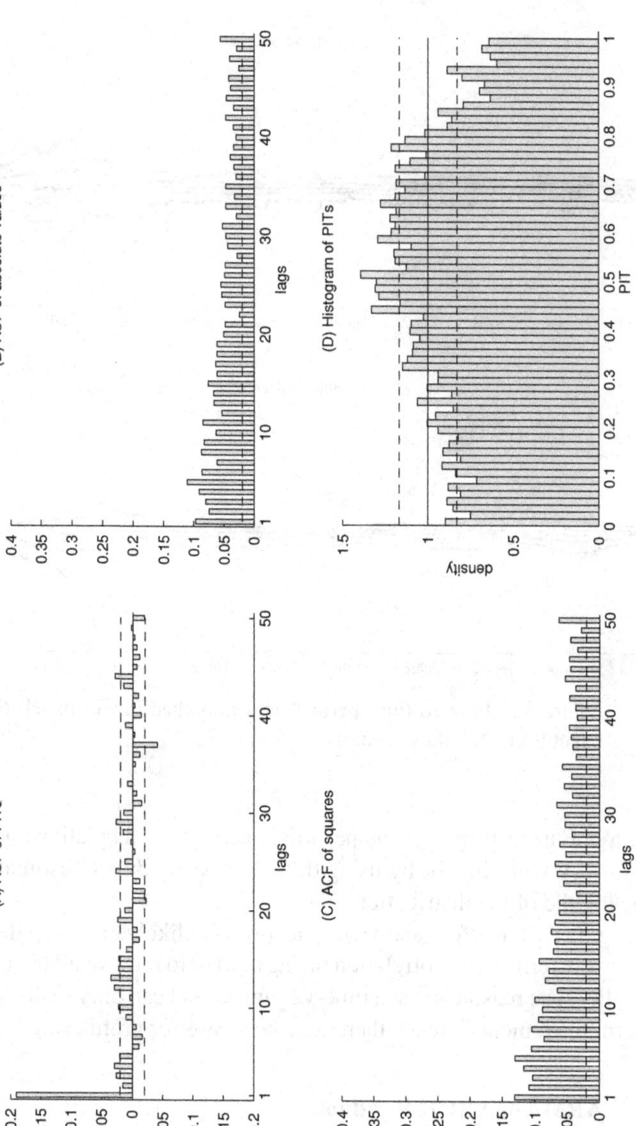

Figure 6.3. ACFs of (A) PITs, (B) their squares and (C) de-meaned absolute values. (D) Histogram of PITs.

time variation. As might be anticipated, the prefiltering effectively renders the median and interquartile range constant. Any remaining time variation is to be found in the high and low quantiles.[4]

Some notion of the way in which tail dispersion changes can be obtained by plotting the ratio of the difference between the τ and the $1-\tau$ quantiles, for small τ, to the interquartile range, that is

$$\widetilde{\alpha}_t(\tau) = \frac{\widetilde{\xi}_t(1-\tau) - \widetilde{\xi}_t(\tau)}{\widetilde{\xi}_t(0.75) - \widetilde{\xi}_t(0.25)}, \qquad \tau << 0.25,$$

where $\widetilde{\xi}_t(\tau)$ might be obtained by filtering or smoothing. Figure 6.4 shows the plot for $\tau = 0.01$ and 0.05 computed using smoothed quantiles, $\xi_{t|T}(\tau)$. Note that $\alpha(0.05)$ is 2.44 for a normal distribution and 2.66 for t_7; the corresponding figures for $\alpha(0.01)$ are 3.45 and 4.22, respectively.

For a symmetric distribution $\xi_t(\tau) + \xi_t(1-\tau) - 2\xi_t(0.5)$, $\tau < 0.5$, is zero for all $t = 1, \ldots, T$. Hence a plot of the measure of skewness

$$\widetilde{\beta}_t(\tau) = \frac{\widetilde{\xi}_t(1-\tau) + \widetilde{\xi}_t(\tau) - 2\widetilde{\xi}_t(0.5)}{\widetilde{\xi}_t(1-\tau) - \widetilde{\xi}_t(\tau)}, \qquad \tau < 0.5,$$

shows how the asymmetry captured by the complementary quantiles, $\xi_t(\tau)$ and $\xi_t(1-\tau)$, changes over time. The statistic $\beta(0.25)$ was originally proposed by Bowley in 1920. The maximum value of $\widetilde{\beta}_t(\tau)$ is one, representing extreme right (positive) skewness, and the minimum value is -1, representing extreme left skewness. Figure 6.4 plots $\widetilde{\beta}_t(\tau)$ for $\tau = 0.01$, 0.05 and 0.25 for the smoothed quantiles. There is substantial time variation in skewness: it is high in the late 70s, whereas around 2002–2005, the distribution is almost symmetric.

The ACFs of the PITs of the residuals, their squares and absolute values showed far less serial correlation than before. The histogram of PITs displayed the same hump-shaped pattern as was evident in the PITs from the raw data, but arguably to a lesser extent.

6.4.3 Bandwidth and Tails

The application to the NASDAQ index not only shows the attractions of the dynamic kernel but also exposes its limitations. In particular, the methods are only appropriate for monitoring distributions that change relatively slowly over time, because otherwise the effective sample size is too small. Short bursts of volatility may have to be accommodated by fitting a GARCH model.

A second limitation is that the bandwidth chosen by maximising the predictive likelihood or the likelihood cross-validation criterion appears to result in a degree of oversmoothing, which manifests itself in the hump-shaped histogram of the probability integral transforms. It may be possible to mitigate this effect

[4] It might be worth considering the use of the DCS model of Section 4.15 in this situation.

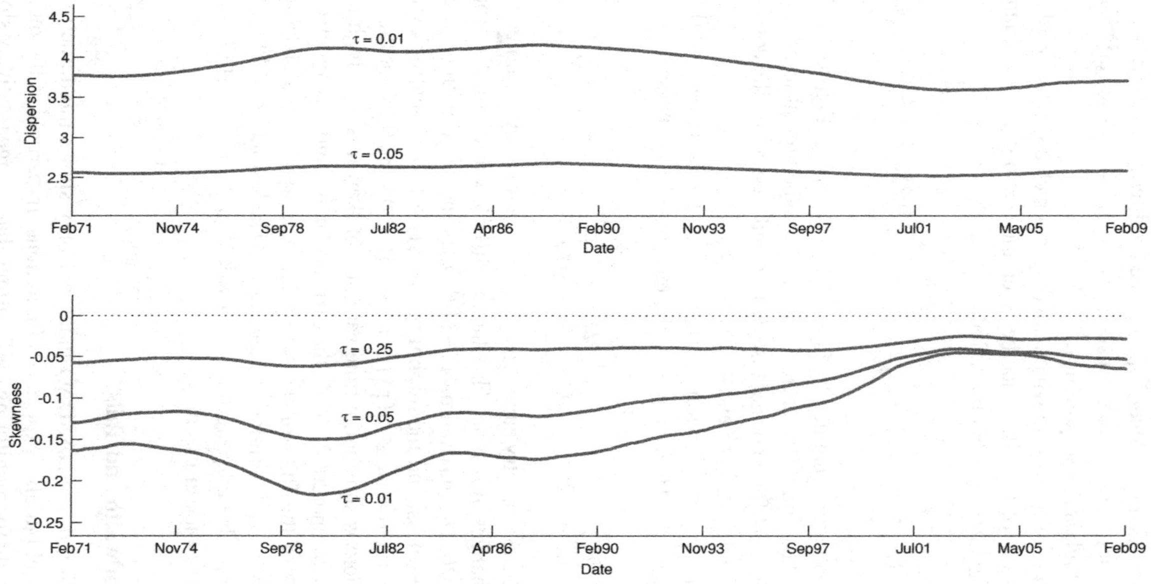

Figure 6.4. Changing dispersion (top panel) and skewness for NASDAQ residuals.

by letting the bandwidth vary over the distribution, but the fundamental problem is that there is not enough information to provide an accurate description of tail behaviour.

Modifications, such as combining kernel estimators with extreme value distributions for the tails, may be worth exploring. There is some discussion of this issue in Markovich (2007, pp. 101–11), but only for static models. Here, beyond a particular time-varying quantile, we might use the generalized Pareto distribution, as in Sub-section 5.3.5, with the scale subject to the same dynamics as in the part of the distribution estimated by the kernel.

CHAPTER 7

Multivariate Models, Correlation and Association

Dynamic conditional score models extend quite naturally to deal with changing location and scale in multivariate time series. Although a full treatment requires extensive use of matrix algebra, the main practical issues concern the nature and scope of restrictions on the parameter matrices governing the dynamics. The asymptotic theory of ML estimation is straightforward in principle, though the details are not always easy to work out.

The main challenge lies in constructing and analyzing models that embody changing relationships between variables. In this case, the asymptotic theory is no longer straightforward, even for Gaussian models. Nevertheless, even when it is not possible to develop a full asymptotic theory, the structure of the information matrix, and the conditions under which it is positive definite, provides a good indication of how well different models and parameterizations might work in practice.

There are important reasons for wishing to use multivariate models in finance. Understanding and measuring the relationship between movements in different assets play a key role in designing a portfolio. The standard theory is based on the multivariate normal distribution, and it shows how to construct a portfolio that gives minimum variance for a given expected return. Unfortunately, the multivariate normal distribution is not usually suitable for this task for two reasons: asset returns are not normally distributed, and their comovements are not adequately captured by correlation coefficients. More specifically, heavy tails are a feature of marginal distributions, and the probability of two asset prices exhibiting big movements in the same direction may be much higher than it would be with a bivariate normal. Taken together, these two observations suggest a relatively high probability that two markets experience large falls at the same time. The implications for many asset allocation strategies are quite serious.

Models based on the multivariate t distribution offer one way forward; Kotz and Nadarajah (2004, p. 243) briefly discuss the use of the multivariate t in asset allocation models. However, the association between any two variables in a multiivariate t distribution depends on a single correlation coefficient, just as in the multivariate normal. Copulas are more general and flexible. The DCS approach offers opportunities for constructing dynamic models for copulas that evolve over time.

Multivariate models play a central role in macroeconometrics. Models that are able to deal with extreme values are less prominent than in finance, but the economic turmoil in recent years and the volatility of many macroeconomic indicators makes such issues far from academic. Furthermore, there is the possibility that economic relationships may change over time. Models in which correlations are dynamic offer a new line of attack on the treatment of time-varying parameters in regression.

The first section in this chapter reviews multivariate distribution theory and sketches out the issues involved in constructing dynamic models for location, scale and association. Dynamic location models are discussed in Section 7.2, and it is shown how some of the main ideas of structural time series models carry over to multivariate DCS models. Section 7.3 examines time-varying correlation models by focussing on bivariate series in which the volatilities are constant; Section 7.4 looks at the situation in which correlations are constant, but volatility is time-varying; and models in which both correlation and volatility are time-varying are discussed in Section 7.5. The final section provides a short introduction to copulas and explains how they are able to capture the association between variables. The issues involved in modelling changing association by dynamic copulas are then explored.

7.1 MULTIVARIATE DISTRIBUTIONS

A multivariate normal distribution for an $N \times 1$ vector $\mathbf{y}_t$ is parameterized in terms of an $N \times 1$ mean vector, $\boldsymbol{\mu}$, and an $N \times N$ covariance matrix, $\boldsymbol{\Sigma}$. The PDF is

$$f(\mathbf{y}_t; \boldsymbol{\mu}, \boldsymbol{\Sigma}) = (2\pi)^{-N/2} |\boldsymbol{\Sigma}|^{-1/2} \exp(0.5(\mathbf{y}_t - \boldsymbol{\mu})\boldsymbol{\Sigma}^{-1}(\mathbf{y}_t - \boldsymbol{\mu})). \quad (7.1)$$

The marginal distributions of y_i are $N(\mu_i, \sigma_i^2)$, $i = 1, 2, \ldots, N$. The distribution of a subset of variables conditional on the other is also multivariate normal.

The most common multivariate t distribution has PDF

$$f(\mathbf{y}_t; \boldsymbol{\mu}, \boldsymbol{\Omega}, \nu) = \frac{\Gamma((\nu + N)/2)}{(\pi\nu)^{N/2}\Gamma(\nu/2)\, |\boldsymbol{\Omega}|^{1/2}\, w_t^{(\nu+N)/2}},$$

where $w_t = 1 + (1/\nu)(\mathbf{y}_t - \boldsymbol{\mu})'\boldsymbol{\Omega}^{-1}(\mathbf{y}_t - \boldsymbol{\mu})$ and $\boldsymbol{\Omega}$ is the scale matrix; see Lange et al. (1989) and Kotz and Nadarajah (2004). The scale matrix may be decomposed as $\boldsymbol{\Omega} = \mathbf{DRD}$, where $\mathbf{R}$ is a correlation matrix and $\mathbf{D}$ is a diagonal matrix with the i-th diagonal element equal to a scale parameter, φ_i. The covariance matrix, when it exists, is $\boldsymbol{\Sigma} = \nu(\nu - 2)^{-1}\boldsymbol{\Omega}$, $\nu > 2$. The distribution may be derived from a multivariate normal and an independent chi-square with ν degrees of freedom, thereby generalizing a fundamental property of Student's univariate t distribution. Specifically, if $\mathbf{x} \sim N(\boldsymbol{\mu}, \boldsymbol{\Sigma})$ and $z \sim \chi^2_\nu$, then $\mathbf{x}\sqrt{\nu/z} \sim t(\boldsymbol{\mu}, \boldsymbol{\Omega})$.

7.1.1 Estimation

Estimation of the parameters in a multivariate Gaussian model is straightforward, with the ML estimators given by the first and second moments. In a bivariate model, the estimator of the correlation, ρ, is the sample correlation coefficient, r.

ML estimation of the multivariate t model requires numerical optimization. The information matrix of the location vector $\boldsymbol{\mu}$ is

$$\mathbf{I}_{\mu\mu} = E\left(\frac{\partial \ln f}{\partial \boldsymbol{\mu}}\frac{\partial \ln f}{\partial \boldsymbol{\mu}'}\right) = \frac{\nu + N}{\nu + N + 2}\boldsymbol{\Omega}^{-1}. \tag{7.2}$$

The derivation can be found in Lange et al. (1989, appendix); see also Kotz and Nadarajah (2004).

The ML estimator of $\boldsymbol{\mu}$ is distributed independently of the ML estimators of elements of the scale matrix and of the degrees of freedom parameter; compare (2.18) for the univariate model. Lange et al. (1989) give analytic expressions for the block of the information matrix for the ν and the distinct elements of $\boldsymbol{\Omega}$. When time variation is introduced into $\boldsymbol{\Omega}$, it will prove advantageous to decompose it into a scale matrix and a correlation matrix.

7.1.2 Regression

Suppose that y_{1t} and y_{2t} are jointly normal with zero means and covariance matrix

$$\boldsymbol{\Sigma} = \begin{bmatrix} \sigma_1^2 & \sigma_{12} \\ \sigma_{12} & \sigma_2^2 \end{bmatrix} = \begin{bmatrix} \sigma_1^2 & \rho\sigma_1\sigma_2 \\ \rho\sigma_1\sigma_2 & \sigma_2^2 \end{bmatrix}.$$

The distribution of y_{1t} conditional on y_{2t} is also normal, and the regression equation can be written as

$$y_{1t} \mid y_{2t} = \beta y_{2t} + \varepsilon_t, \quad \varepsilon_t \sim NID\left(0, \sigma_\varepsilon^2\right), \qquad t = 1, \ldots, T, \tag{7.3}$$

where $\beta = \sigma_{12}/\sigma_2^2 = \rho\sigma_1/\sigma_2$ and ε_t is distributed independently of y_{2t} with variance $\sigma_\varepsilon^2 = \sigma_1^2 - \rho^2\sigma_2^2$. When β is the parameter of interest, it can be estimated efficiently by regressing y_{1t} on y_{2t}. In the terminology of Engle, Hendry and Richard (1982), y_{2t} is said to be weakly exogenous.

When y_{1t} and y_{2t} have a bivariate t distribution with common scale φ, the regression relationship is again linear. Provided $\nu > 2$, the model can be written as in (7.3), but with $\varepsilon_t = \varphi\sqrt{1-\rho^2}t_\nu$, where t_ν is a standard t variate; see Johnson and Kotz (1972, p. 135). However, simply regressing y_{1t} on y_{2t} is no longer efficient compared with maximizing the likelihood function obtained from the joint density of the two variables. Indeed, from the standpoint of estimation, thinking about the problem in single-equation terms is not helpful because outlying and influential observations are a feature of the bivariate t distribution, and only by considering the joint distribution are they dealt with properly.

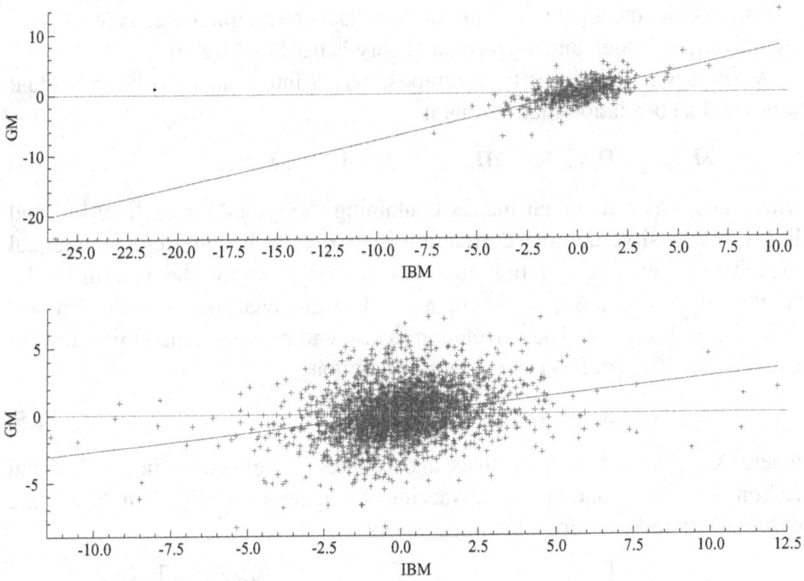

Figure 7.1. Daily returns for IBM plotted against daily returns for General Motors.

Example 19 *Figure 7.1 shows scatter plots of 3397 daily returns for IBM and General Motors from 7th April 1986 to 7th April 1999. The top graph is for the first 500 observations, whereas the bottom graph is for the remainder. The correlation of 0.74 and slope of 0.76 for the earlier period contrasts with a correlation of 0.26 and a slope of 0.27 for the later one. The pair of observations for the crash of 1987, seen in the bottom left-hand corner of the top graph, has had a considerable influence. Making allowance for conditional heteroscedasticity will not change the basic message.*

7.1.3 Dynamic Models

The extension of the DCS-t location model to multivariate time series is described in Section 7.2. No new issues of principle are involved. On the other hand, the treatment of a time-varying scale matrix, $\mathbf{\Omega}_{t|t-1}$, in a Gaussian or multivariate-t model does raise some fundamental issues. The direct extension of Beta-t-EGARCH to multivariate series is to let the scale matrix, $\mathbf{\Omega}_{t|t-1}$, depend on a time-varying matrix, $\mathbf{\Theta}_{t|t-1}$, by a matrix exponential link function, that is, $\mathbf{\Omega}_{t|t-1} = \exp \mathbf{\Theta}_{t|t-1}$. As a result, $\mathbf{\Omega}_{t|t-1}$ is always positive definite, and if $\mathbf{\Theta}_{t|t-1}$ is symmetric, then so is $\mathbf{\Omega}_{t|t-1}$; see Kawakatsu (2006). Unfortunately, the relationship between the elements of $\mathbf{\Omega}_{t|t-1}$ and those of $\mathbf{\Theta}_{t|t-1}$ is complicated and hard to disentangle. In particular, it is difficult to separate scale from association. Issues of interpretation aside, differentiation of the matrix exponential is needed to obtain the score, and this is not straightforward. Although not impossible, the algebraic manipulations lack the simplicity and elegance of the univariate model, and asymptotic theory is hard to develop.

A better way forward is to decompose $\boldsymbol{\Omega}_{t|t-1}$ into scales for the individual series and a correlation matrix, that is,

$$\boldsymbol{\Omega}_{t|t-1} = \mathbf{D}_{t|t-1}\mathbf{R}_{t|t-1}\mathbf{D}_{t|t-1}, \quad t = 1, \ldots, T, \tag{7.4}$$

where $\mathbf{D}_{t|t-1}$ is a diagonal matrix containing the scales for each series, and $\mathbf{R}_{t|t-1}$ is a positve definite correlation matrix with diagonal elements equal to unity. An exponential link function can be used for the volatilities by setting $\mathbf{D}_{t|t-1} = \exp \boldsymbol{\Lambda}_{t|t-1}$, where $\boldsymbol{\Lambda}_{t|t-1}$ is a diagonal matrix with elements $\lambda_{i,t|t-1}, i = 1, \ldots, N$. The correlation matrix can be constrained by following Creal et al. (2011, p. 557) and decomposing it as

$$\mathbf{R}_{t|t-1} = \mathbf{X}'_{t|t-1}\mathbf{X}_{t|t-1}, \quad t = 1, \ldots, T, \tag{7.5}$$

where $\mathbf{X}_{t|t-1}$ is a matrix of sines and cosines as defined as in Jaeckel and Rebonato (1999), and the time-varying parameters contained in $\mathbf{X}_{t|t-1}$ are expressed in radians. For a bivariate model,

$$\mathbf{R}_{t|t-1} = \begin{bmatrix} 1 & \rho_{t|t-1} \\ \rho_{t|t-1} & 1 \end{bmatrix} = \begin{bmatrix} 1 & \cos \zeta_{t|t-1} \\ \cos \zeta_{t|t-1} & 1 \end{bmatrix},$$

with the dynamic equation set up for $\zeta_{t|t-1}$. Even though $\zeta_{t|t-1}$ evolves over time, $\rho_{t|t-1}$ will always lie between -1 and one. Sub-section 7.3.1 analyses a different link function, which is easier to manipulate[1] but unfortunately does not easily generalize to more than two series.[2]

An alternative way of capturing the correlation dynamics is by setting up a model for a symmetric positive definite matrix, $\mathbf{Q}_{t|t-1}$. The dynamic correlations are then given by

$$\mathbf{R}_{t|t-1} = \boldsymbol{\Delta}^{-1}_{t|t-1}\mathbf{Q}_{t|t-1}\boldsymbol{\Delta}^{-1}_{t|t-1}, \quad t = 1, \ldots, T, \tag{7.6}$$

where $\boldsymbol{\Delta}_{t|t-1}$is a diagonal matrix with non-zero elements equal to the square root of the diagonal elements of $\mathbf{Q}_{t|t-1}$. The transformation not only ensures that $\mathbf{R}_{t|t-1}$, like $\mathbf{Q}_{t|t-1}$, is symmetric and positive definite, but also that it has off-diagonal elements in the range [−1,1].

The simplest specification of $\mathbf{Q}_{t|t-1}$ takes the same form as that of the dynamic conditional correlation (DCC) model of Engle (2002), that is,

$$\mathbf{Q}_{t+1|t} = (1 - \alpha - \beta)\mathbf{Q} + (1 - \beta)\mathbf{Q}_{t|t-1} + \alpha\mathbf{x}_t\mathbf{x}'_t, \alpha + \beta < 1, \quad t = 1, \ldots, T,$$

where $\mathbf{x}_t = \mathbf{D}^{-1}_{t|t-1}\mathbf{y}_t$, $\alpha, \beta \geq 0$ and $\mathbf{Q}$ is symmetric and positive definite. A disadvantage of the DCC formulation is that, as with a univariate GARCH

[1] The angle ζ is only identified within the region $[-\pi, \pi]$. This constraint can be imposed on $\zeta_{t|t-1}$, though, according to Creal et al. (2011, p. 557), numerical problems do not seem to occur when this is not done.

[2] Simply having off-diagonal elements in the range [−1,1] does not guarantee a positive definite matrix.

model, the restrictions on the parameters constrain the type of dynamics that might be entertained. This point is still relevant when $\mathbf{Q}_{t|t-1}$ is driven, not by moments, but by the conditional score, as described in Creal et al. (2011, Subsection 3.2, p. 556). Thus there is a strong case for working with models that combine the conditional scores with trigonometric link functions, as in (7.5), just as scores are combined with exponential link functions in modelling scale.

7.2 MULTIVARIATE LOCATION MODELS

Before looking at DCS models, the nature and scope of multivariate Gaussian UC models are briefly discussed.

7.2.1 Structural Time Series Models

Multivariate structural time series models are described in some detail in Harvey (1989, Chapter 8) and implemented in the STAMP 8 package of Koopman et al. (2009). The prototypical model is a direct generalization of (1.1), that is

$$\begin{aligned} \mathbf{y}_t &= \boldsymbol{\omega} + \boldsymbol{\mu}_t + \boldsymbol{\varepsilon}_t, \quad \boldsymbol{\varepsilon}_t \sim NID(\mathbf{0}, \boldsymbol{\Sigma}_\varepsilon), \quad t = 1, \ldots, T \qquad (7.7) \\ \boldsymbol{\mu}_{t+1} &= \boldsymbol{\Phi}\boldsymbol{\mu}_t + \boldsymbol{\eta}_t, \quad \boldsymbol{\eta}_t \sim NID(\mathbf{0}, \boldsymbol{\Sigma}_\eta). \end{aligned}$$

The statistical treatment of all such models is based on the Kalman filter.

The breakdown into signal and noise provides the basis for a rich description of multivariate time series. Setting $\boldsymbol{\Phi} = \mathbf{I}$ gives the multivariate local level model and letting $\boldsymbol{\Sigma}_\eta$ have rank less than N gives rise to common trends and hence co-integration. If the rank of the covariance matrix $\boldsymbol{\Sigma}_\eta$ is $J < N$, an appropriate ordering of the series enables the model to be written with J common levels, or trends, $\boldsymbol{\mu}_t^\dagger$. Thus

$$\begin{aligned} \mathbf{y}_{1t} &= \boldsymbol{\mu}_t^\dagger + \boldsymbol{\varepsilon}_{1t} \qquad (7.8) \\ \mathbf{y}_{2t} &= \boldsymbol{\Pi}\boldsymbol{\mu}_t^\dagger + \overline{\boldsymbol{\mu}} + \boldsymbol{\varepsilon}_{2t}, \end{aligned}$$

where $\boldsymbol{\Pi}$ is an $(N-J) \times J$ matrix of coefficients, $\overline{\boldsymbol{\mu}}$ is an $(N-J) \times 1$ vector of constants, and

$$\boldsymbol{\mu}_t^\dagger = \boldsymbol{\mu}_t^\dagger + \boldsymbol{\eta}_t^\dagger, \quad \boldsymbol{\eta}_t^\dagger \sim NID(\mathbf{0}, \boldsymbol{\Sigma}_\eta^\dagger),$$

where $\boldsymbol{\Sigma}_\eta^\dagger$ is positive definite.

The presence of common trends implies co-integration. In the above local level model, there exist $R = N - J$ (non-unique) co-integrating vectors, such that premultiplication of (7.8) by these vectors yields R stationary time series. For example, if the matrix of co-integrating vectors is $\mathbf{A} = (-\boldsymbol{\Pi}, \mathbf{I}_R)$, the equations for $\mathbf{y}_{2t}$ become

$$\mathbf{y}_{2t} = \boldsymbol{\Pi}\mathbf{y}_{1t} + \overline{\boldsymbol{\mu}} + \boldsymbol{\varepsilon}_t, \qquad (7.9)$$

where $\boldsymbol{\varepsilon}_t = \boldsymbol{\varepsilon}_{2t} - \boldsymbol{\Pi}\boldsymbol{\varepsilon}_{1t}$.

When there is only one common trend, $\mu_t^{\dagger}$, the matrix $\mathbf{\Pi}$ is an $(N-1) \times 1$ vector, $\boldsymbol{\pi}$. There are $N-1$ co-integrating vectors, but these can be chosen in different ways. Restricting $\boldsymbol{\pi}$ to be a vector of ones gives *balanced growth.*

Example 20 *National income, consumption and investment exhibit balanced growth when there is a single common trend for their logarithms. If the common trend is associated with income and the two co-integrating equations correspond to the 'great ratios' of consumption and investment to income, then*

$$\mathbf{A} = [-\boldsymbol{\pi} \quad \mathbf{I}_2] = \begin{bmatrix} -1 & 1 & 0 \\ -1 & 0 & 1 \end{bmatrix}.$$

The Gaussian noise in (7.7) could be replaced by heavy-tailed noise with multivariate t distribution, that is, $\boldsymbol{\varepsilon}_t \sim t_\nu(\mathbf{0}, \boldsymbol{\Omega}_\varepsilon)$. Once the Gaussianity assumption is dropped, computer-intensive techniques are needed. A DCS model offers an alternative.

7.2.2 DCS Model for the Multivariate t

The DCS-t model for changing location can be formulated as

$$\mathbf{y}_t = \boldsymbol{\omega} + \boldsymbol{\mu}_{t|t-1} + \boldsymbol{\nu}_t, \quad \boldsymbol{\nu}_t \sim t_\nu(\mathbf{0}, \boldsymbol{\Omega}), \quad t = 1, \ldots, T,$$

$$\boldsymbol{\mu}_{t+1|t} = \boldsymbol{\Phi}\boldsymbol{\mu}_{t|t-1} + \mathbf{K}\mathbf{u}_t, \tag{7.10}$$

where $\mathbf{K}$ is an $N \times N$ matrix and the vector $\mathbf{u}_t$ depends on the score. The log-density for the t-th observation is

$$\ln f_t(\boldsymbol{\omega}, \boldsymbol{\Phi}, \mathbf{K}, \boldsymbol{\Omega}, \nu) = \ln(\Gamma(\nu+N)/2) - \ln\Gamma(\nu/2) - \frac{N}{2}\ln \pi\nu$$
$$- \frac{1}{2}\ln|\boldsymbol{\Omega}| - \frac{\nu+N}{2}\ln w_t,$$

where

$$w_t = 1 + (1/\nu)(\mathbf{y}_t - \boldsymbol{\mu}_{t|t-1})'\boldsymbol{\Omega}^{-1}(\mathbf{y}_t - \boldsymbol{\mu}_{t|t-1}), \qquad t = 1, \ldots, T.$$

The score vector with respect to $\boldsymbol{\mu}_{t|t-1}$ is

$$\frac{\partial \ln f_t}{\partial \boldsymbol{\mu}_{t|t-1}} = \frac{1}{w_t}\frac{\nu+N}{\nu}\boldsymbol{\Omega}^{-1}(\mathbf{y}_t - \boldsymbol{\mu}_{t|t-1}). \tag{7.11}$$

If $\mathbf{u}_t$ is set equal to the score vector in the multivariate dynamic equation of (7.10), an outlier in any one series will affect the others because they are connected by $\boldsymbol{\Omega}$, but the effect will be mitigated because of the consequent downweighting from w_t. This weight is the same for all series – even if they are uncorrelated with each other. The intuition lies in the fact that the multivariate t is constructed from normal variates with a common chi-squared denominator.

The $\mathbf{u}_t$ vector may be modified by premultiplying by the inverse of the information matrix. Dropping constant terms then gives a generalization of the variable, (3.1), used in the univariate location model, namely,

$$\mathbf{u}_t = w_t^{-1}(\mathbf{y}_t - \boldsymbol{\mu}_{t|t-1}), \quad t = 1, \ldots, T.$$

An outlier in one series will not now affect the other elements of $\mathbf{u}_t$ directly, although there is still the downweighting from w_t. How the different models will finally work out depends on the constraints put on $\mathbf{K}$. If $\mathbf{K}$ is diagonal, the specification of $\mathbf{u}_t$ will be crucial, but this will not be the case if $\mathbf{K}$ is merely constrained to be symmetric.

A multivariate local level DCS model can be specified by setting $\mathbf{\Phi} = \mathbf{I}$. The specification can be adapted to allow for common trends (levels). Thus (7.8) becomes

$$\begin{aligned}\mathbf{y}_{1t} &= \boldsymbol{\mu}^{\dagger}_{t|t-1} + \boldsymbol{\nu}_{1t}, \quad t = 1, \ldots T, \\ \mathbf{y}_{2t} &= \mathbf{\Pi}\boldsymbol{\mu}^{\dagger}_{t|t-1} + \overline{\boldsymbol{\omega}} + \boldsymbol{\nu}_{2t}, \\ \boldsymbol{\mu}^{\dagger}_{t+1|t} &= \mathbf{\Phi}\boldsymbol{\mu}^{\dagger}_{t|t-1} + \mathbf{K}^{\dagger}\mathbf{u}_t,\end{aligned}$$

where $\boldsymbol{\mu}^{\dagger}_{t|t-1}$ is now a $J \times 1$ vector and $\mathbf{K}^{\dagger}$ is a $J \times N$ matrix. For a single common, $\mathbf{K}^{\dagger\prime} = \boldsymbol{\kappa}$ is an $N \times 1$ vector. In a balanced growth model, it may be appropriate to let $\boldsymbol{\kappa}$ be proportional to a vector of ones times the inverse of the information matrix.

An alternative approach to common trends would be to work directly with the $N \times 1$ vector $\boldsymbol{\mu}_{t|t-1}$, as in (7.10) and then constrain the $N \times N$ matrix $\mathbf{K}$ to be symmetric, but with rank J. This may be done by letting $\mathbf{K} = \mathbf{K}^*\mathbf{K}^{*\prime}$, where $\mathbf{K}^*$ is an $N \times J$ matrix in which the first J rows are a lower triangular $J \times J$ matrix. A balanced growth model would have $\mathbf{K}^{*\prime} = \boldsymbol{\kappa}$.

7.2.3 Asymptotic Theory*

The properties of the score vector and its derivatives are a generalization of the properties found in Chapter 3.

Proposition 39 *The distribution of the score does not depend on $\boldsymbol{\mu}_{t|t-1}$ because $\mathbf{y}_t - \boldsymbol{\mu}_{t|t-1}$ and w_t^{-1} are distributed independently of $\boldsymbol{\mu}_{t|t-1}$. Furthermore,*

$$b_t = \frac{(1/\nu)(\mathbf{y}_t - \boldsymbol{\mu}_{t|t-1})'\mathbf{\Omega}^{-1}(\mathbf{y}_t - \boldsymbol{\mu}_{t|t-1})}{1 + (1/\nu)(\mathbf{y}_t - \boldsymbol{\mu}_{t|t-1})'\mathbf{\Omega}^{-1}(\mathbf{y}_t - \boldsymbol{\mu}_{t|t-1})} = 1 - \frac{1}{w_t}$$

is distributed as $beta(N/2, \nu/2)$ (and w_t^{-1} is distributed as $beta(\nu/2, N/2)$). The scores are (multivariate) IID with mean vector zero and covariance matrix given by the information matrix, $\mathbf{I}_{\mu\mu}$ of (7.2).

Proof. The matrix $\mathbf{\Omega}$ can be decomposed as $\mathbf{\Omega} = \mathbf{\Omega}^{1/2}\mathbf{\Omega}^{1/2}$, where $\mathbf{\Omega}^{1/2}$ is positive definite. Thus $\mathbf{\Omega}^{-1/2}(\mathbf{y}_t - \boldsymbol{\mu}_{t|t-1}) \sim t_\nu(\mathbf{0}, \mathbf{I})$. Because $(\mathbf{y}_t - \boldsymbol{\mu}_{t|t-1})'\mathbf{\Omega}^{-1}(\mathbf{y}_t - \boldsymbol{\mu}_{t|t-1})$ is the sum of N independent t variates, it is the ratio of a χ^2_N variable to an independent χ^2_ν variable divided by ν. The fact that b_t is $beta(N/2, \nu/2)$ now follows from Lemma 3, with the details along the lines of those in Corollary 2. ■

The matrix of second derivatives of the log-density – the Hessian – is

$$\frac{\partial^2 \ln f_t}{\partial \boldsymbol{\mu}_{t|t-1} \partial \boldsymbol{\mu}'_{t|t-1}} = -(1-b_t)\frac{\nu+N}{\nu}\boldsymbol{\Omega}^{-1} + 2\frac{\nu+N}{\nu^2}(1-b_t)^2\boldsymbol{\Omega}^{-1}(\mathbf{y}_t - \boldsymbol{\mu}_{t|t-1})(\mathbf{y}_t - \boldsymbol{\mu}_{t|t-1})'\boldsymbol{\Omega}^{-1}.$$

Like the score vector, the Hessian is distributed independently of $\boldsymbol{\mu}_{t|t-1}$.

The fact that the score vector and its first derivative matrix, the Hessian, are independently and identically distributed and depend on bounded variables (which are functions of beta distributed variables at the true parameter values) suggests that the results of Sections 2.3, 2.4 and 3.3 can be extended to find the conditions under which the ML estimators of the unknown parameters in the $\boldsymbol{\omega}$, $\boldsymbol{\Phi}$, $\mathbf{K}$, $\boldsymbol{\Omega}$ and ν will be consistent and asymptotically normal. The first step is to apply Lemma 10 by noting that $\boldsymbol{\mu}_{t|t-1}$ depends on a set of n_1 parameters, which are the distinct elements of the matrices $\boldsymbol{\Phi}$ and $\mathbf{K}$. In the notation of Lemma 10, $\boldsymbol{\mu}_{t|t-1} = \boldsymbol{\theta}_{t|t-1}$ and the parameters are contained in the $n \times 1$ vector $\boldsymbol{\psi}$. Thus the conditional score is

$$\frac{\partial \ln f_t}{\partial \boldsymbol{\psi}} = \frac{\partial \ln f_t}{\partial \boldsymbol{\mu}'_{t|t-1}} \frac{\partial \boldsymbol{\mu}_{t|t-1}}{\partial \boldsymbol{\psi}}$$

and, using (7.2),

$$E_{t-1}\left(\frac{\partial \ln f_t}{\partial \boldsymbol{\psi}}\frac{\partial \ln f_t}{\partial \boldsymbol{\psi}'}\right) = \frac{\partial \boldsymbol{\mu}'_{t|t-1}}{\partial \boldsymbol{\psi}}\mathbf{I}_{\mu\mu}\frac{\partial \boldsymbol{\mu}_{t|t-1}}{\partial \boldsymbol{\psi}} = \frac{\nu+N}{\nu+N+2}\frac{\partial \boldsymbol{\mu}'_{t|t-1}}{\partial \boldsymbol{\psi}}\boldsymbol{\Omega}^{-1}\frac{\partial \boldsymbol{\mu}_{t|t-1}}{\partial \boldsymbol{\psi}'};$$

compare Lange et al. (1989, p. 894) and the top left-hand matrix in (2.54). The elements of the information matrix are then given by the unconditional expectations of the preceding expression; see the discussion in Sub-Section 2.3.7.

7.2.4 Regression and Errors in Variables

Sub-section 7.1.2 explained why regression was inadequate for dealing with a bivariate t distribution. The case for multivariate modelling again becomes apparent when unobserved components enter the picture. The underlying relationship between y_{1t} and y_{2t} in the bivariate Gaussian model of (7.7) may be between the serially correlated signals, μ_{1t} and μ_{2t}, whereas the disturbances ε_{1t} and ε_{2t} represent noise terms that are essentially uncorrelated with each other as well as being serially independent. In the local level model, μ_{1t} and μ_{2t} may be thought of as permanent components, whereas ε_{1t} and ε_{2t} are transitory.

The regression relationship between the signal components is

$$\mu_{1t} \mid \mu_{2t} = \beta_\mu \mu_{2t} + \eta_t, \quad t = 1, \ldots, T,$$

where $\beta_\mu = Cov(\eta_{1t}, \eta_{2t})/Var(\eta_{1t})$. An efficient estimator of β_μ cannot be obtained by regressing y_{1t} on y_{2t} unless the covariances matrices of the $\varepsilon_t' s$ and the $\eta_t' s$ are proportional. When this is the case, y_{2t} is weakly exogenous, but more generally, the ordinary least squares estimator of β_μ will be inconsistent in a stationary model because, in an equation like (7.3), y_{2t} is correlated with ε_t; see Harvey (1989, p. 458). Consistency may be achieved when μ_{1t} and μ_{2t} are random walks, but there is still the matter of efficiency.

In the classic errors in variables model, both components are serially independent, and it is not possible to obtain consistent estimators of the parameters of the underlying relationship unless there is prior information. When the dynamic properties of the components of interest are different from those of the errors, the problem is resolved. An example is given by the bivariate model of GDP and inflation reported in Harvey (2011), where the Phillips curve relationship is extracted from the joint cyclical component. In this case, trend and seasonal components, as well as the irregular, can be taken out of the picture because their dynamics differ from those of the cycle.

Heavy tails do not, in principle, complicate the errors in variables issue. A multivariate DCS-t model provides a solution, and the only difficulty is the practical one of estimating a model with several components.

7.3 DYNAMIC CORRELATION

Changes in correlation in the GM-IBM data set used in Figure 7.1 are not just associated with the 1987 crash observations. When the first 3,000 observations are divided into six groups of 500, and the remaining 397 observations are assigned to a seventh group, the correlation coefficients and Kendall's tau are as in Table 7.1. The correlations are higher at the beginning than at the end. The same is true of Kandall's tau, but because Kandall's tau is a robust measure of association, it is less influenced by outliers, and the differences are not so marked.

Tests for the significance of movement in correlation and other measures of association are proposed in Sub-section 7.3.4. The question of how to model changing correlations is first addressed, and the implications for time-varying

Table 7.1. *Correlations and Kendall's tau for GM-IBM daily returns*

Group	1	2	3	4	5	6	7
r	0.74	0.51	0.42	0.16	0.18	0.10	0.36
tau	0.37	0.34	0.26	0.10	0.15	0.08	0.22

parameters in regression are then analyzed. The emphasis is primarily on bivariate models because no matrix algebra is required, and the consequent transparency provides more insight and understanding.

7.3.1 A Bivariate Gaussian Model

In order to focus on the issues involved in modelling changing correlation, a bivariate model with a conditional Gaussian distribution will be assumed. The means will be set to zero and the variances taken to be time-invariant. In the notation of (7.1), $N = 2$, $\boldsymbol{\mu} = \mathbf{0}$ and

$$\boldsymbol{\Sigma} = \begin{bmatrix} \sigma_1^2 & \rho_{t|t-1}\sigma_1\sigma_2 \\ \rho_{t|t-1}\sigma_1\sigma_2 & \sigma_2^2 \end{bmatrix}.$$

The principal questions are then: how to drive the dynamics of the filter for changing correlation, $\rho_{t|t-1}$, and with what link function?

A simple moment approach, similar to that in the DCC model, would use

$$x_{1t}x_{2t}, \quad t = 1, \ldots, T, \tag{7.12}$$

where $x_{it} = y_{it}/\sigma_i$, $i = 1, 2$, but the effect of $x_1 = x_2 = 2$ is the same as that of $x_1 = 1$ and $x_2 = 4$. The score of the correlation coefficient contains an extra term that effectively resolves the problem.

Rather than work directly with $\rho_{t|t-1}$, a transformation will be applied so as to keep it in the range, $-1 < \rho_{t|t-1} < 1$. The link function

$$\rho_{t|t-1} = \frac{\exp(2\gamma_{t|t-1}) - 1}{\exp(2\gamma_{t|t-1}) + 1}, \quad t = 1, \ldots, T, \tag{7.13}$$

is eminently suitable in that it allows the new variable, $\gamma_{t|t-1}$, to be unconstrained. The inverse,

$$\gamma = \frac{1}{2}\ln\frac{1+\rho}{1-\rho} = \tanh^{-1}\rho,$$

is the arctanh transformation originally proposed by R.A. Fisher to create the z-transform (his z is our γ) of the sample correlation coefficient, r. The asymptotic distribution theory supports this choice because, as Fisher showed, $\tanh^{-1} r$ is asymptotically normal with mean $\tanh^{-1}\rho$ and variance $1/T$. On the other hand, r has a variance that depends on ρ.

It is convenient to specify the standard deviations (the same as scale for a normal distribution) using an exponential link function, particularly as they will be allowed to be dynamic at a later stage. The covariance matrix, $\boldsymbol{\Sigma}_{t|t-1}$, is the same as the scale matrix in (7.4), but the diagonal matrix $\mathbf{D}_{t|t-1} = \mathbf{D}$ is time-invariant with elements $\exp(\lambda_1)$ and $\exp(\lambda_2)$. Following on from (7.13), the correlation matrix can be written

$$\mathbf{R}_{t|t-1} = \begin{bmatrix} 1 & \rho_{t|t-1} \\ \rho_{t|t-1} & 1 \end{bmatrix} = \begin{bmatrix} 1 & \overline{g}_{t|t-1}/g_{t|t-1} \\ \overline{g}_{t|t-1}/g_{t|t-1} & 1 \end{bmatrix}, \tag{7.14}$$

where

$$g_{t|t-1} = \frac{\exp(\gamma_{t|t-1}) + \exp(-\gamma_{t|t-1})}{2} \quad \text{and}$$

$$\overline{g}_{t|t-1} = \frac{\exp(\gamma_{t|t-1}) - \exp(-\gamma_{t|t-1})}{2}.$$

In what follows the subscripts on $g_{t|t-1}$ and $\overline{g}_{t|t-1}$ will be dropped where there is no ambiguity. The inverse of $\mathbf{R}_{t|t-1}$ is

$$\mathbf{R}_{t|t-1}^{-1} = g^2 \begin{bmatrix} 1 & -\overline{g}/g \\ -\overline{g}/g & 1 \end{bmatrix}$$

because $g^2 - \overline{g}^2 = 1$ and so $|\mathbf{R}_{t|t-1}| = 1 - \overline{g}^2/g^2 = 1/g^2$.

The log-density in the static model is

$$\ln f(\rho, \sigma_1^2, \sigma_2^2) = -\ln 2\pi - \frac{1}{2}\ln\sigma_1^2 - \frac{1}{2}\ln\sigma_2^2 - \frac{1}{2}\ln(1-\rho^2)$$
$$- \frac{1}{2(1-\rho^2)}\left(\frac{y_1{}^2}{\sigma_1^2} - \frac{2\rho y_1 y_2}{\sigma_1\sigma_2} + \frac{y_2{}^2}{\sigma_2^2}\right),$$

but, with the transformations for ρ, σ_1^2 and σ_2^2,

$$\ln f(\gamma, \lambda_1, \lambda_2) = -\ln 2\pi - \lambda_1 - \lambda_2 + \ln g$$
$$- \frac{1}{2}\left(\frac{y_1{}^2}{\exp(2\lambda_1)}g^2 - \frac{2y_1y_2}{\exp(\lambda_1+\lambda_2)}g\overline{g} + \frac{y_2{}^2}{\exp(2\lambda_2)}g^2\right).$$

Because $\partial g/\partial\gamma = \overline{g}$ and $\partial\overline{g}/\partial\gamma = g$, the score for γ is

$$\begin{aligned}\frac{\partial \ln f}{\partial \gamma} &= \frac{\overline{g}}{g} - \frac{y_1{}^2}{\exp(2\lambda_1)}g\overline{g} + \frac{y_1y_2}{\exp(\lambda_1+\lambda_2)}(g^2+\overline{g}^2) - \frac{y_2{}^2}{\exp(2\lambda_2)}g\overline{g} \\ &= \frac{\overline{g}}{g} + \frac{y_1y_2}{\exp(\lambda_1+\lambda_2)}(2g^2-1) - \left[\frac{y_1{}^2}{\exp(2\lambda_1)} + \frac{y_2{}^2}{\exp(2\lambda_2)}\right]g\overline{g}\end{aligned} \tag{7.15}$$

and it is not difficult to confirm that the expectation at the true parameter values is zero.

The first-order dynamic equation for correlation is defined as

$$\gamma_{t+1|t} = (1-\phi)\omega + \phi\gamma_{t|t-1} + \kappa u_{\gamma t}, \quad t = 1, \ldots, T, \tag{7.16}$$

where $u_{\gamma t}$ is the score, $\partial \ln f_t/\partial\gamma_{t|t-1}$, and the condition $|\phi| < 1$ is all that is required to ensure that $\gamma_{t+1|t}$, and hence $\rho_{t+1|t}$, is stationary. The score reduces to (7.12) when $\rho_{t|t-1} = \gamma_{t|t-1} = 0$, but more generally, the term involving squared observations makes important modifications.

Setting $x_{it} = y_{it}\exp(-\lambda_i)$, $i = 1, 2$, gives

$$\frac{\partial \ln f_t}{\partial \gamma_{t|t-1}} = \frac{1}{2}(x_{1t} + x_{2t})^2 \exp(-2\gamma_{t|t-1}) - \frac{1}{2}(x_{1t} - x_{2t})^2 \exp(2\gamma_{t|t-1}) + \rho_{t|t-1} - x_{1t}x_{2t}, \tag{7.17}$$

where $(x_{1t} - x_{2t})^2$ and $(x_{1t} + x_{2t})^2$ are uncorrelated. The second term is zero when $x_{1t} = x_{2t}$, whereas the first term gets larger as the correlation moves from being strongly positive, that is, $\gamma_{t|t-1}$ large, to being strongly negative. In other words, $x_{1t} = x_{2t}$ is evidence of positive correlation, so there is little reason to change $\gamma_{t|t-1}$ when $\rho_{t|t-1}$ is close to one. On the other hand, if $x_{1t} = -x_{2t}$, the first term is zero and the second term is strongly negative if the correlation is positive, but approaches zero as it becomes more and more negative. The last term is relatively small when $\rho_{t|t-1}$ is close to ± 1. As regards the case of $x_{1t} = x_{2t} = 2$ compared with $x_{1t} = 1$ and $x_{2t} = 4$, it is readily seen that the effect of the latter will be to engineer a significant reduction in the correlation when the current correlation is strongly positive because the second term is dominant.

The information matrix for the ML estimators of λ_1, λ_2 and γ in the static model depends only on γ.

Proposition 40 *The information matrix for the static bivariate Gaussian model is*

$$\mathbf{I}\begin{pmatrix}\lambda_1\\ \lambda_2\\ \gamma\end{pmatrix} = \begin{bmatrix} 1+g^2 & 1-g^2 & -\overline{g}/g \\ 1-g^2 & 1+g^2 & -\overline{g}/g \\ -\overline{g}/g & -\overline{g}/g & 2-1/g^2 \end{bmatrix}. \tag{7.18}$$

Proof. Differentiating (7.15) gives

$$\frac{\partial^2 \ln f}{\partial \gamma^2} = \frac{g^2 - \overline{g}^2}{g^2} - \frac{{y_1}^2}{\exp(2\lambda_1)}(g^2 + \overline{g}^2) + \frac{y_1 y_2}{\exp(\lambda_1 + \lambda_2)} 4g\overline{g} - \frac{{y_2}^2}{\exp(2\lambda_2)}(g^2 + \overline{g}^2)$$

and so

$$-E\frac{\partial^2 \ln f}{\partial \gamma^2} = \frac{-1}{g^2} + 2g^2 + 2\overline{g}^2 - 4\overline{g}^2 = 2(g^2 - \overline{g}^2) = 2 - \frac{1}{g^2}.$$

The score for the scale parameters can be written as

$$\frac{\partial \ln f}{\partial \lambda_i} = -1 + \frac{{y_i}^2}{\exp(2\lambda_i)} g^2 - \frac{y_1 y_2}{\exp(\lambda_1 + \lambda_2)} g\overline{g}, \qquad i = 1, 2. \tag{7.19}$$

Therefore,

$$E\frac{\partial \ln f}{\partial \lambda_i} = -1 + g^2 - \overline{g}^2 = 0, \qquad i = 1, 2,$$

and

$$\frac{\partial^2 \ln f}{\partial \lambda_i^2} = -\frac{2{y_i}^2}{\exp(2\lambda_i)}g + \frac{y_1 y_2}{\exp(\lambda_1 + \lambda_2)}\overline{g}$$

so

$$-E\frac{\partial^2 \ln f}{\partial \lambda_i^2} = 2g^2 - \overline{g}^2 = g^2 + 1, \qquad i = 1, 2.$$

Furthermore,

$$-E\frac{\partial^2 \ln f}{\partial \lambda_1 \partial \lambda_2} = -E\frac{y_1 y_2}{\exp(\lambda_1 + \lambda_2)}g\overline{g} = -\overline{g}^2 = 1 - g^2.$$

Also, for $i = 1, 2$,

$$\begin{aligned} -E\frac{\partial^2 \ln f}{\partial \gamma \partial \lambda_i} &= -E\frac{{y_i}^2}{\exp(2\lambda_i)}2g\overline{g} + E\frac{y_1 y_2}{\exp(\lambda_1 + \lambda_2)}(2g^2 - 1) \\ &= -2g\overline{g} + 2\overline{g}g - \frac{\overline{g}}{g} = -\frac{\overline{g}}{g}. \end{aligned}$$

■

The limiting distribution of the ML estimators is multivariate normal with covariance matrix,

$$Var\begin{pmatrix} \widetilde{\lambda}_1 \\ \widetilde{\lambda}_2 \\ \widetilde{\gamma} \end{pmatrix} = \frac{1}{2}\begin{bmatrix} 1 & 1 - 1/g^2 & \overline{g}/g \\ 1 - 1/g^2 & 1 & \overline{g}/g \\ \overline{g}/g & \overline{g}/g & 2 \end{bmatrix} \tag{7.20}$$

$$= \frac{1}{2}\begin{bmatrix} 1 & \rho^2 & \rho \\ \rho^2 & 1 & \rho \\ \rho & \rho & 2 \end{bmatrix}, \tag{7.21}$$

obtained by inverting (7.18). The asymptotic variances of the ML estimators of λ_1 and λ_2 are the same as for univariate models, whereas the asymptotic distribution of $\widetilde{\gamma}$ is the same as that of $\tanh^{-1} r$. Indeed, the ML estimators of λ_1 and λ_2 are just the logarithms of the individual sample variances, whereas $\widetilde{\gamma} = \tanh^{-1} r$; see Johnson and Kotz (1972, pp. 103–4).

Premultiplying the score vector by the inverse of the information matrix, (7.20), gives

$$u_{it} = \frac{1}{2}\left(\frac{{y_{it}}^2}{\exp(2\lambda_i)} - 1\right), \qquad i = 1, 2, \tag{7.22}$$

for the volatilities, together with the modified score for $\gamma_{t|t-1}$,

$$u_{\gamma t} = \frac{2y_{1t}y_{2t}}{\exp(\lambda_1 + \lambda_2)}g^2 - \left[\frac{{y_{1t}}^2}{\exp(2\lambda_1)} + \frac{{y_{2t}}^2}{\exp(2\lambda_2)}\right]g\overline{g}. \tag{7.23}$$

These variables are simpler than the raw scores and may be more attractive candidates for inclusion in the dynamic models for scale and correlation.

The modified score of (7.23) can be rearranged as

$$u_{\gamma t} = (x_{1t} + x_{2t})^2 \exp(-2\gamma_{t|t-1}) - (x_{1t} - x_{2t})^2 \exp(2\gamma_{t|t-1}),$$

which is a little neater than (7.17).

Corollary 32 *When location parameters are introduced, their ML estimators are distributed independently of the estimators of scale, correlation and degrees of freedom. The covariance matrix of the limiting distribution of the ML estimator of the vector* $\boldsymbol{\mu}$ *is* $Var(\widetilde{\boldsymbol{\mu}}) = \boldsymbol{\Sigma}$. *Thus for the bivariate model, the asymptotic distribution of the ML estimators of* μ_1 *and* μ_2 *depends on* γ, *as well as on* λ_1 *and* λ_2.

7.3.2 Time-Varying Parameters in Regression

Time-varying parameters are usually modelled in a regression framework by letting the coefficient of an explanatory variable change over time. Thus

$$y_t = \beta_t x_t + \varepsilon_t, \quad t = 1, \ldots, T, \tag{7.24}$$

where β_t follows a stochastic process, such as an AR(1) or random walk; see Harvey (1989, pp. 408–11) and the test procedure proposed by Nebeya and Tanaka (1988). This model is valid if the explanatory variable is non-stochastic, for example, if it is a function of time. If the explanatory variable is stochastic, then it needs to be independent of β_t and ε_t in all time periods. Not only is this assumption restrictive, but if x_t is a linear process, then y_t will, in general, be nonlinear. Furthermore, there are concerns about the path followed by the dependent variable when the explanatory variable is integrated; see the discussion in Harvey (1989, pp. 409–10).

A bivariate model provides a better starting point. Suppose that y_{1t} and y_{2t} are jointly normal with zero means and constant variances, but a correlation that changes over time. The regression equation in (7.3) then becomes

$$y_{1t} \mid y_{2t} = \rho_t(\sigma_1/\sigma_2)y_{2t} + \varepsilon_t, \quad t = 1, \ldots, T,$$

where ε_t is distributed independently of y_{2t} with variance $\sigma_1^2 - \rho_t^2\sigma_2^2$. Similarly for the DCS model,

$$y_{1t} \mid y_{2t} = \rho_{t|t-1}(\sigma_1/\sigma_2)y_{2t} + \varepsilon_t, \quad t = 1, \ldots, T.$$

The time-varying parameter is $\beta_{t|t-1} = \rho_{t|t-1}(\sigma_1/\sigma_2)$, and if $\rho_{t|t-1}$ is constrained to lie in the interval $(-1, 1)$, perhaps by letting it evolve as in (7.16), the range of $\beta_{t|t-1}$ is $-\sigma_1/\sigma_2$ to σ_1/σ_2.

When the means are non-zero,

$$y_{1t} \mid y_{2t} = (\mu_y - \rho_{t|t-1}\mu_x) + \rho_{t|t-1}(\sigma_1/\sigma_2)y_{2t} + \varepsilon_t, \quad t = 1, \ldots, T,$$

so the movements in the constant term also depend on those of $\rho_{t|t-1}$. There are similar implications when y_{1t} and y_{2t} depend on exogenous explanatory variables.

By formulating the model in terms of changing correlation, the marginal distributions are unaffected. If both y_{1t} and y_{2t} are linear univariate processes, they remain so. Furthermore, the bivariate process for y_{1t} and y_{2t} is strictly stationary if $\gamma_{t|t-1}$, and hence $\rho_{t|t-1}$, is stationary. On the other hand, there is nothing to stop $\gamma_{t|t-1}$ being non-stationary, because although this makes $\rho_{t|t-1}$ non-stationary, it is still confined to the range $(-1, 1)$.

The model can be generalized to deal with more than two variables, and EGARCH effects can be added.

Autoregressive models with time-varying parameters have also been employed in econometrics. A recent example can be found in Cogley et al. (2010). The prototypical case is

$$y_t = \mu + \phi_t(y_{t-1} - \mu) + \varepsilon_t, \quad t = 1, \ldots, T,$$

$$\phi_t = \xi\phi_{t-1} + \eta_t, \qquad |\xi| < 1,$$

where ε_t and η_t have independent normal distributions, and μ and ξ are parameters. The properties of this model are examined in Weiss (1985), where conditions under which y_t has a finite variance are derived. Although the model is nonlinear, it is conditionally Gaussian, and the likelihood function can be obtained from the Kalman filter. However, constraints need to be imposed on ϕ_t to prevent the model becoming explosive and, as with (7.24), there is the question of what kind of process y_t follows. These difficulties can be avoided by setting $y_{1t} = y_t$ and $y_{2t} = y_{t-1}$ and assuming that they have a bivariate Gaussian distribution with covariance matrix

$$\boldsymbol{\Sigma} = \exp(\lambda)\begin{bmatrix} 1 & \rho_t \\ \rho_t & 1 \end{bmatrix}.$$

Then, because $\sigma_1 = \sigma_2 = \exp(\lambda)$,

$$y_t = \mu + \phi_t(y_{t-1} - \mu) + \varepsilon_t, \quad t = 1, \ldots, T,$$

with $\phi_t = \rho_t$.

In the DCS model

$$y_t = \mu + \rho_{t|t-1}(y_{t-1} - \mu) + \varepsilon_t, \quad t = 1, \ldots, T,$$

and if $\rho_{t|t-1}$ evolves through $\gamma_{t|t-1}$ the constraints on the autoregressive coefficient are automatically satisfied because of the transformation, (7.13). The variance of y_t is still given by $\exp(2\lambda)$, and the process remains strictly stationary.

7.3.3 Multivariate *t* Distribution

For the multivariate t distribution, the Gaussian scores are amended by modifying the observations so that they enter as

$$y_{it}^* = y_{it}\sqrt{\frac{\nu+N}{\nu}\frac{1}{w_t}}, \quad i = 1, 2, \ldots, N, \qquad t = 1, \ldots, T. \quad (7.25)$$

The effect of dividing by w_t is to downweight the influence of an outlier in any of the series. The filtered correlations will evolve more smoothly than they would under an implicit assumption of Gaussianity and can therefore be more easily tracked.

7.3.4 Tests of Changing Correlation

Before fitting a model, tests of changing correlation can be based on the score of γ, evaluated at the sample autocorrelation, r. The variable

$$u_{\gamma t} = \frac{y_{1t}y_{2t}}{\exp(\lambda_1+\lambda_2)}(2g^2-1) - \left[\frac{y_{1t}{}^2}{2\exp(2\lambda_1)} + \frac{y_{2t}{}^2}{2\exp(2\lambda_2)}\right]g\overline{g} + r, \quad (7.26)$$

where g and $\overline{g}$ now have γ replaced by $\tanh^{-1} r$, can be used to construct test statistics. The stationarity tests of Nyblom and Mäkeläinen (1983) or Kwiatkowski et al. (1992) will have power against (7.16) when ϕ is one, or close to one. For a stationary alternative, the Ljung-Box test, based on the Q-statistic, (2.73), may be used. The null hypothesis is that (y_{1t}, y_{2t}) is a sequence of IID variables.

Test procedures may need to be modified to take account of conditional heteroscedasticity. Two options are available. One is to fit (E)GARCH models and correct for heteroscedasticity. The other is to robustify the tests against heteroscedasticity as in Sub-section 4.13.2. Which approach is better is a matter for investigation. Further changes are needed if the observations are thought to come from a multivariate-t distribution. The modification in (7.25) makes the test statistics more robust to outliers.

7.4 DYNAMIC MULTIVARIATE SCALE

Suppose that, in contrast to the previous section, scale evolves while association remains constant. Thus (7.4) becomes $\mathbf{\Omega}_{t|t-1} = \mathbf{D}_{t|t-1}\mathbf{R}\mathbf{D}_{t|t-1}$. The general formulation has the logarithms of the diagonal elements of $\mathbf{D}_{t|t-1}$ given by $\boldsymbol{\omega} + \boldsymbol{\lambda}_{t|t-1}$, where $\boldsymbol{\omega}$ is an $N \times 1$ vector of constants, and

$$\boldsymbol{\lambda}_{t+1|t} = \mathbf{\Phi}\boldsymbol{\lambda}_{t|t-1} + \mathbf{K}\mathbf{u}_t, \qquad t = 1, \ldots, T. \quad (7.27)$$

When the conditional scores are standardized with the information matrix, as in (7.22), the interpretation is more straightforward. For example, restricting the $\mathbf{\Phi}$ and $\mathbf{K}$ matrices to be diagonal leads to simple univariate filters.

When only the volatilities change, it is, in principle, possible to derive the asymptotic distribution of the ML estimator. To do so requires building on Theorem 1 in Creal et al. (2011), where general expressions for the score and the information matrix of the multivariate t distribution are given.

Example 21 *For the bivariate Gaussian model, in which*

$$\begin{aligned}\lambda_{1,t+1|t} &= \phi_{11}\lambda_{1,t|t-1} + \phi_{12}\lambda_{2,t|t-1} + \kappa_{11}u_{1t} + \kappa_{12}u_{2t},\\ \lambda_{2,t+1|t} &= \phi_{21}\lambda_{1,t|t-1} + \phi_{22}\lambda_{2,t|t-1} + \kappa_{21}u_{1t} + \kappa_{22}u_{2t},\end{aligned} \tag{7.28}$$

the information matrix can be obtained from the general expression, (2.54). The block involving the volatilities is

$$E\left[\left(\frac{\partial\lambda_1}{\partial\boldsymbol{\psi}}\ \frac{\partial\lambda_2}{\partial\boldsymbol{\psi}}\right)\begin{bmatrix}1+g^2 & 1-g^2\\ 1-g^2 & 1+g^2\end{bmatrix}\left(\frac{\partial\lambda_1}{\partial\boldsymbol{\psi}}\ \frac{\partial\lambda_2}{\partial\boldsymbol{\psi}}\right)'\right],$$

where $\boldsymbol{\psi}$ contains the full set of dynamic parameters. When the $\mathbf{\Phi}$ and $\mathbf{K}$ matrices are diagonal, $\boldsymbol{\psi}_i = (\omega_i, \phi_{ii}, \kappa_{ii})'$, $i = 1, 2$, the sub-matrices $\partial\boldsymbol{\lambda}_1'/\partial\boldsymbol{\psi}_2$ and $\partial\boldsymbol{\lambda}_2'/\partial\boldsymbol{\psi}_1$ are null and the expression simplifies, as in (2.55), so that

$$\mathbf{I}\begin{pmatrix}\boldsymbol{\psi}_1\\ \boldsymbol{\psi}_2\end{pmatrix} = \begin{bmatrix}(1+g)E\left(\frac{\partial\lambda_1}{\partial\boldsymbol{\psi}_1}\frac{\partial\lambda_1}{\partial\boldsymbol{\psi}_1'}\right) & (1-g^2)E\left(\frac{\partial\lambda_1}{\partial\boldsymbol{\psi}_1}\frac{\partial\lambda_2}{\partial\boldsymbol{\psi}_2'}\right)\\ (1-g^2)E\left(\frac{\partial\lambda_2}{\partial\boldsymbol{\psi}_2}\frac{\partial\lambda_1}{\partial\boldsymbol{\psi}_1'}\right) & (1+g^2)E\left(\frac{\partial\lambda_2}{\partial\boldsymbol{\psi}_2}\frac{\partial\lambda_2}{\partial\boldsymbol{\psi}_2'}\right)\end{bmatrix}.$$

All that is needed in addition to terms found for the univariate model is

$$E\left(\frac{\partial\lambda_1}{\partial\boldsymbol{\psi}_1}\frac{\partial\lambda_2}{\partial\boldsymbol{\psi}_2'}\right).$$

Evaluation of the above expression requires terms such as $E(u_1u_2) = -\overline{g}^2$.

In the single-factor volatility model, the elements of $\mathbf{D}_{t|t-1}$ are $\omega_i + \lambda_{t|t-1}$, $i = 1, \ldots, N$, where $\lambda_{t|t-1}$ is common to all series. It is convenient to write

$$\mathbf{\Omega} = \exp(2\lambda_{t|t-1})\overline{\mathbf{\Omega}},$$

where $\overline{\mathbf{\Omega}}$ is standardized so as to contain $N(N+1)/2$ free parameters, consisting of the $N(N-1)/2$ distinct elements of the correlation matrix, $\mathbf{R}$, together with the N constant terms, $\omega_i, i = 1, \ldots, N$. For computational purposes, it is useful to set $\overline{\mathbf{\Omega}} = \mathbf{L}\mathbf{L}'$, where $\mathbf{L}$ is a lower triangular matrix. A slightly different parameterization would treat ω_1 as part of the volatility factor, included in the dynamic equation. If this is done, the first element in $\mathbf{L}$ is set to unity.

The score with respect to $\lambda_{t|t-1}$ in the multivariate t model is

$$\frac{\partial \ln f_t}{\partial\lambda_{t|t-1}} = \frac{1}{w_t}\frac{\nu+N}{\nu}\exp(-2\lambda_{t|t-1})\mathbf{y}_t'\overline{\mathbf{\Omega}}^{-1}\mathbf{y}_t - N,$$

where $w_t = 1 + (1/\nu)\exp(-2\lambda_{t|t-1})\mathbf{y}_t'\overline{\boldsymbol{\Omega}}^{-1}\mathbf{y}_t$. The score can be written in the same form as in the univariate Beta-t-EGARCH model, that is,

$$u_t = (\nu + N)b_t - N, \qquad t = 1, \ldots, T,$$

where, as in the DCS-t location model, b_t is distributed as $beta(N/2, \nu/2)$. The expectation of b_t is $N/(\nu + N)$, confirming that $E(u_t) = 0$. The derivative of u_t is a simple generalization of the univariate formula, namely,

$$\partial u_t/\partial\lambda = -2(\nu + N)b_t(1 - b_t), \tag{7.29}$$

and the necessary conditions for the asymptotic theory to go through are satisfied. An analytic expression for the information matrix of the parameters in the dynamic equation for $\lambda_{t|t-1}$ can be obtained as in Section 4.6 by using formula (2.5) to find the expectation of $\partial u_t/\partial\lambda$, its square and $u_t\partial u_t/\partial\lambda$ and so evaluate a, b and c. The expression for the full information matrix is complicated a little by the estimation of the constant scale terms in $\overline{\boldsymbol{\Omega}}$, as well as by the degrees of freedom.

The general case of several factors is discussed in Creal et al. (2011).

7.5 DYNAMIC SCALE AND ASSOCIATION

Joint modelling of dynamic scale and association can be based on the multivariate conditional t model $\mathbf{y}_t \sim t_\nu\left(\mathbf{0}, \boldsymbol{\Omega}_{t|t-1}\right)$, where $\boldsymbol{\Omega}_{t|t-1}$ depends on a set of time-varying parameters, which in the first-order case evolve according to

$$\boldsymbol{\theta}_{t+1|t} = (\mathbf{I} - \boldsymbol{\Phi})\boldsymbol{\omega} + \boldsymbol{\Phi}\boldsymbol{\theta}_{t|t-1} + \mathbf{K}\mathbf{u}_t, \quad t = 1, \ldots, T,$$

The preferred way forward for this multivariate Beta-t-EGARCH model is to proceed as in (7.4) and break down the parameter vector into parameters governing volatility and those concerned with association. Thus $\boldsymbol{\theta}_{t|t-1} = (\boldsymbol{\lambda}_{t|t-1}', \boldsymbol{\gamma}_{t|t-1}')'$, where $\boldsymbol{\lambda}_{t|t-1}$ is as in (7.27), whereas the vector $\boldsymbol{\gamma}_{t|t-1}$ contains the $N(N-1)/2$ parameters that determine $\mathbf{R}_{t|t-1}$ through $\mathbf{X}_{t|t-1}$ in (7.5).

In a bivariate model, there is only one element in $\boldsymbol{\gamma}_{t|t-1}$, and the arctanh transformation of (7.13) is possible. The vector $\boldsymbol{\theta}_{t|t-1}$ contains only three elements: $\lambda_{1,t|t-1}$, $\lambda_{2,t|t-1}$ and $\gamma_{t|t-1}$. Specifying the score as in (7.22) makes it easier to investigate the implications of restrictions on $\boldsymbol{\Phi}$ and $\mathbf{K}$. For the blocks governing the volatilities, letting $\boldsymbol{\Phi}$ and $\mathbf{K}$ be diagonal so as to give univariate filters is a possibility, as is the weaker restriction of symmetry. Although block diagonality for volatility and correlation parameters in $\boldsymbol{\Phi}$ and $\mathbf{K}$ is a sensible option, there is a case for arguing that high volatility could lead to bigger changes in correlation. The converse is less plausible.

A satisfactory treatment of volatility may require two components. On the other hand, a single long-run component is recommended for modelling correlations.

Example 22 *Creal et al. (2011, Section 6) fit a multivariate Beta-t-GARCH model to daily returns on four equity series. The score is multiplied by the*

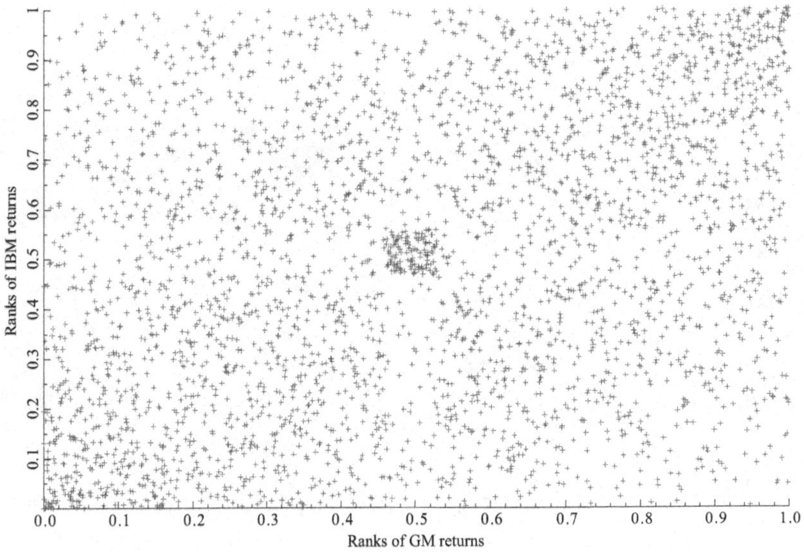

Figure 7.2. Scatter plot of ranked GM and IBM returns.

inverse of the information matrix, and $\mathbf{\Phi}$ *and* $\mathbf{K}$ *are constrained to be diagonal. The parameters in the equations governing the correlations are specified to be the same for each series. There are major differences in the filtered series of correlations and volatilities for the DCS model and conventional models. Gaussianity is rejected, and the DCS model outperforms conventional models in terms of goodness of fit. Specifying the dynamic equation with the score is crucial to the performance of Beta-t-GARCH: simply having a conditional-t distribution is not enough.*

7.6 COPULAS

When two series are non-Gaussian, correlation may not be the best way of capturing the association between them. The multivariate t distribution is a partial attempt to break out of the Gaussian mould in that it accommodates heavy tails, but association is still measured by correlation. Copulas offer a more radical and flexible way of modelling association between variables that is independent of their marginal distributions. Modelling the relationship between two variables in this way exploits the fact that the PIT of any random variable has a uniform distribution.

7.6.1 Copulas and Quantiles

Figure 7.2 shows a scatter plot of the ranked GM and IBM returns of Figure 7.1. There is more association in the upper and lower tails than can be captured by a bivariate Gaussian distribution.

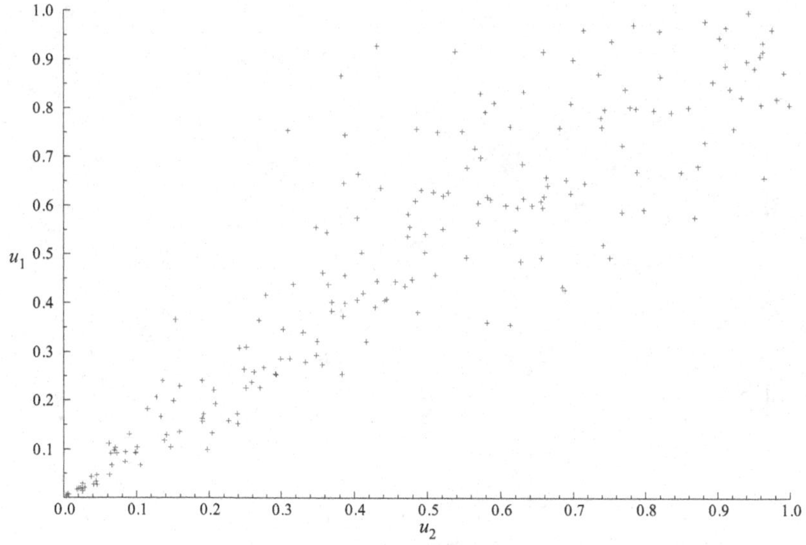

Figure 7.3. Scatter plot of 200 ranked observations from a Clayton copula with $\theta = 5$.

In population terms, the probability that an observation from the first series is less than the τ_1–quantile, $\xi(\tau_1)$, at the same time as the corresponding observation from the second series is below the τ_2–quantile, $\xi(\tau_2)$, is

$$\Pr(Y_1 \le \xi(\tau_1), Y_2 \le \xi(\tau_2)) = F(\xi(\tau_1), \xi(\tau_2)), \quad 0 \le \tau_1, \tau_2 \le 1.$$

Such probabilities are given by the *copula,* $C(\tau_1, \tau_2)$.

The copula is a joint distribution function of standard uniform random variables, that is,

$$C(\tau_1, \tau_2) = \Pr(U_1 \le \tau_1, U_2 \le \tau_2), \quad 0 \le \tau_1, \tau_2 \le 1.$$

Example 23 *The Clayton copula is defined as*

$$C(\tau_1, \tau_2) = \begin{cases} (\tau_1^{-\theta} + \tau_2^{-\theta} - 1)^{-1/\theta}, & \theta \in [-1, \infty),\ \theta \neq 0 \\ \tau_1 \tau_2, & \theta = 0. \end{cases} \tag{7.30}$$

Figure 7.3 shows a scatter plot of 200 observations generated with $\theta = 5$*. The concentration of points in the lower left-hand corner indicates tail dependence.*

Because the PIT, $F(Y)$, of a random variable has a uniform distribution, the copula may be combined with the marginal distribution functions to give the full joint distribution function. Specifically, a copula computed at $\tau_1 = F_1(y_1)$,

$\tau_2 = F_2(y_2)$ gives $F(y_1, y_2)$ because

$$C(F_1(y_1), F_2(y_2)) = \Pr(U_1 \leq F_1(y_1), U_2 \leq F_2(y_2)) \qquad (7.31)$$
$$= \Pr(F_1^{-1}(U_1) \leq y_1, F_2^{-1}(U_2) \leq y_2)$$
$$= \Pr(Y_1 \leq y_1, Y_2 \leq y_2) = F(y_1, y_2).$$

When y_1 and y_2 are the quantiles $\xi(\tau_1)$ and $\xi(\tau_2)$, the copula is $C(\tau_1, \tau_2)$.

Sklar's theorem states that if $F(y_1, y_2)$ is a joint distribution function with continuous marginals $F_1(y_1)$ and $F_2(y_2)$, then there exists a unique copula. Marginal distributions do not need to be of the same form, nor is the choice of copula constrained by the choice of marginals. Hence, given the joint distribution function, the univariate marginals and the dependence structure can be separated, with the dependence structure represented by the copula.

Example 24 *When a Clayton copula is combined with marginal distributions of Y_1 and Y_2, both of which are exponential and so have CDF's $F_i(y) = 1 - \exp(-y_i/\alpha_i)$, $i = 1, 2$, the joint distribution function of Y_1 and Y_2 is*

$$F(y_1, y_2) = ((1 - \exp(-y_1/\alpha_1)^{-\theta} + (1 - \exp(-y_2/\alpha_2)^{-\theta} - 1)^{-1/\theta}.$$

The copula density is

$$c(\tau_1, \tau_2) = \frac{\partial^2 C(\tau_1, \tau_2)}{\partial \tau_1 \partial \tau_2}, \quad 0 \leq \tau_1, \tau_2 \leq 1.$$

Example 25 *For a Clayton copula*

$$c(\tau_1, \tau_2) = (1 + \theta)\tau_1^{-\theta-1}\tau_2^{-\theta-1}\left(\tau_1^{-\theta} + \tau_2^{-\theta} - 1\right)^{-(1+2\theta)/\theta}, \quad 0 \leq \tau_1, \tau_2 \leq 1. \qquad (7.32)$$

Figure 7.4 shows the conditional distribution of τ_2 given that $\tau_1 = 0.1$ for $\theta = 1$, $\theta = 5$ and $\theta = 0$. When $\theta = 5$, the probability that τ_2 is close to the value taken by τ_1 is quite high. In contrast, τ_2 and τ_1 are independent when $\theta = 0$ and $c(\tau_2 \mid \tau_1) = 1$ for $0 \leq \tau_2 \leq 1$.

The joint probability density function of y_1 and y_2 is

$$f(y_1, y_2) = c(F(y_1), F(y_2)).f_1(y_1).f_2(y_2). \qquad (7.33)$$

If the marginal densities are uniform, the joint density function is the copula density. If not, its shape is stretched and contracted by the form of the probability density functions.

When the variables are independent $C(\tau_1, \tau_2) = \tau_1\tau_2$. This is the product copula. The *copula density*, $c(\tau_1, \tau_2)$, is unity and so $f(y_1, y_2) = f_1(y_1).f_2(y_2)$.

As noted earlier, the variables in a bivariate normal or bivariate t distribution are linearly related. However, linear relationships are the exception rather than the rule. Bouyé and Salmon (2009) showed how to derive the distribution of one variable conditional on another when they are related by a given parametric copula.

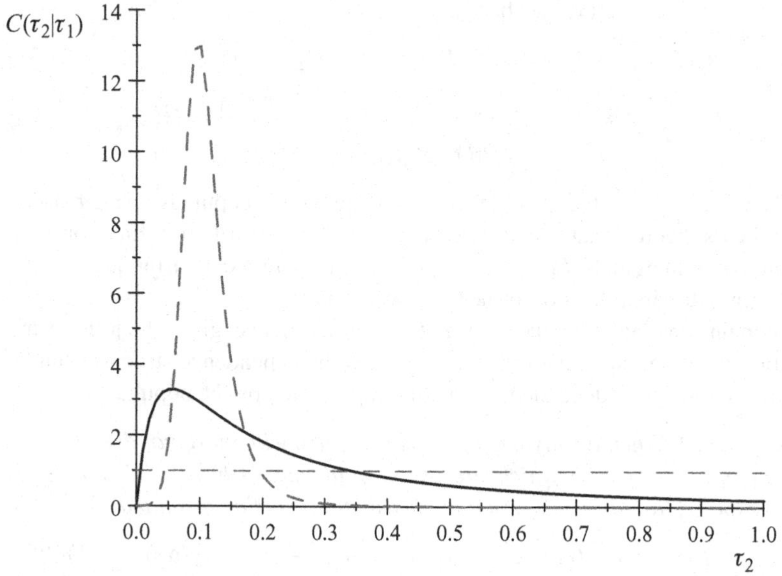

Figure 7.4. Conditional distribution of τ_2 given that $\tau_1 = 0.1$ for a Clayton copula with $\theta = 1$ (solid line), $\theta = 5$ (thick dashed) and $\theta = 0$ (thin dashed).

7.6.2 Measures of Association

The *survival function*

$$\overline{C}(u_1, u_2) = \Pr(U_1 > \tau_1, U_2 > \tau_2),$$

gives the probability that two variables both lie above preassigned quantiles, that is, $\overline{C}(\tau_1, \tau_2) = \Pr(y_{1t} > \xi_1(\tau_1), y_{2t} > \xi_2(\tau_2))$. The quadrant association,

$$\overline{C}(\tau_1, \tau_2) + C(\tau_1, \tau_2), \quad 0 \leq \tau_1, \tau_2 \leq 1,$$

gives a measure of dependence in the range [0, 1]. However, it can be shown that quadrant association depends only on $C(\tau_1, \tau_2)$ and is equal to $1 - \tau_1 - \tau_2 + 2C(\tau_1, \tau_2)$; see Cherubini et al. (2004, p. 75) or McNeil et al. (2005, p. 196).

There is *positive quadrant dependency* if $C(\tau_1, \tau_2) \geq \tau_1\tau_2$. *Blomqvist's beta,* $4C(0.5, 0.5) - 1$, is the quadrant association at $\tau_1 = \tau_2 = 0.5$, standardized so as to lie in the range $[-1, 1]$ and to be zero when the series are independent.

Conditional probabilities for measuring dependence depend on the copula. The probability that an observation from the first series is less than a given quantile, $\xi(\tau_1)$, given that the corresponding observation from the second series is below a given quantile, $\xi(\tau_2)$, is

$$F(\xi(\tau_1), \xi(\tau_2))/F(\xi(\tau_2)) = C(\tau_1, \tau_2)/\tau_2.$$

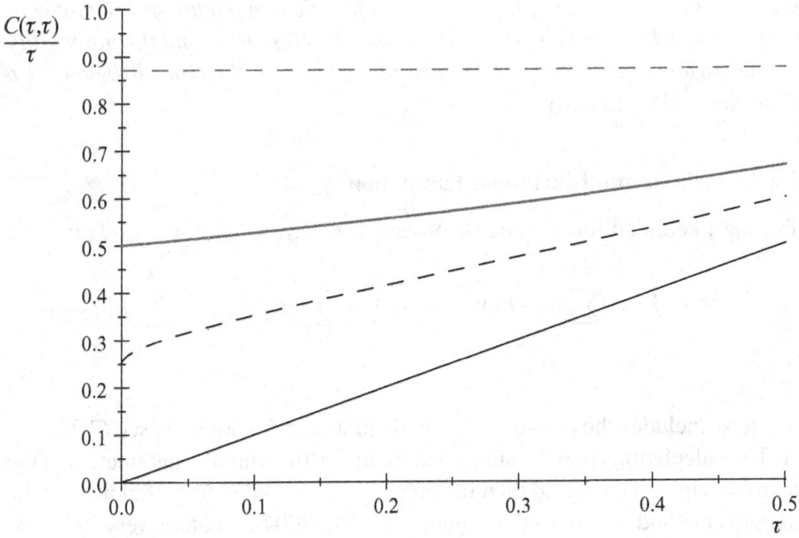

Figure 7.5. Lower tail dependence, $C(\tau, \tau)/\tau$, for Clayton copula for $\theta = 1$ (thick line), $\theta = 5$ (upper) and $\theta = 0.5$ (dashed) and independent (lower thin line).

Example 26 *For the Clayton copula with* $\tau_1 = \tau_2 = \tau$

$$C(\tau, \tau)/\tau = \left(2 - \tau^{\theta}\right)^{-1/\theta} \tag{7.34}$$

Figure 7.5 plots $C(\tau, \tau)/\tau$ *for three values of* θ. *When* $\theta = 1$, *the tail dependence for* $\tau = 0.10$ *is 0.526, but if* $\theta = 5$, *as in Figure 7.3, it goes up to 0.870. The conditional density of Figure 7.4 gives a complementary picture of the association.*

The coefficients of tail dependence provide measures that depend only on copula shape parameters; see McNeil et al. (2005, p. 208). The *coefficient of lower (left) tail dependence*, or *lower tail index*, is

$$\lambda_L = \lim_{\tau \to 0} C(\tau, \tau)/\tau,$$

whereas the *coefficient of upper (right) tail dependence* is

$$\lambda_U = \lim_{\tau \to 1} \overline{C}(\tau, \tau)/(1 - \tau).$$

If two variables have a bivariate normal distribution, with $|\rho| < 1$, they are asymptotically independent in the tails, as the coefficients of tail dependence are both zero.

Example 27 *For* $\theta > 0$, *the Clayton copula exhibits lower tail dependence, with* $\lambda_L = 2^{-1/\theta}$, *as is easily seen from (7.34). For* $\theta = 1$, $C(\tau, \tau)/\tau \simeq 1/2$ *for small* τ *and* $\lambda_L = 0.5$. *For* $\theta = 5$, $\lambda_L = 0.870$, *the same as was calculated for*

$\tau = 0.1$. *As* $\theta \to \infty$, $C(\tau,\tau)/\tau \to 1$. *The practical implications are that with a small* τ, *such as 0.05 or 0.01,* $C(\tau,\tau)$ *may be close to* τ, *and the probability of one variable being below its* τ *quantile, given that the other is below its* τ *quantile, is close to unity.*

7.6.3 Maximum Likelihood Estimation

The log-likelihood function of the observations $y_{1t}, y_{2t}, t = 1, \ldots, T$, is

$$\ln L(\boldsymbol{\psi}) = \sum_{t=1}^{T} \ln c(F(y_{1t}), F(y_{2t})) + \sum_{t=1}^{T} \ln f_1(y_{1t}) + \sum_{t=1}^{T} \ln f_2(y_{2t}), \tag{7.35}$$

where $\boldsymbol{\psi}$ includes the parameters of both copula and marginals; see (7.33).

The calculations may be simplified by first estimating the parameters in the marginal distributions and then the copula. This is called the inference for the margins method. According to Cherubini et al. (2004), it entails very little loss in efficiency.

7.6.4 Dynamic Copulas

Time-varying copulas can be modelled using the conditional score to drive a dynamic equation for the shape parameter. Because the conditional score takes account of the specification of the copula, it would seem to be a better way of proceeding than the essentially ad hoc approach of Patton (2006). Creal et al. (2012) illustrated the viability and relevance of the DCS approach in an application of dynamic Gaussian copulas to exchange rate data.

The specification for a first-order dynamic equation is of the form (7.17), but with $\gamma_{t|t-1}$ replaced by the shape parameter, labeled $\theta_{t|t-1}$ in the Clayton case. As should be clear from (7.33), the form of the score for the joint density function depends only on the copula, but the marginal distributions affect its value through the probability integral transforms applied to the raw data. Unfortunately, the information quantity is not usually easy to derive, and so there is little hope of developing an asymptotic theory for ML estimation as in Chapter 2. Nevertheless, the simulation results for the Clayton copula reported by Creal et al. (2012) show that ML estimation works well.

Example 28 *The conditional score for the Clayton copula is*

$$\begin{aligned}\frac{\partial \ln f_t(y_{1t}, y_{2t}; \theta_{t|t-1})}{\partial \theta_{t|t-1}} &= -\ln(\tau_{1t}\tau_{2t}) + (1+\theta_{t|t-1})^{-1} \\ &\quad + \theta^{-2}\ln(\tau_{1t}^{-\theta_{t|t-1}} + \tau_{2t}^{-\theta_{t|t-1}} - 1) \\ &\quad + \left(\frac{1+2\theta_{t|t-1}}{\theta_{t|t-1}}\right)\frac{(\tau_{1t}^{-\theta_{t|t-1}}\ln\tau_{1t} + \tau_{2t}^{-\theta_{t|t-1}}\ln\tau_{2t})}{\tau_{1t}^{-\theta_{t|t-1}} + \tau_{2t}^{-\theta_{t|t-1}} - 1},\end{aligned}$$

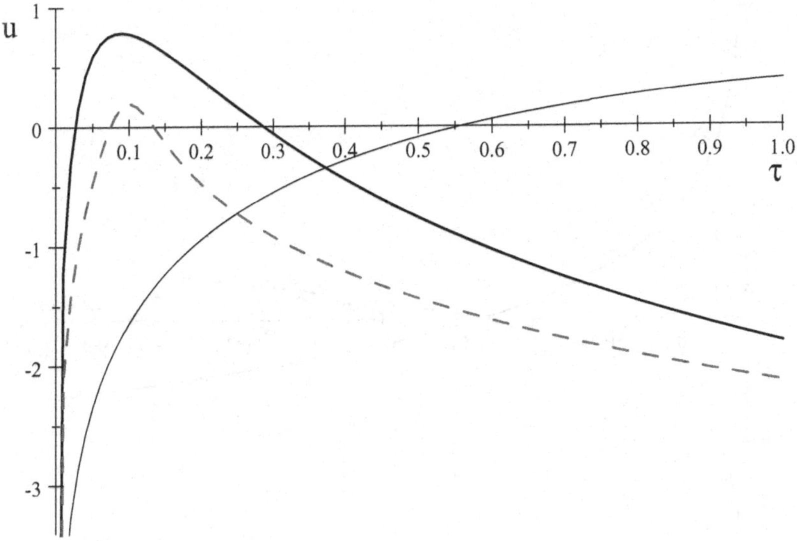

Figure 7.6. Response of score for $\theta = 1$ when τ_2 varies, but τ_1 is fixed at 0.1 (thick line) or 0.9 (thin line). The dashed line shows the response for $\theta = 5$ and τ_1 fixed at 0.1.

where $\tau_{it} = F(y_{it})$, $i = 1, 2$. The response to a pair of observations is not as readily interpretable as it is for the bivariate normal distribution. However, the basic point to note is that the first term involves the product $\tau_{1t}\tau_{2t}$, and so is a little like the product $x_{1t}x_{2t}$ in (7.12). In the Gaussian model, the score modifies the impact of $x_{1t}x_{2t}$ by taking account of how the product was formed and the current parameter value. The same is true here. Figure 7.6 shows the response of the score when τ_2 varies, but τ_1 is fixed. Two points are worth noting. First, as expected, the response is asymmetric in the sense that the behaviour with τ_1 fixed at 0.9 is not a mirror image of the behaviour for τ_1 fixed at 0.1. Second, when $\tau_1 = 0.1$, the score is only positive for values of τ_2 close to 0.1, the effect being more pronounced when $\theta = 5$, as opposed to $\theta = 1$. This behaviour is entirely consistent with the conditional density shown in Figure 7.4: if τ_2 is not close to 0.1, it suggests that $\theta_{t|t-1}$ is too big, and the role of the negative score in the dynamic equation is to make $\theta_{t+1|t}$ smaller. The response shown in Figure 7.7 is very different. Here $\theta = 0.0001$, so τ_1 and τ_2 are almost independent. When $\tau_1 = 0.1$, the score increases as τ_2 gets closer to zero and decreases as it goes towards one. The opposite is true for $\tau_1 = 0.9$.

A full maximum likelihood approach can, in principle, be used to jointly estimate dynamic volatility and copula parameters by defining (7.35) in terms of distributions conditional on past observations. However, a two-step procedure may be more appealing in practice. If a univariate Beta-t-EGARCH is fitted

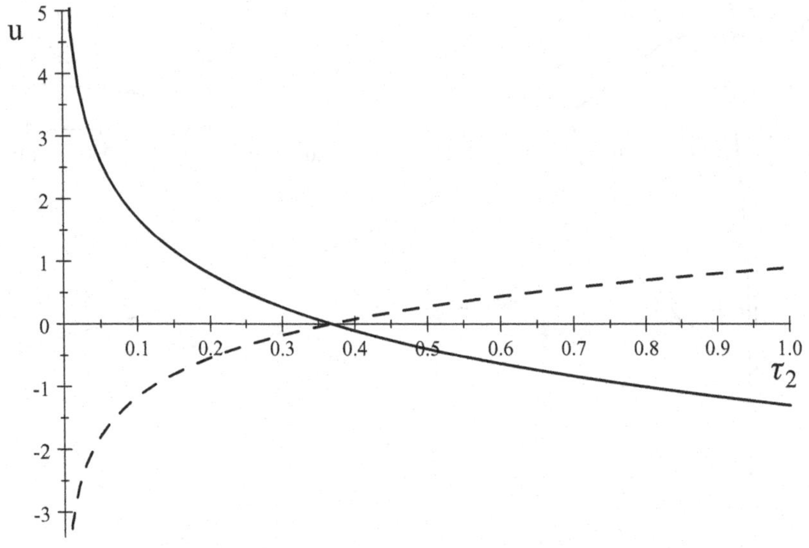

Figure 7.7. Response of score, u, for $\theta = 0.0001$ when τ_2 varies, but τ_1 is fixed at 0.1 (solid line) or 0.9 (dashed line).

to each series, the PITs can be computed using a subroutine for a regularized incomplete beta function.

Probabilities associated with a constant copula can be estimated nonparametrically simply by counting the number of pairs of observations with the required property, for example, both being below a certain quantile. A changing copula can be tracked by using a time series filter, such as an EWMA, to estimate the copula probabilities. Filtering to allow for changing volatility can be done nonparametrically, as described in Chapter 6, or parametrically, by using an EGARCH model. The application described in Harvey (2010) shows how the association between the Hong Kong (Hang Seng) and Korean stock market indices increased in the late 1990s.

7.6.5 Tests against Changing Association

General tests against time-varying copulas are investigated in Busetti and Harvey (2011). The idea is to look at how the proportion of observations in particular quadrants changes over time. The default is to use a test based on medians, thereby essentially detecting movements in Blomqvist's beta. Such a test will be more robust than one based on the Gaussian score of (7.26). However, scores derived from the multivariate t will be less affected by outliers.

A test against time variation in a given parametric copula could be based on the scores constructed by estimating a static copula from the PITs obtained from fitting univariate Beta-t-EGARCH models.

CHAPTER 8

Conclusions and Further Directions

Many nonlinear unobserved components models can be approximated by analogous observation-driven models in which the dynamics are driven by the score of the conditional distribution. Given a judicious choice of link function, everything falls into place. When the dynamic conditional score model is taken to be the true model, the asymptotic theory for maximum likelihood estimation can be developed, and in many cases, an analytic expression can be derived for the information matrix. Furthermore, maximum likelihood estimation seems to work well in practice. In the applications reported here, convergence of the likelihood function for the models estimated was fast and reliable.

In much of the literature, the way in which observation-driven models are constructed is essentially arbitrarily. The use of the conditional score in models associated with unobserved components parameter-driven models provides guidance and discipline, as well as a unified approach to nonlinear time series modelling. Even when the asymptotic theory cannot be developed along the lines set out here, as is the case with any parameter associated with the distributions typically employed for count data and qualitative observations, the evidence suggests that the conditional score is still the best way forward.

A theory of testing, both before and after model estimation, is also developed, and the evidence suggests that it is appropriate and effective. For example, the Lagrange multiplier tests for serial correlation are robust to heavy tails, and the tests based on the probability integral transform are useful for assessing the validity of distributional assumptions. The numerical standard errors computed for the parameters in models estimated from real data were sometimes found to be unreliable, particularly for shape parameters. On the other hand, analytic standard errors require moderate size samples to be close to the values indicated by Monte Carlo experiments. Nevertheless, it should be borne in mind that even when the standard errors are reliable, care has to be exercised in testing certain hypotheses, particularly those that pertain to a parameter being zero, because identifiability issues may render Wald tests invalid.

The principle underlying the class of models which includes GARCH is that the dynamics are driven by a variable whose expectation is equal to the moment of interest. Thus in GARCH itself the dynamics depend on past squared observations and the model is autoregressive in the sense that the predictor of variance is a linear combination of them. When the mean is the moment of interest, it is the levels of the observations that drive the dynamics. Fitting a time series model is a way of weighting the observations in order to estimate a moment that may be changing over time. However, once the notion of a conditional distribution that is neither Gaussian nor gamma is entertained, the case for focussing on moments is seriously weakened. The structure of DCS models is based on likelihood principles. As a result, forecasts of location and scale are not necessarily formed by simply weighting past observations, or their squares, because attention is shifted to the full conditional distribution.

If there are doubts about a suitable parametric specification, a kernel density estimator may be allowed to change over time by weighting the observations using standard time series filters. As is the case for observation-driven models, the likelihood function may be obtained from predictive distributions, thereby enabling the parameters governing the dynamics of the kernel to be estimated, together with the bandwidth. The example in Chapter 6 illustrates how this approach works in practice. If there is time variation in asymmetry and the tails, tracking the changes in certain quantiles, together with measures of skewness and kurtosis, may be informative.

Extending dynamic conditional score modelling to multivariate time series appears to be relatively straightforward for time-varying location models based on the multivariate t distribution. Generalizing Beta-t-EGARCH to multivariate series is more difficult. The best approach seems to be to decompose the covariance, or scale, matrix into two parts, one of which is for the correlations. If only the volatilites change over time, the statistical treatment is relatively straightforward. It is evolving correlations which pose the challenge, particularly with regard to asymptotic theory. At the same time, the modelling of dynamic correlations, with or without heavy-tailed distributions, offers a rich opportunity for extending the scope of time series econometrics. Rather than approaching modelling changing relationships from the standpoint of time-varying regression parameters, the signal extraction framework adopted in this monograph suggests that modelling changing correlations is likely to provide a more fruitful line of attack. More generally, copulas offer a flexible way of capturing the association between two variables that is independent of their marginal distributions. When a time-varying copula is to be modelled, letting the dynamic equations be driven by the conditional score has significant attractions.

APPENDIX A

Derivation of Formulae in the Information Matrix

A.1 UNCONDITIONAL MEAN PARAMETERIZATION

The LIE is used to evaluate the outer products in the $\mathbf{D}(\boldsymbol{\psi})$ matrix of (2.40). The formula for κ was derived in the main text. For ϕ

$$E_{t-1}\left(\frac{\partial\theta_{t+1|t}}{\partial\phi}\right)^2 = E_{t-1}\left(x_t\frac{\partial\theta_{t|t-1}}{\partial\phi}+\theta_{t|t-1}-\omega\right)^2 \tag{A.1}$$

$$= b\left(\frac{\partial\theta_{t|t-1}}{\partial\phi}\right)^2 + (\theta_{t|t-1}-\omega)^2 + 2a\frac{\partial\theta_{t|t-1}}{\partial\phi}(\theta_{t|t-1}-\omega).$$

The unconditional expectation of the last term is found by writing

$$E_{t-2}\left(\frac{\partial\theta_{t|t-1}}{\partial\phi}(\theta_{t|t-1}-\omega)\right)$$

$$= E_{t-2}\left(x_{t-1}\frac{\partial\theta_{t-1|t-2}}{\partial\phi}+\theta_{t-1|t-2}-\omega\right)\left(\phi(\theta_{t-1|t-2}-\omega)+\kappa u_{t-1}\right)$$

$$= \phi E_{t-2}\left(x_{t-1}\frac{\partial\theta_{t-1|t-2}}{\partial\phi}(\theta_{t-1|t-2}-\omega)\right) + \phi(\theta_{t-1|t-2}-\omega)^2$$

$$+\kappa E_{t-2}\left(u_{t-1}x_{t-1}\frac{\partial\theta_{t-1|t-2}}{\partial\phi}\right) + \kappa E_{t-2}(u_{t-1}(\theta_{t-1|t-2}-\omega)).$$

The last term is zero, as $\theta_{t-1|t-2}$ depends on $u_t's$ prior to u_{t-1}, and the penultimate term is also zero. The unconditional expectation of the second term is ϕ times the variance of $\theta_{t|t-1}$, which is $\sigma_u^2\kappa^2/(1-\phi^2)$. Hence

$$E\left(\frac{\partial\theta_{t|t-1}}{\partial\phi}(\theta_{t|t-1}-\omega)\right) = \frac{\phi\sigma_u^2\kappa^2}{(1-a\phi)(1-\phi^2)}. \tag{A.2}$$

Taking unconditional expectations in (A.1) and substituting from (A.2) gives

$$E\left(\frac{\partial\theta_{t+1|t}}{\partial\phi}\right)^2 = bE\left(\frac{\partial\theta_{t|t-1}}{\partial\phi}\right)^2 + \frac{\sigma_u^2\kappa^2}{1-\phi^2} + \frac{2a\phi\sigma_u^2\kappa^2}{(1-a\phi)(1-\phi^2)},$$

which leads to B.

Now consider ω. We have

$$E_{t-1}\left(\frac{\partial\theta_{t+1|t}}{\partial\omega}\right)^2 = b\left(\frac{\partial\theta_{t|t-1}}{\partial\omega}\right)^2 + 2a(1-\phi)\left(\frac{\partial\theta_{t+1|t}}{\partial\omega}\right) + (1-\phi)^2.$$

Taking unconditional expectations gives C.

As regards the cross-products

$$\begin{aligned}
&E_{t-1}\left(\frac{\partial\theta_{t+1|t}}{\partial\kappa}\frac{\partial\theta_{t+1|t}}{\partial\phi}\right)\\
&= E_{t-1}\left[\left(x_t\frac{\partial\theta_{t|t-1}}{\partial\kappa} + u_t\right)\left(x_t\frac{\partial\theta_{t|t-1}}{\partial\phi} + \theta_{t|t-1} - \omega\right)\right]\\
&= E_{t-1}\left[x_t\frac{\partial\theta_{t|t-1}}{\partial\kappa}\frac{\partial\theta_{t|t-1}}{\partial\phi}\right] + E_{t-1}\left[\left(x_t u_{t-1}\frac{\partial\theta_{t|t-1}}{\partial\phi}\right)\right]\\
&\quad + E_{t-1}\left[\left(x_t\frac{\partial\theta_{t|t-1}}{\partial\kappa}(\theta_{t|t-1} - \omega)\right)\right] + E_{t-1}\left[(\theta_{t|t-1} - \omega)u_t\right]\\
&= b\left[\frac{\partial\theta_{t|t-1}}{\partial\kappa}\frac{\partial\theta_{t|t-1}}{\partial\phi}\right] + c\frac{\partial\theta_{t|t-1}}{\partial\phi} + a\frac{\partial\theta_{t|t-1}}{\partial\kappa}(\theta_{t|t-1} - \omega) + 0.
\end{aligned}$$

The unconditional expectation of the second term is zero, and the third term is found by writing

$$\begin{aligned}
&E_{t-2}\left(\frac{\partial\theta_{t|t-1}}{\partial\kappa}(\theta_{t|t-1} - \omega)\right)\\
&= E_{t-2}\left[\left(x_{t-1}\frac{\partial\theta_{t-1|t-2}}{\partial\kappa} + u_{t-1}\right)\left(\phi(\theta_{t-1|t-2} - \omega) + \kappa u_{t-1}\right)\right]\\
&= a\phi\left(\frac{\partial\theta_{t-1|t-2}}{\partial\kappa}(\theta_{t-1|t-2} - \omega)\right) + \kappa\sigma_u^2.
\end{aligned}$$

Thus

$$E\left(\frac{\partial\theta_{t|t-1}}{\partial\kappa}(\theta_{t-1|t-2} - \omega)\right) = \frac{\kappa\sigma_u^2}{1 - a\phi}$$

leading to D.

For ω and ϕ,

$$\begin{aligned}
&E_{t-1}\left(\frac{\partial\theta_{t+1|t}}{\partial\omega}\frac{\partial\theta_{t+1|t}}{\partial\phi}\right)\\
&= E_{t-1}\left[\left(x_t\frac{\partial\theta_{t|t-1}}{\partial\omega} + 1 - \phi\right)\left(x_t\frac{\partial\theta_{t|t-1}}{\partial\phi} + \theta_{t|t-1} - \omega\right)\right]\\
&= b\left[\frac{\partial\theta_{t|t-1}}{\partial\omega}\frac{\partial\theta_{t|t-1}}{\partial\phi}\right] + (1-\phi)(\theta_{t|t-1} - \omega) + a(1-\phi)\frac{\partial\theta_{t|t-1}}{\partial\phi}\\
&\quad + a\frac{\partial\theta_{t|t-1}}{\partial\omega}(\theta_{t|t-1} - \omega).
\end{aligned}$$

Taking unconditional expectations gives

$$E\left(\frac{\partial\theta_{t+1|t}}{\partial\omega}\frac{\partial\theta_{t+1|t}}{\partial\phi}\right) = bE\left(\frac{\partial\theta_{t|t-1}}{\partial\omega}\frac{\partial\theta_{t|t-1}}{\partial\phi}\right) + aE\left(\frac{\partial\theta_{t|t-1}}{\partial\omega}(\theta_{t|t-1}-\omega)\right), \tag{A.3}$$

but we first require

$$\begin{aligned}
E_{t-2}&\left(\frac{\partial\theta_{t|t-1}}{\partial\omega}(\theta_{t|t-1}-\omega)\right)\\
&= E_{t-2}\left[\left(x_{t-1}\frac{\partial\theta_{t-1|t-2}}{\partial\omega}+1-\phi\right)\left(\phi(\theta_{t-1|t-2}-\omega)+\kappa u_{t-1}\right)\right]\\
&= a\phi\left(\frac{\partial\theta_{t-1|t-2}}{\partial\omega}(\theta_{t|t-1}-\omega)\right)+(1-\phi)\phi(\theta_{t-1|t-2}-\omega)\\
&\quad+\kappa c\frac{\partial\theta_{t-1|t-2}}{\partial\omega}+\kappa(1-\phi)E_{t-2}(u_{t-1})\\
&= a\phi\left(\frac{\partial\theta_{t-1|t-2}}{\partial\omega}(\theta_{t|t-1}-\omega)\right)+0+\kappa c\frac{\partial\theta_{t-1|t-2}}{\partial\omega}+0.
\end{aligned}$$

Taking unconditional expectations in the above expression then yields

$$E\left(\frac{\partial\theta_{t|t-1}}{\partial\omega}(\theta_{t|t-1}-\omega)\right) = a\phi E\left(\frac{\partial\theta_{t-1|t-2}}{\partial\omega}(\theta_{t|t-1}-\omega)\right)+\frac{\kappa c}{1-a}$$

and so

$$E\left(\frac{\partial\theta_{t|t-1}}{\partial\omega}(\theta_{t|t-1}-\omega)\right) = \frac{\kappa c}{(1-a\phi)(1-a)}.$$

Substituting in (A.3) gives F (divided by $1-b$).

Finally,

$$E_{t-1}\left(\frac{\partial\theta_{t+1|t}}{\partial\omega}\frac{\partial\theta_{t+1|t}}{\partial\kappa}\right) = E_{t-1}\left[\left(x_t\frac{\partial\theta_{t|t-1}}{\partial\omega}+1-\phi\right)\left(x_t\frac{\partial\theta_{t|t-1}}{\partial\kappa}+u_t\right)\right].$$

Expanding and taking unconditional expectations give E.

A.2 PARAMERIZATION WITH δ

The evaluation of the $\mathbf{D}(\boldsymbol{\psi})$ matrix in (2.44) follows along similar lines to that of (2.40). The formula for κ is as in the ω paramerization. For ϕ

$$E_{t-1}\left(\frac{\partial\theta_{t+1|t}}{\partial\phi}\right)^2 = E_{t-1}\left(x_t\frac{\partial\theta_{t|t-1}}{\partial\phi}+\theta_{t|t-1}\right)^2 \tag{A.4}$$

$$= b\left(\frac{\partial\theta_{t|t-1}}{\partial\phi}\right)^2+\theta^2_{t|t-1}+2a\frac{\partial\theta_{t|t-1}}{\partial\phi}\theta_{t|t-1}.$$

The unconditional expectation of the last term is

$$E\left(\frac{\partial\theta_{t|t-1}}{\partial\phi}\theta_{t|t-1}\right) = \frac{\phi E(\theta^2_{t|t-1})}{1-a\phi} + \frac{\omega(\delta+\kappa c)}{(1-a)(1-a\phi)}. \tag{A.5}$$

Taking unconditional expectations in (A.4) and substituting from (A.5) gives

$$E\left(\frac{\partial\theta_{t+1|t}}{\partial\phi}\right)^2 = bE\left(\frac{\partial\theta_{t|t-1}}{\partial\phi}\right)^2 + E(\theta^2_{t+1|t}) + \frac{2a\phi E(\theta_{t+1|t})}{1-a\phi}$$
$$+\frac{2a\delta(\delta+\kappa c)}{(1-a)(1-\phi)(1-a\phi)},$$

which leads to B on substituting for $E\left(\theta_{t+1|t}\right) = \delta^2/(1-\phi)^2 + \sigma_u^2\kappa^2/(1-\phi^2)$.

As regards δ,

$$E_{t-1}\left(\frac{\partial\theta_{t+1|t}}{\partial\delta}\right)^2 = b\left(\frac{\partial\theta_{t|t-1}}{\partial\delta}\right)^2 + 2a\left(\frac{\partial\theta_{t+1|t}}{\partial\delta}\right) + 1.$$

Unconditional expectations give

$$E\left(\frac{\partial\theta_{t+1|t}}{\partial\delta}\right)^2 = \frac{1+a}{(1-a)(1-b)}$$

For the cross-products

$$E_{t-1}\left(\frac{\partial\theta_{t+1|t}}{\partial\kappa}\frac{\partial\theta_{t+1|t}}{\partial\phi}\right) = E_{t-1}\left[\left(x_t\frac{\partial\theta_{t|t-1}}{\partial\kappa} + u_t\right)\left(x_t\frac{\partial\theta_{t|t-1}}{\partial\phi} + \theta_{t|t-1}\right)\right]$$
$$= b\left[\frac{\partial\theta_{t|t-1}}{\partial\kappa}\frac{\partial\theta_{t|t-1}}{\partial\phi}\right] + c\frac{\partial\theta_{t|t-1}}{\partial\phi}$$
$$+ a\left(\frac{\partial\theta_{t|t-1}}{\partial\kappa}\theta_{t|t-1}\right) + 0.$$

The unconditional expectation of the last non-zero term is found by writing

$$E_{t-2}\left(\frac{\partial\theta_{t|t-1}}{\partial\kappa}\theta_{t|t-1}\right)$$
$$= E_{t-2}\left[\left(x_{t-1}\frac{\partial\theta_{t-1|t-2}}{\partial\kappa} + u_{t-1}\right)\left(\phi\theta_{t-1|t-2} + \delta + \kappa u_{t-1}\right)\right]$$
$$= a\phi\left(\frac{\partial\theta_{t-1|t-2}}{\partial\kappa}\theta_{t-1|t-2}\right) + \kappa\sigma_u^2.$$

Thus

$$E\left(\frac{\partial\theta_{t|t-1}}{\partial\kappa}\theta_{t|t-1}\right) = \frac{\kappa\sigma_u^2}{1-a\phi}$$

leading to D.

For δ and ϕ,

$$E_{t-1}\left(\frac{\partial\theta_{t+1|t}}{\partial\delta}\frac{\partial\theta_{t+1|t}}{\partial\phi}\right) = b\left[\frac{\partial\theta_{t|t-1}}{\partial\delta}\frac{\partial\theta_{t|t-1}}{\partial\phi}\right]$$

$$+\,\theta_{t|t-1} + a\frac{\partial\theta_{t|t-1}}{\partial\phi} + a\frac{\partial\theta_{t|t-1}}{\partial\delta}\theta_{t|t-1}.$$

Taking unconditional expectations gives

$$E\left(\frac{\partial\theta_{t+1|t}}{\partial\delta}\frac{\partial\theta_{t+1|t}}{\partial\phi}\right) = bE\left(\frac{\partial\theta_{t|t-1}}{\partial\delta}\frac{\partial\theta_{t|t-1}}{\partial\phi}\right) + \gamma + \frac{a\gamma}{1-a}$$

$$+\,aE\left(\frac{\partial\theta_{t|t-1}}{\partial\delta}\theta_{t|t-1}\right). \tag{A.6}$$

Because

$$E_{t-1}\left(\frac{\partial\theta_{t|t-1}}{\partial\delta}\theta_{t|t-1}\right) = E_{t-1}\left[\left(x_{t-1}\frac{\partial\theta_{t-1|t-2}}{\partial\delta}+1\right)\left(\delta+\phi\theta_{t-1|t-2}+\kappa u_{t-1}\right)\right]$$

$$= a\phi\left(\frac{\partial\theta_{t-1|t-2}}{\partial\delta}\theta_{t-1|t-2}\right) + \delta a\frac{\partial\theta_{t-1|t-2}}{\partial\delta} + \delta$$

$$+\,\phi\theta_{t-1|t-2} + \kappa c\frac{\partial\theta_{t-1|t-2}}{\partial\delta} + 0,$$

we obtain

$$E\left(\frac{\partial\theta_{t|t-1}}{\partial\delta}\theta_{t|t-1}\right) = a\phi E\left(\frac{\partial\theta_{t-1|t-2}}{\partial\delta}\theta_{t-1|t-2}\right)$$

$$+\,\frac{\delta - a\phi\delta + \kappa c - \phi\kappa c}{(1-a)(1-\phi)}$$

and so

$$E\left(\frac{\partial\theta_{t|t-1}}{\partial\delta}\theta_{t|t-1}\right) = \frac{\delta - a\phi\delta + \kappa c - \phi\kappa c}{(1-a\phi)(1-a)(1-\phi)}$$

Substituting in (A.6) gives F.

Finally,

$$E_{t-1}\left(\frac{\partial\theta_{t+1|t}}{\partial\delta}\frac{\partial\theta_{t+1|t}}{\partial\kappa}\right) = E_{t-1}\left[\left(x_t\frac{\partial\theta_{t|t-1}}{\partial\delta}+1\right)\left(x_t\frac{\partial\theta_{t|t-1}}{\partial\kappa}+u_t\right)\right]$$

Expanding and taking unconditional expectations give E.

A.3 LEVERAGE

To derive B^* in (4.39), replace θ by λ in (A.1) and observe that the conditional expectation of the last term, that is, $2aE_{t-1}\left((\partial\lambda_{t|t-1}/\partial\phi)(\lambda_{t|t-1}-\omega)\right)$, is now $2a$ times

$$
\begin{aligned}
&E_{t-2}\left(x_{t-1}^{*}\frac{\partial\lambda_{t|t-1}}{\partial\phi}+\lambda_{t|t-1}-\omega\right)\\
&\quad\times\left(\phi(\lambda_{t|t-1}-\omega)+\kappa u_t+\kappa^{*}sgn(-y_{t-1})(u_t+1)\right)\\
&=\phi E_{t-2}\left(x_{t-1}^{*}\frac{\partial\lambda_{t|t-1}}{\partial\phi}(\lambda_{t|t-1}-\omega)\right)+\phi(\lambda_{t|t-1}-\omega)^2\\
&\quad+\kappa E_{t-2}\left(u_t x_{t-1}^{*}\frac{\partial\lambda_{t|t-1}}{\partial\phi}\right)+\kappa E_{t-2}(u_t(\lambda_{t|t-1}-\omega))\\
&\quad+\kappa^{*}E_{t-2}\left(x_{t-1}^{*}\frac{\partial\lambda_{t|t-1}}{\partial\phi}sgn(-y_{t-1})(u_t+1)\right)\\
&\quad+\kappa^{*}E_{t-2}(sgn(-y_{t-1})(u_t+1)(\lambda_{t|t-1}-\omega))
\end{aligned}
$$

The last two terms are zero. Substituting in (A.1) and noting that $Var(\lambda_{t|t-1})$ is now given by (4.24) gives B^*.

APPENDIX B

Autocorrelation Functions

B.1 BETA-t-EGARCH

The autocorrelations of the powers of a stationary model are

$$\rho(\tau; |y_t|^c) = \frac{E\left(|y_t|^c\,|y_{t-\tau}|^c\right) - E\left(|y_t|^c\right)E\left(|y_{t-\tau}|^c\right)}{E\left(|y_t|^{2c}\right) - E\left(|y_t|^c\right)E\left(|y_{t-\tau}|^c\right)}. \tag{B.1}$$

When $\lambda_{t|t-1}$ in (4.1) is covariance stationary, it follows from Corollary 15 that

$$E\left(|y_t|^c\right) = E\left(|\varepsilon_t|^c\right)e^{c\omega}\prod_{j=1}^{\infty}E\left(e^{\psi_j(\nu+1)b_{t-j}c}\right).$$

To obtain the autocovariances it is necessary to find

$$E\left(|y_t|^c\,|y_{t-\tau}|^c\right) = E\left(|\varepsilon_t|^c\,e^{\lambda_{t|t-1}c}\,|\varepsilon_{t-\tau}|^c\,e^{\lambda_{t-\tau|t-\tau-1}c}\right), \quad \tau = 1, 2, \ldots.$$

Evaluating this expression is not straightforward because of the dependence between $e^{\lambda_{t|t-1}}$ and $|\varepsilon_{t-\tau}|^c$, but we may write

$$E\left(|y_t|^c\,|y_{t-\tau}|^c\right) = C.E(|\varepsilon_t|^c))B_\tau(c)\prod_{j=1}^{\tau-1}E\left(e^{\psi_j(\nu+1)b_{t-j}c}\right)$$

$$\times\prod_{i=1}^{\infty}E\left(e^{(\psi_{\tau+i}+\psi_i)(\nu+1)b_{t-\tau-i}c}\right), \tag{B.2}$$

where $C = \exp(2c(\omega - \Sigma\psi_j))$ and

$$B_\tau(c) = E_{t-\tau-1}(|\varepsilon_{t-\tau}|^c\,e^{\psi_\tau(\nu+1)b_{t-\tau}c}), \quad \tau = 1, 2, \ldots.$$

For $\tau = 1$, the product over j is set to one. Rearranging (4.3) yields $|\varepsilon_t|^c = \nu^{c/2}b_t^{c/2}/(1-b_t)^{c/2}$. Therefore, dropping subscripts on b and ψ,

$$B_\tau(c) = \nu^{c/2}E\left(\frac{b^{c/2}}{(1-b)^{c/2}}e^{\psi(\nu+1)bc}\right).$$

Because b has a $beta(1/2, \nu/2)$ distribution, it follows from Lemma 1 that

$$B_\tau(c) = \nu^{c/2}\frac{B(1/2 + c/2, \nu/2 - c/2)}{B(1/2, \nu/2)}E(e^{\psi(\nu+1)bc})$$

with the second expectation taken with respect to a $beta((1 + c)/2, \nu/2 - c/2)$ distribution. Thus $1 + 2r$ is replaced by $1 + c + 2r$ in the product term of the expansion, (4.13), to give $\beta_{\nu,c}(\psi_\tau c)$. Furthermore, from (2.12),

$$B_\tau(c) = E(|\varepsilon_{t-\tau}|^c).E(e^{\psi_\tau(\nu+1)b_{t-\tau}c}), \quad \tau = 1, 2, \ldots,$$

and so substituting for $B_\tau(c)$ in (B.2) gives

$$E\left(|y_t|^c\,|y_{t-\tau}|^c\right) = C.(E(|\varepsilon_t|^c))^2\beta_{\nu,c}(\psi_\tau c)\prod_{j=1}^{\tau-1}\beta_\nu(\psi_j c)\prod_{i=1}^{\infty}\beta_\nu((\psi_{\tau+i}+\psi_i)\,c).$$

After dividing the numerator and denominator of (B.1) by $\left[E\,|y_t|^c\right]^2$, a little rearrangement leads to (4.18).

B.2 GAMMA-GED-EGARCH

When g has a $gamma(\alpha, \gamma)$ distribution, (2.9), and $w(g)$ is a function of g with finite expectation,

$$E\left(g^h w(g)\right) = \frac{\alpha^h\Gamma(h + \gamma)}{\Gamma(\gamma)}E[w(g)], \tag{B.3}$$

where g on the right-hand side is now understood to have a $gamma(\alpha, h + \gamma)$ distribution. The result, which is similar to that in Lemma 1, follows because

$$E\left(g^h w(g)\right) = \frac{\alpha^{-\gamma}}{\Gamma(\gamma)}\int_0^\infty g^h g^{\gamma-1}e^{-g/2}w(g)dg$$

$$= \frac{\alpha^{-\gamma}}{\Gamma(\gamma)}\frac{\Gamma(h+\gamma)}{\alpha^{-(h+\gamma)}}\left[\frac{\alpha^{-(h+\gamma)}}{\Gamma(h+\gamma)}\int_0^\infty w(g)g^{h+\gamma-1}e^{-g/2}dg\right].$$

To derive the ACF of $|y_t|^c$ it is necessary to find $E_{t-\tau-1}\left(|\varepsilon_{t-\tau}|^c\, e^{\psi_\tau|\varepsilon_{t-\tau}|^\upsilon \upsilon c/2}\right)$, $\tau = 1, 2, \ldots$. From Lemma 4, $g_t = |\varepsilon_t|^\upsilon$ has a $gamma(1/2, 1/\upsilon)$ distribution. Dropping subscripts, formula (B.3), with $h = c/\upsilon$, can be used to write

$$E\left(g^{c/\upsilon}e^{\psi\upsilon gc/2}\right) = \frac{2^{c/\upsilon}\Gamma((c + 1)/\upsilon)}{\Gamma(1/\upsilon)}E\left(e^{\psi\upsilon gc/2}\right).$$

The last term can be evaluated from the formula for the MGF of a $gamma(1/2, (c + 1)/\upsilon)$ distribution. Thus, using (2.10) to rewrite the first term gives

$$E\left(g^{c/\upsilon}e^{\psi gc/2}\right) = E(|\varepsilon_t|^c)(1 - \upsilon c\psi)^{-(c+1)/\upsilon}, \quad \psi < 1/\upsilon c.$$

B.3 BETA-t-GARCH

The derivation of $\rho(\tau; y_t^2)$ follows from first taking conditional expectations at time $t-1$ of

$$y_t^2 y_{t-\tau}^2 = z_t^2 \sigma_{t|t-1}^2 z_{t-\tau}^2 \sigma_{t-\tau|t-\tau-1}^2, \qquad \tau = 1, 2, \ldots,$$

to give

$$E_{t-1}\left(y_t^2 y_{t-\tau}^2\right) = \sigma_{t-1|t-2}^2(\phi + \kappa u_{t-1}) z_{t-\tau}^2 \sigma_{t-\tau|t-\tau-1}^2 + \delta z_{t-\tau}^2 \sigma_{t-\tau|t-\tau-1}^2.$$

Applying the LIE we obtain

$$E_{t-\tau-1}\left(y_t^2 y_{t-\tau}^2\right) = \phi^{\tau-1} \sigma_{t-\tau|t-\tau-1}^2 (\phi + \kappa E_{t-\tau-1}(z_{t-\tau}^2 u_{t-\tau})) + \delta(1 + \phi + .. + \phi^{\tau-1}) \sigma_{t-\tau|t-\tau-1}^2.$$

Now $z_t^2 = (\nu - 2) b_t / (1 - b_t)$. Proceeding as in Lemma 1,

$$E_{t-\tau-1}\left(z_{t-\tau}^2 u_{t-\tau}\right) = \frac{(\nu-2)(\nu+1)}{B(1/2, \nu/2)} \int \frac{b^2}{1-b} b^{-1/2} (1-b)^{\nu/2-1} db - 1 = \frac{B(5/2, \nu/2 - 1)}{B(1/2, \nu/2)} - 1 = 2.$$

Noting that $Ey_t^2 = E(z_t^2 \sigma_{t|t-1}^2) = E\sigma_{t|t-1}^2 = \delta/(1-\phi)$, and that $Ey_t^4 = E(z_t^4 \sigma_{t|t-1}^4) = \kappa_\nu E\sigma_{t|t-1}^4$, the autocorrelations are as in (4.47).

APPENDIX C

GED Information Matrix

Differentiating the log-density for the GED gives

$$\frac{\partial \ln f_t}{\partial \upsilon} = \frac{\ln 2}{\upsilon^2} - \upsilon^{-2}\psi\left(1+1/\upsilon\right) - \frac{1}{2}\left|y_t \exp(-\lambda_{t|t-1})\right|^{\upsilon} \ln\left|y_t \exp(-\lambda_{t|t-1})\right|.$$

Hence

$$\frac{\partial^2 \ln f_t}{\partial \upsilon^2} = \frac{-2\ln 2}{\upsilon^3} - g(\upsilon) - \frac{1}{2}\left|y_t \exp(-\lambda_{t|t-1})\right|^{\upsilon} (\ln\left|y_t \exp(-\lambda_{t|t-1})\right|)^2$$

and

$$\frac{\partial^2 \ln f_t}{\partial \upsilon \partial \lambda_{t|t-1}} = (1/2)\left|y_t \exp(-\lambda_{t|t-1})\right|^{\upsilon}\left(1+\ln(\left|y_t \exp(-\lambda_{t|t-1})\right|)^{\upsilon}\right)$$

Taking expectations, and recalling that $g_t = \left|y_t \exp(-\lambda_{t|t-1})\right|^{\upsilon}$ is gamma distributed, gives

$$\begin{aligned} E\left(\frac{\partial^2 \ln f_t}{\partial \upsilon^2}\right) &= \frac{-2\ln 2}{\upsilon^3} - g(\upsilon) - \frac{1}{2}E(g_t(\ln g_t)^2) \\ &= \frac{-2\ln 2}{\upsilon^3} - g(\upsilon) - \frac{\Gamma(2/\upsilon)((\psi(2/\upsilon))^2 - \psi'(2/\upsilon))}{2\upsilon^2\Gamma(1/\upsilon)} \end{aligned}$$

and

$$\begin{aligned} E\left(\frac{\partial^2 \ln f_t}{\partial \upsilon \partial \lambda_{t|t-1}}\right) &= (1/2)(E(g_t) + E(g_t \ln g_t)) \\ &= \upsilon^{-1} + \upsilon^{-1} 0.5\Gamma(2/\upsilon)\psi(2/\upsilon)/\Gamma(1/\upsilon)). \end{aligned}$$

APPENDIX D

The Order of GARCH Models

The classic $GARCH(p, q)$ model in Bollerslev(1986) is $y_t = \sigma_{t|t-1}\varepsilon_t$, with

$$\sigma^2_{t|t-1} = \delta + \beta_1\sigma^2_{t-1|t-2} + \cdots + \beta_p\sigma^2_{t-p|t-p-1} + \alpha_1 y^2_{t-1} + \cdots \alpha_q y^2_{t-q}. \tag{D.1}$$

Alternatively,

$$\sigma^2_{t|t-1} = \delta + \phi_1\sigma^2_{t-1|t-2} + \cdots \phi_p\sigma^2_{t-p|t-p-1} \cdots + \alpha_1\sigma^2_{t-1|t-2}u_{t-1} + \cdots + \alpha_m\sigma^2_{t-m|t-m-1}u_{t-m},$$

where $u_t = y_t^2/\sigma^2_{t|t-1} - 1$ and $m = \max(p, q)$ and $\phi_j = \alpha_j + \beta_j$, $j = 1, \ldots, m$.

Substituting for $\sigma^2_{t|t-j}$, $j = 1, \ldots, p$ in (D.1) using the identity $y_t^2 = \sigma^2_{t|t-1} + \sigma^2_{t|t-1}u_t$ gives

$$y_t^2 = \delta + \phi_1 y^2_{t-1} + \cdots \phi_q y^2_{t-m} + \sigma^2_{t|t-1}u_t + \theta_1\sigma^2_{t-1|t-1}u_{t-1} + \cdots + \theta_m\sigma^2_{t-p|t-p-1}u_{t-p}, \tag{D.2}$$

which is $ARMA(m, p)$ with $\theta_j = -\beta_j$, $j = 1, \ldots, m$. The heteroscedasticity makes the equation inconvenient for some purposes, such as ML estimation, but it can be used for forecasting, and as such it provides a useful parallel with using an ARMA model to forecast location. It is also the standard route for deriving the ACF of the squared observations.

The starting point for GARCH could be the signal extraction equation

$$\sigma^2_{t+1|t} = \delta + \phi_1\sigma^2_{t|t-1} + \cdots \phi_p\sigma^2_{t-p+1|t-p} \cdots + \kappa_0\sigma^2_{t|t-1}u_t + \cdots + \kappa_r\sigma^2_{t-r|t-r-1}u_{t-r}.$$

Following Nelson (1991), and the convention adopted throughout this book, the model would be labelled $GARCH(p, r)$; see (1.17). The $ARMA(p, m)$ model for the squares then has $m = \max(p, r + 1)$ and $\theta_j = \kappa_{j-1} - \phi_j$, $j = 1, \ldots, m$. The length of the state vector in the state space form is also m.

In his original article, Engle (1982) had only lagged squared observation in the dynamic equation. He called the model $ARCH(p)$ because the forecasts have the form of an $AR(p)$. (In GARCH notation, the $ARCH(p)$ model is $GARCH(0, p)$.) Thus for the $ARCH(1)$ model, the process for y_t^2 is AR(1), rather than the ARMA(1,1) model suggested by (D.2), as

$$y_t^2 = \delta + \phi y_{t-1}^2 + \left(y_t^2 - \sigma_{t|t-1}^2\right) = \delta + \alpha y_{t-1}^2 + \sigma_{t|t-1}^2 u_t$$

and the forecast function for y_t^2 still behaves like that of an AR(1), that is $y_{T+\ell|T}^2 = \alpha^l y_T^2$, $\ell = 1, 2, 3, \ldots$, when $\delta = 0$.

The signal extraction equation can only give an $ARCH(p)$ model if it is set up to be of order (p, p) and subject to the constraints $\phi_j = \kappa_{j-1}$, $j = 1, \ldots, p$. For example, the $ARCH(1)$ model is

$$\sigma_{t+1|t}^2 = \delta + \alpha y_{t-1}^2 = \delta + \phi \sigma_{t|t-1}^2 + \kappa \sigma_{t|t-1}^2 u_t,$$

with $\alpha = \kappa$ and $\phi = \kappa$. Thus if signal extraction is seen as the starting point for GARCH modelling, the pure ARCH formulation appears as an unlikely special case.

APPENDIX E

Computer Programs

The menu-driven programs listed here are available or in the process of being developed at the time of writing. All run in Oxmetrics and are available from Timberlake consultants; see www.timberlake.co.uk/software/?id=64.

i) STAMP estimates linear Gaussian structural time series models; see Koopman et al. (2009).
ii) G@RCH 7 estimates a wide range of GARCH models, including Beta-t-EGARCH; see Laurent (2013).
iii) DySco estimates DCS model with generalized gamma and beta distributions; see Andres (2012).

In addition, an R-program for Beta-t-EGARCH, including skew-t, is available on the Web site in Sucarrat (2012).

Bibliography

Alizadeh, S., Brandt, M. W. and F. X. Diebold (2002). Range-based estimation of stochastic volatility models. *Journal of Finance* **57**, 1047–92.

Altman, N. and C. Léger (1995). Bandwidth selection for kernel distribution function estimation. *Journal of Statistical Planning and Inference* **46**, 195–214.

Andersen, T. G., Bollerslev, T., Christoffersen, P. F. and F. X. Diebold (2006). Volatility and correlation forecasting. In Elliot, G., Granger, C. and A. Timmerman (eds.), *Handbook of Economic Forecasting*, 777–878. Amsterdam: North Holland.

Andersen, T. G. and T. Bollerslev (1998). Deutsche Mark-Dollar volatility: intraday activity patterns, macroeconomic announcements, and longer run dependencies. *Journal of Finance* **53**, 219–65.

Andres, P. K. (2012). Computation of maximum likelihood estimates for score driven models for positive valued observations. Memeo.

Andres, P. and A. C. Harvey (2012). The dynamic location/scale model. Cambridge Working Papers in Economics, CWPE 1240.

Andrieu, C., Doucet, A. and R. Holenstein (2010). Particle Markov chain Monte Carlo methods (with discussion). *Journal Royal Statistical Society B* **72**, 269–342.

Asmussen, S. (2003). *Applied Probability and Queues*. Berlin: Springer Verlag.

Azzalini, A. (1981). A note on the estimation of a distribution function and quantiles by a kernel method. *Biometrika* **68**, 326–8.

Bauwens, L., Giot, P., Grammig, J. and D. Veredas (2004). A comparison of financial duration models via density forecasts. *International Journal of Forecasting* **20**, 589–609.

Bauwens, L. and N. Hautsch (2009). Modelling high frequency data using point processes, in T. G. Andersen et al., *Handbook of Financial Time Series*, 953–79. Berlin: Springer.

Bauwens, L. and D. Veredas (2004). The stochastic conditional duration model: A latent factor model for the analysis of financial durations. *Journal of Econometrics* **119**, 381–412.

Berkowitz, J. (2001). Testing density forecasts, with applications to risk management. *Journal of Business and Economic Statistics* **19**, 465–74.

Bollerslev, T. (1986). Generalized autoregressive conditional heteroskedasticity. *Journal of Econometrics* **31**, 307–27.

Bollerslev, T. (1987). A conditionally heteroskedastic time series model for security prices and rates of return data. *Review of Economics and Statistics* **59**, 542–7.

Bollerslev, T. and H. O. Mikkelsen (1996). Modelling and pricing long memory in stock market volatility. *Journal of Econometrics* **73**, 151–84.

Bowman, A., Hall, P. and T. Prvan (1998). Bandwidth selection for the smoothing of distribution functions. *Biometrika* **85**, 799–808.

Bowsher, C. G. and R. Meeks (2008). The dynamics of economic functions: Modelling and forecasting the yield curve. *Journal of the American Statistical Association* **103**, 1419–37.

Bouyé, E. and M. Salmon (2009). Dynamic copula quantile regression and tail area dynamic dependence in Forex markets. *European Journal of Finance* **15**, 721–50.

Box, G. E. P. and G. M. Jenkins (1976). *Time Series Analysis: Forecasting and Control*, revised edition. San Francisco: Holden-Day.

Brandt, A. (1986). The stochastic equation Yn+1 = AnYn + Bn with stationary coefficients. *Advances in Applied Probability* **18**, 211–20.

Brandt, M. W. and C. S. Jones (2006). Volatility forecasting with range-based EGARCH models. *Journal of Business and Economic Statistics* **24**, 470–86.

Brown, B. M. (1971). Martingale central limit theorems. *Annals of Mathematical Statistics* **42**, 59–66.

Brownlees, C. T. and G. M. Gallo (2010). Comparison of volatility measures: A risk management perspective. *Journal of Financial Econometrics* **8**, 29–56.

Brownlees, C. T., Cipollini, F. and G. M. Gallo (2011). Intra-daily volume modelling and prediction for algorithmic trading. *Journal of Financial Econometrics* **9**, 489–518.

Busetti, F. and A. C. Harvey (2011). When is a copula constant? A test for changing relationships. *Journal of Financial Econometrics* **9**, 106–31.

Chernoff, H. (1954). On the distribution of the likelihood ratio. *Annals of Mathematical Statistics* **25**, 573–78.

Cherubini, U., Luciano, E. and W. Vecchiato (2004). *Copula Methods in Finance*. Chichester: John Wiley and Sons.

Cogley, T., Primiceri, G. E. and T. J. Sargent (2010). Inflation-gap persistence in the US. *American Economic Journal: Macroeconomics* **2**, 43–69.

Cox, D. (1981). Statistical analysis of time series: some recent developments. *Scandinavian Journal of Statistics* **8**, 93–105.

Creal, D. (2012). A survey of sequential Monte Carlo methods for economics and finance. *Econometric Reviews* **31**, 245–96.

Creal, D., Koopman, S. J. and A. Lucas (2008). A General Framework for Observation Driven Time-varying Parameter Models. Tinbergen Institute Discussion Paper, TI 2008-108/4, Amsterdam.

Creal, D., Koopman, S. J. and A. Lucas (2011). A dynamic multivariate heavy-tailed model for time-varying volatilities and correlations. *Journal of Business and Economic Statistics* **29**, 552–63.

Creal, D., Koopman, S. J. and A. Lucas (2012). Generalized autoregressive score models with applications. *Journal of Applied Econometrics* (to appear). Earlier version appeared as Creal et al. (2008).

Davidson, J. (2000). *Econometric Theory*. Oxford: Blackwell.

Davis, R. A., Dunsmuir, W. T. M. and S. Streett (2003). Observation driven models for Poisson counts. *Biometrika* **90**, 777–90.

De Livera, A. M., Hyndman, R. J. and R. D. Snyder (2011). Forecasting time series with complex seasonal patterns using exponential smoothing. *Journal of the American Statistical Association* **106**, 1513–27.

Deo, R., Hurwich, C. and Y. Lu (2006). Forecasting realized volatility using a long memory stochastic volatility model: Estimation, prediction and seasonal adjustment. *Journal of Econometrics* **131**, 29–58.

De Rossi, G., and A. C. Harvey (2006). Time-varying Quantiles. University of Cambridge, Faculty of Economics, Cambridge Working Papers in Economics (CWPE) 0649.

De Rossi, G. and A. C. Harvey (2009). Quantiles, expectiles and splines. *Journal of Econometrics* **152**, 179–85.

Diebold, F. X., Gunther, T. A. and A. S. Tay (1998). Evaluating density forecasts. *International Economic Review* **39**, 863–83.

Ding, Z., Engle, R. F. and C. W. J. Granger (1993). A long memory model of stock market returns and a new model. *Journal of Empirical Finance* **1**, 83–106.

Doornik, J. A. (2007). *Ox: An Object-Oriented Matrix Language*, 5th edition. London: Timberlake Consultants Press.

Durbin, J. and S. J. Koopman (2012). *Time Series Analysis by State Space Methods*, 2nd edition. Oxford: Oxford Statistical Science Series.

Engle (1982). Autoregressive conditional heteroskedasticity with estimates of the variance of United Kingdom inflation. *Econometrica* **50**, 987–1007.

Engle, R. F. and V. K. Ng (1993). Measuring and testing the impact of news on volatility. *Journal of Finance* **48**, 1749–78.

Engle, R. F. and G. G. J. Lee (1999). A long-run and short-run component model of stock return volatility. In Engle, R. F. and H. White (eds.), *Cointegration, Causality, and Forecasting: A Festschrift in Honour of Clive W.J. Granger*. Oxford: Oxford University Press.

Engle, R. F. (2002). New frontiers for ARCH models. *Journal of Applied Econometrics* **17**, 425–46.

Engle, R. F. and J. G. Rangel (2008). The spline-GARCH model for low frequency volatility and its global macroeconomic causes. *Review of Financial Studies* **21**, 1188–222.

Engle, R. F. and G. M. Gallo (2006). A multiple indicators model for volatility using intra-daily data. *Journal of Econometrics* **131**, 3–27.

Engle, R. F. and S. Manganelli (2004). CAViaR: conditional autoregressive value at risk by regression quantiles. *Journal of Business and Economic Statistics* **22**, 367–81.

Engle, R. and J. Russell (2010). Analysis of high frequency and transaction data. In Ait-Sahalia, Y. and L. P. Hansen (eds.), *Handbook of Financial Econometrics*. Amsterdam: North Holland.

Engle, R. and M. E. Sokalska (2012). Forecasting intraday volatility in the US equity market. Multiplicative component GARCH. *Journal of Financial Econometrics* **10**, 54–83.

Escanciano, J. C. and I. N. Lobato (2009). An automatic portmanteau test for serial correlation. *Journal of Econometrics* **151**, 140–9.

Fernandez, C. and M. F. J. Steel (1998). On Bayesian modeling of fat tails and skewness. *Journal of the American Statistical Association* **99**, 359–71.

Fiorentini, G., Calzolari, G. and I. Panattoni (1996). Analytic derivatives and the computation of GARCH estimates. *Journal of Applied Econometrics* **11**, 399–417.

Francq, C. and J.-M. Zakoïan (2009). A tour in the asymptotic theory of GARCH estimation, in Andersen, T. G., Davis, R. A., Kreiß, J.-P. and T. Mikosch (eds.), *Handbook of Financial Time Series*. Berlin: Springer.

Francq, C. and J. M. Zakoïan (2004). Maximum likelihood estimation of pure GARCH and ARMA-GARCH processes. *Bernoulli* **10**, 605–37.

Francq, C. and J.-M. Zakoïan (2010). *GARCH Models: Structure, Statistical Inference and Financial Applications*. New York: John Wiley and Sons.

Franses, P. H., van Dijk, D. and A. Lucas (2004). Short patches of outliers, ARCH and volatility modelling. *Applied Financial Economics* **14**, 221–31.

Gallant, A. R. (1984). The Fourier flexible form. *American Journal of Agricultural Economics* **66**, 204–8.

Giot, P. and S. Laurent (2003). Value at risk for long and short trading positions. *Journal of Applied Econometrics* **18**, 641–64.

Glosten, L. R., Jagannanthan, R. and D. E. Runckle (1993). On the relationship between the expected value and the volatility of the nominal excess return on stocks. *Journal of Finance* **48**, 1779–801.

Grammig, J. and K.-O. Maurer (2000). Non-monotonic hazard functions and the autoregressive conditional duration model. *Econometrics Journal* **3**, 16–38.

Gregory, A. and J. J. Reeves (2010). Estimation and inference in ARCH models in the presence of outliers. *Journal of Financial Econometrics* **8**, 547–69.

Greene, W. H. (2012). *Econometric Analysis*, 7th edition. Boston: Prentice-Hall.

Gourieroux, C. and J. Jasiak (2008). Dynamic quantile models. *Journal of Econometrics* **147**, 198–205.

Hall, P. and P. Patil (1994). On the efficiency of on-line density estimators. *IEEE Transactions on Information Theory* **40**, 1504–12.

Hall, P. and Q. Yao (2003). Inference in ARCH and GARCH models with heavy-tailed errors. *Econometrica* **71**, 285–317.

Hamilton, J. D. (1994). *Time Series Analysis*. Princeton: Princeton University Press.

Harvey A. C. (1989). *Forecasting, Structural Time Series Models and the Kalman Filter*. Cambridge: Cambridge University Press.

Harvey A. C. (1993). *Time Series Models* (2nd ed). Hemel Hempstead: Harvester-Wheatsheaf.

Harvey A. C. (2005). A unified approach to testing for stationarity and unit roots. In Andrews, D. W. K. and J. H. Stock (eds.), *Identification and Inference for Econometric Models*, 403–25. New York: Cambridge University Press.

Harvey, A. C. (2006). Forecasting with unobserved components time series models. In Elliot, G., Granger, C. and A. Timmermann (eds.), *Handbook of Economic Forecasting*. Amsterdam: North Holland.

Harvey, A. C. (2010). Tracking a changing copula. *Journal of Empirical Finance* **17**, 485–500.

Harvey, A. C. (2011). Modelling the Phillips curve with unobserved components. *Applied Financial Economics*, special issue in honour of Clive Granger **21**, 7–17.

Harvey, A. C. and T. Chakravarty (2009). Beta-t-EGARCH. Working paper. Earlier version appeared in 2008 as a Cambridge Working Paper in Economics, CWPE 0840.

Harvey, A. C. and S. J. Koopman (1993). Forecasting hourly electricity demand using time-varying splines. *Journal of American Statistical Association* **88**, 1228–36.

Harvey, A. C. and A. Luati (2012). Filtering with Heavy Tails Cambridge Working Papers in Economics, CWPE 1255.

Harvey, A. C. and V. Oryshchenko (2011). Kernel density estimation for time series data. *International Journal of Forecasting* **28**, 3–14.

Harvey A. C., E. Ruiz and N. Shephard (1994). Multivariate stochastic variance models. *Review of Economic Studies* **61**, 247–64.

Harvey A. C. and N. Shephard (1996). Estimation of an asymmetric stochastic volatility model for asset returns. *Journal of Business and Economic Statistics* **14**, 429–34.

Harvey, A. C. and M. Streibel (1998). Testing for a slowly changing level with special reference to stochastic volatility. *Journal of Econometric* **87**, 167–89.

Harvey, A. C. and G. Sucarrat (2012). EGARCH Models with Fat Tails, Skewness and Leverage. Cambridge Working Paper in Economics, CWPE 1236.

Harvey, A. C. and T. Trimbur (2003). General model-based filters for extracting cycles and trends in economic time series. *Review of Economics and Statistics* **85**, 244–55.

He, C. and T. Teräsvirta (1999). Properties of moments of a family of GARCH processes. *Journal of Econometrics* **92**, 173–92.

He, C., Teräsvirta, T. and H. Malmsten (2002). Moment structure of a family of first order exponential GARCH models. *Econometric Theory* **18**, 868–85.

Jaeckel, P. and R. Rebonato (1999). The most general methodology for creating a valid correlation matrix for risk management and option pricing purposes. *Journal of Risk* **2**, 17–28.

Jensen, S. T. and A. Rahbek (2004). Asymptotic inference for nonstationary GARCH. *Econometric Theory* **20**, 1203–26.

Johnson, N. L. and S. Kotz (1972). *Distributions in Statistics: Continuous Multivariate Distributions*. New York: Wiley.

Kawakatsu, H. (2006). Matrix exponential GARCH. *Journal of Econometrics* **134**, 95–128.

Kleiber, C. and S. Kotz (2003). *Statistical Size Distributions in Economics and Actuarial Sciences*. New York: Wiley.

Koenker, R. (2005). *Quantile Regression*. Cambridge: Cambridge University Press.

Kohn, R., Ansley, C. F. and C.-H. Wong (1992). Nonparametric spline regression with autoregressive moving average errors. *Biometrika* **79**, 335–46.

Koopman, S. J. (1993). Disturbance smoother for state space models. *Biometrika* **80**, 117–26.

Koopman, S. J. Harvey, A. C., Doornik, J. A. and N. Shephard (2009). *STAMP 8.2 Structural Time Series Analysis Modeller and Predictor*. London: Timberlake Consultants Ltd.

Koopman, S. J. and A. C. Harvey (2003). Computing observation weights for signal extraction and filtering. *Journal of Economic Dynamics and Control* **27**, 1317–33.

Koopman, S. J., Lucas, A. and M. Scharth (2012). Predicting Time-Varying Parameters with Parameter-Driven and Observation-Driven Models. Tinbergen Institute Discussion Paper, TI 2012-020/4, Amsterdam.

Kotz, S. and S. Nadarajah (2004). *Multivariate T Distributions and Their Applications*. Cambridge: Cambridge University Press.

Kwiatkowski, D., Phillips, P. C. B., Schmidt, P. and Y. Shin (1992). Testing the null hypothesis of stationarity against the alternative of a unit root: How sure are we that economic time series have a unit root? *Journal of Econometrics* **44**, 159–78.

Kuester, K., Mittnik, S. and C. H. Paolella (2006). Value-at-risk prediction: a comparison of alternative strategies. *Journal of Financial Econometrics* **4**, 53–89.

Lange, K. L., Little, R. J. A. and M. G. Taylor (1989). Robust statistical modelling using the t distribution. *Journal of the American Statistical Association* **84**, 881–96.

Lange, T., Rahbek, A. and S. T. Jensen (2010). Estimation and asymptotic inference in the AR-ARCH model. *Econometric Reviews* **30**, 129–53.

Laurent, S. (2007). *GARCH 5*. London: Timberlake Consultants.

Laurent, S. (2013). *GARCH 7*. London: Timberlake Consultants.

Li, W. K. (2004). *Diagnostic Checks in Time Series*. London: Chapman and Hall.

Lin, T. I. and Y. J. Wang (2009). A robust approach to joint modelling of the mean and scale covariance for longitudinal data. *Journal of Statistical Planning and Inference* **139**, 3013–26.

Ling, S. and M. McAleer (2002). Stationarity and the existence of moments of a family of GARCH processes. *Journal of Econometrics* **106,** 109–17.

Lobato, I., Nankervis, J. C. and N. E. Savin (2001). Testing for autocorrelation using a modified Box-Pierce Q test. *International Economic Review* **42**, 187–205.

Malmsten, H. and T. Teräsvirta (2010). Stylized facts of financial time series and three popular models of volatility. *European Journal of Pure and Applied Mathematics* **3**, 443–77.

Maronna, R., Martin, D. and Yohai, V. (2006). *Robust Statistics: Theory and Methods*. John Wiley & Sons.

Markovich, N. (2007). *Nonparametric Analysis of Univariate Heavy-tailed Data. Research and Practice*. New York: John Wiley and Sons.

Martens, M., Chang, Y. C. and S. J. Taylor (2002). A comparison of seasonal adjustment methods when forecasting intraday volatility. *Journal of Financial Research* **25**, 283–99.

Masreliez, C. J. (1975). Approximate non-Gaussian filtering with linear state and observation relations. *IEEE Transactions on Automatic Control* **20**, 107–10.

McCullagh, P. and J. A. Nelder (1989). *Generalised Linear Models*, 2nd edition. London: Chapman and Hall.

McLeod, A. I. and W. K. Li (1983). Diagnostic checking ARMA time series models using squared-residual autocorrelations. *Journal of Time Series Analysis* **4**, 269–73.

McNeil, A. J., Frey, R. and P. Embrechts (2005). *Quantitative Risk Management*. Princeton, NJ: Princeton Series in Finance.

Mitchell, J. and K. F. Wallis (2011). Evaluating density forecasts: Forecast combinations, model mixtures, calibration and sharpness. *Journal of Econometrics* **26**, 1023–40.

Muler, N., Peña, D. and V. J. Yohai (2009). Robust estimation for ARMA models. *Annals of Statistics* **37**, 816–40.

Muler, N. and V. J. Yohai (2008). Robust estimates for GARCH models. *Journal of Statistical Planning and Inference* **138**, 2918–40.

Nabeya, S. and K. Tanaka (1988). Asymptotic theory of a test for the constancy of regression coefficients against the random walk alternative. *Annals of Statistics* **16**, 218–35.

Nadaraya, E. A. (1964). Some new estimates for distribution functions. *Theory of Probability and Its Applications* **9**, 497–500.

Nelson, D. B. (1990). Stationarity and persistence in the GARCH (1,1) model. *Econometric Theory* **6**, 318–24.

Nelson, D. B. (1991). Conditional heteroskedasticity in asset returns: A new approach. *Econometrica* **59**, 347–370.

Nelson, D. B. and D. P. Foster (1994). Asymptotic filtering theory for univariate ARCH models. *Econometrica* **62**, 1–41.

Newey, W. and D. McFadden (1994). Large sample estimation and hypothesis testing. *Handbook of Econometrics* **4**, 2111–245.

Nyblom, J. and T. Makelainen (1983). Comparison of tests for the presence of random walk coefficients in a simple linear model. *Journal of the American Statistical Association* **78**, 856–64.

Ozkok, E. Sreftaris, G., Waters, H. R. and A. D. Wilkie (2012). Bayesian modelling of the time delay between diagnosis and settlement for critical illness insurance using a Burr generalised linear type model. *Insurance: Mathematics and Economics* **50**, 266–79.

Ord, J. K., Koehler, A. B. and R. D. Snyder (1997). Estimation and prediction for a class of dynamic nonlinear statistical model. *Journal of the American Statistical Association* **92**, 1621–29.

Patton, A. J. (2006). Modelling asymmetric exchange rate dependence. *International Economic Review* **47**, 527–56.

Robert, C. and G. Casella (2010). *Introducing Monte Carlo Methods with R*. New York: Springer Verlag.

Russell, J. R. and R. F. Engle (2010). Analysis of high-frequency data. In Ait-Sahalia, Y. and L. P. Hansen (eds.), *Handbook of Financial Econometrics* Volume 1 – *Tools and Techniques*. 383–427. Amsterdam: North-Holland Publishing.

Sakata, S. and H. White (1998). High breakdown point conditional dispersion estimation with application to S&P 500 daily returns volatility. *Econometrica* **66**, 529–67.

Schick, I. C. and S. K. Mitter (1994). Robust recursive estimation in the presence of heavy-tailed observation noise. *Annals of Statistics* **22**, 1045–80.

Schmidt, P. and P. C. B. Phillips (1992). LM tests for a unit root in the presence of deterministic trends. *Oxford Bulletin of Economics of Statistics* **54**, 257–87.

Sheather, S. J. and J. S. Marron (1990). Kernel quantile estimators. *Journal of the American Statistical Association* **85**, 410–16.

Shephard, N. G. and T. G. Andersen (2009). Stochastic volatility: origins and overview. In Andersen, T. G., Davis, R. A., Kreiss, J. P. and T. Mikosch (eds.), *Handbook of Financial Time Series*. New York: Springer.

Shephard, N. G. and A. C. Harvey (1990). On the probability of estimating a deterministic component in the local level model. *Journal of Time Series Analysis* **11**, 339–47.

Siegal, A. (1956). *Nonparametric Statistics*. New York: McGraw Hill.

Silverman, B. (1986). *Density Estimation for Statistics and Data Analysis*. London: Chapman and Hall.

Slater, L. J. (1965). Confluent hypergeometric functions. In Abramowitz, M. and I. A. Stegun (eds.), *Handbook of Mathematical Functions*, 503–35, New York: Dover Publications.

Straumann, D. (2005). Estimation in conditionally heteroskedastic time series models. *Lecture Notes in Statistics* **181**, Berlin: Springer.

Straumann, D. and T. Mikosch (2006). Quasi-maximum-likelihood estimation in conditionally heteroscedastic time series: a stochastic recurrence equations approach. *Annals of Statistics* **34**, 2449–95.

Stuart, A. and J. K. Ord (1987). *Kendall's Advanced Theory of Statistics*, originally by Sir Maurice Kendall. Fifth Edition of Volume 1, Distribution Theory. London: Charles Griffin & Company.

Sucarrat, G. (2012). betategarch: Estimation and simulation of the first-order Beta-t-EGARCH model. R package version 1.2. http://cran.r-project.org/web/packages/betategarch/

Tadikamalla, P. R. (1980). A look at the Burr and related distributions. *International Statististical Review* **48**, 337–44.

Taylor, J. and A. Verbyla (2004). Joint modelling of location and scale parameters of the t distribution. *Statistical Modelling* **4**, 91–112.

Taylor, S. J. (1986). *Modelling Financial Time Series*. Chichester: John Wiley & Sons.

Taylor, S. J. (2005). *Asset Price Dynamics, Volatility, and Prediction*. Princeton: Princeton University Press.

Tsay, R. (2010). *Analysis of Financial Time Series*, 3rd edition. New York: Wiley.

Teräsvirta, T. (2006). Forecasting economic variables with nonlinear models. In Elliott, G., Granger, C. W. J. and A. Timmermann (eds.), *Handbook of Economic Forecasting*, 413–53. Amsterdam: North Holland. Publishing

Teräsvirta, T., Tjostheim, D. and C. W. J. Granger (2010). *Modelling Nonlinear Time Series*. Oxford: Oxford University Press.

Wegman, E. J. and H. I. Davies (1979). Remarks on some recursive estimators of a probability density. *The Annals of Statistics* **7**, 316–27.

Weiss, A. A. (1985). The stability of the AR(1) process with an AR(1) coefficient. *Journal of Time Series Analysis* **6**, 181–6.

Whittle, P. (1983). *Prediction and Regulation*, 2nd edition. Oxford: Blackwell.

Yu, K., and M. C. Jones (1998). Local linear quantile regression. *Journal of the American Statistical Association* **93**, 228–37.

Zhu, D. and J. W. Galbraith (2010). A generalized asymmetric Student-*t* distribution with application to financial econometrics. *Journal of Econometrics* **157**, 297–305.

Zhu, D. and J. W. Galbraith (2011). Modelling and forecasting expected shortfall with the generalised asymmetric Student-*t* and asymmetric exponential power distributions. *Journal of Empirical Finance* **18**, 765–78.

Zhu, D. and V. Zinde-Walsh (2009). Properties and estimation of asymmetric exponential power distribution. *Journal of Econometrics* **148**, 86–99.

Author Index

Subject Index

Other titles in the series (continued from page iii)

Eric Ghysels, Norman R. Swanson, and Mark Watson, Editors, *Essays in econometrics: Collected papers of Clive W. J. Granger (Volume I)*, 9780521772976, 9780521774963

Eric Ghysels, Norman R. Swanson, and Mark Watson, Editors, *Essays in econometrics: Collected papers of Clive W. J. Granger (Volume II)*, 9780521792073, 9780521796491

Cheng Hsiao, *Analysis of panel data, second edition*, 9780521818551, 9780521522717

Mathias Dewatripont, Lars Peter Hansen, and Stephen J. Turnovsky, Editors, *Advances in economics and econometrics – Eighth World Congress (Volume I)*, 9780521818728, 9780521524117

Mathias Dewatripont, Lars Peter Hansen, and Stephen J. Turnovsky, Editors, *Advances in economics and econometrics – Eighth World Congress (Volume II)*, 9780521818735, 9780521524124

Mathias Dewatripont, Lars Peter Hansen, and Stephen J. Turnovsky, Editors, *Advances in economics and econometrics – Eighth World Congress (Volume III)*, 9780521818742, 9780521524131

Roger Koenker, *Quantile regression*, 9780521845731, 9780521608275

Charles Blackorby, Walter Bossert, and David Donaldson, *Population issues in social choice theory, welfare economics, and ethics*, 9780521825511, 9780521532587

John E. Roemer, *Democracy, education, and equality*, 9780521846653, 9780521609135

Richard Blundell, Whitney K. Newey, and Thorsten Persson, Editors, *Advances in economics and econometrics – Ninth World Congress (Volume I)*, 9780521871525, 9780521692083

Richard Blundell, Whitney K. Newey, and Thorsten Persson, Editors, *Advances in economics and econometrics – Ninth World Congress (Volume II)*, 9780521871532, 9780521692090

Richard Blundell, Whitney K. Newey, and Thorsten Persson, Editors, *Advances in economics and econometrics – Ninth World Congress (Volume III)*, 9780521871549, 9780521692106

Fernando Vega-Redondo, *Complex social networks*, 9780521857406, 9780521674096

Itzhak Gilboa, *Theory of decision under uncertainty*, 9780521517324, 9780521741231

Krislert Samphantharak and Robert M. Townsend, *Households as corporate firms: An analysis of household finance using integrated household surveys and corporate financial accounting*, 9780521195829, 9780521124164

Rakesh Vohra, *Mechanism design: A linear programming approach*, 9781107004368, 9780521179461

Daron Acemoglu, Manuel Arellano, and Eddie Dekel, Editors, *Advances in economics and econometrics – Tenth World Congress (Volume I)*, 9781107016040, 9781107638105

Daron Acemoglu, Manuel Arellano, and Eddie Dekel, Editors, *Advances in economics and econometrics – Tenth World Congress (Volume II)*, 9781107016057, 9781107674165

Daron Acemoglu, Manuel Arellano, and Eddie Dekel, Editors, *Advances in economics and econometrics – Tenth World Congress (Volume III)*, 9781107016064, 9781107627314

Printed in the United States
By Bookmasters